Inside America's Opioid Crisis

Inside America's Opioid Crisis

12 Hard Lessons for Today's Drug War

Richard J. Baum

BLOOMSBURY ACADEMIC
NEW YORK • LONDON • OXFORD • NEW DELHI • SYDNEY

BLOOMSBURY ACADEMIC
Bloomsbury Publishing Inc, 1385 Broadway, New York, NY 10018, USA
Bloomsbury Publishing Plc, 50 Bedford Square, London, WC1B 3DP, UK
Bloomsbury Publishing Ireland, 29 Earlsfort Terrace, Dublin 2, D02 AY28, Ireland

First published in the United States of America 2026

Cover design: Sally Rinehart
Cover image © iStock.com/tomazl; Walter Bibikow/DigitalVision/Getty Images

Library of Congress Cataloging-in-Publication Data
[to come]

ISBN: HB: 978-1-5381-8640-4
PB: 978-1-5381-8641-1
ePDF: 979-8-8818-6583-2
eBook: 978-1-5381-8642-8

Typeset by Deanta Global Publishing Services, Chennai, India

For product safety related questions contact productsafety@bloomsbury.com.

To the workforce – whether employed in public health or public safety – who give their all every day to save lives, reduce the suffering caused by drugs, and to support those on the road to recovery, however long it takes.

To the families who have lost a loved one – for courageously sharing their stories and helping all of us to understand the challenge we must face together.

To my own family, my wife Linda and our children Ally and Matthew, for the love, support, joy, and meaning they bring to every aspect of my life.

Contents

Acknowledgments

During my education and career, I have had the benefit of many teachers, mentors, colleagues, and friends who have enlightened and challenged me to think carefully about my own views. My original mentor was my late father, Michael Baum, who sparked in me a deep curiosity to understand how the world worked and as long as he lived sent me news articles on a wide array of subjects. It is a tradition I carry on today with my own kids, and with my students and friends.

Teaching at Georgetown University's McCourt School of Public Policy this past decade had given me the gift of engaging with many brilliant students who challenged me through their written work and in class discussion. Let me reference specifically those students who reviewed book chapters or sections: Makana Meyer, Kathleen Semansky, Erin Fitzpatrick, Gina Malagold, Jack Resnick, Jacob Al Muaber, Deborah Covert, and Ben Eichberg.

Friends who shaped my thinking include Steve Allsop, Steve Alm, Aaron Arnold, Dave Aronberg, Bill Bailey, Jen Brophy, Bob Brown, Allan Clear, Nancy Rosen Cohen, Charlotte Colman, Roger Conner, Dan Cuzzolino, Jerry Daley, Jennifer de Vallance, James Derderian, Chris Dishman, Creighton Drury, Melissa Fitzgerald, Matt Gerson, Mark Gold, Brady Granier, Heather Haase, Jacqueline Hackett, Rene Hanna, Carolyn Hardin, Tom Hill, David Holtgrave, Alex Inman, Steve Johnston, Regina LaBelle, Kelly Lieupo, Barry Logan, Bertha Madras, Mac McConahie, Carol McDaid, Robert Morrison, Jessica Nickel, Rick Ohrstrom, Bryce Pardo, Michel Perron, Rossen Popov, Daniel Raymond, Jon Rice, Fred Ryan, Paul Samuels, Jane Sanville, Alan Santos, June Sivilli, Bill Smith, Cecelia Spitznas, Sue Thau, Doug Tieman, Jonathan Thompson, Tom Umberg, John Walsh, Sarah Wattenberg, Tom Welch, Sis Wenger, Chuck Wexler, Chris Williamson, James Winnefeld, John Zadrozny, and Terry Zobeck.

Mark Kleiman, whose writing on drug policy sparkles with his genius, leaves behind an amazing legacy. Although he died in 2019, his policy innovations and personal courage to take on difficult issues has long inspired me.

General Barry McCaffrey, who set a high mark for leadership as the first ONDCP Director I worked for, demonstrated every day how to make government work.

A special mention for Dr. Robert Dupont, whose deep intellect and great personal warmth always shines through, no matter what the subject.

There are also many writers and academics who I owe a huge debt to. They are cited throughout the book, and I am grateful for their tremendous scholarship on drug policy and related issues. Any errors are mine alone.

Introduction

Why and how. Those are the two questions that have been keeping me up at night as I look at the wreckage in the United States caused by the disastrous opioid epidemic. *Why* did this happen—what vulnerabilities, mistakes, ways of thinking, and gaps in our programs, policies, and resources enabled this opioid crisis to harm so many. Secondly, *how,* with fatal overdoses down from peak levels, but still extremely high and drug addiction rates unchanged, do we fix it? What will it take, building on existing efforts and knowledge, to get us to a point where the problems caused by dangerous, addictive, and often deadly drugs will be greatly reduced nationwide? Let me say plainly that I intend to answer both questions in this book.

No, there is not a single simple bumper sticker type solution that can solve the interconnected set of challenges that constitute the opioid crisis. But for those who are looking for ways to better understand what is happening, why, and what must be done about it, I will offer a roadmap—an exit strategy to guide us permanently out of this crisis. The path forward requires us to recognize and understand *12 hard lessons* and then implement approaches to address them.

Why do I believe I know how to take on this problem that so many people all over the country have been debating for decades, but especially since 2013 when drug dealers started selling products containing fentanyl, a synthetic opioid fifty times more potent[1] than heroin? Well, I have seen and learned a lot during the 35 years I have spent working on the country's drug problem, including 28 years at the White House Office of National Drug Control Policy (ONDCP), the agency responsible for coordinating the government-wide fight against drugs on behalf of the President. Between 2017 and 2018, I served as the country's Acting Director (often referred to as America's "Drug Czar"). Because I wanted to speak freely about the ideas in this book and the need for major changes in American drug policy, I decided to retire from government in late 2025.

My career in drug policy began during the crack cocaine epidemic as a Congressional staffer in the late 1980s. When I started, to be honest, I didn't know much. Like a lot of young Congressional staffers, I got a job after college—in my case at the House of Representatives Select Committee on Narcotics Abuse and Control in 1988—and jumped on the tasks assigned to me. I was not looking for a drug policy job specifically, but that was the first paid job that I was offered, and I gladly accepted the position. It was interesting work, preparing for hearings, writing speeches, drafting memos, and traveling with the Committee Members to drug-producing and trafficking countries. Initially, I did not feel a need to understand the roots of America's relationship with drugs. However, over time, I began to read more widely and think more deeply.

For a few years, I was out of government after the House Narcotics Committee was, unfortunately, eliminated in 1993. I started a pair of newsletters, *Drug Policy Report* and *Crime and Drug Report,* serving as editor/publisher as well as chief correspondent. I would cover events around Washington, including Attorney General Janet Reno's weekly briefing with reporters in her cavernous office. When I went back to the Department of Justice (DOJ) twenty-five-years later as White House Drug Czar to meet with Attorney General Jeff Sessions in that same room—to argue against ONDCP's drug enforcement task force program getting moved to DOJ—I had quite the flashback. The room looked the same, except my seat was better. During this period in the 1990s, I began working for the nonprofit group, the Center for Community Interest, leading a six-city study of homelessness, crime, and street disorder. In 1997, I was hired by ONDCP at a time when the agency's director, General Barry McCaffrey, was restaffing the office after President Bill Clinton made major cuts early in his first term.

At ONDCP, my first job was with the Office of Supply Reduction. Initially, I was focused on combating cocaine production and trafficking, traveling multiple times with General Barry McCaffrey to Peru, Bolivia, and Colombia. But soon I was promoted to lead a team working on international policy and developing national strategic documents, including the first of several southwest border strategies. Later, I received a great assignment—for over a decade I led ONDCP's planning for the world's largest annual global drug conference, the United Nations Commission on Narcotic Drugs in Vienna, Austria.

Two parts of this work proved to be quite instrumental in my deepening education. The first part was identifying model domestic US drug programs to highlight at the annual meeting through negotiated resolutions (to guide global drug policy) and panel discussions. I loved this opportunity to search for the best anti-drug initiatives that the United States had to offer the world. Under my leadership, the United States shared our experiences with alternatives to incarceration such as drug courts, the need for a recovery-specific programs, and the risks posed by prescription opioid painkillers. The second part was learning what drug policy reformers who also attended the conference were up to. At first, I was wary, seeking to understand why these people—mostly Americans—were critiquing US drug policy on the global stage. Although back then, and still today, I oppose radical reforms, such as legalization of hard drugs, by attending their events and getting to know the advocates personally, I gained a deeper understanding about drug policy problems that needed to be addressed.

As the opioid epidemic evolved, starting with prescription opioids and expanding to heroin and later fentanyl, I sought the opportunity to develop a graduate course at Georgetown University's McCourt School of Public Policy. I started to teach the class—*The War on Drugs: Causes, Consequences and Alternatives*—a decade ago. To do a good job as a teacher, I had to confront the reality of the country's early drug war history and reflect on the impact of policies instituted during the crack epidemic, including my own role in it. As I integrated more information into the course on the worsening opioid crisis my students and I grappled with how to turn around the shocking loss of life. They challenged me, and I challenged myself, to assess why the situation had gotten so bad and to come up with specific ways to address it.

From many years working in drug policy, as well as from teaching, reading, and talking to a wide range of experts, and reflecting on what I have seen about how government works, I've learned a lot. Knowledge is a wonderful thing. I respect those who gather knowledge primarily for academic pursuits. That's a tremendous public service on its own. But for me, knowledge is something to put into practice, to utilize to solve problems. I did what I could to use what I had learned while still in government, especially while serving as the lead federal official for President Trump's *Commission on Combating Drug Addiction and the Opioid Crisis*. But I have much more to say about what needs to be done.

Let me share something that surely won't surprise readers of this book—some very serious mistakes were made in the development and implementation of the War on Drugs. These mistakes have left a legacy still not fully addressed. Moving forward requires us to look closely at past decisions and approaches that do not serve us well today, particularly during the crack cocaine epidemic during the 1980s. There are also more recent challenges to unpack regarding causes of the opioid crisis. Although the atrocious practices of Purdue Pharma in addicting so many Americans to prescription opioids (see chapter 3) unleashed the opioid epidemic, public policy responses to address it also require review (see chapter 4).

I don't condemn anyone working in drug policy at the federal, state, or local level for getting something wrong. These issues are complex and the political pressure to act is intense. But on the other hand, once it becomes clear that something is not working, these problems need to be directly addressed, not swept under the rug, to be ignored as the years tick by and the consequences mount.

There is much that needs to be done today. Across the country there are many significant initiatives to address the domestic drug problem, as well as important efforts to combat the global illicit drug supply. But there are reasons why current efforts are falling short. There are troubling gaps in how the country is responding to the drug problem that must be understood and taken on. That is what *Inside America's Opioid Crisis* is all about.

The book has eleven chapters, covering the spectrum of drug policy. Each chapter has a specific "Hard Lesson" that summarizes the challenges discussed in that chapter and at least one recommendation. A final hard lesson, number 12, is in the conclusion. Although the recommendations are designed to assist the 28.2 million Americans who meet the medical definition of a drug use disorder, many of the recommendations will also apply to the 27.9 million Americans who have an alcohol use disorder.[2] Similarly, the recommendations will also help the 21.2 million adults with a co-occurring mental health and substance use disorder.[3] Taken together, that's a lot of our fellow Americans who need help.

In this introduction, I will highlight five cross-cutting themes that are core elements of the whole book:

- *The racial bias and over-reliance on incarceration* have both harmed many individuals and damaged the police-community trust necessary to effectively combat today's drug markets.

- *The deep flaws in our country's approach to addiction treatment* which discourage most chronic drug users from seeking or receiving the care they need for this complex and widely stigmatized condition.
- *The unforgiving risks posed by today's lethal drugs* that underscore the urgent need to better focus global supply control efforts and to rapidly expand prevention and early intervention initiatives.
- *Why the most effective anti-drug programs fail to reach national scale* due to the lack of a systemic effort and the "curse of knowledge" (explained below).
- *The vastly under-resourced response to today's drug crisis* guarantees, absent new investments, greater human suffering and economic costs tomorrow.

Before introducing these key themes, which can be seen as a critique of the traditional approach to the US "War on Drugs" let me define what this famous phrase means. The US War on Drugs encompasses all efforts, international and domestic, intended to reduce or mitigate the production, trafficking, sale, and consumption of illicit drugs as well as to prevent the misuse of licit pharmaceutical products. The phrase incorporates everything done at every level of government to address drug-related problems.

The War on Drugs term was popularized after President Richard Nixon declared drugs "public enemy number one" in 1971.[4] I believe that date is a good demarcation point for the modern War on Drugs, but a more appropriate start date for America's long history with drugs is when the first international meeting on drugs was convened, at US request, in Shanghai, China on February 1, 1909. Since this meeting drugs has been both a global and domestic concern for the United States government. The War on Drugs is a dated term, infused with a supply reduction focus and an underemphasis on the large public health effort critical to addressing today's drug crisis. Most people working on drug-issues have replaced the famous phrase with the more neutral "drug policy," yet the original term endures, although now weighed down with the many mistakes, excesses, and failures since 1909. At ONDCP, General McCaffrey banned the use of the term, and it has long since been dropped from all official documents.

Racial Bias and Over-Reliance on Incarceration

The entanglement of racism with drug policy was present at the very start of the drug war. I recognize these are sensitive issues, and it might be tempting to gloss over them, but I think it's best to adopt the stoic expression, "the only way out is through." To build a broad consensus for new approaches to the drug problem, it's important *not* to ignore history, but rather to bring it out into the sunlight and address it straight on. The failure to acknowledge problems, past and present, creates obstacles to progress.

To give one example of the legacy of racial bias, one can simply look back a few decades to the crack cocaine epidemic. The crack epidemic and the opioid epidemic are different, complex problems, but a fair observer must recognize that far more compassion has been offered to white people suffering from opioid addiction in the 21st century than it was to African Americans suffering from crack cocaine addiction in the 1980s and 1990s. To deny this is to deny reality. As Heather McGhee wrote in 2021 about the crack epidemic:

> Dehumanizing and unpitying stereotypes about the dangers of drug use in the inner cities fueled a new era of harsher sentencing and post-release penalties to create a system of mass incarceration. While the so-called crack epidemic is far behind us, the system rolls on. . . The racist nature of our mass incarceration system has been well documented. White and black people are equally likely to use drugs, but the system is six times as likely to incarcerate black people for a drug crime. . .[5]

Race is very much entangled with drug policy. A better drug policy must not just accept this reality but also act to rectify past mistakes and combat racially influenced decision-making today. This is not just a theoretical or academic matter. Years of excessive reliance on arrest and incarceration have damaged police/community relationships. However, efforts to address the sale of dangerous drugs today require close cooperation between police and the community. Police cannot do their job unless community members provide information about what is happening in their neighborhood. Community members cannot be expected to provide such information if trust is not established with law enforcement and they believe that their family members, especially their teenage children, will be treated with respect by local police.

There are specific mechanisms that have been developed to facilitate reconciliation between communities impacted by drugs and police (discussed in chapter 7). Once honest communication is established, past mistakes are acknowledged, and better, more targeted initiatives are adopted to control drug sales, positive change can happen. It's a good thing too, because reconciliation between police and community members is the key to unlocking a fairer and more effective drug enforcement approach.

Let me also highlight that when the opioid epidemic emerged, it was initially disproportionately impacting whites. However as the epidemic has evolved, African Americans have been severely impacted as well. Black overdoses rates have been trending up for a decade, and by 2022, they outpaced white fatal drug overdoses.[6] This reality is another reminder that there is no time to lose in embracing strategies to rebuild damaged relationships between minority communities and the police charged with protecting them.

Of course, drugs remain a societal-wide problem, and the same initiatives that are needed in minority communities, such as police/community engagement, reduced reliance on long sentences for drug offenses, and far more diversion of drug users to treatment, will help all Americans. States need robust alternatives to incarceration, including court-supervised treatment and pre-arrest police facilitated referrals to treatment. These options were in short supply during the crack cocaine epidemic, but are needed now, everywhere, for those whose criminal behavior is driven by their addiction. This is not just about getting more people into treatment; widespread drug sales and use contribute to community crime problems. Every neighborhood needs and deserves safety and security. Reforming sentencing strategies and providing better access to treatment, both in the community and within the justice system, as outlined in this book, are designed to make us all safer.

The Deep Flaws in Our Country's Approach to Addiction Treatment

There is a long history in America of attacking and criticizing people who become dependent on drugs. Stigma can be defined as "a set of negative attitudes and beliefs that often lead to unjust treatment. The stigma associated with addiction can lead to social isolation and may discourage people from seeking help."[7]

We need to find ways to move beyond this outdated and unfair mindset because it harms rather than helps. Those struggling with addiction to powerful narcotics should not be subjected to criticism, neglect, or mistreatment, especially by health service providers who are supposed to be helping them. This sentiment to end stigma is not an excuse to ignore unsafe behavior—quite the opposite—it's the best path to directly take on risky drug use in a far more effective manner.

The American Society of Addiction Medicine (ASAM) defines addiction as "a treatable, chronic medical disease involving complex interactions among brain circuits, genetics, the environment, and an individual's life experiences. People with addiction use substances or engage in behaviors that become compulsive and often continue despite harmful consequences."[8]ASAM explains that addiction can be prevented and treated, and evidence-based treatments are as successful for those with a diagnosed substance use disorder (this encompasses both alcohol and drug dependence) as with other chronic diseases. This is a good definition, but it is also fair to say that addiction involves an array of social, behavioral, and genetic risk factors, which makes it hard to define simply.

Not everyone believes that "disease" is the right word, and some worry that use of the word undermines the reality that, unlike many diseases, those with a substance use disorder have a demonstrated capacity to take actions to improve their condition. The author of *What it is Like to be an Addict* observes that a reason for using "disease, disorder, and dysfunction is that these are the words used in laws and insurance guidelines ...that provide rights to medical and/or psychiatric treatment and to subsidize costs." However, he prefers to describe addiction as "something that involves a person with a substance use habit that undermines their success at living the life that they want to live."[9]

Psychiatrist Gabor Mate, with his son Daniel, wrote in *The Myth of Normal*,[10] that viewing addiction as a disease is an improvement over the longstanding historical approach that considers chronic drug use as a personal moral failure. However, they believe that the disease model should be thought of as a helpful metaphor, rather than a perfect description. Addiction is, they explain, primarily a coping mechanism with features of disease, such as:

> physical symptoms, impairment of certain brain circuits, cycles of remission and relapse, even death. But to call them disease is to miss both the point and the opportunity to deal with them intelligently. Addictions represent in their onset the defenses of an organism against suffering it does not know how to endure. In other words, we are looking at a natural response to unnatural circumstances, an attempt to soothe the pain of injuries incurred in childhood and stresses sustained in adulthood.

This description refers to chronic, daily, heavy drug use—not early, episodic use by those who consume drugs at parties or otherwise may never develop a pattern of use that would be diagnosed as a substance use disorder. However, if drug use, especially fentanyl, heroin, methamphetamine, or cocaine, becomes a routine part of one's life, the consequences and dependence inevitably mount. Later in the book I will be discussing marijuana, a substance that can lead to dependence and quite serious health consequences, but requires a different set of public policies than other drugs, since so much of the country has embraced legalization, allowing for licit sales to adults of very high potency forms of the drug consumed in a variety of new smokable and edible products.

If one thinks of daily drug use as a way of coping with problems, of enabling people to feel normal, to be able to manage life's pressures, then stigmatizing chronic drug consumers is an extremely unhelpful way to address it. "When it comes down to it, all addiction can be summed up as an escape from the confines of the self . . . of being uncomfortable and isolated in one's own skin."[11] What people with a serious substance use disorder need are better, safer, healthier coping mechanisms—which they can learn through treatment—not stigmatization and criticism—which often worsens the psychic suffering that caused them to rely on drugs to cope with life in the first place.

The implications of this understanding of the high price society pays for stigmatizing drug users should drive drug policy reform across a wide range of issues. People who chronically consume drugs do not benefit from stigma. Nor do they benefit from having their addiction ignored. What they need is help to work through the process of finding new coping mechanisms along with support to unpack and address underlying problems that contributed to their development of a substance use disorder.

People with substance use disorders require a range of treatment options. Some seek and benefit from strict programs with clear rules and are ready and able to commit to immediate abstinence. Many others prefer to initiate treatment more gradually, after building a trusting relationship with a doctor, addiction counselor, social worker, peer or recovery coach with past lived experience with addiction. Such positive relationships, which are so often lacking in the lives of those impacted by addiction, can spark real progress towards recovery.

Ideally individuals, with the advice of their family and friends, will decide on their own to seek treatment. Treatment providers and the health system must make treatment entry as easy as possible. But that doesn't mean that those who initiate treatment through the justice system won't succeed. Often, they do quite well. A key factor is that arrestees are given a choice: treatment or jail. Although this choice is under pressure, individuals retain their agency and recognize that by agreeing to treatment and avoiding a jail sentence, they are receiving an important benefit. This type of *leveraged* treatment entry, such as through a drug court, has far better outcomes than forced or "compulsory treatment" which offers "questionable therapeutic benefits and raises serious concerns about potential due process."[12] The idea that someone can just be thrown in jail and that will solve their drug problem does not have any credible evidence to support it. Treatment outcomes depend on the fairness of the *entry process* as well as the *quality* and *duration* of treatment programs. The subject of how the justice system can improve its engagement with those impacted by addiction is a major focus of the book.

Although justice system interventions can be effective, it is vital that the country create a far better environment for voluntary treatment entry and provide many more easily accessible points for those with drug problems to receive care. The reality that the health system has not done this is troubling and must change. Stigma in society and among many health service providers has impeded the development of the types of treatment entry opportunities many people with drug problems tell us they want. Yes, addiction is complex, and not always the easiest problem for the the health system to deal with. But with so many people dying and many more suffering from this problem it's long since time for the health system, with the support of government, to update its approach based on the evidence of what works, even when it's not what is most convenient for them.

The Unforgiving Risks Posed By Today's Lethal Drugs

The country has never seen a drug supply like the one we face today. Fentanyl and other powerful synthetic opioids have rapidly penetrated much of supply of illicit drugs consumed in the United States. Although initially an additive to heroin, it has now largely replaced heroin on the black market—meaning even those seeking heroin and trying to avoid fentanyl will often end up purchasing and consuming fentanyl. Let me note that I will continue to refer to "fentanyl" to mean all potent synthetic opioids, but there are numerous similar opioids that are sold as fentanyl. Also, as described below, there is a wide range of substances used in combination with opioids, many added to drug products by traffickers unknown to drug buyers, and some consumed by drug users intentionally. All of these substances used with opioids should be thought of as part of the "the opioid crisis."

There are logical, market-driven reasons why fentanyl now dominates drug markets. Fentanyl consumers experience a more intense high, but one that doesn't last as long as heroin. They will begin to suffer unpleasant withdrawal symptoms in six hours or less, requiring them to purchase and consume fentanyl more often than heroin—which lasts 8–10 hours—enabling drug dealers to make more frequent sales.[13] In addition, fentanyl, as a synthetic chemical, is much cheaper to produce and smuggle into the United States. No opium crop in the field is required to be grown, harvested, and processed.

Fentanyl is often combined with methamphetamine or cocaine. Stimulant users who are not accustomed to regular use of opioids can overdose far more easily and are much less likely to have the opioid antidote, naloxone (commonly referred to under the brand name, Narcan), on hand to reverse an overdose. They are also less likely to follow the guidelines for those taking opioids today—such as never use alone, start with a low dose, and test the drugs with fentanyl test strips if seeking to avoid it. Individuals who use both opioids and stimulants have double the risk of "overdoses compared to indivdiuals who only use opioids"[14] and the role of methamphetamine and cocaine is an underappreciated component of the current opioid crisis.

Regardless of whether it began as a consumer's decision or as a supplier's business strategy, use of fentanyl with other substances results in serious consequences. In addition to greater risks for overdose and death, treatment approaches are complicated by the need to manage withdrawal of and treatment for dependence on multiple drugs.

It is not just drugs sold as powders to experienced drug consumers that represent a deadly overdose threat. Fraudulent prescription drugs, whether they are sold as opioid painkillers or other common pharmaceutical drugs taken for anxiety, insomnia, or attention deficit disorder, often contain fentanyl. Pills are frequently how new consumers experiment with drugs for the first time, especially youth. This is particularly terrifying for parents who worry that their high school or college-age kids will buy or be given fake prescription drugs purchased on the internet or through social media. Adolescent overdoses have increased because of these fraudulent fentanyl pills.[15]

We must tell our kids, as many times as it takes, to never, ever consume a pill they did not get themselves from a pharmacy. But also, parents know that any kid can make a mistake. Young people deal with a lot today: family, social and academic pressures, and a variety of mental health challenges, sometimes triggered by toxic social media or just the normal ups and downs of a teenager or young adult. It's terrifying that one mistake can cost someone their life. But that's the harsh reality we live with.

Opioid painkiller prescriptions, still a serious problem for many Americans who become dependent after painful injuries or surgeries, have been reduced from their peak. Nevertheless, Americans do not need corrupt pharmaceutical companies to help them initiate opioid consumption. Fentanyl pills and powders are widely available. Primarily Chinese pharmaceutical manufacturing companies sell the precursor chemicals needed to manufacture fentanyl to Mexican drug cartels, who complete the production within Mexico. The finished product—highly concentrated and compact— is smuggled into the United States the same way as other illicit drugs, across the border through points of entry hidden in a tiny percentage of the 200,000 cars and 50,000 pedestrians that enter the United States from Mexico every day, as well as via cargo containers in ships, trucks, and trains, through tunnels under the border, and sometimes via low flying drones or other aircraft.

It's a formidable challenge, but there are actions that can be taken to better combat the fentanyl supply that is killing so many Americans (see chapter 9). Fentanyl has supercharged drug misuse in the United States, increasing risks and costs across the board. People with drug problems used to have more time to find their way to effective treatment and recovery. Unfortunately, the dangerous drug supply has shortened the window that people who use drugs have to access help. Yes, thankfully, many are saved every day by the heroic work of first responders. However, that does not eliminate the breathtaking risk. Far more can and must be done to warn those who acquire drugs, or fraudulent medications, from friends or through social media platforms, about the highly lethal drug supply the country faces today.

Why the Most Effective Anti-Drug Programs Fail to Reach National Scale

There is so much that still needs to be done. Widespread addiction, co-occurring mental health problems, crime, homelessness, and tragic, heartbreaking overdoses are devastating families from every state at every socio-economic level. Urban, suburban, and rural counties are all impacted and struggling to keep people alive and get them help. But on the other hand, there are also very promising signs. All over the country the unrelenting pressure of the opioid epidemic has motivated local officials to develop new approaches, new programs, new ways of facilitating collaboration between groups that in the past did not work together. Once rare, law enforcement and public health partnerships have become far more common. Important new pathways into treatment have been opened. These new interventions must be spread throughout the country, but it's just not happening at a sufficient scale or speed.

When one visits a model program, talks to the people who built it, hears about their lessons learned and the challenges they have overcome, it's deeply inspiring. Seeing these model programs and visiting the individuals who have benefited from them is one of the great joys of working in drug policy today. So many fantastic Americans, from every corner of the country, are doing amazing, life-changing work.

It is, however, painful for me to admit that although model programs are exhilarating to visit, we greatly underestimate how difficult it is to take what is working in one place and replicate these innovations everywhere they are needed. I had once thought that if policy experts wrote up case studies on model programs, researchers performed an evaluation study, and the media spread the news of a promising program, then the innovation would rapidly spread naturally. Unfortunately, the world doesn't work this way.

Social policy innovations don't usually spread like wildfire. Instead, they require the development of formal and informal mechanisms to transfer an initiative from one place to other places effectively. The process, which will often require adaptation of the intervention to local circumstances, needs financial resources, political backing, and the development of a supportive coalition or network. This can be advanced through dedicated, federally funded "Centers of Excellence" to bring everyone together to drive specific innovations into practice (discussed in chapter 10). However, experts, academics and practitioners must first overcome our own temptation to believe that good policies and programs can spread just by talking or writing about them. They don't.

I first read about the "Curse of Knowledge" in Chip and Dan Heath's 2007 book, *Made to Stick: Why Some Ideas Survive and Others Die,*[16] and I never forgot it. They wrote, "Once we know something, we find it hard to imagine what it was like not to know it. Our knowledge has 'cursed us.' And it becomes difficult for us to share our knowledge with others,"[17] and this is because, in our minds, the brilliant innovation that first amazed us, quickly becomes something we believe is easy to explain to everyone —a no-brainer. We believe everyone will instantly get it, but we are, unintentionally, fooling ourselves.

That unique set of circumstances that excited us, which includes not just what we saw in person, but our own previous knowledge brought to the revelatory experience, cannot be transferred to others just by describing the program or by producing a written description. Also, when we see a highly functional program, we tend to overlook the underlying factors that contributed to its success. The trial-and-error process, the organizations that found ways to work together, the funders that got behind the initiative, the community champions that boosted it, and the background, training, and talents of the workforce that keep it all going.

It is hard, serious work to convert model programs to widespread implementation, and we are not doing a good job at it. But once we appreciate this reality, we can get much better. Read on, and I will lay out how to transform a model program producing excellent results in a few places into an effective nationwide initiative.

The Vastly Under-Resourced Response to Today's Drug' Crisis

I left this theme to last because I believe it's important to emphasize that the continuing severity of the drug crisis is not all about money. Still, resources matter. Agencies must fight hard to fund their priorities, even when the country is not facing a daunting crisis. I was unpleasantly surprised to face my own highly public funding crisis at ONDCP when I served as Drug Czar, just when fentanyl overdoses were rapidly climbing."[18]

There has been a fair bit of excitement over the new funds that are coming to the drug fight because of the opioid litigation settlement. Understandably, people are encouraged by the $50 billion that will become available over the next eighteen years to address the drug crisis. These funds, averaging out to $2.8 billion a year, represent an urgently needed and helpful infusion of funds into state and local efforts. It's encouraging that many states and localities are thinking carefully about how to use these resources and that several non-profit groups have written excellent guidance on the use of the settlement funds.[19] However, these funds will not be nearly enough to solve the current crisis. This amount of money, 85 percent of which must be used on drug-related projects and programs, represents only about a 5 percent increase over the 2025 federal drug budget. During the heart of the crack cocaine epidemic the entire drug budget almost *tripled* from 1986 to 2000.[20] There is no way around the reality that today's drug crisis requires a considerably greater investment.

As I describe in more detail throughout the book, those struggling with addiction need a lot more help than they are getting. The types of assistance they require include not only addiction treatment, recovery support, mental health, and trauma-informed counseling, but also access to housing, work or other sources of income, educational opportunities, transportation, childcare, healthy food, etc. Similar support is needed for many of the 600,000[21] individuals with substance use disorder who leave prison or jail each year. A critical point to emphasize is that even when individuals get quality drug treatment services, it's just not for an extended enough time. Acute care, the most likely to be covered by health insurance, is often limited to just 30 days. However, individuals with severe substance use disorder often need 12 months of treatment followed by several years of recovery support.[22] The "dose" of treatment that most individuals receive is woefully short of what is required. The transition of a daily consumer of addictive drugs to stable recovery can be a long, difficult process, even when individuals are participating in a high-quality addiction treatment program. A helpful way to think about the process is through the *Stages of Change* theory, described by its developer, psychologist Carlo C. DiClemente, in his book, *Addiction and Change*:

> The road that leads individuals to change an established behavior pattern begins in the Precontemplation stage, where they have no current interest in change. A person moves through the Contemplation, Preparation, and Action states before arriving at the Maintenance states. Maintenance becomes the final stage in the transition to the new pattern of behavior and ultimately can lead to a termination of the change process.[23]

These stages are a lot to work through and highlight why extended treatment programs, and quite often more than one attempt at treatment, as well as ongoing recovery support, are vital for many. The country has quite a bit more work to do in funding such extended treatment and moving beyond the short-term focus of many health insurance programs. The current treatment system reaches only a quarter of those struggling with drug addiction, and with uneven results.

Because addiction has long been such a stigmatized illness, a great deal of the health services provided in this space are financed through federal and state grants to service providers. The trend more recently, especially in Medicaid expansion states and for those with high-quality health insurance, is for more coverage to be funded through the mainstream medical system. Nearly 2 million Americans, 35 percent of all those treated for opioid addiction, received their care through Medicaid in 2021.[24] Considering the huge need and the pressure to reduce Medicaid costs, increased direct federal grants to states will be essential for the foreseeable future. Although well-meaning experts can debate the best funding mechanisms, leaving addiction treatment services severely underfunded would be quite a costly error. If the federal government does not invest smartly up front, it will certainly pay far more later as addiction, drug-related crime, and other consequences mount.

I will make the case in detail that investing in taking on the opioid crisis will provide a significant return on investment. The result will not just be a large reduction in the tremendous suffering of individuals and their families due to addiction, but also a reduction in net costs to taxpayers over time.

However, again, it's not just about spending more money. Congress cannot just pour federal resources into existing initiatives; they must reform outdated efforts and establish new programs, policies, and institutions that will ensure that the money is well spent. This means financing not just more services through grants, but also building policy and program infrastructure for key drug policy areas that can foster strong coalitions organized around major priorities. Modest federal support for these coalitions is necessary to enable the key components of an effective drug policy do not just survive, but also nimbly adapt both to the evolving drug problem and work to improve and refine program implementation. No program is perfect, but initiatives deserving of continued funding have to commit to continuous improvement, fixing weaknesses and addressing gaps to maximize effectiveness. That's why *both* increased funding to states to run anti-drug programs *and* national policy coaltions run by non-governmental organizations to support high-quality program implementation are necessary.

Recognizing the huge debt the country faces and the struggle in finding new sources of funding, I am proposing a 2 percent annual *opioid crisis fee* on the entire $500 billion pharmaceutical industry to finance the range of new initiatives needed to overcome today's drug crisis. Someone must cover these significant upfront costs, and big pharma is a logical source. Throughout the rest of the book, I will detail how this additional $10 billion a year for the next decade can enable the country to address what is a far different, and much more dangerous problem than what we faced before the opioid crisis.

An Overdue Reckoning

Drug policy, like many issues today, results in people falling into competing camps. By no means do I suggest that the intense debate over drug policy needs to end and that elected officials, advocacy groups, experts in the field, and the public should stop sharing their ideas and their opinions. That dynamic friction can be productive. But I do think it's overdue for the country to look beyond the debate between a "law enforcement" or "public health" approach. We need both, and both areas are overdue for reform and restructuring. Although many reforms can be initiated at the state and local level, the federal government needs to make systemic changes. I am proposing a new joint House/Senate Congressional Committee empowered to put together a comprehensive legislative reform package to undo past errors and reform our drug policies and programs.

When I started working on drug issues in 1988, the country was experiencing about 5,000 fatal drug overdoses annually. In recent years total fatal overdoses have peaked at over 100,000. That level of death should truly shock and appall us. The world is not supposed to work this way.

The decline in fatal overdose cases in late 2024 and 2025, is encouraging. As of this writing, it appears that traffickers are selling their fentanyl pills and powders with reduced amounts of fentanyl due to pressure on their existing supply chain. However, profit-driven drug traffickers are resilient. They are actively recruiting new chemists to manufacture the fentanyl precursors they need to produce a more potent product and to reduce their dependence on imports from China.[25] Further, today's drug markets are evolving to include more risky combination products. This window, while there is a somewhat less lethal mix of opioid street drugs reaching retail markets should compel us to redouble efforts to reach those struggling with drugs now. Odds are this respite won't last long.

Further, fatal overdoses are just one measure; many people are experiencing high rates of addiction-related diseases and hospitalizations, co-occurring mental health challenges, loss of their jobs, homes, and families, as well as arrest, and incarceration. As one scientist who has studied how behavior and biology interact put it: "Addiction does not always kill in dramatic fashion. Sometimes it kills slowly and invisibly. It moves like a shadow, through the quiet repetition of damage that adds up."[26]

I appreciate that many fighting America's opioid crisis on the front lines are exhausted. The daily work of trying to dismantle drug markets and to help those with substance use disorders initiate treatment and get started on the road to recovery is difficult. Seeing repeated overdoses, the loss of life, and the heartbreak of families takes a huge emotional and physical toll. The existing workforce, both public health and public safety, has been under unrelenting stress for over a decade. Still, there is hope, not just from declining fatal overdoses, but also from the initiatives that have been effective in empowering individuals to enter recovery. The question for us is: will we bring the assistance, policies, programs, and collaborations that are working in some places everywhere they are needed?

It is time to reckon seriously with the hard lessons that have emerged from the country's battle with drugs and to equip every community with what they need to to take on today's drug crisis. There is no time to wait. We must build a brighter future for those struggling with drugs today, and for the next generation that very much deserves to grow up in a better, safer world.

Author's Note

Let me just add a few words for those impacted directly by drug use, including families and friends of individuals with a substance use disorder. Although this book is about policy, it is also about bringing care to those in need in every possible way. Families and friends are an important part of this effort. When someone we love is affected by addiction, it can be terrifying, frustrating, and confusing. But it is important to emphasize that everyone deserves support, assistance, and continued love from the people in their lives. The outdated ideas that people who use drugs cannot be helped until they "hit bottom" or that it makes sense to "cut off" those struggling with a substance use disorder from their closest family and friends are wrong. Absent a safety risk, it is important to keep our loved ones as close as we can. They need us more than ever.

This doesn't mean that any of us automatically know how to communicate effectively with someone who is struggling with an addiction or the best techniques to persuade them to access the help they need. Our instincts to confront our loved ones, to tell them to stop, and to raise our voices out of fear or worry can backfire. Fortunately, there has been a great deal learned about how to help. This book will provide important context about addiction and how people can recover. But I would also encourage families to access Community Reinforcement and Family Training (CRAFT), via a guidebook[27] or an online course. Your efforts could save your family or a friend's life and empower them to take those first few difficult steps toward recovery.

Let me also encourage those who have been impacted by addiction, directly or indirectly, to use this book, combined with their first-hand knowledge of conditions where you live, to support drug policy reform. Most of the book's recommendations can be adapted to specific community needs to improve existing efforts. If you are concerned about what is happening, or not happening, where you live, take action. Visit with local officials to encourage them to support new pilot programs, join or establish a community organization, advocate for evidence-based prevention, treatment, recovery, and justice system programs, engage with the media, and encourage businesses to hire those in recovery. Let your voice be heard. Don't let anyone tell you that more people can't be helped or more lives saved. Where there is a will, there is a way. If I can help in any way, please contact me through my website (RichardJBaum.com). We are all in this together.

Richard J. Baum, Falls Church, Virginia. January, 2026

1

The Longest War

America Launches Drug Fight with Supply Control, Propaganda, and Prejudice

Chapter Introduction: What Can Marvel's Iron Man Teach Us about the Early War on Drugs?

When we look back at the first hundred years of the War on Drugs, from the aftermath of the Civil War until the start of the Nixon Administration, it's instructive to ask if there are lessons from this now distant past that we should heed today. Perhaps there was some wrong turn, some systematic misunderstanding that led us down the wrong path, or some lost insights that could help us grapple with the awful reality of losing a football stadium full of people a year from opioid overdoses.

This question reminds me of one of my all-time favorite movie scenes. In the middle of *Iron Man 2,* Tony Stark watched an old black and white video of his long dead father, Howard Stark, describing his ambitious plans for the future of Stark Industries. The elder Stark, looking like Walt Disney mapping out plans for Disney World in Florida, takes a break from reading the script of his promotional video and talks directly to the camera, to his son. Howard explains to Tony that he didn't have the technology needed to accomplish great things, but that one day, with the clues he left behind, his son would change the world. In the film Tony figures out that his dad had designed a new atomic element into the plans for the new Stark Industries campus that would create a great energy source. Tony, with the help of his artificial intelligence computer, Jarvis, used the wisdom of his long dead father, to bring into existence that new element and power his Iron Man suit.

What about us and the drug war—are there lessons from the old days that would allow us to, like Tony, bring a brighter future for the millions of Americans impacted by drugs? Turns out there are. Applying these lessons won't be as easy as asking Jarvis, or ChatGPT, to tell us what to do. There is no miracle cure for today's deadly fentanyl/polydrug crisis, but if we dig deep and look for clues, we can indeed find a few important lessons from the first century of the War on Drugs to guide us today.

Hard Lesson: We must confront the two original sins of the drug war—racism and stigma—to effectively combat today's crisis

Race-based or stigmatizing rhetoric or actions regarding drugs, whether explicit or implicit, is an ugly stain on past and present drug policies. All Americans, whatever their background, face risks from regular use of dangerous drugs. Those with fewer means or who live in a highly policed area may be perceived as the ones struggling with addiction, but wealthier Americans are also consuming illegal drugs at similar rates. Racist stereotypes and the stigmatization of addiction—long key components of America's drug war—must be addressed to effectively take on this massive problem.

The country needs to create an environment within which those struggling with addiction know that they can come forward to seek help, and not hold back due to stigma, shame, or fear of racial bias. This is urgent because drugs continue to pose a grave threat. The longstanding racism and stigma intertwined with the drug war imposes costs. Racial bias, whether reflected in rhetoric or unfair treatment within the justice system, has not only impacted many individuals and families over the last century, but it also makes it harder to build the type of trusted partnerships between minority communities and police essential to address today's brutal drug crisis. Stigma deters people who use drug from seeking drug treatment and can hamper those who successfully address their substance use to sustain recovery and reintegrate into society. To make progress on today's daunting drug challenges, it is necessary to honestly address this longstanding dark legacy of the War on Drugs.

Note that this chapter ranges from the very start of the country's turn of the 20th century drug crisis over a hundred years ago and brings us through the Nixon era. The subsequent chapter covers the cocaine epidemic, and then chapter three turns to today's opioid crisis, which is the focus of the remainder of this book and most of its thirty-two recommendations.

The Ancient Power of the "Milk of the Poppy" to Heal and to Harm

Opium, extracted from the poppy plant, has been utilized for pain relief for thousands of years, with references to it as early as 2100 BC. The milk of the poppy, as it is referred to in *Game of Thrones* and *House of the Dragon*, has been used in surgery for over a thousand years. In 1900, when L. Frank Baum (alas, no relation) published the *Wonderful Wizard of Oz,* the ability of the poppy plant to heal and to harm was well understood by the public. He wrote:

> Now it is well known that when there are many of these flowers together their odor is so powerful that anyone who breathes it falls asleep, and if the sleeper is not carried away from the scent of the flowers, he sleeps on and on forever. But Dorothy did not know this, nor could she get away from the bright red flowers that were everywhere about; so presently her eyes grew heavy, and she felt she must sit down to rest and to sleep... "If we leave her here, she will die," said the Lion. "The smell of the flowers is killing us all."[1]

The naturally occurring opioids became more potent and dangerous once the alkaloids in the resin of the poppy plant were isolated and later synthesized. Morphine, extracted from the naturally occurring poppy resin back in 1806, was utilized in the form of "morphine salts" that could be directly applied to a wound or injury. The drug was used widely in this way during the civil war. After morphine's chemical formula was identified and the hypodermic needle was invented[2] morphine came into common use in the 1860s. Later, in 1898, heroin was introduced by the pharmaceutical company Bayer as, they claimed, a safer, less addictive substance made from morphine. The natural alkaloids—also referred to as opiates—include opium, morphine and codeine. Semi-synthetic derivatives include "heroin, fentanyl, hydromorphone, methadone, and buprenorphine."[3]

It is important to highlight that in the era before modern medicine when, like today, people suffered from many painful ailments, morphine effectively reduced pain. It was a valuable and important tool that addressed suffering all over the world. Over time, however, morphine's expanding sales and unregulated consumption led to misuse and addiction. A movement grew to control the drug.

The Unregulated Drug Market Results in Misuse, Addiction

In the 1800s and early 1900s, morphine was easily available in the United States without a prescription as a component in a growing array of products sold to adults and children to ease their aches and pains. Traveling salesmen marketed these dangerous, fraudulent, and often ineffective cures for pain and suffering. However, urban dwellers did not need to wait for one of these "snake oil salesman" to ride into town on their horse. Morphine, as well as cocaine, was also easily available from pharmacies for 5–10 cents a dose.

Mrs. Winslow's Soothing Syrup, a popular product also sold in pharmacies, contained morphine and alcohol and was advertised for parents to give to their children to ease their teething pain or other ailments. Unfortunately, the risks were not carefully explained. Some children given Mrs. Winslow's Soothing Syrup by mom or dad went to bed and never woke up. The reality is that morphine could be fatal to children, even in small amounts.[4]

Cocaine, a stimulant derived from coca bush leaves grown in Colombia, Bolivia, and Peru, was also commonly sold as an ingredient in drugstore products or in powder form. It was a popular product, included in the original recipe for Coca-Cola, from its first introduction in 1886—until the coca alkaloid was removed in 1903.[5] Over time the sales of these substances, whether sold individually or mixed into to drug combination products, led to growing misuse and addiction throughout the United States.

In the early 1900s, journalists referred to as "Muckrakers" dug deep into scandals of the day via long-form investigative journalism. One publication, *Colliers*, produced an 11-part series called *The Great American Fraud*, which focused on the dangers of patent medications (the name stuck, but the products were not actually patented) and called for supply control and regulation.[6] A particular concern were the doctors who specialized in prescribing morphine to opioid dependent adults. Some, like the opioid painkiller pill mills which emerged early in our current opioid epidemic, saw hundreds of patients a day for brief visits. As described in *Colliers*, many of the Americans who developed a morphine addiction were women who were recklessly prescribed and dispensed legal opiates by physicians and pharmacist for "female problems." Eventually the government acted to control these narcotics.

The original *Pure Food and Drugs Act* was signed into law by President Teddy Roosevelt in 1906. The new law required sellers of over-the-counter medications to list the ingredients by amount in their products, revealing to consumers for the first time how much morphine, opium, heroin, alcohol, cocaine, and cannabis[7] that were in their medications. This curtailed misuse by reducing accidental consumption of these powerful substances. But enforcement mechanisms for illegal sales were extremely limited and a push for further controls accelerated.

President Teddy Roosevelt Launches the Global War on Drugs

Even though the United States did not yet dominate the world stage in the early 1900s as it did after the Second World War, it nonetheless helped to establish the global drug control system which led to the set of three United Nations Drug Conventions[8] that govern global drug policy. President Teddy Roosevelt knew an opportunity to lead when he saw it.

American interest in drug diplomacy originated due to the work of missionaries in the Philippines. The island nation in the pacific had become a US territory in 1898 and was a producer and consumer of opium. Although at first the United States appointed Governor of the Philippines (and later US president), William Howard Taft, was planning to allow traditional use of opium to continue, local missionaries launched a petition to oppose the move. With President Roosevelt's support, Governor Taft appointed a three-person commission to investigate opium issues. Charles Brent, the Episcopal Bishop of Manila, led the commission and pushed for the prohibition of opium production and consumption over a three-year period. In 1906, Brent wrote to Roosevelt and requested that the United States call an international conference to support international opium control efforts. The President agreed and the Shanghai Opium Commission[9] took place in China on 1909.

The US Commissioners returned to the United States from Shanghai with a clear understanding that to lead the drug war on the global stage, the American government had to get its own house in order. At this time there were, according to historian David Musto, "little or no legal controls over the sale and distribution of narcotics" and the United States "was one of the few" countries in the more developed western world to "allow unregulated drug use."[10]

It is important to remember that drug control in the United States, along with other local health and public safety matters, had long been understood as a state, not a federal matter. That was beginning to change. Work began in earnest to draft the first federal drug law controlling illicit drugs. The message from the US Commissioners to Shanghai to the American Government was clear—Washington had to get their act together and join the new international consensus—which they helped forge—to crack down on drugs.

First Federal Drug Law Comes Down Hard on Doctors, Dealers, and Users

There is a certain irony that the United States called for global drug control before it had enacted its own domestic drug laws. Teddy Roosevelt's successor, President Taft, was committed to addressing that problem. Although at this point it was unclear exactly where the US Constitutional limits were on expanding federal police powers, there was a head of steam to find out. Another Commissioner to the Shanghai Convention, Hamilton Wright, conducted research to support development of the new law by sending questionnaires to police departments, prisons, state boards of health, pharmacies, and morphine manufacturers to collect information on drug trends.

Wright put together draft legislation, working with Congressman Francis Burton Harrison, Democrat of New York. Their plan was to develop controls that would be effective, while still overcoming potential resistance from doctors, pharmacists, and drug manufacturers who were concerned over a loss of income. The drug stores and other commercial interests established an association, the National Drug Trade Conference, to stop or at least weaken the legislation. The resulting legislation created some confusion over exactly what the law required. There was a debate after the law was adopted on whether it was appropriate for doctors to continue to provide narcotics to those already dependent. Over time US courts interpreted the Harrison Act to mean that doctors could prescribe narcotics for "medical treatment," but not to treat addiction—which was not considered a disease at this time. There were several Supreme Court cases challenging the law, but at the end of the day prohibition won out. David Musto concluded that the Harrison Act ended in triumph for supporters who opposed the use of narcotics for the maintenance of "mere addiction."[11] The law also required that those who imported or sold narcotics had to keep detailed records. This requirement facilitated the prosecution of "unregistered narcotics distributors such as saloon keepers and street peddlers."[12]

Although the Harrison Act was a major landmark, it is also interesting to note that it did not signal a sudden change in what most people thought about drugs. Even prior to its enactment, narcotics prescribing and consumption was already in decline due to growing concerns over addiction.[13] Further, drug enforcement was not controversial among the American people. There was widespread consensus that trafficking, and the sale of narcotics had to be controlled at home and abroad. There was no mass movement opposing drug control. Unlike the national arguments and widespread public protests associated with alcohol prohibition (adopted by Constitutional amendment in 1920 and revoked in 1933), narcotics lacked the widespread social acceptance of alcohol. For those interested in this history of prohibition there is an excellent book called *Last Call* by Daniel Okrent. But regarding regular use of drugs, the risks of addiction had become quite clear. Those who had developed what we would refer to today as a substance use disorder, garnered little sympathy.

The Harrison Act empowered the federal government to stop the prescription of morphine or other drugs of addiction for those dependent on these substances. The feds were committed to shutting down doctors who sought to "maintain" drug users with continuing prescriptions. Most doctors complied; those who didn't were prosecuted. With enforcement of the Harrison Act people who continued to desire newly illegal drugs had to turn to the black market, that to the surprise of the authorities, rapidly emerged. Soon local police started arresting drug users and sellers, filling up their jails.

The Trouble with Drug Treatment—There Isn't Any

As I became involved in participating in the annual meeting in Vienna, Austria, to review implementation of the U.N. drug treaties, the Commission on Narcotic Drugs (CND) in the early 2000s, something that is odd to us today, became apparent to me. The U.N. drug treaties are dominated by supply control, with demand reduction barely mentioned in the actual text of the treaties. The key objective of the U.N. drug treaties was to foster international cooperation in reducing the illegal drug trade, not on what countries did in terms of domestic treatment, prevention and recovery. The drafters of the U.N. drug treaties believed that once the supply was addressed through international cooperation, there would not be much consumption to worry about. They were sadly mistaken.[14]

Domestically, the Harrison Act crackdown led to the creation of new, illegal drug markets, posing a new kind of problem. Instead of doctors and pharmacists providing low-cost morphine or cocaine, drug peddlers emerged to meet market demand. It was not unusual for drug sellers to use their own products. Both consumers and dealers were locked up. Something had to be done with all the arrestees. The federal government stepped in to develop two large, locked jail campuses referred to as "narcotics farms" administered by the United States Public Health Service, in the hope that hard work and fresh air would cure their addiction. It didn't work. Almost everyone relapsed immediately after serving their sentence at the drug farms.[15]

At this time, there was no evidence-based treatment for opioid addiction. Later, in 1935, recognizing the problem, a small research facility was established at the Lexington, Kentucky narcotics farm to study the problem. It became the Addiction Research Center in 1948. Although some of this research was ethically questionable, it did result over time in the development of much greater knowledge about drug addiction and provided useful insight into methadone as a treatment medication. Eventually it was this tiny research center that formed the core of what was to become the National Institute of Drug Abuse (NIDA). This organization, a part of the National Institute of Health, is today the global leader in scientific research on addiction with an annual budget of $1.7 billion and a broad and important research portfolio.

Although this gradual progress in understanding how to treat addiction that emerged over the last half century is a critically important accomplishment, it was of no help to those who suffered from addiction in the decades after the Harrison Act took effect. Doctors had no credible, proven methods to provide addiction treatment. If they experimented with gradually weaning drug-dependent people off morphine or cocaine, they were subject to arrest. Although various treatment methods were advertised, they were either deliberate frauds or simply ineffective in treating addiction.

Self-help groups eventually emerged as an option. Alcoholics Anonymous (AA) started in 1935. Narcotics Anonymous (NA) was established in 1953. For many who struggled with addiction, these programs, known for their twelve steps,[16] offered fellowship, hope and strategies that worked for some to address their addiction. Of course, it's not the same thing as going to a doctor or a counselor utilizing a set of evidence-based, research-tested best practices and Food and Drug Administration (FDA) approved medications. In a time when the medical profession had nothing to offer them and the criminal justice system was locking them up, it was a welcome, often life-saving new option for a stigmatized and suffering population.

Learning from Alcohol Prohibtion's Failure, New Federal Drug Agency Focuses on Public Relations and Supply Control

The Department of the Treasury's Federal Bureau of Narcotics was established in 1930[17] as a separate agency from the department's struggling Bureau of Prohibition, whose controversial work on alcohol was subject to much criticism. Although separating drug enforcement from alcohol enforcement was a wise move, drug cops would soon find themselves challenged by the same smugglers who established criminal organizations during alcohol prohibition. When prohibition ended in 1933 many of these alcohol bootleggers moved into the drug business full time.

Harry Anslinger was appointed by President Herbert Hoover as the first commissioner of the new anti-drug agency. He had been managing the drug portfolio in the Treasury's Probation Bureau, and earlier in his career he served as an intelligence officer in post-First World War Europe. When the decision was made to separate the Prohibition and Narcotics Bureaus, just three years before the end of prohibition, Anslinger was a logical choice to run the agency.

Anslinger served as the first federal drug czar through the Roosevelt, Truman, and Eisenhower Administrations and left the job in 1962 during the Presidency of John F. Kennedy. Even after leaving Treasury, he represented the US government at the United Nations Commission on Narcotic Drugs. There is a lot that can be said about his more than three decades in the role as the country's top official on narcotics,[18] operating well before the DEA or the White House Office of National Drug Control Policy was established.

Anslinger viewed addiction as "a kind of contagious lunacy that sprang inevitably from exposure to drugs and drug users"[19] explains Matthew Pembleton in his masterful study of the Federal Bureau of Narcotics. Doctors and pharmacists, now banned from distributing morphine and heroin, were no longer the problem. Rather, international production and trafficking of opioids into the United States was the primary threat. Anslinger believed that the only way to stop continued use at home was to stop the supply at the source. He said that there are "no national boundaries in our work … you can't afford national sovereignty when you are trying to break up the narcotics racket."[20] The Bureau sent agents abroad, first as "roving ambassadors" to push for tougher drug enforcement and later established permanent offices in key countries. Heroin was the top concern, leading to a focus on countries such as Turkey, Lebanon, Italy, and France. Anslinger put little faith on border controls, considering the task of effectively defending all American sea, land, and air points of entry as a mission impossible.

The presence of American agents working on foreign soil was often controversial, but as American political and economic power expanded after the Second World War, it was difficult for countries to deny repeated requests from the Narcotics Bureau to open a field office. The Bureau opened in Italy its "District 17" office in 1951 to cover Europe, the Middle East, and North Africa—the first-time drug agents were permanently based abroad—a tradition maintained by the Drug Enforcement Administration today. One of their cases became well known, thanks to the 1971 movie, "The French Connection" based on a book of the same name by Robin Moore. What Anslinger's agents discovered by 1959 was that opium and morphine were being smuggled from around the Mediterranean to the Marseille region of France. It was processed into heroin there before being trafficked across the Atlantic. The Narcotics Bureau got a big break in the case when they arrested a diplomat from Guatemala and his French associate, leading to further arrests and additional focus on the regions drug processing center in Marseille.

Anslinger's international agents were often frustrated by what they saw as a lack of enthusiasm for fighting drugs and toleration of drug corruption in the areas where they were based. Nonetheless, they worked hard to develop relationships with local police as well as informants, utilizing incentives such as equipment, training, and occasional small gifts, such as cigars and liquor. These efforts led to some arrests. The local relationships built by Anslinger's international agents also provided the Narcotics Bureau with a decent picture of the heroin supply chain that impacted the United States. Despite a few successes, it did not prove possible to keep heroin out of the country. The international work did, however, burnish the bureaucratic reputation of Mr. Anslinger and provide invaluable media attention for the agency.

The publicity machine that Anslinger built would impress any government official. Decades before reality TV was invented, he kept the Bureau's work in the news by authorizing popular journalistic accounts of major cases pursued by the Bureau and turning some of his best agents into public figures. The message was consistent: drugs were not a homegrown problem but a subversive foreign menace that had to be fought. Well before Richard Nixon took office Anslinger set the tough tone in talking about the drug problem. The lesson Anslinger learned from the failure of alcohol prohibition was that maintaining strong public support for the agency's mission was essential. It is a lesson he never forgot. Anslinger published scores of articles and three books, *The Traffic in Narcotics* (1953), *The Murderers* (1961) and *The Protectors* (1964).

Anslinger was a highly skilled bureaucrat. He knew of the poor reputation of the Treasury's Prohibition Bureau and intended for the Narcotics Bureau to not suffer the same fate. He did not hesitate to exaggerate the drug threat, employ heated—and racist—rhetoric, and to overpromise what his relatively small band of federal agents could accomplish to maintain Congressional and public support. As Pembleton observes, Anslinger's fear mongering was effective in bolstering his agency's support because, unfortunately, it resonated with much of the public.

The Ugly Racism of Harry Anslinger

The man who dominated federal drug policy for over thirty years was a notorious racist. Even for the pre-civil rights, Jim Crow era, he stood out for his crude public use of rhetoric targeting African Americans. Anslinger, seeking support for the drug war from white Americans, which in 1930 represented 87.8 percent of the US population,[21] sought to associate drug use with minorities. Anslinger emphasized heroin addiction as an urban, African American problem, stating that heroin use was mostly an issue among "young hoodlums and about 80 percent of them are colored."[22]

A strange obsession with the corrupting influence of music also shows up repetitively in his writings. In his now infamous pamphlet on marijuana, *Assassin of Youth*,[23] he wrote:

> Along the Mexican border and in southern seaport cities it had long been known that the drug has a strangely exhilarating effect upon the musical sensibilities. The musician who uses it finds that the musical beat seemingly comes to him quite slowly, thus allowing him to interpolate improvised notes with comparative ease. He does not realize that he is tapping the keys with a furious speed impossible for one in a normal state. Soon a song was written about the drug. Perhaps you remember: *Have you seen that funny reefer man? He says he swam to China; any time he takes a notion, he can walk across the ocean.*

Although some of these quotes are comical today, his enforcement operations could be shockingly cruel. One of the saddest stories concerns Anslinger's obsession with legendary jazz singer Billie Holiday. She was a mainstream success as a recording artist and performer from the 1930s to the 1950s, including appearances at Carnegie Hall. Holiday was well known for performing the song, Strange Fruit,[24] which hauntingly describes the images of lynched African Americans hanging from a tree after their murder. Johann Hari tells this story in detail in his book, *Chasing the Scream*.[25] The book was turned into a film entitled *The U.S. vs. Billie Holiday*.[26] Hari writes that Billie Holiday received her first threat of arrest from Anslinger's Narcotics Bureau after performing Strange Fruit in 1939 in New York City.

Anslinger had heard she was consuming heroin, and he launched an investigation. The Narcotics Bureau relied heavily on undercover investigations. Although Anslinger didn't like to hire Black agents, he recruited one specifically to go undercover to find out about Holiday's drug use. Anslinger was also assisted by Holiday's husband, a man who resented his wife's success and physically abused her. Holiday was arrested, put on trial, and sentenced to a year in prison, served in West Virginia. But her punishment didn't end there. Hari writes: ". . . as a former convict, she was stripped of her cabaret performer's license, on the grounds that listening to her might harm the morals of the public. This meant she wasn't allowed to sing anywhere that alcohol was served—which included all the jazz clubs in the United States."[27]

Opioids and marijuana were not the only drugs unfairly associated with blacks. Published reports charged black "cocaine fiends" with causing havoc.[28] Whites pushed the ideas in the early Jim Crow era that "cocaine use prompted African Americans to act uppity" and caused them refuse to accept their purported social inferiority.[29] Anslinger surely knew that white cocaine use was just as common as minority use, but that didn't stop him from using this racist trope to maintain support for his work.

Anslinger also associated marijuana with Mexicans. What he wrote, also in *The Assassin of Youth,* sounds quite odd today. Here is one example:

> In Florida, police found a youth staggering about in a human slaughterhouse. With an ax he had killed his father, mother, two brothers, and a sister. He had no recollection of having committed this multiple crime. Ordinarily a sane, rather quiet young man, he had become crazed from smoking marijuana. In at least two dozen comparatively recent cases of murder or degenerate sex attacks, marijuana proved to be a contributing cause.

This racist attitude and approach to the drug problem was baked into the original governmental campaign to stigmatize drug use and rally support among Congress and the public for the drug war. It has left an ugly legacy that still has not been reckoned with.

At age seventy, in 1962, Anslinger was forced into mandatory retirement. He was replaced by a long-time Narcotics Bureau veteran, Henry Giordano. However, Giordano was unable to manage changing public opinion toward drug use in the 1960s. President Lyndon Johnson in 1968 brought all federal drug enforcement duties into the Department of Justice's (DOJ) new Bureau of Narcotics and Dangerous Drugs. Anslinger, with his long tenure, imposing personal presence and strong public profile was a hard man to replace. As Pembleton concludes, "the Bureau would not have survived nearly forty years without a leader of Anslinger's political acumen and strange charisma." From today's perspective his racism, propaganda, and rejection of the public health perspective on addiction invites well-deserved criticism, in his day it was a different story.

Anslinger was a widely respected figure, described as the "world's greatest authority on dope," nominated for a Nobel Peace Prize, and was on Adlai Stevenson's short list for Vice President in 1952.[30] There is no question that his agents did score some drug enforcement victories, even if tales of their heroics were exaggerated. Nor was Anslinger wrong about the risks of heroin use in the days before evidence-based treatment. However, his harsh rhetoric, prejudice, and his steadfast objection to seriously researching and piloting addiction treatment programs did a disservice to the country. Anslinger did not help the government prepare for a much more complex and diverse drug environment that his successors would inherit.

Anslinger was not the only long-serving, prominent federal law enforcement official well known for his racism. J. Edgar Hoover, who served as director of the Federal Bureau of Investigation (FBI) from 1924 until his death in 1972, famously sought to undermine the civil rights movement and spied on and harassed Martin Luther King. In her authoritative 2022 biography Beverly Gage describes how Hoover had equal disdain for civil rights activists and the murderous Ku Klux Klan. After nearly two decades of tracking southern racial conflicts,

> He had come to view civil rights activists and Klansman as part of the same debilitating turn towards law breaking and disorder. The fact that one group used torture, intimidation, and murder as its methods while the other practiced non-violence, was almost incidental to him. Both groups, in his view, broke the law and assaulted the status quo and both created unwelcome problems for federal officials . . . by promoting conflict and instability.[31]

Increasing Drug Use in the 1960s Raises Anxiety in a Troubled Time

The American approach to drugs faced a challenge when the post-Second World War baby boomers reached their teenage years in the 1960s. A youth counterculture emerged with new attitudes and behaviors regarding clothing, sexuality, and drugs. This was a complicated time in US history. The United States was struggling in the Vietnam War and young adults, opposing the war, and fearing the draft, joined widespread public protests. The civil rights movement—the intensifying campaign for

African Americans to finally win rights that were denied in the aftermath of the civil war—brought hope to millions but raised anxiety among many whites. Assassinations of President Kennedy in 1963, as well as his brother Robert F. Kennedy and civil rights icon Martin Luther King in 1968, shocked the nation. The American people watched these events unfold on television news and wondered what was happening to the country they grew up in.

Harry Anslinger was appalled at the growth of drug use in the 1960s. He launched an intensified public relations approach and further heightened his anti-drug rhetoric. It didn't work. Additional factors challenged those who sought to rein in growing drug use. Harvard psychologist and researcher Timothy Leary promoted the use of psychedelic drugs, famously calling at a public gathering in Golden Gate Park in San Francisco for people to "turn on, tune in, drop out." He encouraged use of LSD, and he consumed psilocybin with some of the well-known writers of the era, including Allen Ginsberg and Jack Kerouac.[32] Although he lost his faculty position at Harvard after reports of him sharing drugs with his students became public in 1963, he continued his advocacy of psychedelics.

To digress for a moment to current times, psychedelics, despite the bad reputation they earned from the theatrics of Timothy Leary, the substances never quite disappeared. Musicians, including country artist Kacey Musgraves has spoken of use of LSD,[33] and the singer Miley Cyrus found ayahuasca helpful.[34] Tech titans today have reported consuming psychedelics in "microdoses" in an interesting but not evidence-based approach to attempt to benefit from the substances while minimizing serious side effects.

However, much more mainstream than psychedelics, starting back in the late 1960s, were the prescription products developed and heavily marketed by big pharma. This growing licit drug use was helped by a drug marketing innovator from a now famous family.

Dr. Arthur Sackler transformed Hoffman-La Roche's Valium into the top-selling drug in the United States between 1968 and 1982.[35] The Rolling Stones song, "Mother's Little Helper[36]" highlighted the popularity of drugs such as Valium that was widely prescribed, including to many women. As we will explore in Chapter 3, Arthur's Sackler's nephew, Richard Sackler, would later model his marketing campaign after his uncle's successful Valium campaign to turn OxyContin into a blockbuster.

In a pattern that we would see again, both in the 1980s during the crack cocaine epidemic and later, during the opioid crisis, politicians stepped forward to address public concern over rising drug use. Richard Nixon, the former Vice President, who had barely lost the presidency to John F. Kennedy in 1960, and who was defeated for the California Governorship in 1962, turned to the issue in his successful campaign to finally claim the White House geared up in 1968.

Richard Nixon and his Psychiatrists Launch the White House Drug Czar's Office

Today the federal government funds domestic drug treatment programs in all fifty states at the rate of over $20 billion a year, but it wasn't always so. In fact, most politicians in the 1960s still considered addiction treatment primarily a responsibility for state and local health authorities. However, there was an important exception. Washington D.C., as the federal district, had a special status making it the "only local jurisdiction in which federal funding could be made available for municipal crime-reduction programs."[37] In Washington, as well as in other urban areas around the country, the rise in heroin use was associated with an increase in crime and methadone treatment emerged as a potential solution to address the crime wave and the addiction crisis.

Harvard-trained psychiatrist Robert DuPont started working in Washington's Department of Corrections in 1968. Dr. Dupont and colleagues studied inmates in D.C. jails and found that nearly half of them had a history of heroin use. Although it was not necessarily news that drug use and crime was linked, the concrete evidence produced by the D.C. jail study[38] made a strong impression in Washington. Based on the study, Dupont developed in 1970 for D.C. a federally funded methadone maintenance program under a new organization called the Narcotics Treatment Administration (NTA).[39] Methadone, a synthetic morphine substitute, can satisfy the craving for heroin, without producing a high. As a medication it can be prescribed by a doctor. It was taken once a day, as a powder dissolved in a fruit-flavored drink. The program, which served a population that was 95 percent African American, was shown to substantially reduce heroin use—and crime. Dupont shared the results widely, including during April 1971 testimony before the House Select Committee on Crime. The program quickly came to the attention of the Nixon Administration.

A young Nixon aide surveyed several drug treatment programs around the country, including one run by psychiatrist Jerome Jaffe in Chicago, which, like the NTA, utilized methadone. Jaffe was asked to provide recommendations on treatment for heroin consumers and, unsurprisingly, recommended utilization of methadone. The Nixon Administration supported the proposal and integrated it into its formal launch of the new Drug Czar's office, bringing leadership of drug policy into the White House.

On June 17, 1971, in a public speech[40] and a more detailed written statement[41] Nixon unleashed major changes in the federal approach to drugs. Nixon instituted through an Executive Order the *Special Action Office for Drug Abuse Prevention* and concurrently asked Congress to enact legislation to broaden the authority of the new office. Although later in his administration there was a greater focus on promoting law enforcement action, this new White House office was squarely focused on demand reduction. Its mission was to develop a federal drug strategy, establish program goals and objectives, implement prevention and treatment programs and to support the collection of data on drug use and to promote research.

President Nixon brought Jaffe to D.C. to run the office. Dr. Dupont supported the work from his federal post running the NTA, and later became Jaffe's successor. Nixon, although he did also, of course, utilize tough law and order rhetoric, was explicitly focused on treatment and rehabilitation in a manner no other previous US president ever was. He wrote in his 1971 Message to Congress that drug enforcement must be "coupled with a rational approach to the reclamation of the drug user himself. . . . We must rehabilitate the drug user if we are to eliminate drug abuse and all the antisocial activities that flow from drug abuse."[42]

Together, with President Nixon's strong support, Jaffe and Dupont led the development of a network of methadone treatment facilities all over the United States as the core part of the $105 million requested in his 1972 budget to be used "for the treatment and rehabilitation of drug-addicted individuals."[43] The Nixon Administration continued to invest in treatment programs, spending two-thirds of the government's drug funding[44] on demand reduction. The results in reducing both heroin use and crime nationally mirrored the success of the D.C. program.

Harry Anslinger, still alive but out of government, did not approve of the federal support for methadone, calling it a monstrous development. As time passed, investment in Nixon's program ebbed and enforcement efforts became more central in the anti-drug fight. Nonetheless, as a model for an effective federal treatment program, and the first national program funding medication for opioid use disorder, it stands out today as an important breakthrough worth remembering.

Nixon Era Drug Enforcement

Although I believe it is important to emphasize the Nixon Administration's innovation in establishing the country's first national treatment program, drug enforcement also became a Nixon priority. The Office of Drug Abuse Law Enforcement (ODALE) was established at the Department of Justice by an Executive Order 1972.[45] ODALE was charged with disrupting the domestic heroin market at street level. Patterned after the DOJ's Organized Crime Strike Forces, it included task forces of federal, state, and local enforcement officers. Myles J. Ambrose, the agency's director served concurrently as a consultant to the President and a special assistant attorney general, an unusual arrangement. ODALE established task forces in thirty-four cities in 1972.

Their agents were criticized for conducting drug raids involving unauthorized forcible entries into private homes. The office did not operate at a scale to have an impact on national arrest rates, but it did provide increased visibility of federal drug enforcement efforts that the White House could highlight. ODALE was folded in with DOJ's Narcotics and Dangerous Drugs Bureau and later became part of the newly established Drug Enforcement Administration (DEA) in 1973.

It's fair to say that Richard Nixon launched the modern War on Drugs, but more in terms of increasing the political salience of the drug issue, rather than in the sense of widespread use of incarceration. His harsh law and order rhetoric set a tone and other political leaders, not just on the federal level, but also on the state level, went along, and some even upped the ante. It was New York state Governor Nelson

Rockefeller, a moderate republican planning his own run for the White House, who established what became known as the harsh "Rockefeller Drug Laws" in 1973. The new penalties mandated fifteen-year sentences for possession of heroin, cocaine, and marijuana and filled the state's prisons with drug offenders. The last of these laws were not repealed by the New York state legislature until 2009. This punitive approach became a nationwide phenomenon during the crack cocaine epidemic, discussed in the next chapter.

Discussing Racism in Nixon's Drug War

The reality that ugly racism was central to Harry Anslinger's thirty-year reign as the top federal drug official is well documented. The case regarding the Nixon Administration is more complicated. The largest drug program his administration funded was treatment focused, albeit explicitly connected with the objective of reducing crime. Still, Nixon did not hesitate to roll out tough rhetoric. During his Presidential campaign in 1967 Nixon published "What Happened to America" in *Readers Digest*, at that time the nation's largest circulation magazine. Nixon wrote:

> The symptoms are everywhere manifest: in the public attitude toward police, in the mounting traffic in illicit drugs, in the volume of teen-age arrests, in campus disorders and the growth of white-collar crime. The fact that whites looted happily along with Negroes in Detroit is ample proof that the affliction is not confined to one race. The shocking crime and disorder in American life today flow in large measure from two fundamental changes that have occurred in the attitudes of many Americans. First, there is the permissiveness toward violation of the law and public order by those who agree with the cause in question. Second, there is the indulgence of crime because of sympathy for the past grievances of those who have become criminals. Our judges have gone too far in weakening the peace forces as against the criminal forces.[46]

There is another quote about racism in the Nixon Administration that has become well known. It is from a magazine article by author Dan Baum (no relation). Here is what former Nixon White House Counsel and domestic policy adviser John D. Ehrlichman was quoted as saying:

> The Nixon campaign in 1968, and the Nixon White House after that, had two enemies: the antiwar left and black people. You understand what I'm saying? We knew we couldn't make it illegal to be either against the war or blacks, but by getting the public to associate the hippies with marijuana and blacks with heroin, and then criminalizing both heavily, we could disrupt those communities. We could arrest their leaders, raid their homes, break up their meetings, and vilify them night after night on the evening news. Did we know we were lying about the drugs? Of course we did.[47]

This quote, provided in a 1994 interview, more than two decades after Nixon resigned from office, does not provide a full picture of Nixon's drug policy and perhaps reflects a mistaken reminiscence. I include it here because it is now in the public record, but because I was concerned about its accuracy, I reached out to Dr. Jaffe and Dr. Dupont to ask their perspective, since they both worked directly with President Nixon on drug policy. Jerome Jaffe told me[48] that he never saw that racist side of Richard Nixon. Dr. Jaffe later emailed me that Ehrlichman's comments were "entirely inconsistent with every contact I ever had with" President Nixon and "inconsistent with what he did" in terms of supporting significant federal funding for drug treatment.

Dr. Dupont, when I asked him about the quote, told me: "I never felt that any of the people I related to in the Nixon staff were racist or that there were lies about anything involving drugs or drug policy. Blacks were about 90 percent of our Narcotics Treatment Administration's patients and three of my bosses in five years working for the D.C. government were Black."[49]

As in the historical record for many public policy issues, the truth is complicated. What is clear is that there is a longstanding and troubling relationship between racism and drug policy in the United States.

The Harsh Legacy of Stigma Directed at People Who Need Drug Treatment

Stigmatization of drug use, present at the beginning of the drug war, continues to impede progress in the effort to reduce overdoses, foster treatment entry and to create an environment where people can openly pursue recovery from addiction. Studies have found that stigma is a fact of life for those with substance use disorders and that "these experiences can negatively impact feelings and beliefs about treatment" and have a negative effect on treatment outcomes by reducing "feelings of self-efficacy."[50]

Stigma, besides being cruel and unfair, stands as a major obstacle to progress. Stigma "manifests in labeling of people, negative stereotyping, status loss, and discrimination . . . At the individual level, anticipation of being stigmatized can lead to a desire to hide one's substance use, contributing to social isolation and high-risk practices such as solitary use of drugs."[51] Reducing stigma toward addicted individuals is an essential requirement for making progress in addressing today's crisis.

Stigma is a tough problem, but not an impossible one to address. Effective stigma-reduction efforts would seek to amplify and publicize the benefits of high-quality substance use disorder treatment and increase treatment providers' and the medical profession's "enthusiasm for caring for patients with addiction and improving patients' experiences with the health care system."[52] Stigma is a long-standing, complex, and consequential problem. Efforts to study and test different strategies to address it must be made in earnest.

Stigma does not just severely impact people who use drugs, but also their families and closest friends or roommates in the aftermath of an overdose. The grief of parents, children, and siblings is acute and can be long lasting.[53] This close circle surrounding the individual who passed away may face not just the painful loss always associated with an unexpected death, but also shame and guilt about their inability to prevent the death. Naturally, much of drug policy is focused on helping people with a current drug problem find a path to treatment and recovery, but it is critical that those who may be suffering grief and loss also receive the support they need.

Recommendations

1. **Establish an *Opioid Crisis Memorial Museum and Education Center* in Washington**

   The country needs a dedicated place where visitors can learn about the country's evolving opioid crisis as well as about the individuals who have lost their struggle with drugs and those who have navigated their way to recovery. Information about anti-drug programs and policies, past and present, including those that have racist and stigmatizing impacts, the causes, and implications of addiction, and the new initiatives that are working today to bring hope for a better tomorrow need to be shared. The whole story, good, bad, and ugly should be accessible to all. Far more Americans have died in this war than in all foreign wars combined. Yes, this is not the same type of war as what American servicemen have faced overseas, but it is nonetheless important, complex, and worthy of all our citizens learning about it.

   This *Opioid Crisis Memorial Museum* would have four related functions. *First*, it would provide a place to permanently remember those who have died from drugs, both from the ongoing opioid epidemic, and from earlier epidemics. A digital biography, along with photos or videos, can be provided by families. *Second*, the museum's education center will develop permanent exhibits on the opioid crisis, programs for students, and host speakers and events. *Third*, the museum will support families who have lost a loved one, facilitate their access to grief counseling, and aid those seeking to establish a family foundation to educate the public about addiction. These families are uniquely powerful witnesses to the costs of overdoses, the country needs to amplify their voices. *Fourth*, the museum will run an anti-stigma campaign and serve as the base for a new Center of Excellence on studying and combating drug-related stigma. *An initial appropriation of $100 million is proposed to begin planning for the museum, set up virtual exhibits, provide services to families, and establish for $5 million an anti-stigma Center of Excellence and social media initiative. Like other memorials and museums on the National Mall, this museum will be built with private funds and once constructed operate as part of the Smithsonian.*

Chapter Summary

2

Coked Up

Building Washington's Drug War Infrastructure in the Crack Cocaine Era

Chapter Introduction: This Scourge Will Not End

When President George H.W. Bush stepped forward to be sworn in and then prepared to deliver his inaugural address on the top of the Capitol Steps, I was out in the crowd watching. On this day, January 20, 1989, I walked the few blocks from the Congressional staff building known by the not so impressive name House Annex #2 (later renamed the Ford House Office Building) to join the gathered masses. I was in my second year on the Republican staff at the House Select Committee on Narcotics Abuse and Control, working for the Ranking Republican, Congressman Ben Gilman from New York State. I started interning for Representative Gilman after graduating from Georgetown University in 1987 as I looked for a full-time paid job. I had sought out Gilman since he was a moderate Republican from my home state, and he served on the House Foreign Affairs Committee. My goal was to get a staff position at Foreign Affairs, but when he offered me a Committee Staff job at the Narcotics Committee in early 1988, I was happy to accept it. The issue was hot, and the work turned out to be interesting. Of course, I did not appreciate that I would still be grappling with a similar set of policy issues thirty-eight years later.

When I started the new job, I had just turned twenty-three and was happy to be able to pay my rent for an apartment just across the Potomac in Rosslyn, Virginia. Life was good—a lot of my college friends stuck around town, and I was excited to start my career on Capitol Hill while frequenting happy hours downtown for the free food and cheap drinks. I dived into the War on Drugs with enthusiasm. During the year before President Bush's inauguration, I had a small junior staffer role in working on the Anti-Drug Abuse Act of 1988 that created the new Drug Czar's office. One of my jobs was to write up and hand out flyers on the House Floor that would advise Republican Members how to vote on amendments, and on final bill passage. It was my hope, as I watched the speech in the crowd, that the new President would highlight the drug issue. I was not disappointed.

George H.W. Bush, (George W. Bush's father) had worked on drug enforcement as the head of the South Florida drug interagency task force and emphasized drugs during his successful presidential campaign against the Democratic nominee, Massachusetts Governor Michael Dukakis. In his inaugural address, President Bush hit the subject hard:

> There are few clear areas in which we as a society must rise up united and express our intolerance. The most obvious now is drugs. And when that first cocaine was smuggled in on a ship, it may as well have been a deadly bacteria, so much has it hurt the body, the soul of our country. And there is much to be done and to be said but take my word for it: This scourge will stop.[1]

When I heard those words, I felt a rush of excitement. Every staffer, on the Hill, in the executive branch, or at a think tank or advocacy group, wants to believe that what they are working on is important. When the President talks about your issue in a speech televised all around the world, it feels good. It meant, from an inside the beltway perspective, that what I was working on mattered, that the chances of having an impact, while also advancing your career, were elevated. As I look back now, I realize how little I knew about addiction and drug policy. There was no boot camp, no manual, no training course when I started. But I didn't notice the absence. Like most young people starting out I would learn on the job. On that sunny day, I could not have been happier to throw myself into fighting America's War on Drugs.

Hard Lesson: Drug policies and programs, built for the crack cocaine epidemic, must be overhauled for the opioid crisis

The troubling increase in the sale and use of crack, open-air drug markets, and related gang violence required new laws, policies, and programs to address the problem. To some extent this is a positive sign of how our democratic system of government works. The public's priorities rise to the top of the agenda and politicians seek solutions. However, in hastily drafting legislation mistakes were made. The most troubling offense was failing to quickly recognize and correct them. Some errors—such as the crack / powder 100–1 sentencing disparity discussed below—were particularly consequential and eventually addressed (in 2022). But others, such as the collateral consequences for drug sentences, the failure to better balance and integrate public safety and public health responses, and the insufficient effort to create the array of accessible, affordable paths into treatment needed remain with us. Yes, progress has been made, but far more still needs to be done. A top to bottom review of federal laws, budgeting priorities, drug sentencing laws and gaps in programs needed to address today's crisis is required. States and counties should also conduct their own reviews. Times have changed and government, at every level, needs to rebuild, restructure, and prepare to take on the increasingly complex opioid epidemic more effectively, which will be with us, unfortunately, for an extended period.

American's Taste for Cocaine Fuels Powerful Colombian Drug Cartels

Cocaine, a stimulant, has long been utilized as a drug to provide energy to those who could afford it and avoid addiction or overdose. Former US President and Civil War General Ulysses S. Grant relied on a cocaine solution to finish his memoirs as he fought late-stage throat cancer."[2]

Sigmund Freud used the drug and prescribed it to his patients in the pre-Harrison Act era. Inventor Thomas Edison enjoyed cocaine infused wine to help him work long hours.[3] Once cocaine was banned, along with opioids, cocaine use became less common. However, that would change when experienced marijuana dealers in the 1970s found a way to feed a growing cocaine market for a wider cross section of American baby boomers who sought out cocaine as a party drug.

Famously, pilot and marijuana trafficker George Jung met Colombian trafficker Carlos Lehder in 1974 behind bars when both were serving prison sentences in Danbury, Connecticut. They hatched a plan to build out a cocaine market utilizing the Bahamas as their base, starting with a single plane before building a drug smuggling hub in the Bahamian island, Norman's Cay. The book *Blow*, which was turned into a film of the same name, starring Johnny Depp, tells their story. They could buy a kilo of cocaine in Colombia from Medellin drug kingpin Pablo Escobar for $2,000 and generate $50,000 in sales inside the United States[4] making them extremely rich, fueling Escobar's rapidly growing cartel and eventually turning these trafficking innovators into top targets of the DEA. Jung and Lehder were arrested in 1987.

Their downfall, however, not surprisingly, did not end cocaine trafficking to the United States. By the time of their arrest many other organizations were involved in the cocaine trafficking business, having learned from Jung and Lehder about the efficiency of small planes to transport a growing volume of cocaine, and about the lucrative American cocaine market. Pablo Escobar continued to expand his cartel, before being killed in 1993. In Cali, Colombia, the Orejuela brothers built a more discreet business-minded cartel that lasted until 2006. Netflix's *Narcos* series depicts the violent rise, evolution, and fall of these two powerful cartels, including the cruel torture and murder of DEA agent Enrique Camarena. These organizations vastly expanded Colombia's ability to move cocaine north to the United States, as well as to other drug markets around the world.

In a significant change from past practices, Colombian drug traffickers by the 1990s, fearing potential indictment and extradition to the United States, sought to limit their exposure to US law enforcement by selling their cocaine directly to Mexican cartels. This led to the development of the powerful and violent cartels we face today across our Southern border. The home base and names of the top cocaine traffickers changed, and many have been killed—by trafficker rivals or the Mexican Government—or arrested. Nonetheless, the massive production of cocaine continues in Colombia, as does its large scale flow into Mexico and on to the United States.

Powder Cocaine Becomes the Elite's Drug of Choice

Many drug policy experts in Washington in the 1960s and 1970s initially did not believe that cocaine posed a serious health risk. This was true during both Republican and Democratic administrations. A 1975 white paper on drugs published by the Ford Administration[5] concluded, incorrectly, that cocaine "is not physically addictive" and that the drug "usually does not result in serious consequences such as crime, hospital emergency room admissions or death." Peter Bourne, President Jimmy Carter's close friend and a psychiatrist by training who worked from 1973–1974 for Nixon's drug anti-drug office, was appointed as Carter's Drug Czar in 1977. Bourne famously said: "Cocaine is probably the most benign of illicit drugs. At least as strong a case could be made for legalizing it as for legalizing marijuana."[6] To be fair, they were relying on the data available to them at the time, which indicated that cocaine was less addictive compared to heroin. The level of concern about cocaine, however, would soon elevate.

As the supply of cocaine increased, the US domestic market evolved. In the 1970s, cocaine was a drug for the wealthy who had the funds to spend $100 for a gram of the substance. At first there were few serious law enforcement or societal obstacles for those who had the funds to purchase it. It was frequently consumed by rock stars, Hollywood elite and the titans of Wall Street, both for energy and stamina, and to stay up late at private parties and famous night clubs such as Studio 54 in New York City. Before Robert Downey Jr. became Iron Man, he struggled with cocaine addiction and received treatment for it. Legendary 1970s band Fleetwood Mac (the inspiration for the book and Amazon Prime streaming show *Daisy Jones and the Six*) was infamous for their cocaine use, reportedly consuming a bump (one dose) before every concert.[7]

Growing demand by a broader group of Americans with money to spend was met by increased supply and reduced prices as cocaine became more mainstream. Cocaine, according to a 1981 *Time* magazine cover story, became the "drug of choice for perhaps millions of solid, conventional and often upwardly mobile citizens."[8] This widespread drug use, although it did over time cause serious behavioral and health problems among regular users, did not become a top priority for local police because of the people who consumed it. As an expensive drug, sales were relatively discrete, consumption was behind closed doors and its use was not seen as a driver of local crime, violence, or street disorder. Observed one law enforcement official in Chicago: "These people are not the dregs of society. They tend to be legitimate business people."[9] This is not to say that federal officials were not concerned about international cocaine smuggling, they were, but it did not become a dominant national priority for the federal government until crack emerged.

The Development and Rapid Spread of Crack Cocaine

Before there was crack cocaine, some people learned how to smoke cocaine via "freebasing" powder, which was done by combining cocaine with ether, heating the combination, and then smoking the fumes of the crystallized substance through a water pipe. Famously comedian Richard Pryor in June 1980 caught on fire free-basing cocaine and was found by police running down the street in Northridge, California near his home. Pryor later, in 1982, described the incident in one of his televised comedy specials that were extremely popular. The incident was national news, educating Americans about the risks of smoking cocaine in this manner. Pryor's description of the incident is available on YouTube.[10]

However, for smokable cocaine really to take off, there was a need to develop a more easily accessible product. Drug traffickers were aware of the potential market for smokable cocaine and experimented with different ways to process cocaine powder in to smokable crystalized rocks. Historian David Farber concludes that the recipe for crack was probably developed around the same time by multiple traffickers in major cities around the country, but that a group of Dominican drug distributors in New York were likely first. Their recipe cooked up a combination of cocaine, baking soda, and a variant of the prescription drug lidocaine. As Farber describes: "Crack's fierce and nearly instant high was a huge hit with coke users of all kinds, especially poorer folks who could not afford the price of a gram of powder cocaine but could buy a cheap hit of the highly potent" new drug.[11] The product quickly spread to major cities all over the country.

Selling crack was a tempting opportunity to earn money in communities that offered little in terms of job opportunities. For young people, particularly boys, struggling with underfunded schools in impoverished neighborhoods and who didn't have access to the employment opportunities available to those living in wealthier neighborhoods, dealing crack cocaine "seemed like an economic lifeline, an improbable but readily available ticket to the good life."[12] It was a rapidly growing business. A crack dealer quoted by Farber notes with a sense of wonder: "That shit took off. I mean like a rocket ship."

Open Air Crack Markets, Gang Violence, and Growing Public Fear

The crack cocaine market was very different from the powder cocaine market. Although dealers could also sell smaller amounts, powder was often sold in relatively large volume, such as an eighth of an ounce—called an 8-ball (equal to 3.5 grams). One gram would provide a regular user with over a dozen large doses, and new users with up to a hundred small doses. In contrast to the $100 cost of a gram of powder, a dose of crack was cheap, around $10. It was quick and easy to consume and hit the brain and body faster than powder, providing a near instantaneous high.

This type of low-cost, high-volume product required a much different approach to retail sales. The large number of transactions led to open-air drug markets in many communities, initially just in the big cities but over time spreading around the country to mid-sized cities and smaller towns as drug dealers sought their own territory to control. As the drug became more popular and the profits rolled in, dealers and traffickers had to protect their profits and their area of operations, resulting in drug sellers carrying guns and business rivalries leading to shootouts in the streets. With so many people armed, even non-drug related conflicts, over women or other personal beefs, that might once have been settled by a fist fight, were addressed with guns. Naturally this type of violence was of concern to communities and prominently featured on the nightly local news, raising fears even for those who lived far away from these crack markets.

There is no doubt that communities that involuntarily hosted violent crack markets were troubled by the negative impact of open-air drug markets on their neighborhoods. Local officials demanded that the police take action to shut down these markets and protect their families from the violence. Many citizens also bravely sought to organize neighborhood watches or community patrols to make it difficult for drug transactions to occur. At the House Select Narcotics Committee, these local efforts drew our attention as something both important and politically useful to highlight. I organized a hearing on this subject for the Committee in 1992 (called "Community-Based Anti-Drug Initiatives") and later produced a guide for how other communities could directly reduce drug sales through protests, marches, or just occupying the space where drug markets were based. I was happy with the title I came up with for it: *Block by Block: A Community Guide to Retaking Our Streets and Neighborhoods from Drug Dealers*. This approach, developed by courageous and persistent community activists, would scare away customers and at least temporarily paralyze drug markets. These efforts did have a meaningful impact, but it was difficult to permanently shut down drug markets, which moved locations or waited out activists. Nonetheless residents' bravery in the face of potential violence in the effort to reclaim their neighborhoods was something to this day I admire. Learning directly from these community leaders and innovative organizers opened my eyes to how seriously residents from many impacted communities sought to rid their neighborhoods of the impact of open-air crack markets.

The violence associated with crack markets, although sensationalized by news portrayals, was real. As described in a 2006 study[13] the homicide rate for young black makes (between fourteen and seventeen) more than doubled during the peak of the crack era, with slightly older black men (eighteen to twenty-four) experiencing nearly the same rate of increase. Many African American communities suffered greatly during this era, and not just from the violence. The spreading crack use and the rapidly escalating arrests were both highly consequential. There was a doubling of children in foster care, and an increase in fetal deaths and low birth weight babies in minority communities. As the crack epidemic ebbed in the late 1990s these impacts faded away, and by 2000 fell back to their pre-crack levels. Yet the laws, policies and beliefs developed in this era would persist.

Drugs, AIDS, and the Reagans

Ronald Reagan took office as the 40th US President in 1981. His landslide over Jimmy Carter was seen as a significant shift to a more conservative approach to governing. This included strong support for proactive law enforcement and tough language against drugs. President Reagan said in an address to the International Association of Chiefs of Police:

> Studies of prison inmates have found that at least half admitted to using drugs in the month prior to their arrest. And it's still estimated that 50 to 60 percent of property crimes are drug related. From these statistics about youthful offenders and the impact of drug addiction on crime rates, a portrait emerges. The portrait is that of a stark, staring face, a face that belongs to a frightening reality of our time—the face of a human predator, the face of the habitual criminal. Nothing in nature is more cruel and more dangerous.[14]

Notably, as the Reagan Administration turned to taking on drug use as part of their broader advocacy for traditional values, crack cocaine had yet to emerge as a crisis. In fact, when First Lady Nancy Reagan launched her "Just Say No" anti-drug prevention messaging campaign, the focus was very much on youth marijuana consumption. Her efforts, begun in 1982, with Mrs. Reagan coming up with the phrase in answering a student's question about what to do if someone offers you drugs, took off. She traveled the country giving speeches, made television appearances on then popular family television shows, Diff'rent Strokes and Punky Brewster, and helped to foster the establishment of over 5,000 Just Say No school-based clubs by student groups.

The approach was widely ridiculed as the 1980s wore on and the addiction and violence of the crack epidemic became the focus of drug policy. Nonetheless, in the era when there was a much less developed body of research on prevention science, it was a way to talk to young children about drugs. Once someone had already initiated drug use these types of simple messaging are not effective. However, youth drug use, particularly for marijuana, did decline sharply in the Reagan era, suggesting that the consistent anti-drug messaging—although of no help to those urgently needing vastly underfunded treatment for crack addiction—perhaps had some impact in reducing or delaying initiation of substance misuse by young people. It is hard to make a strong causal case, but it's important to keep in mind when debating these types of public campaigns who the target audience is. Over time, in some anti-drug media campaigns, a far more rigorous effort was made to utilize focus groups and surveys to test the ads. This type of prevention science was not widely used in the 1980s.

Later, ONDCP's *Above the Influence* campaign, which reflected lessons learned from earlier media campaigns, was working quite well. However, it was defunded by Congress in 2014. When I told President Trump, at a briefing on opioid policy at his New Jersey golf resort, that we could make a real difference on drug use with a $100 million media campaign, he told me, "You need a billion." I laughed with appreciation at his genuine enthusiasm. Unfortunately, we were never able to get a large-scale, well-funded, research-based anti-drug media campaign going.

Turning back to Ronald Reagan's Presidency, although the Reagans were focused on tough anti-drug messaging, another epidemic threatened the health of Americans—AIDS. The AIDS epidemic in the United States was formally declared in 1981 by the Centers for Disease Control and Prevention (CDC). The disease, although it impacted both men and women, had a devastating impact on gay men. AIDS was spread not just by sexual contact, but also through blood transfusions and the sharing of needles with someone who had been infected. There is much in books, films, television, and theater about the tragedy of AIDS, the breathtaking loss of life, the search for an effective treatment, and the battle for attention and respect for stigmatized communities. To get a sense of the times watch the 1983 Oscar winning film *Philadelphia* starring Tom Hanks, with a beautiful title song by Bruce Springsteen, or the book by Randy Shilts, *And the Band Played On*, which was turned into a film in 1983.

The slow response to the AIDS epidemic by the Reagan Administration is a theme of both the academic and popular literature of the era. Particularly important for drug policy is the development of harm reduction techniques, such as providing clean syringes, to reduce the spread of AIDS. Over time, veteran harm reduction experts and activists moved into the drug policy space bringing a new approach that was initially fiercely resisted by the anti-drug community. Much more on this in Chapter Five.

The Political Earthquake From the Cocaine Overdose of College Basketball Star Len Bias

Two days after he was selected on June 17, 1986, as the number two NBA draft choice by the Boston Celtics, star college basketball forward at the University of Maryland, Len Bias, overdosed and died from a cocaine overdose. Although Bias consumed powder cocaine, not crack, the political reaction focused largely on the emerging crack epidemic. The overdose of a young athlete in peak physical condition received widespread media coverage and overnight sharply intensified political pressure in Washington to come forward with solutions. Soon cocaine was seen as the number one problem the country faced and was the subject of cover stories in national magazines. Once the crack cocaine crisis reached public consciousness as a crisis, it stayed that way for an extended period. According to a June 1989 Gallup poll, drugs were the top concern by a 3–1 ratio over any other issue. The same poll found that 92 percent of Americans wanted tougher laws against drug sellers and 77 percent supported tougher laws against drug users.[15]

The Len Bias overdose did not predate the crack epidemic, since before his death crack was widely consumed in most large cities and federal drug use surveys indicated rising use and emergency room reports of crack related visits, more overdoses, and heightened treatment demand. The dramatic increases in cocaine related visits to hospital emergency room from 1983 to 1986 were particularly alarming (from 10,000 to over 600,000) and fatalities increasing from 500 to 3,500.[16] Urban residents didn't need a data report to know what was happening—they were seeing it on their streets and everyone else was watching on their nightly news. The media coverage of Bias's death, the disturbing survey data, and firsthand accounts of the crack epidemic combined to create a strong political reaction.

As described in a classic public administration text[17] by John Kingdon, a policy proposal gets on the political agenda when three conditions are met: (1) the issue must be perceived as a problem; (2) a viable solution must already exist; (3) and the political environment must be willing to allow a policy change. After Bias's death conditions 1 and 3 were met. Congress quickly went to work to come up with newly proposed solutions.

The United States Congress, like other legislative bodies, has a traditional way of developing legislation to update US laws. The process would generally start with the exploration of a problem and possible solutions through public hearings and staff consultations with experts in academia, think tanks and executive branch agencies. Based on the hearings and discussions draft legislation is put together by committee staff and then shared with interested groups, such as national associations—for drug policy matters—in the health and justice fields. Proposed changes in criminal law could be sent to the Department of Justice for review, as well as to current or retired judges, prosecutors, defense lawyers, and non-governmental organizations (NGOs) with an interest in the subject. This process would refine the draft legislation, correct any mistakes, and help to build consensus on the best way forward. In the case of developing legislation to address the crack cocaine crisis this careful process was tossed out the window.

After the death of Len Bias, members of the Congress from all over the country were hearing from their constituents. The public's concerns rapidly escalated, with the percentage of American adults calling drugs the country's top problem jumping from 2 percent to 13 percent in just the few months after Bias's overdose.[18] Then Speaker of the House, Thomas "Tip" O'Neil was quoted as saying "send me some goddamn legislation" to his caucus.[19] President Ronald Reagan signed the Anti-Drug Abuse Act of 1986 into law on October 27, 1986, five months after the death of Len Bias. An incredibly short period for such a comprehensive piece of newly drafted federal legislation.

Most African American Members of Congress strongly supported the law. That is not to say that over the next decade, when the cumulative impact of the series of laws enacted by Congress became clearer, minds did not change. But in the heat of the Len Bias overdose, representatives from hard hit Congressional districts helped lead the charge. "There is simply no federal program in place to address this serious public health and law enforcement crisis," Rep. Charles B. Rangel (D-N.Y.), Chairman of the House Select Committee on Narcotics Abuse and Control stated at a hearing on July 18, 1986.[20] Rangel was certainly not alone among black leaders outraged by what crack was doing to their communities. The most well-known civil rights leader in the country at this time, the Reverend Jesse Jackson stated bluntly: "Ropes never killed as many of our young people as the pushers of drugs."[21]

The 100–1 Crack Cocaine Sentencing Disparity Fiasco

The 1986 Anti-Drug Abuse Act was enacted with widespread bipartisan support. The House, on September 11, 1986, voted 391–16 while a few weeks later, the Senate voted 97–2. After some negotiation, the final bill easily passed Congress and was signed into law by President Reagan a week prior to the November fourth mid-term Congressional elections. House Members and Senators were surely happy to have some tough new drug laws to campaign on.

There were significant drug laws previously, such as the 1970 Controlled Substances Act, which authorized federal enforcement against all controlled substances and established the five-part drug scheduling system and the 1984 Sentencing Reform Act which reduced judicial discretion in sentencing and abolished federal parole. However, the Anti-Drug Abuse Act of 1986 was a whopper. It increased mandatory minimum prison sentences, as well as current maximum allowable sentences for all major drugs of abuse across the board.[22] Federal sentences involving any Schedule I or II drug, except for marijuana, were increased to twenty years to life when death or bodily injury resulted from use of the drug sold. Drug trafficking offenses that were committed while armed would now be punished by a mandatory fifteen years in prison.

The law also increased the authorities of the armed forces, the Customs Service (today Customs and Border Protection) to address drug trafficking, expanded law enforcement's civil forfeiture authority, broadened drug intelligence support, and widened the scope of federal money laundering laws. The legislation created what would become the very controversial international narcotics certification law, requiring cuts in foreign assistance to major drug producing and trafficking countries that did not combat drugs sufficiently. A new program for state and local drug enforcement was funded at $230 million a year. Substantial funds were also included for drug treatment. The overall price tag for the law was $1.7 billion. But no single element of the bill was more consequential than the new crack penalties.

How Congress ended up inserting into US law a 100–1 ratio between crack and powder drug sentencing is quite a story. As described by then House Judiciary Committee counsel Eric Sterling, Congress sought to identify what would be a credible weight of crack cocaine to be considered a trafficking amount. They asked someone whom they had relied on as an expert on street sales of drugs and had claimed to hold a degree in pharmacology from the University of Maryland. As it turns out, the expert was a fraud, who never completed any academic degree programs. But even his estimate, of 20 grams of crack for a five-year sentence, was seen by Senate Republicans as too lenient, and they decreased it to 5 grams. This meant that someone caught with $225 worth of crack faced the same prison sentence as a trafficker found with $50,000 work of powder. As Sterling concludes: "It was completely detached from science. Nobody could say that crack was 100 times more dangerous than powder."[23]

The long-term consequences of this and related sentencing decisions will be explored in chapter 7. But let me emphasize that the tragedy was not just the poor drafting of one law, but the inability of Congress to find a way to take a second look and fix what should have been seen as a drafting error suitable for non-controversial technical corrections a year or two later. It was a reckless abandonment of serious policy making. The disparity was reduced to 18–1 in 2010 and finally eliminated in 2022.

Although President Nixon is credited with launching the War on Drugs, drug war fueled mass incarceration did not kick into gear until after these legislative changes triggered by the political response to the crack epidemic. It is important to highlight that although the reach of the federal justice system did start rapidly growing in late 1980s and 1990s, the federal justice system is relatively small compared to the combined state systems. As a rule of thumb, the federal justice system is about one tenth the size of the criminal justice systems of all states combined.

Congress incentivized states to take a tougher posture toward drugs through increased federal support for police, prosecutors, and prisons, but regardless, state legislatures were subject to the same political pressures as Congress to increase their own penalties for drug crimes.

Local officials adapted to this intense focus on drug enforcement by taking actions that led to aggressive crackdowns in hard hit urban communities and major increases in incarceration. In 1984, Washington state adopted the country's first "truth-in-sentencing" laws that required inmates to complete 85 percent of their sentences—a major increase for the typical inmates who previously could be paroled after serving just over half their sentences. As the crack era hit hard, twenty-seven other states followed Washington state to also increase the length of drug sentences served.[24]

A careful analysis of how urban areas responded to the emergence of major crack cocaine markets and political pressure to address the crisis is instructive. Until pushed into a position of grappling with crack, prosecutors and courts did not have the capacity nor the desire to lock up large number of its citizens. Previously they dealt with most local crimes by locking people up for a night in jail, but under the pressure of a hot War on Drugs, and new state laws, cities like Chicago changed their approach. Cook County's state's attorney, Richard Daley, a future mayor who learned politics from his father, a local political boss, reorganized the district attorney's office to closely track cases, tightened cooperation between police and prosecutors, and built a "highly efficient incarceration machine."[25] Skeptical judges that raised concerns faced ridicule in the media from Daley.

Drug arrests in Chicago rose from just 4 percent of all arrests in 1983 to 9 percent by 1985, and to 13 percent in 1987. This percentage reached a peak of 23 percent by 1998. This massive effort in Chicago in the 1980s nonetheless was unable to control drug sales, gang activity, or drug-related violence. Looking back, it is hard not to agree with historian David Courtwright who wrote in his book, *Dark Paradise*, "What we think about addiction very much depends on who is addicted."[26]

The accelerated incarceration process featured a heavy reliance on negotiated plea bargains between prosecutors and defense attorneys. Plea bargains, which resolve about 97 percent of cases, also reflect a disproportionate impact on African Americans. One recent study concluded that the "structure and process of plea bargaining makes it more likely that the historical racial bias that exists against African American male defendants will taint the negotiation process and justice outcomes."[27]

Police stop and frisk practices are also generally concentrated in minority communities. From 2002 to 2019 "the New York City Police Department (NYPD) conducted over five million pedestrian stops. Approximately 85% of those stops were initiated against blacks and Latinos."[28] For many years political leadership in New York assumed that stop and frisk policies were essential for reducing crime. However, when stop and frisks were reduced from an annual peak to 685,724 in 2011 to 11,629 in 2017[29] there was no measurable increase in crime—in fact felony offenses declined.[30]

Cocaine Myths and Legends

There are a fair number of myths about drugs that have entered the public consciousness. Let me highlight four of them, including two major conspiracy theories suggesting that the United States Government was directly involved in fueling widespread cocaine use in minority neighborhoods.

One theory was that US intelligence agencies were involved in a scheme with supporters of the Nicaraguan Contras—then fighting a civil war in their Central American nation—to spread crack cocaine throughout urban America. This hypothesis, proposed by reporter Gary Webb in his series of stories published in the *San Jose Mercury News* in 1996 under the title "Dark Alliance: The Story Behind the Crack Explosion" has been credibly disproven. Michael Massing in his book *The Fix*, called it "ludicrous,"[31] observing that there was no question that the vast bulk of the then seventy tons moving into the country each year was controlled by Colombians, not Nicaraguans or any organizations linked to US government agencies. A strong overview of this matter was published in 2014 by the *Washington Post*, which reiterated that although the CIA may have had relationships with the Nicaraguan rebels who profited from drug trafficking, there was not a CIA role in a drug ring.[32]

A similar but more diffuse theory reflects the view that the far-flung American law enforcement and security system, internationally, on the border, and domestically in states, cities and towns must have the ability to stop the continuing flow of drugs into neighborhoods. Since drugs keep showing up, day after day, particularly in impoverished communities where people of color reside, it must because that's the way the government wants it to be. It is an understandable thought, considering the under-investment in many minority neighborhoods in terms of public services and the long history of racism in America, but as will be discussed in later chapters, controlling the drug supply is wickedly difficult and there is no evidence to suggest that government at any level was intentionally and systematically channeling or otherwise allowing drugs to reach certain communities.

Another important myth that emerged from the crack epidemic was the fear that children of mothers consuming crack while pregnant would face a lifetime of physical and mental disabilities. Although any drug or alcohol prenatal exposure has risks, the racist undertones directed at minority pregnant women struggling with crack cocaine addiction were a focus of the narrative. A more sympathetic, although still mixed, societal attitude emerged when white women were exposing their babies to opioids a couple decades later. Nonetheless, researchers found that the impact on brain development and behavioral health from mother's crack use during pregnancy turned out to be relatively modest, fading over time.[33]

That doesn't take away from the reality that pregnant mothers with a substance use disorder need to be a significant focus of drug policy, both in terms of protecting the mother and the child. A destigmatized approach that enables honest conversations between expecting moms and their doctor and encourages substance use disorder treatment for the mom without threats of punitive enforcement actions is appropriate, regardless of the drug or the background of the woman involved.

Finally, let me highlight a phrase that echoed through the decades but is rooted in the crack epidemic: "Superpredators." The expression originated from an academic and later political appointee John DiLulio in a 1995 article[34] and picked up by numerous politicians and journalists. It suggested that the emerging generations of teenagers, born into homes struggling with addiction, poverty, and lack of a strong moral education were going to become a new generation of violent, unfeeling criminals threatening America. The phrase was associated with African Americans and helped drive the push for longer prison sentences. As it turned out, in the 1990s, as the crack epidemic faded away, crime dropped sharply. By 2001 DiLulio, to his credit, said his theory was wrong and apologized for it.[35]

The Crack Era Ends, But Much of the Policy Infrastructure Built for it Remains

The crack crisis, which emerged in the early 1980s, was in retreat by the early 1990s. The wreckage regular crack consumption caused in people's lives made the drug appear far less attractive. Young people saw the drug damage or destroy the lives of their older brothers and sisters, parents, aunts and uncles and friends. As David Farber concludes: "Crack was hard on the body and the soul. Customers were lost to arrests, to death, to illness, destitution, detoxification and simply to age."[36]

The crack cocaine epidemic ended, but even with improvements in many sentencing laws, serious crack era collateral consequences remain for those convicted of drug offenses. A cursory review of the National Inventory of Collateral Consequences of Conviction[37] shows a daunting array of challenges to those seeking to reintegrate into society. Perhaps most importantly is the obstacle posed by simply having a felony conviction on one's criminal history, creating serious hurdles for those who have completed their sentence, entered stable recovery, and are seeking to rebuild their lives. To a lesser extent, but still a concern are the collateral consequences for those with a misdemeanor sentence, which in certain states can be quite severe.

This is a problem that deserves more attention. A way needs to be found to relieve those who have served their time, and demonstrated good behavior to break free from this heavy burden. Those coming out of prison face tremendous barriers, internal and external. The fact that past crimes follow people the rest of their lives seems quite un-American and a cruel catch-22. Society expects those who complete their prison sentence to work and maintain a law-abiding life, but also restricts their ability to work or find a home. This type of permanent penalty should be removed; this scarlet letter of a felony conviction should not haunt people the rest of their lives.

Recommendations

2. **<u>Create a *Drug Policy Reform Congressional Committee* to correct past errors and establish new initiatives to address today's opioid crisis</u>**

   We are still too reliant on laws, institutions, and funding mechanisms built for the cocaine era and must reorganize to effectively take on the fentanyl/polydrug threat that challenges us today. The entire drug sentencing approach should be restructured, eliminating the reliance on the weight of drugs seized and removing collateral consequences that persist even after a drug sentence is completed. The federal government is not set up to adequately fund and manage important areas of drug policy, including providing low-threshold, flexible treatment; recovery support; diversion of drug offenders; recovery housing; expanding the addiction workforce; ensuring universal access to evidence-based youth drug prevention programs, and disrupting covert and internet-based drug markets. New capacities, staffing, and authorities are also needed at ONDCP, as I describe in subsequent chapters. Another outside advisory commission report is *not* needed. Rather, a legislative body empowered to enact changes must be established to modernize the drug war infrastructure, address long-festering problems, and chart a path for the future. *A bicameral, bipartisan Committee should be established to draft a comprehensive legislative reform package that would eliminate unhelpful legacy legislation remaining from the crack cocaine era and create a governance system that fully meets today's needs. Congress should also re-establish the Select Committee on Narcotics, eliminated in 1993, to help monitor implementation of reforms and to expand the number of House Members and specialized Congressional staff closely tracking drug policy on Capitol Hill.*

Chapter Summary

3

Prescription for Disaster

Purdue Pharma's Crime of the Century

Chapter Introduction: Risky Business

There is a lot of blame to go around for the slow and inadequate response to the opioid epidemic. This crisis revealed weaknesses in government at the federal, state, and local level that still have not been fixed. Much of this book focuses on examining these hard lessons. Nonetheless, that is not to suggest in any way that government was the primary driver for launching the relentless, cascading killer waves of the opioid epidemic. That blame has rightly been fixed at the door of Purdue Pharma. So, this examination of the opioid crisis starts with reviewing the actions of this greedy and cruel corporation and other bad actors who along with Purdue seeded and profited from prescription drug misuse. But it doesn't end there. After a review of how Purdue launched this tidal wave of overdoses across every part of the country we will turn in the next chapter to the government's response, look at what went wrong and why, and explore how to make sure the government is equipped with the capabilities and resources it needs to take on this crisis.

How this happened—how one company started the most lethal drug epidemic in world history—is a breathtaking tale. It's a warning and reminder of how powerful organizations, driven by their own business goals, can alter the trajectories of millions of individual lives and bring suffering to so many families. Many outstanding writers have produced well-researched books on Purdue Pharma. I will draw upon their work in the pages ahead to lay out the key elements of what was unleashed on the United States by a single profit-driven pharmaceutical company.

On a personal note, let me highlight that I am by no means anti-business, nor do I question the great achievements of innovative companies and their hard working executives, boards of directors, and employees. My late father, Michael, was a personal financial advisor, spending his days researching new companies, advising clients, and excitedly telling me and my brother about new products and services. He spurred my curiosity about the private sector by bringing home samples of new breakfast cereals offered by General Mills, buying one of the first Apple Computers, and tracking the early development of Disney World and EpCot Center in the 1970s. I still remember, four decades ago, when he shared a news article with me about this crazy idea of combining a pizza restaurant with a giant arcade. Later, when the first Chuck E. Cheese opened, he took the family to try it out—a tradition I proudly continued when my kids were young.

The private sector has an incredible history of bringing new products and services to Americans, creating new jobs, and enabling our country to grow, thrive, and develop. The pharmaceutical industry has produced tremendously important products and treatments, enabling people everywhere to live longer and fuller lives. Those companies that kept front and center their higher purpose to improve health have been a wonderful part of the modern world. Effective medications can be like miracles, saving lives that in an earlier era would have been lost, and preserving the quality and lifespan of beloved family members. There are many exceptional pharmaceutical companies. Purdue Pharma was not one of them. Instead, they sparked a deadly fire which spread across the Nation, one that, two decades after OxyContin was introduced, is still burning hot.

Hard Lesson: Big pharma's reckless marketing of opioids has severely and permanently worsened America's drug problem

The opioid epidemic was not caused by the government, rather it was launched by the leaders of one company, Purdue Pharma. Other profit hungry corporations jumped into the opioids business in the wake of OxyContin's release. This is not to imply that all of the critical individual actors with an important role in the profitable opioid supply chain were intentionally harming patients. Surely most doctors, pharmacists, patient advocates, hospitals, and medical clinics in this national tragedy sought to help patients experiencing pain. However, the entire health care system was operating in an environment skillfully manipulated by Purdue Pharma to favor increased prescribing of opioids and to discount the increasingly clear evidence of a crisis. The fact that Purdue's marketing, lobbying, and advertising efforts were so successful is disturbing and raises many questions about how some large for-profit companies operate. Perhaps the government can't fix all these problems, but it certainly can make sure the pharmaceutical industry doesn't forget their central role in causing the deadliest drug epidemic in world history.

The Spark: Release of OxyContin in 1996

Purdue Pharma knew it faced an obstacle to getting doctors to jettison their long-standing reluctance to prescribe an opioid outside a highly controlled hospital setting when it prepared to release its new drug. This work on changing attitudes was informed by the company's experience with the release of the OxyContin precursor, MS Contin, in 1987, a drug containing morphine. Purdue's innovation was adding a coating (referred to as "Contin"), which slowed absorption of the drug and, they claimed, made the opioid safer than other formulations of morphine in both prolonging the pain-relieving duration of the medication, and in reducing the potential of addiction.

Nonetheless, Purdue, even with its special coating, had some work to do to convince doctors that lengthy opioid prescriptions would be safe. As recounted by Patrick Radden Keefe in his 2021 book *Empire of Pain*, back in 1984, in Toronto, Richard Sackler organized an International Symposium on Pain Control. One of the doctors at the event asserted that addiction "is a psychological malady" and only occurs when morphine was misused by "those who do not need it."[1] This conference and other marketing initiatives were very effective. MS Contin was a hit for Purdue Pharma. But as MS Contin's twenty-year patent was getting closer to running out, Purdue Pharma began looking for another opioid formulation that they could profit from.

After some debate, Purdue Pharma settled on the drug oxycodone. It was much stronger than morphine but was not a new drug. Oxycodone had only been sold as part of a combination product with acetaminophen (Percocet) or aspirin (Percodan). In these formulations the dose of oxycodone was relatively low, and the medications that were combined with it made taking the drug for an extended time not feasible due to the health consequences of excessive consumption of acetaminophen or aspirin. However, Purdue Pharma argued that if pure oxycodone could be slowly absorbed by the body due to the addition of its Contin coating system a much stronger dose of oxycodone could be provided, resulting in better pain relief, no risk of toxicity because of the removal of acetaminophen or aspirin, and, according to Purdue, no serious risk of addiction. Thus, the concept of OxyContin was born. Now all they had to do was get it through the FDA drug approval process.

Did they conduct years of careful research or conduct human trials for safety and efficacy as normally were required for new drugs? No. They didn't have to, the company successfully argued that Purdue Pharma was just reformulating an existing drug and that therefore would not need to work through those lengthy and expensive new drug review processes. They made their case for approval to the FDA utilizing an almost impossible to believe thin research base. Purdue Pharma highlighted a one paragraph summary of a study of opioid misuse by 40,000 patients in hospital settings. The 1980 short article, entitled *Addiction Rare in Patients Treated with Narcotics* concluded: ". . . that despite widespread use of narcotic drugs in hospitals, the development of addiction is rare in medical patients with no history of addiction."[2] Even though Purdue's plan was to have doctors prescribe OxyContin for extended home use, they leaned heavily on this large hospital study. Another smaller study, of thirty-eight patients prescribed a variety of opioids outside a hospital setting, but not including OxyContin, was pointed to by Purdue Pharma concluded that: "opioid maintenance therapy can be a safe, salutary and more humane alternative to the options of surgery or no treatment in those patients with intractable non-malignant pain and no history of drug abuse."[3]

One might have thought that Purdue would conduct at least a few comprehensive new studies of OxyContin use outside hospital settings, but they didn't. Purdue carefully negotiated the approval process with the key FDA official charged with reviewing and approving new opioid products. Curtis Wright, who later went to work directly for Purdue, collaborated on the documentation required for approval with his future employer. They negotiated on the fine print of the booklet of information that would be included with the drug, summarizing the available research and describing the safety of the drug. OxyContin was formally approved by the FDA on December 28, 1995. The whole approval process took less than a year. If the substance was treated like a new drug it would have taken over ten years.[4] Richard Sackler bragged to his team: "This just didn't happen. It was a deftly coordinated, planned event."[5] A year later Curtis Wright started work at Purdue, making a cool $400,000 a year.

Critical to the approval process was Purdue's reliance on their previously developed pill coating. They argued that, as with MS Contin, their technology curtailed the risk of addiction. They even produced a chart[6] illustrating this theory which they showed doctors to illustrate how and why their drug was safer than other products. The first half of their chart illustrated how traditional opioids work, with rapid cycles of sedation and euphoria, followed by the effect wearing off and pain returning. This cycle contributes to addiction. However, Purdue Pharma said they solved that problem with their Contin system, turning pharmaceutical opioids into long-acting painkillers, as they illustrated with their second part of the chart, which showed consistent, steady pain relief over twelve hours. Many patients found that OxyContin pain relief wore off earlier, compelling them to start taking more of the drug early and launching them on a path toward excessive use, dependence, and addiction. The chart was brilliant medical marketing, reassuring doctors, even if it was not validated by research and was meaningless once patients discovered how to peel off the coating, crush and snort the pills, or dissolve them in water and inject the solution.

A *Los Angeles Times* investigation of OxyContin's exaggerated pain relief found the following:

> As OxyContin's popularity grew, a handful of scientists outside Purdue published research raising questions about the 12-hour claim. Scientists affiliated with the Oklahoma University College of Medicine found in 2002 that nearly 87% of those prescribed OxyContin at a school pain clinic were taking it more frequently than every 12 hours. The reason, researchers wrote, was 'perceived end-of-dose failure.' A separate study underwritten by a Purdue competitor, Janssen Pharmaceutical, reached a similar conclusion. Researchers surveyed chronic pain patients treated with OxyContin and reported that less than 2% said the drug lasted 12 hours

and nearly 85% said it wore off before eight, according to a 2003 journal article detailing the research.[7]

If you were like me, you probably thought that multi-billion-dollar pharmaceutical companies would be investigated by government regulators in the promulgation of a data-based chart without clear evidence to back it up. Turns out, they got away with it. The same newspaper article also reported that when doctors expressed concern that OxyContin was not lasting twelve-hours for their patients the Purdue marketing reps were instructed to advise them to just increase the dose, but not alter the frequency. "There is no ceiling on the amount of OxyContin a patient can be prescribed, sales reps were to remind doctors, according to the presentation and other training materials." This pattern of use was particularly awful for patients who well before twelve hours suffered both the return of pain and the emergence of serious withdrawal symptoms.

In addition to the problem of the duration of the pain relief provided by OxyContin, there is the related and serious problem of how the coating can be defeated by those either seeking more immediate pain relief or otherwise misusing the drug. A 2013 analysis confirmed that OxyContin consumers were easily evading the coating and thus absorbing the medication rapidly.[8] This type of use greatly increased the risk of addiction and overdose. It also made Purdue's simple coating solution to protect against excessive use of opioids worthless to the many patients, who discovered through internet chat rooms or word of mouth easy work arounds. This would lead to tragic consequences. By the time Purdue Pharma came up with a solution, meaning a far more effective abuse deterrent reformulation of OxyContin, it was far too late for many, and as we shall see below, ultimately also ended up making matters worse.

The Spread: Purdue's Pharmaceutical Marketing Tornado

OxyContin was an incredible blockbuster sales success for Purdue Pharma. How'd they do it? With a breathtaking and fraudulent marketing campaign. Their focus, naturally, was doctors. Between 1996 and 2001, Purdue conducted more than forty national pain-management conferences, flying in physicians to resorts and teaching them about the benefits of OxyContin. Although many doctors do not believe that their prescription decisions are influenced by such events, the research,[9] and Purdue's escalating profits, indicated otherwise. Court documents filed by the Attorney General of Massachusetts in 2019 suggested that "doctors who met with Purdue Pharma drug reps were *ten times* more likely to have prescribed opioids to patients who later died of an overdose than physicians who prescribed opioids without having met the company's drug reps."[10]

But it wasn't just large gatherings that were used to convince doctors to start utilizing OxyContin; they also sent sales representatives to visit, often bringing small gifts, such as lunch for the staff or stuffed animals. John Oliver highlights some of these tokens of appreciation in his brilliant three-part series[11] on opioids (see https://www.judgeforyourselves.info/). These sales representatives were highly incentivized with annual bonuses averaging $71,500 in 2001, which were well more than their average annual base salary of $55,000.[12] This was in addition to a continuing campaign of print advertising, promotional videos, public relations efforts to defend the company, and a well-funded legal and lobbying campaign to protect Purdue Pharma's interests.

The OxyContin marketing effort was a huge national campaign, and Purdue staffed up, building up its team of sales representatives and coaching them how to increase sales and overcome any skepticism toward the new drug. Although the sales reps were not trained or credentialed health professionals, they were quite good at their jobs. As Keefe explains:

> Sales reps aren't doctors. They're salespeople: bright, often physically attractive. These qualities might not be essential prerequisites, but they're helpful in a job that is in some ways pretty challenging. The pharmaceutical rep spends her days dropping in on doctors, surgeons, pharmacists, anyone who can influence the prescribing of a drug. As a rule, the people she is calling on are busy and overworked, so they may not welcome the unsolicited intrusion in an already hectic day. Reps are door to door missionaries. The good ones are naturally persuasive. Each sales rep is prepared: drilled by instructors, coached on talking points, armed with

serious-looking medical literature that spoke to the revolutionary properties of OxyContin. They were on a mission.[13]

These missionaries were unleashed on the country and got to work. OxyContin hit the market in 1996. That first year it earned $45 million in sales, but by the year 2000 sales exploded to $1.1 billion and continued to grow.[14] By 2010, sales reached $3.1 billion—Richard Sackler's dream had come true. He had the biggest hit in his company's fifty-year history, surpassing his uncle Arthur Sackler's success with Valium.[15]

In his assessment of the causes of the epidemic, Malcolm Gladwell writes in his 2024 update of his first book, *The Revenge of the Tipping Point*, that Purdue Pharma marketed OxyContin "with more enthusiasm and audacity than anyone had ever marketed a painkiller before." He also emphasizes that the company, even after widespread reports of sharply rising fatal overdoses, closely followed the expert advice of their consulting firm, McKinsey, to focus its army of marketers on the highest-rate prescribers. Richard Sackler wrote in an email that the "discoveries of McKinsey are astonishing"[16] and utilized them to turbocharge sales with mounting fatal consequences for the country.

Further, Purdue Pharma and other distributors of opioid pharmaceuticals had more tools in the toolbox to keep expanding sales, even when the risks had become clear. *The New York Times* revealed in late 2024 that pharmacy benefit managers, the critical middlemen between health insurance companies and pharmacies, received generous financial incentives to keep opioid pharmaceuticals flowing to the American people. Purdue "didn't want doctors to have to provide additional justification for prescribing a powerful narcotic, and it didn't want strict limits on the number of pills that could be dispensed"[17] and used payments to pharmacy benefit managers such as Express Scripts, CVS Caremark and Optum Rx—$400 million a year by 2012—to effectively block sales restrictions.

What Purdue and their well-compensated collaborators were selling wasn't much different from the pharmacists peddling ten cents worth of morphine a century earlier. The trick wasn't the drug, it was the skillful evasion of the guardrails put in place after the original opioid epidemic to protect Americans from easy, long-term, non-hospital access to powerful opioids.

The Accelerant: Industry Funded Pain Advocacy Groups Push for More Use of Opioids

Perhaps the most manipulative aspect of Purdue Pharma's multifaceted marketing campaign concerns their discreet funding of what appeared to be public-interest campaigns addressing the undertreatment of pain in the United States. Although a typical consumer of news in America would have quite logically assumed that when changes in how pain was treated were publicly announced and instituted that they were driven largely by medical associations and independent experts, the truth was otherwise. Purdue Pharma helped push for the establishment of the Joint Commission on Pain and influenced its deliberations through its funding of anti-pain advocacy groups. Of course, this is not to suggest that all actors in this process had bad motives. Surely many had genuine compassion for suffering patients and were trying to promote policies they believed in. But regardless, the driving force behind the scenes was the large companies making a killing selling pain pills.

Fourteen pain advocacy organizations were identified in a US Senate report, from 2012 to 2017, to have received big pharma financing. Purdue and four other opioid producers were the largest donors. Several of the pain groups went out of business soon after the primary source of their funding was revealed. Nonetheless, it was a good return on investment for Purdue Pharma. Although the US Pain Foundation received just $2.9 million, and the Academy of Integrative Pain Management and the American Pain Society just $1 million,[18] these targeted investments helped clear away obstacles to Purdue Pharma turning OxyContin into a billion dollar a year blockbuster drug.

The marketing lift Purdue Pharma and other companies selling similar opioid products received from these influential pain groups was stunning. The Joint Commission on Pain, which likely would not have been created if not for Purdue Pharma, promulgated in 2001 Pain Management Standards which promoted the concept of pain as the "fifth vital sign." The standards led to the widespread distribution of "smiley face" pain rating patient charts[19] into medical facilities across the country. It also effectively encouraged hospitals to survey patients on their degree of pain relief and linked results of these patient surveys to levels of hospital reimbursement for medical treatment. The message was clear—the doctors and hospitals insisted that sufficient medications be provided so that patients were 100 percent pain free. This goal resulted in pressure to increase opioid dosage regardless of the long-term consequences.[20]

Pain is a serious subject, and I by no means want to suggest that it isn't a vital concern for the health and well-being of tens of millions of Americans. Many individuals in pain were recovering from significant injuries or surgeries, or wounds acquired by defending the United States in military service. Of course, nobody wants people to suffer unnecessarily. But the establishment of the goal that such patients should have zero pain set unrealistic expectations and created increased risks of dependency and overdose. What was really was necessary for these patients were alternative pain treatments and a supervised plan for gradually titrating down their opioid use. Too often this type of individualized care was not provided.

The Jump: Prescription Opioid Users, Cutoff from Legal Access, Turn to Black Market Heroin and Fentanyl

Purdue Pharma wasn't the only profit-driven enterprise that saw opportunities in selling more opioids. Drug trafficking organizations based in Mexico also watched with interest how big pharma was reshaping the drug business. For drug cartels, seeing declining revenue from marijuana as many states approved medical use and then recreational use of marijuana, the message was clear, plant more poppies and produce more heroin to supply America's now rapidly expanded appetite for opioids.

When Americans were cut off from their opioid prescriptions, they had an easily available and affordable alternative in heroin. For those resistant, at least at first, to injection drug use, the Mexican heroin was pure enough to be smoked. The traffickers, as Sam Quinones highlighted in his 2016 book, *Dreamland*, often targeted for heroin sales the demographic that first were addicted to prescription opioids: white middle-class Americans living in old industrial towns. The dealers found a lot of customers in these economically struggling areas. Also, the new generation of drug dealers tended to be far more discrete, less violent, and less public in their drug sales than crack cocaine sellers. This approach made it harder for police to find and arrest them, and easier for the traffickers to keep selling more heroin. Thanks to the drug market Purdue Pharma shaped, many prescription opioid consumers converted to reliance on black market heroin. The result was mountains of cash smuggled back to the world's most dangerous drug cartels based in Mexico.

Mexico rapidly increased its annual heroin production, which accelerated from an estimated 26 metric tons in 2012 to 111 metric tons in 2017.[21] A quadrupling of their production was a stunning change. The Mexican drug cartels, recognizing the huge surge in potential new customers, moved swiftly to take advantage of an incredibly lucrative market opportunity. There was little doubt about where that Mexican heroin would end up. Almost all the heroin consumed in the United States is produced in Mexico. Although Afghanistan has traditionally been by far the largest producer of heroin in the world, it has never been a significant supplier to the United States due to issues of cost, distance, and established trafficking networks and routes. More recently heroin production in Afghanistan has been dropping sharply due to a crackdown on opium growing by the ruling Taliban Government. This will not impact the US drug market, which has already seen major reductions in heroin consumption as fentanyl use has largely supplanted heroin, but could provide an opportunity for fentanyl producers to increase their sales in Europe, Asia, and the Middle East if they do end up facing a prolonged heroin shortage.

The next chapter will go into more detail about the government's response to the epidemic, but it's clear that as the ramifications of the large expansion of opioid prescribing came into focus, the government acted on multiple fronts. Those actions deserve scrutiny. However, before we leave this topic of the emergence of the opioid crisis, it's important to emphasize again that the launch of the opioid epidemic was primarily the responsibility of Purdue Pharma. However, as evident from the opioid litigation and settlements, once Purdue expanded the opioid market, other prominent companies also profited. The 2025 book *No More Tears* highlights how Johnson & Johnson, the country's largest pharmaceutical company,[22] partnered with Purdue Pharma to promote long-term use of opioids, marketed their own opioid painkillers (the Duragesic patch and Nucynta tablet), and supplied the bulk of opium used by American companies to manufacture their opioid pharmaceutical products. Below are a pair of recommendations designed to sharply reduce the chances that the hard lessons from Purdue Pharma's crime of the century will not have to be re-learned anytime soon.

Recommendations

3. **Impose a lifetime ban on pharmaceutical company employment for former FDA officials with responsibility for key regulatory decisions over narcotics**

   The failure to prevent the opioid epidemic is the most painful hard lesson from *Inside America's Opioid Crisis*. As highlighted throughout this chapter, the primary offenders are the companies that recklessly marketed powerful prescription painkillers to so many Americans. Nonetheless, there is no avoiding the fact that a government official who later went to work for Purdue Pharma appears to have gone easy in the regulatory review of OxyContin. These regulatory decisions are complex, and I do not want to suggest that these agencies, nor their expert staff, intentionally made decisions to harm public health. Still, the reality is that the collective governmental decision-making process surrounding OxyContin contributed to an extremely large loss of life. Stronger guardrails need to be installed. Even subtle actions by those with a vague thought of potential future employment can influence decision-making. Let's not take that risk, the price is too high. This threat was well summarized back in 2011 *in Critical Criminology*: "The failure of the state to protect its people is important in understanding the harm created by the promotion and widespread diversion of OxyContin. Simply focusing on the actions of the corporation [Purdue Pharma] would neglect a very important aspect of this tragedy."[23]

   It is a tremendous honor to work for the American people. Government salaries and benefits, especially for senior officials, are sufficient to make a good living, raise a family, and finance retirement. FDA does very important work and should have the resources, staffing and independence they need across the board. Nonetheless, the risks involved in continuing to enable the few dozen officials in the most sensitive drug approval positions to benefit from highly lucrative post-government careers working for large pharmaceutical companies with interests before their agencies are too great to allow it to continue. *Congress should require the Health and Human Service (HHS) departmental inspector general to designate which regulatory officials at the FDA should be subject to lifetime bans on post-government employment with pharmaceutical companies. FDA should be authorized to provide pay supplements to those subject to the ban to ensure the agency can continue to attract and retain top talent. Five million dollars should be appropriated to pay for the salary supplements.*

4. **Impose a $10 billion annual "opioid crisis fee" on the pharmaceutical industry to help pay for the huge costs of the opioid epidemic**

The pharmaceutical industry has a term describing reports of individuals suffering negative reactions to their products—adverse consequences. Such outcomes are expected from almost all medications, as we hear when we watch those pharmaceutical commercials and someone speed-reads at the end a long list of what these products can do to our bodies. It is not fair to expect any company to produce a perfect product—adverse consequences are part of the system we must live with to benefit from lifesaving and health-improving medications. Still, the costs to society from addiction, financial and human, are monumental. Later in the book, I am going to dive into some of these cost estimates for the opioid epidemic and how much the federal government really needs to spend to address the current threat. However, estimates of the costs to society of the opioid crisis are over $1 trillion a year, and the lives lost since the start of this opioid epidemic are approaching one million. These are unacceptable adverse consequences. Sure, one can argue that through litigation settlements the involved companies have offered compensation for their actions. But keep in mind that even with the significant reduction in opioid prescribing over the last decade, the medical system is still producing 1.5 million[24] new opioid misusers a year, with an estimated total of 7.6 million Americans misusing pain relievers and another 4.6 million misusing pharmaceutical sedatives and 3.9 million misusing prescription stimulants.[25] The US pharmaceutical industry overall has over $500 billion in annual revenue.[26] It's time they provide 2 percent back to help address the tremendous adverse consequences from addiction to prescription medications. This ten billion, targeted appropriately, would over time reduce costs to government at every level without burdening individual taxpayers with higher taxes. *Congress should impose a 2 percent "opioid crisis fee" on the pharmaceutical industry for ten years to finance new programs to combat drugs.*

Chapter Summary

4

Fatal Errors

The Consequences of Pushing Prescription Drug Consumers into the Illicit Drug Market

Chapter Introduction: Pain Management—Too Close to Home

Looking back, it now seems clear that in the rush to impose opioid painkiller prescription limits, government officials seriously under-appreciated the highly consequential implications of such changes. I should have known better. In 2017 I had an up close and personal experience with prescription opioids. My wife had complex and extremely painful foot surgery. She needed around the clock pain relief to get through that first month after surgery. Without the opioids, or some other pain relief, she couldn't sleep. Her suffering was acute.

One time, when her prescription for oxycodone was about to run out, I went to Rite Aid in Falls Church, Virginia, to get her refill. The pharmacist told me that it was too soon for her to get the prescription filled and said that I should come back in a week. I thought to myself, "I'm the Drug Czar, you have to give me these pills," but of course, I did not say that as it would clearly be inappropriate behavior for a government official. Instead, I explained that she was about to run out and that my wife was anxious about not having her medication. The pharmacist said she was sorry, but my insurance wouldn't cover it.

I politely debated it a bit more, and then she said to me, you could just pay for it. How much, I asked? The pharmacist looked at her computer and said with available coupons and discounts I was eligible for it would be $50. I knew I couldn't come home empty handed to my suffering wife, so I handed over my credit card and got the pills. Let me add, that my wife hated needing the opioids and at one point quit cold turkey. I was very worried by the disturbing opioid withdrawal symptoms which quickly emerged and had to convince her to more gradually reduce her use, which she did. Later, as she described how I found her shivering and miserable, suffering from withdrawal, she said she knew she was in trouble when "the drug czar made me take oxy."

Was I a hypocrite? At the time, I did not think so and the reason was simple. The seven-day limit on initial prescriptions that was being promoted by states, anti-drug advocates, and others in government trying to reduce the prescription opioid epidemic was not envisioned as a ban on doctors prescribing more medications. Rather, it was considered a guardrail on the initial prescription, requiring the patient to consult with their doctor about any continuing pain control issues after that first week. If the doctor decided that their patient needed additional opioids, or some other non-opioid treatment for their pain, they could discuss the best and safest way forward. Such individualized care could stop the risky automatic offering of lengthy prescriptions and would allow for safe and appropriate management of each individual case.

As events unfolded, I was wrong about the behavior of actors throughout the health care system regarding how prescription limits would be managed. Those limits were widely locked in as hard caps by state laws and insurance companies. Prescribers got the message that they had to dial back prescribing, often abandoning their patients who needed help with pain care, opioid dependence, or both. Many patients were not properly transitioned off opioids and sought opioids through cash and carry pill mills, or the illicit drug market. Individualized non-opioid pain treatments or effective initiatives to get evidence-based substance use disorder treatments to these patients were not delivered.

In a world where there was not easily available cheap and highly potent heroin (and later fentanyl) produced in Mexico, this approach might have been more effective. Or imagine a world where busy doctors would have the time and resources to individually assess patients, offer a range of alternative pain treatments, and the obligation to utilize gradual withdrawal management and, as necessary, addiction treatment. Unfortunately, we didn't, and we still don't, live in this world. Systematically cutting off so many patients without carefully assessing them and routing them to the medical care they needed—better pain treatment and/or drug treatment—was not sound drug policy or health policy.

A thorough accounting of the outcomes, an assessment of alternative approaches that would have produced better results, and careful consideration of corrective measures still needed to address flawed policy approaches are appropriate. Although this exercise inevitably assigns some blame, that is not the primary objective. The higher purpose is to clearly identify the hard lessons that still need to be addressed. The questions that I believe require answers are:

- Why were major policy changes not tested before being applied everywhere?
- As negative consequences emerged, why were there not significant adjustments made?
- Which alternative approaches to the problem could have produced better outcomes and need to be instituted now?
- What tools, capacities, staffing, resources, and mindset are needed going forward?

These questions can only be answered if we take a closer look at the prescription opioid controls instituted and face head-on the searing realities of the long-term results. As we look at the implementation of these opioid controls it is important to reflect on what it would have taken to identify and respond to these problems more effectively. As I look back in frustration at policy failures, I keep thinking of the classic public administration book, *Groupthink*, which explores the disastrous 1961 Bay of Pigs US invasion of Cuba and the failure of President John F. Kennedy's national security team to challenge their assumptions and or consider alternative approaches.[1] President Kennedy's solution was to assign his brother, Attorney General Robert F. Kennedy, to take the opposing view in policy debates to push all participants to think deeply and avoid a rush to judgment. These reform efforts are credited with ensuring a safe outcome when the Soviet Union and the United States came disturbingly close to nuclear war during the 1962 Cuban Missile Crisis.

The intelligence community at times avoids the risks of groupthink by assigning a "red team" of analysts to propose alternatives to intelligence assessments. It's long overdue for drug policy officials to similarly work harder to avoid groupthink and deliberately assess alternatives before driving major national changes. Further, when negative consequences mount, there needs to be an intensive examination of what is happening, and mechanisms instituted to address problems. At the end of this chapter, I will propose some ways to do this. It's late in the drug war to add this capacity, but never too late. But first let's zero in on the primary set of government policies rolled out to reduce inappropriate prescribing and describe the troubling outcomes. Four policy interventions will be addressed in turn, and then the cumulative impact will be discussed.

Hard Lesson: Restrictions on opioid painkillers were recklessly applied and led to many unnecessary drug overdose deaths

We are twenty-five years into the devastating opioid epidemic. There is a lot known now that we didn't know about this crisis at its start, especially regarding the spread of lethal fentanyl into much of the illicit drug supply. The purpose of this book is not to throw rocks at policymakers and government staff. Those working on various aspects of the opioid issue in the dozens of agencies and offices involved in drug policy did not have a crystal ball. Decisions were made based on information available at the time, and of course, there was huge political pressure to reverse the misuse of prescription opioids. As highlighted in the previous chapter, Purdue Pharma deserves the bulk of the responsibility for this disaster. Still, one's stomach churns when examining missed opportunities for the government to have stopped or slowed this national disaster. Looking back at the wreckage in lives lost and families devastated is excruciating, but learning from such consequential errors and missed opportunities by the government is necessary and long overdue.

Prescription Drug Monitoring Programs

There is a very strong logic behind electronic Prescription Drug Monitoring Programs (PDMPs). Many pain patients were seeking opioid painkillers by fraudulently requesting the same medication from multiple physicians visiting numerous pharmacies, or falsifying prescriptions. The problem, referred to as "doctor shopping" had to be dealt with. What these patients were doing was illegal, dangerous to them, and posed a problem for the doctors charged with managing their health.

One might have thought that, before the opioid epidemic, there would have already been an electronic system to keep track of individual's prescriptions, if only to prevent counter-indications of different medications. Many Americans, especially those that are older, regularly take quite a few medications. Nearly 20 percent of senior citizens take ten prescriptions or more—that's a lot to keep track of, especially when patients are seeing multiple doctors for different issues.[2] However, although some prescription chains maintained an electronic database for their own stores, there was, when the opioid painkiller epidemic emerged in the 1990s, no system-wide electronic prescription tracking. Considering the worsening overdose crisis, concerned actors on the federal level quite logically began to offer federal grant funds to incentivize and support states to begin building out their PDMPs.

The concept of a PDMP was not new, nor was its connection to addiction. The first one was established in 1918 in New York State. As described by *Pharmacy Times*, this initial PDMP was utilized to "monitor prescriptions for cocaine, codeine, heroin, morphine, and opium."[3] This early PDMP relied on paper records. The first electronic PDMP was launched in Oklahoma in 1989. Electronic PDMPs initially spread gradually, but then at a faster rate when federal funds for them became available in 2003. Although Missouri was a hold out until 2023, now every state has one.

From the start, it was clear that there was a challenge to link different states databases so patients couldn't beat the system by crossing state lines. Because in our federal system states have broad control of health and medical matters within their own jurisdiction, there was little support for building a national PDMP. Many countries with a national health care system don't have this problem because they have a unified national healthcare system, and their data is automatically linked. But in the United States, those connections between states had to be built one at a time, through two software platforms that were developed, one by a private company and a seperate one by the federal government.

Let me emphasize that PDMPs were not controversial. There was widespread consensus that they were needed, and the only issue was how quickly state governments, with federal assistance, could get them up and running. Once states built their systems, there was a lot of focus on upgrading the software and the interfaces to facilitate their consistent utilization by busy doctors, physician assistants, nurses, and pharmacists.

How the PDMP works is straightforward. Before a prescription was written or dispensed, doctors' offices and pharmacists would check the PDMP database. If there was no record of doctor shopping or fraud, the prescription was provided. If there was a record of a problem, the prescription would be denied. Over time, out of frustration that the health-care actors were not always looking patients up and making sure that the prescription was legitimate, many states made checking the PDMP mandatory.

One might assume, as I did at first, that if a doctor's office found a patient trying to get extra prescription opioids, there would be a very serious effort by the doctor to get in touch with the patient and offer guidance or a referral to a pain clinic or addiction treatment. Clearly, doctor shopping behavior indicated that there was something alarming happening with that patient. Unfortunately, whatever efforts were made were woefully insufficient in terms of addressing the realities faced by those struggling with pain issues or opioid addiction. No doubt many busy doctors' offices were worried about the health and safety of their doctor shopping patients. Perhaps they asked these patients to come in for a consultation about their opioid use or encouraged them to seek addiction treatment. Unfortunately, this type of simple suggestion from a doctor or nurse practitioner is not going to be effective for many who have developed opioid dependence.

The result was that many doctors, relieved to have stopped an illegitimate, illegal prescription, essentially fired their patients and washed their hands of their fate. Nonetheless, the lack of a deeper curiosity and a more fulsome response to the problem is concerning. Here is my description of the three categories of behavior doctor shoppers fall into.

1. They are suffering pain patients who believe they medically require more opioids than their doctor is prescribing.
2. They have an opioid use disorder and need evidence-based addiction treatment, including medications for opioid use disorder.
3. They are selling their prescription for cash and ought to face justice system consequences, including, if they also have an addiction problem, court-supervised treatment programs.

Each type of patient deserved a different type of response, but they received basically the same one. All types of patients seeking an opioid prescription that was not authorized were stopped from getting it. PDMPs worked as designed. The problem was the system was not set up to effectively get help to individuals in desperate need of it.

Of course, these are complicated patients, lying to their doctors and pharmacists and committing fraud. The medical practice that provided the opioid prescription, for example, an orthopedic surgeon, may believe they are not equipped to manage their ongoing pain problems or drug dependence. One can't automatically assume the right course of treatment or the correct specialist to refer these individual patients to. Did they need alternative pain therapies (different medications, physical therapy, massage, chiropractic care) or did they just need coaching on gradually reducing their opioid use? Had they developed a serious opioid use disorder and required appropriate detoxification (i.e., medically supervised withdrawal management) and an addiction treatment program, including medications for opioid use disorders? Alas, as patients were cut off across the country, there did not seem to have been much of an effort to answer these questions. Doctors, facing pressure to reduce prescribing, did so. The whole approach seems to miss the bigger picture, as one study of PDMP implementation in three states concluded:

> Reducing opioid prescribing does not address the issue of people addicted to and misusing opioids. Many participants shared the opinion that the PDMP and new opioid prescribing recommendations have become a reason for doctors to avoid treating problematic patients while also

avoiding being marked as someone who prescribes excessive amounts of opioids.[4]

Below, I will explore the cumulative impact of mistakes made on how opioid prescribing was restricted. In the recommendations section, I will offer suggestions on how to reform PDMPs. The country needs them, but changes are required, not so much in the database, but how prescribers, state agencies, and pharmacists utilize them. Some programs have already initiated promising reforms, but much more work is necessary to ensure these systems help save and support patients, rather than drive them to the lethal black market.

Abuse Resistant Drug Formulations of Opioid Medications

As the prescription opioid epidemic became more visible and threatening to Purdue Pharma, the company sought to differentiate good patients from bad. The good patients were following doctors' instructions to treat their pain, while the bad patients were "drug addicts" consuming far more pills than prescribed. These bad patients failed to use the drugs properly and their problems were their fault. Richard Sackler wrote in a 2001 email later discovered during litigation: "We have to hammer on the abusers in every way possible. They are the culprits and the problem. They are reckless criminals."[5]

As the deaths continued to pile up, Purdue offered a solution that appealed to federal officials searching for a way to slow the epidemic. Purdue would alter the pills so that when crushed they would become a slimy gel that could not be snorted or injected. Thus, the most dangerous routes of administration for prescription opioids could be prevented. This new, alternative technology to prevent misuse was far more effective than the thin coating from the Contin system that was so helpful to Purdue Pharma in getting OxyContin approved by federal regulators.

It was an interesting idea—one that was embraced by government officials anxious for any way to contain the prescription drug epidemic. Federal regulatory agencies got on board and pushed through the adoption of abuse-resistant formulations. It was a classic Washington compromise—

companies making billions could keep selling their pain pills while the government could highlight the actions they were taking to reduce misuse. There was also a bonus for Purdue Pharma. Their new abuse resistant formulation changed their drug formula enabling Purdue to extend their patent. The original OxyContin patent was supposed to expire in 2013, but the new abuse resistant formulations and other minor changes to the chemical structure of the drug[6] extended that until 2030. Apparently, a great victory for all.

Unfortunately, government officials did not sufficiently recognize the emerging trend of widespread transitioning of pharmaceutical opioids to the illicit market for heroin. As often occurred in the history of the War on Drugs, the real-world outcomes were not anticipated. One analysis attributed a quadrupling of heroin death rates to the reformulation of OxyContin in August of 2010. This study found the following:

> The new abuse-deterrent formulation led many consumers to substitute to an inexpensive alternative, heroin. . . [W]e find that opioid consumption stops rising in August 2010, heroin deaths begin climbing the following month, and growth in heroin deaths was greater in areas with greater pre-reformulation access to heroin and opioids. The reformulation did not generate a reduction in combined heroin and opioid mortality—each prevented opioid death was replaced with a heroin death.[7]

Another study found that the introduction of abuse-deterrent OxyContin led to an increase in hepatitis C infections in the United States. The infections increased at three times the rate in states "most affected by the reformulation—states with above-median rates of initial OxyContin misuse—than in states with below-median rates, and this differential increase began immediately after the reformulation in 2010."[8] Before the reformulation, there was almost no difference in hepatitis C infection rates across the two groups of states.

The results of the new formula were increased heroin use, more dangerous infections for IV drug users, and no net change in opioid overdoses. In addition, the patient became lost to the black market, no longer engaged in receiving medical care from the doctors who had been prescribing opioid painkillers. At least when connected to medical practices, those patients had a place to go to ask for help. Once they started relying on street drugs, they were lost to the health system and the risks to their survival rapidly escalated.

Strict Limits on Opioid Prescribing

The data was clear about the risks of long-term prescription opioid use for many patients. Those who left the hospital after a medical procedure with an opioid prescription for over a week faced growing odds of still consuming opioids a year later. Those odds continued to rise with increases in the length of prescription. One study noted that for those whose use of opioids lasted at least eight days 13.5 percent were still on opioids after a year. Those who continued use for at least thirty-one days experienced a 29.9 percent rate of continued use.[9]

Something had to be done. Anti-drug organizations proposed strict limits and government officials jumped on the bandwagon. On March 18, 2016, the CDC published its *Guideline for Prescribing Opioids for Chronic Pain*, recommending that no more than three to seven days of opioids be prescribed for acute pain, accelerating imposition of new restrictions. One former CDC official emphasized that no guideline "had ever been implemented this swiftly, this thoroughly, this specifically, and this zealously" by public and private sector actors.[10]

There were patients' rights groups that raised concerns, arguing that the limits were arbitrary and would put patients at risk. Later, government agencies and officials received numerous complaints and questions from family members of those cut off from medications. Regardless, the idea picked up momentum around the country, not just in federal and state government, but also within health insurance companies, to impose an opioid painkiller limit. The whole environment toward opioid prescribing rapidly shifted toward cutting patients off, enforced by new state laws and private insurance company practices.

This issue is an especially resonant example of a kind of panic taking over what should have been a much more rigorous policy debate. It was right for policy officials to recognize the scale of the prescription drug epidemic crisis and to propose new approaches, but driving a national solution without mechanisms set up to validate the approach had severe consequences, explored in greater detail below. A good question to consider is how to find a balance to still enable "energy in the executive" that Alexander Hamilton called for in Federalist Paper No. 70, while also creating credible guardrails to catch problems. Too often government agencies are skilled at announcing and launching new initiatives, less so in testing them in the field or going back and overhauling them when problems and complications mount. Further, the cascading impact of national policies on other actors also must be accounted for. Federal health officials supported strict limits on prescribing, but it was state legislation and insurance companies' practices that implemented them.

Shutting Down Pill Mills

I used to spend a lot of time in Florida as a kid and young adult. My late grandparents owned a small condo in Royal Palm Beach, and my parents kept it so the family could use it. When we drove those last few miles inland from West Palm Beach down Okeechobee Boulevard to Royal Palm Beach, I loved to see what changed year to year. What was once a relatively undeveloped area of palm trees, orange groves and a handful of homes when I was young transformed from the 1970s to the 1990s. It was exciting to see the new movie theaters, restaurants, and stores crop up—but I do miss the orange groves where you could pick your own fruit. I remember driving down Okeechobee with my wife, before we had kids, looking at what had opened at the strip malls that had replaced the tropical fauna. I noticed a pattern—the signs for "pain clinics" showed up multiple times on that twenty-minute drive. By then I had been working on drug policy for quite a few years already, so I certainly had an idea of what the clinics were. But what I saw in Florida startled me—this was a trend that looked like trouble.

The state of Florida had become the epicenter of a reckless business of medical practices selling pain pills to patients. It was not uncommon for purchasers to resell some (or all) of their opioid medications on the black market in high opioid use states, such as West Virginia, Ohio, Tennessee, Pennsylvania, and Kentucky. At their 2010 peak, ninety of the nation's 100 largest prescribers of opioid pharmaceuticals were physicians based in Florida and 85 percent of the nation's oxycodone was prescribed in the state.[11] A local newspaper noted that there were at least twice as many pain clinics in Florida as McDonalds.[12] There is no question that these clinics had to be shut down. But the question that also needs to be asked is, "what happened to the patients?" That is a sad story.

When law enforcement agencies identify health service organizations that are corruptly or carelessly dispensing powerful, addictive opioid pharmaceuticals, they have a duty to act. These pill mills are dangerous, harm-causing entities staffed by doctors violating their ethical obligations to their patients and breaking the law. Many were nothing more than drug dealers, turning their practices into a lucrative cash business. These doctors deserved to have their medical licenses suspended and their facilities shut down. However, the consequences for the patients receiving these pills must be considered.

The police departments—in Florida and elsewhere—that investigated pill mills, built their cases, and shut down the clinics were doing important work. Some of the customers at these clinics were re-selling the pain pills to others, not buying them for personal use. However, many of the patients were seeking pain relief they sincerely believed they needed and deserved. Others had developed a substance use disorder and were utilizing the pain clinics as a source of the drug their bodies needed to avoid withdrawal.

These corrupt clinics were not sophisticated practices seeking to develop, implement, and oversee a safe pain control regime for suffering patients. The country needs facilities with caring doctors, physical therapy, non-addictive medications, and other support for those in chronic pain. These cash and carry centers deserved to be eliminated. What was the plan for those who showed up seeking a refill of the powerful medication they may have been consuming daily for many months or years? Generally, these opioid seekers faced a sealed clinic front door with a notice instructing patients on where they could get copies of their medical records. Where were the health workers to counsel these patients, or the recovery coaches and addiction counselors to guide people into treatment? Nowhere. Patients, many soon to be in severe withdrawal and in a desperate search for a new drug supplier, were on their own.[13]

Actions Have Consequences

Unfortunately, too many believed during the first decade of the prescription opioid crisis that the barrier to patients shifting from pills to injecting heroin use was sufficient to deter a transition to black market opioids. Further, the untested assumption was that those who had an opioid pill problem and lost their access would just stop misusing opioids or seek treatment. As I will explore in more depth in the next chapter, this mistaken view reflects a poor understanding of addiction. We should have known better.

Research has shown that many prescription opioid consumers transitioned to heroin or fentanyl when they were cut off. Only now, many years past the peak of opioid prescribing, are we truly assessing this process more closely. This is a mistake we can't make again. The authors of one study described the process people who used opioids went through as they grappled with changing access to the prescription opioids (POs) they had once relied on:

> Many participants reported that their physicians cut off their prescriptions, often abruptly, for any of the following reasons: the patient had other drugs in their urine drug screens; the acute need for the prescription ended and doctors felt that participants no longer needed POs; the participant reported to the doctor that they were becoming addicted to the PO; or the doctor cut the prescription because of interactions with other drugs, particularly benzodiazepines. Participants also reported that doctors were less willing to prescribe POs to treat pain, particularly for patients with documented opioid use disorders (OUD) or patients on medications to treat opioid use disorder (MOUD), i.e., buprenorphine or methadone. . . In response, participants reported changing their routes of administration to sniffing or injecting POs, which allows more efficient absorption, switching to heroin or fentanyl, which was cheaper and more accessible than POs, or stopping or slowing down their opioid use.[14]

To state the obvious, the goal of prescription opioid restrictions was to reduce opioid misuse. The fact that so many pre-existing patients moved to the black market when cut off means that for far too many, the policy was a failure. It makes sense for doctors, knowing what we know now, to be much more restrictive in prescribing opioids to *new* patients. But longstanding patients who became dependent on pain pills require a different, more thoughtful approach. The failure to more closely study real-world outcomes for patients that were cut off from opioids was irresponsible. A far more rigorous study of results in states that first imposed restrictions should have been done before the health system launched this experiment on millions of people addicted to prescription opioids all across the country.

It is an important point to make that not everyone, or even a majority, of opioid consumers transition to street drugs. Nonetheless, the total population misusing prescription opioids was so large that even a modest rate of transition triggered a rapid and consequential rise in heroin consumption. Researchers estimate that sixteen percent of opioid users who lost access to prescription opioids "respond by initiating heroin consumption."[15] A study of those who began misusing opioids in the 2000s found that "... 75 percent reported that their first opioid was a prescription drug." Examining national-level general population heroin data (including those in and not in treatment), nearly 80 percent of heroin users reported using prescription opioids prior to heroin."[16] That still leaves many who managed to successfully stop using pharmaceutical opioids. But the consequences for the significant minority who went to the black market were so severe that the overall policy approach was deeply flawed.

The policies described in this chapter did succeed, as intended, in reducing opioid prescribing. As was well summarized by the Bipartisan Policy Center:

> In 2016, the CDC issued a Guideline for Prescribing Opioids for Chronic Pain. The guideline provides information for prescribers on proper opioid prescribing and the potential risks associated with such prescribing. The rate of opioid prescribing in the United States [has] decreased 9.3 percent annually from 2009 to 2016. In 2017, the opioid prescribing rate fell to the lowest rate in 10 years.[17]

These declines, and subsequent ones, were an important accomplishment. It reduced the rate at which the United States was creating new opioid misusers. There is no debate that tightening was required, nor that the government at every level needed to better constrain and monitor access outside the hospital setting prescribing of these powerful medications. Nonetheless, the focus on indiscriminately controlling opioid prescriptions for all consumers without an associated effort to ensure that the patients were handed off to appropriate specialists led to cascading tragic consequences.

As noted in the previous chapter, many patients cut off from their doctors went to the black market first to seek prescription opioids and, when those were either not available or too expensive, they turned to heroin. Overdose rates further accelerated when fentanyl was combined with heroin, and when fraudulent prescription opioid pills containing fentanyl became widely distributed. The fact is that many of these opioid-seeking patients still had a serious health problem, either an opioid addiction or severe, unresolved pain issues. These patients fell through the cracks between the state PDMP programs and the wider health system. The PDMPs were set up for a specific purpose, to stop doctor shopping. In that regard they were successful, but for too many patients they unintentionally inflicted serious, sometimes fatal consequences.

Prescribing has declined and many new patients have been protected from potentially dangerous addiction to prescription opioids. Long-term recipients of opioid painkillers did not fare as well. Some states, recognizing what was happening, began to provide doctors "death notices" after their patients experienced a fatal overdose. Of course, it was too late for the people who had died—and their grieving families.

Recommendations

5. **Reform prescription drug monitoring programs to empower doctors to provide addiction treatment or pain management to their patients to protect them from lethal street drugs**

   PDMPs are an important tool. They provide extremely useful information to prescribers. The question is what is done with that information. Cutting off patients automatically and potentially driving them to the lethal drug market is not a wise option. Several logical steps that should be taken to help those who are identified by PDMPs for misusing their prescriptions. These include screening patients for opioid use disorder or a chronic pain problem and then either treating them for these problems or carefully managing their transfer to a specialist.

   Prescribers need support to effectively execute this approach. States should follow the "hub and spoke" approach innovated by Vermont with substance use disorder patients. In Vermont, the doctors' offices are the spokes, and a more extensive state-supported treatment program is the hub. Doctors start treating patients within their practice with the understanding that the state hubs would take on challenging cases, such as those that require methadone or have complex physical or mental health issues. Additional funds should be made available for patients flagged by PDMPs to pay for screening and treatment. Further, the whole PDMP ecosystem, including all prescribers, state agencies, and pharmacies, need to update their culture. Medical practices need an electronic mechanism to track prescriptions, but the mission must prioritize preserving life. States need to plan a transition and re-train all involved. Federal agencies can provide technical assistance, including a new model PDMP law. The program should be renamed the *Prescription Drug Safety System* which would help emphasize that saving lives and getting people help is the focus of the entire effort. *Congress should appropriate $100 million to support PDMPs in reforming their operations, including $5 million a year to create a Center of Excellence outside government to study, support, and assist in this transition.*

6. **Agencies should designate a senior official to produce *risk assessments* for major new initiatives**

   In government agencies, as in other organizations, there is often enthusiasm for significant new initiatives backed by leadership. It is difficult for agency staff to risk irritating their bosses by being the skunk at the party and critiquing an agency head's big idea. However, if agencies are required to designate someone or a small group of staff to play the role of "red teaming" or raising concerns, like Robert Kennedy did for JFK, it will allow for some reflection and give agency leadership the opportunity to adjust the new policy before it is instituted. Furthermore, it alerts senior agency leadership to be on the lookout for potential adverse outcomes if the initiative goes forward. Policy making is hard, and there is understandably the temptation not to look back once a decision is made. Let's help make sure agencies get it right the first time. *No additional funds are required. Federal legislation should require that all federal drug agencies designate an official to prepare a risk assessment for major new initiatives and brief leadership in writing and in person on their views. A model state law should be produced and disseminated to states to support and encourage them to produce their own state drug policy risk assessments.*

7. **Study state drug policy changes via rapid research before national implementation**

   As Associate Supreme Court Justice Louis Brandeis wrote in his dissent of a case in 1932: "a state may, if its citizens choose, serve as a laboratory; and try novel social and economic experiments without risk to the rest of the country."[18] New policies often emerge at the state level, and this is a good thing. However, just because an initiative gains political support in one or several states, it doesn't mean it's a ready for nationwide adoption. Often states do not sufficiently invest in research at the start of an initiative, failing to collect baseline data, to assess initial outcomes, or to conduct qualitative interviews with those impacted. Long-term research projects, such as those funded by the National Institute of Drug Abuse, are critically important, but are not a substitute for rapid policy implementation assessments. It would be prudent to have a separate, federally controlled funding stream specifically for the purpose of validating state drug policy initiatives of national significance before they are widely implemented. *A federal interagency work group should be established under ONDCP's leadership to identify priority areas for rapid drug policy research, allocate research funds and manage the dissemination of results, inside and outside of government. Congress should appropriate $100 million for this purpose, with the funds residing at ONDCP.*

Chapter Summary

5

The Real Treatment Gap

Why Most People Who Need Treatment Do Not Seek it and What to Do About it

Chapter Introduction: Ground Truth

In the summer, when Stockholm, Sweden, is warm and beautiful, and the layers of ice and snow that cover the Söderström river have long since melted, the city hosts international meetings of the World Federation Against Drugs (WFAD). Sweden has always been known as one of the more conservative anti-drug countries in Europe. One of the reasons why the WFAD organization was set up in Sweden was to combat the drug legalization movement that had been building momentum around western Europe at the start of this century. So it was with some shock that I realized that a group of current drug users, who were represented by their own organization, were coming to participate in the conference.

This was something we certainly did not do in the United States. People in recovery—yes, those who had gone through treatment and committed to a drug-free life, sure. But those in the throes of addiction, who might be intoxicated when they were meeting with us, no way. I didn't get it. Why would government officials want to discuss drug policy with current drug consumers? Well, it's a good question.

There's an expression that came out of the HIV/AIDS prevention and treatment movement, "nothing about us without us." Even a couple of decades ago I understood this expression, but I did not see how it applied to those who were struggling with chronic drug addiction. It felt wrong to me. If they couldn't figure out how to stop using drugs, why should they be advising "drug policy experts" on how to fix the drug problem?

Unfortunately, I had failed to properly understand one very critical point that came into increasingly sharper focus as the opioid crisis worsened in the United States—the single most important issue in drug policy today is how to persuade those with a substance use disorder to successfully enter treatment and take the first critical steps on their recovery journey. Asking those Swedish drug users would have been a good place to start.

Even well before the current crisis, many of us working in drug policy had been focused on increasing investments in evidence-based treatment programs, creating more free treatment slots, improving access to treatment medications, and getting better insurance coverage. All good goals. But I was missing the big picture. People weren't coming. We had not figured out how to persuade most people with a substance use disorder to seek and stay with treatment, and we weren't systematically asking them so that treatment providers could learn what approaches would be most effective. That was a big mistake. I wish I had gone that day to talk to the drug consumers about this in Stockholm, but I didn't, I was too stuck in my own mindset.

As the devastation spreading through our country due to the escalating opioid epidemic unfolded and the cold hard facts about the failure to increase treatment entry became clearer, I reconsidered my views about engaging directly with people who use drugs. Failing to meet with the group of drug consumers in Stockholm was a missed opportunity for me, but it was something I did not forget. It's a funny thing when you have an opinion strongly implanted in your mind and one day you realize you had it wrong. A hard lesson, but one I have taken to heart.

The reality is that if you want someone to voluntarily do something, and they are not doing it, it's essential to talk to them and ask them what they want and need. Some of that information is available through research and surveys, however no ongoing national mechanism exists to systematically collect, analyze, and disseminate it. Acquiring up to date knolwedge of the treatment opportunities that those with a substance use disorder will accept to get started in a treatment program is essential. It's time to stop sitting around, because even when quality treatment slots are created, many people in need are just not coming forward to benefit from them.

There are times when police and courts need to be involved (discussed in chapter 8) in facilitating or leveraging those who pose public safety risks to enter addiction treatment. However, before communities turn to these strategies, they need to make a much more serious effort at promoting *voluntary* treatment entry. It's wrong to think that many with substance use disorders cannot be persuaded to initiate treatment engagement via evidence-based outreach efforts. It is also wrong not to try harder. There is abundant evidence from the experiences of families and friends of those struggling with drugs, as well as through all kinds of interventions by well-meaning, thoughtful individuals that " . . . you change things by changing minds—by persuading."[1]

It is increasingly clear that low-threshold, or low-barrier care, is more appealing than abstinence-based treatment for many people who have become dependent on fentanyl and other synthetic drugs. Low-threshold care is defined as "a model for treatment that seeks to minimize the demands placed on clients and makes services readily available and easily accessible."[2] This approach has a strong track record of facilitating engagement in treatment, addressing directly the core problem of low treatment demand by a large majority of chronic drug consumers (discussed in more detail below).

A lot of rhetoric has been spilled over the years about the term "harm reduction." As I will explain below, there is a sound middle ground between more traditional anti-drug supporters and many harm reduction advocates that the country needs to land on. As highly addictive fentanyl has increasingly penetrated the entire drug supply, many practitioners are moving into this space which, for clarity I have dubbed "harm reduction-informed treatment." What that means is that formal treatment initiation should not always require immediate abstinence. Under a harm reduction-informed approach treatment program participants may choose to gradually cut back their use and start utilizing other health and social services, while concurrently building trusted relationships with a treatment provider, including certified peer counselors or recovery coaches with lived experience. As they begin to access care, build a therapeutic alliance with their treatment counselor, and utilize medications for opioid dependence, those with a substance use disorder can build momentum in their recovery journey and end their drug consumption over time.

This is the way to meet people where they are, but not leave them there. Too many reject traditional treatment because going immediately from daily, chronic use to zero drug consumption—and enduring severe withdrawal symptoms—all at once is too daunting for them to take on. They don't have the belief that they can do it. Many have tried and dropped out or were kicked out of treatment programs previously for continuing some drug use or admitting to a single relapse. Offering options for smaller steps, climbing that mountain to reach recovery gradually, is more manageable and more appealing. Again, traditional abstinence-based treatment is ideal for those who want it and believe they can do it. But for too long we have left the majority who want another path without adequate options. With the drug supply so dangerous, it is not good drug policy. We must get everyone with a substance use disorder engaged in some level of treatment, both to enable them to move forward toward recovery and to reduce the extremely high risk of a fatal overdose they face every day.

Hard Lesson: Most chronic drug users will only voluntarily enter treatment via 'harm reduction-informed' approaches that support a gradual pursuit of recovery

Those of us who work in drug policy, whether in Washington or anywhere else, need to get out of our own heads and learn to walk a few steps in the shoes of those who have become regular consumers of highly addictive drugs. Of course, we want chronic consumers to commit to treatment and recovery. However, daily drug use takes a powerful grip on one's mind and body. Most of those whose regular drug use has become a full-blown substance use disorder are no longer getting much pleasure from drug use. Rather, they continue to consume drugs to avoid painful withdrawal symptoms, to help them feel normal, and to cope with daily life, which may include managing untreated trauma, sexual abuse, or serious health or personal challenges. They will not be freed of their addiction by slogans, television commercials, stern lectures, or stigmatizing disapproval of their behavior. They cannot be "scared straight" or punished into stopping drug use. Although a significant minority of people who use drugs seek abstinence-based drug treatment programs, most do not. Until the country accepts this reality, we will be stuck with an approach that will only reach about a quarter of those who are struggling with addiction. The rest will remain at severe risk of overdose and death.

America's Two Drug Treatment Gaps

Some time ago, when I was working on a presentation for ONDCP, I examined a pie chart that showed how many people who had a substance use disorder received treatment. I wasn't surprised that it was low; I had known that for a while. Since the 1980s when I worked at the House Select Committee on Narcotics, I knew about "the treatment gap." That gap, I thought, was due to the lack of sufficient treatment availability. This is why the country needed to expand treatment availability across the nation and make sure it was affordable and accessible. In my mind I assumed if government, insurers, foundations, private payers, etc., just created one quality treatment slot for each person who needed treatment, the treatment gap would shrink and one day disappear. The country was increasing treatment every year, but the gap wasn't getting smaller, in fact it was growing. What was happening? I looked at the fine print of the data chart and saw the truth that evaded me for too many years—most people with a substance use disorder were not seeking treatment. Those at the most severe risk of a fatal overdose, were not banging down the door of treatment centers. They didn't want the services being offered.

This doesn't mean there still isn't a serious problem with the supply of high-quality treatment slots; there definitely is (more on this below). There are often many individuals who are urgently seeking treatment who still can't get it, due to cost, availability, health insurance restraints, or lack of transportation or time off from work. But these are two separate problems, *two treatment gaps*, that require different solutions. Can't believe I missed that for so long, but once I saw it I began to look at addiction, treatment, and people who use drugs differently.

Why, I wanted to understand, did the people who needed it most not want the substance use disorder treatment that could save their lives? The problem, I came to believe, is with many treatment programs. Most traditional drug treatment programs insist that people commit to stopping all use of drugs when they initiate treatment. This is often a requirement for treatment entry and for remaining in the program. Any violation of that commitment, a single episode of substance use, would get them kicked out of the programs.

For those who are ready to stop and can sustain that commitment to abstinence, that is more than fine; it's a perfect fit. Whatever their journey had been previously, they were done, they were ready and able to fully commit to an abstinence-based treatment program and not look back. Millions of Americans have gone through such drug treatment programs and done well, going back to the first, extremely important treatment program for alcohol and drugs. Narcotics Anonymous (NA), evolved from Alcoholics Anonymous (AA), with their twelve steps, sponsorships, and regular meetings are an incredibly valuable part of the treatment system. The insight on the benefit of having regular opportunities to talk honestly about substance use through group therapy was an important innovation for the treatment field. Many treatment programs, even if they do not follow AA/NA's overall approach, have adopted the concept of group meetings. Every American who wants an abstinence-based program should have access to it, as well as access to an AA/NA meeting, in person or virtual. However, research indicates that those ready and willing to accept immediate abstinence represent only about one-fourth of people with a substance use disorder. This estimate is based on two studies, one that found that 24.6[3] percent of those with a substance use disorder said they were willing to enter drug treatment, and another analysis that found only 27.8[4] percent of people needing it received opioid treatment medications. What about the other 75 percent?

For them, quitting all drug use immediately and permanently, is not something they are willing to commit to. They won't enter a treatment program that requires it. Why? It's because people who consume drugs every day do so to avoid an extremely painful physical withdrawal, and, for many, because they rely on drugs to cope with some other serious problem in their life. As highlighted in the introduction, opioids and other drugs provide relief from not just physical, but also psychic pain or suffering. It's a coping strategy, one that their minds and bodies have been acclimated to. Even if one can get through the withdrawal, the underlying problems that had been masked through drug use, are still there. For those fortunate not to have a history of severe trauma, many years of regular problematic drug use will cause serious life problems regarding work, health, family, and friends that must be dealt with once drug use ends.

Most individuals cannot stop using drugs until they have developed *alternative* coping strategies. Nor will they have confidence in a treatment program that insists they must immediately cease all their drug use on day one. Some, wanting to get help, are put in a position of lying about their ability to quit drugs and end up failing in treatment, dropping out and further adding to the shame and stigma that drug consumers face.

Many people with a substance use disorder have experienced severe physical or emotional trauma as a child. This could include beatings, sexual abuse, severe neglect, or witnessing violence. It is not uncommon for adults with a drug addiction problem to grow up in an abusive or chaotic home with a drug-dependent or otherwise troubled parent. For a child, being harmed by someone they are emotionally dependent on can create feelings of overwhelming anxiety that a young person doesn't understand or know how to cope with. As these children grow up, especially if they do not have access to mental health treatment, drugs may become a method to manage this emotional pain, "a way to feel differently, to not feel, or to get one's mind off the feeling."[5]

Dr. Gabor Mate, who worked as the physician for severely drug-dependent individuals on Vancouver's East Side, described childhood trauma as virtually universal among those diagnosed with a serious substance use disorder. In his recent book, he quotes in agreement, another medical expert on addiction: "Trauma is the foundational factor" in addiction. He adds in his own voice, "whatever the degree of injury, all addiction is a kind of refugee fleeing from intolerable feelings incurred through adversity, and never processed, into a state of temporary freedom even if illusory."[6] This helps to explain why many people who try drugs never become addicted. Absent that underlying trauma many can resist chronic dependence. However, for those with a history of trauma drugs can provide long sought and hoped for relief from deep-seated emotional suffering.

People who use drugs and have a substance use disorder are not dumb, nor are they intoxicated twenty-four-hours a day. They understand that they have a problem; they know that their family and friends are disappointed in them. They also know about treatment, likely having been kicked out or dropped out of treatment programs previously, another thing they have failed at. The only relief they know from this emotional suffering is to continue using drugs.

Many people experience adverse childhood experiences, or ACEs, that occur in the first seventeen years of life. Some young people are resilient or have sources of support that mitigate the impact of childhood trauma, but not everyone. Unfortunately, for others, this trauma can disrupt healthy brain and social development and "lead to substance misuse and other unhealthy coping behaviors."[7]

We should be careful to assess people as individuals. Some people develop a chronic addiction without trauma, they may consume a street drug, a medication, or alcohol for the first time and feel a long-sought sensation of comfort, or over time move from occasional use to daily consumption. Owen Flanagan's book describes how his severe addiction emerged despite a very happy childhood.[8] There are multiple paths to addiction. But regardless of how someone ended up with a substance use disorder, the key is working with them effectively to improve their health and to support their recovery journey. There is much that can and should be done. But first, let's look at the development of the mainstream treatment field to assess how far it's come, and to understand what still needs to change.

Treatment Progress and Challenges

The science of drug treatment has been evolving and improving significantly in the last two decades, but at the same time, the rapidly shifting opioid epidemic has created new challenges to established approaches. It is hard for the treatment workforce to keep up. Remember, when it comes down to it, treatment counselors are people. They have their own experiences, education, and training to rely on. If they are in long-term recovery themselves, some of their own life lessons may be less resonant with drug users today if they are not adapting to current circumstances or received recent training.

It's important to recall that the treatment field is still relatively new.[9] As highlighted in chapter one, when the international drug control treaties were written and during the long tenure of Harry Anslinger astride federal drug policy from 1930 to 1962 the focus was almost exclusively on the supply control side. AA emerged gradually in the 1930s, but not as a medically supervised and research tested intervention, but as a secret self-help fellowship. The Minnesota Model that developed in the 1950s was based on AA's twelve steps and group meetings, but incorporated contributions of professional counselors and psychiatrists.

It wasn't until the early 1970s that the treatment of heroin addiction incorporated a medication, methadone, which greatly increased treatment effectiveness. Buprenorphine was approved for medical use in 1981, and the widely utilized combination of buprenorphine and naloxone, known by the brand name Suboxone was approved by the FDA in 2002. The presence of naloxone makes it very unlikely for someone to overdose on the combination product. But until recently Suboxone and other similar products faced restrictions, including requirements for training by doctors before they could prescribe it, referred to as the "X-waiver" not eliminated until 2022 (as previously mentioned).

Further, the fact that these medications became available did not mean that all providers would utilize them. Significant stigma toward utilizing buprenorphine and methadone continues today. Less controversial—because it does not contain any opioids—has been naltrexone, approved for medical use in the United States in 1984, and today utilized both as a daily medication taken orally and as a monthly injection under the brand name Vivitrol—approved in 2006, but only widely used after 2010. Naltrexone which blocks the effects of opioids and has proven to be effective for many. Considering the potency of fentanyl, methadone remains an under-utilized tool in our efforts to address opioid dependence. Buprenorphine, although not as strong as methadone, is much more easily prescribed, effective for many and sharply reduces the chances that those taking it will suffer a fatal opioid overdose. Considering the potency of the current drug supply providers should be assessing the need for higher buprenorphine doses to ensure its effectiveness. Providers, including those in the justice system, should worry less about buprenorphine diversion or misuse. "Evidence for diversion harm is minimal, yet the consequences of inadequate dosing are predictable and catastrophic."[10] Especially with higher doses, patients experience reduced emergency room visits, use opioids less frequently, and remain engaged in treatment longer. The excessive focus on diversion should be dialed back, since it discourages doctors from prescribing the medication and too often has "spooked pharmacies"[11] from stocking the medication and filling prescriptions. That being said, buprenorphine isn't a cure; its use should be accompanied by counseling, patients who wish to reduce or end their use of the drug should be supported, and states need to regulate buprenorphine clinics to ensure quality. There have been abuses reported by companies that market buprenorphine products, as highlighted by a 2025 book, *Rehab: An American Scandal*.[12]

Treatment medications have become more accessible, and the trendline is moving in the right direction. It is encouraging that the telehealth flexibilities utilized during the COVID-19 pandemic have been permanently extended by a regulation developed jointly by DEA and SAMHSA that went into effect in April of 2024. The regulation "allows patients to receive take-home doses of methadone and the initiation of methadone treatment via audiovisual telehealth and buprenorphine via audio only."[13] This new flexibility creates a range of new opportunities to get medications to patients more simply and quickly, reducing the barriers that create obstacles for people who use drugs to get their first treatment medication prescription. States should use this change to establish medication "hotlines" so that those in crisis can call directly and get linked on the phone with a prescriber—this can include not just doctors, but nurse practitioners and physician assistants. This approach, assessed during COVID-19 in Ohio and Kentucky, was found to be "associated with better retention in treatment"[14] and not associated with any increased risks to the patients. It would be important to continue to study the impact of telehealth over an extended period to refine policy implementation.

Behavioral therapies, although rooted in early psychiatry and developed in the 1960s, became more commonly utilized in addiction treatment in the 1980s. Under the broad umbrella of cognitive behavioral therapy (CBT), there is an array of evidence-based programs utilized on their own or in combination with medications. CBT seeks to alter faulty thinking patterns and negative emotions to replace unhealthy behaviors, such as illicit drug use, with healthier coping skills. CBT includes such specific interventions as motivational interviewing, relapse prevention, and contingency management which incorporates positive incentives into the treatment process to strengthen treatment adherence.

This approach has proven to be especially effective for dependence on methamphetamine and other stimulants.[15] A recent meta-analysis found that 80 percent of studies that tested this approach found that it reduced stimulant use. The California Department of Health Care Services concluded that contingency management "is the only treatment that has demonstrated robust outcomes for individuals living with stimulant use disorder."[16] This limit was raised to $750 per patient each year in January of 2025.[17] This policy should be sustained, and other tax and bureaucratic obstacles need to be addressed. Although some have objected to "paying addicts" to stop using drugs, the costs of the small dollar gift certificates pale compared to the healthcare and criminal justice costs to society, and the individual, of regular methamphetamine or cocaine use. National organizations rightly called on the government to lift the shortsighted $75 limit on treatment funds that can be used for contingency management under many federal grant programs.[18]

Overall, it would be fair to say that today there is a wide range of treatment interventions with a record of effectiveness. There have also been improvements in terms of public and private insurance coverage of substance use disorder treatment and expanding federal funding of treatment through large block grants administered by HHS's Substance Abuse and Mental Health Services Administration (SAMSHA) and other federal grant programs that support a wide variety of state and local efforts. Yet collectively these efforts, especially considering the tidal wave of opioid addiction sparked by Purdue Pharma, remain inadequate. Let's zero in on some of the explanations for this.

When you compare addiction treatment to other medical care, it remains very "program focused." Meaning that many treatment providers and counselors often have a specific program that they utilize with all their clients. This may include elements that are a particularly poor fit for initiating and sustaining engagement in treatment, such as requiring immediate abstinence, kicking people out of the program if they relapse, and inflexible standards that fail to adapt to individual circumstances. Some programs oppose or discourage the use of medications, others rebuke or confront clients who admit they have doubts or fears of ever becoming abstinent. This failure to integrate into treatment programs the realities of individual patients, which may include co-occurring mental health disorders, childhood trauma, and complex personal circumstances, such as difficult polydrug addiction and other health problems, undermines program effectiveness and increases relapse and drop-out risks. Further, rather than helping many patients, the experience in some treatment programs can inflict new trauma and worsen the stigma and shame they experience.

There is an approach developed by psychologist Carl Rogers called "person-centered therapy" that was developed in the 1950s but has not received the attention it deserves. This approach emphasizes respect for the client, treats them with unconditional positive regard, and accepts that the client is the best authority on their own experience. This approach offers benefits over many treatment programs today and is worthy of greater focus within education or training programs for treatment counselors and addiction specialists. It includes some of the elements of the harm reduction-informed treatment described below.

Mainstream treatment programs are too often overly regimented, too focused on following a very specific protocol. With the best of intentions, these programs can end up discouraging and failing patients. The idea that it's necessary to break someone down before they build them up or otherwise confront, challenge, or dictate to them exactly what they must do is not an evidence-based approach. Further, insisting that people who use drugs who may be reluctant to have an abstinence-based program immediately imposed on them are "in denial" or because they have not "hit-bottom" yet is dangerous, cruel, and impractical.

There are many paths to successful recovery; it might involve the AA/NA twelve steps or a twenty-eight-day intensive inpatient program for those that want it, but it doesn't have to. Intensive outpatient, individual psychotherapy, group therapy, behavioral therapy, medications, and a wide range of low-threshold/non-abstinence-based care and services, including SMART Recovery,[19] all have a role. If people who use drugs can engage with a peer counselor, discuss options to improve their health, and select some initial goals to improve their life, then they are taking the first critical steps to a healthier life. As the saying goes, there should be no "wrong door" to accessing treatment.

Stigma—Why it Matters

The issue of stigma directed at people who are struggling with a substance use disorder can be a confusing one. Some argue that if we want individuals and society to avoid the often-devastating consequences of regular drug use, we ought to stigmatize it. There is some truth to this when we are talking about children—we do want to teach kids to avoid drugs, alcohol, and tobacco, especially when they are well under the legal drinking and smoking age. The intent of such anti-drug messaging is to delay and hopefully prevent initiation of illegal substance use, giving time for their brains and bodies to fully develop to avoid serious, perhaps permanent damage to their health. But what about those who have already developed a substance use disorder? At that point, stigmatizing attitudes and approaches are counterproductive.

Consider the difference in the way people react when a family member, neighbor, or friend is diagnosed with cancer. The types of things people do for cancer patients in their social network include calling to check in on them, stopping by to bring some food, or otherwise just offering to walk with them as they go through treatment. With drug addiction it's different, but it shouldn't be. At those times when those impacted by a substance use disorder need love and support, stigma too often keeps people away.

I remember trying to explain to representatives of other governments, such as Russia and China, the meaning of recovery and avoiding stigma at an international meeting. They weren't getting it. Their officials argued stigma is good, we want to send the message that society disapproves. Sure, I conceded, for kids, but not for adults who are already buying and consuming hard drugs every day. Stigma for them doesn't help. The reality is we must hold two ideas in our head at the same time—clearly oppose illicit substance use for young people and for those who have not developed an unhealthy chronic drug dependence. But once someone has a serious, life-threatening, complicated drug problem all of us as individuals, and as a society, need to offer help, kindness, and options to initiate treatment. That is the best way to engage them in genuine dialogue and assist them in taking the often excruciatingly difficult first steps toward creating a healthier life.

It's clear that stigma inflicts harm on people who use drugs. The stigma associated with those who have substance use disorders is a "pervasive phenomenon that has had detrimental effects on treatment outcomes, health care providers, treatments, research, policies, and society as a whole."[20] One good way to start is the language we use to describe drug use. The field has moved from referring to people as an "addict" to those with a substance use disorder (SUD). It's true that some with lived experience choose to refer to themselves as an addict or alcoholic, and that is their choice. But for the rest of us it's good practice to avoid pejorative, stigmatizing words and rely on more neutral or medical language.

Although stigma is often the result of deep-seated beliefs about people who use drugs, that does not mean that it cannot be reduced. The medical profession has an especially important obligation to both address addiction and to avoid stigmatizing language or actions in their practice. "Negative attitudes of health professionals towards patients with substance use disorders are common and contribute to suboptimal health care for these patients."[21] These attitudes reduce patients' feelings of empowerment and impair treatment outcomes. The medical profession needs to significantly increase its commitment to educating those studying to be doctors, nurses, or physician assistance about addiction, including both how to treat it and how to talk about it in a non-stigmatizing matter.

Clinicians and psychologists have "opportunities to promote resilience to stigma to prevent the development of SUDs and leverage acceptance and mindfulness approaches to reduce internalized stigma among people with SUDs."[22] They can also help educate the wider public about substance use disorders and the harms caused by stigma while also advocating for equal coverage by insurance companies for substance use and mental health disorders compared with other medical care. Although this type of approach, referred to as "parity" is now required by law, there are often limits imposed on care such as excessive pre-authorizations, "fail first" approaches and other ways that insurance coverage for substance use disorders are constrained.

Although training programs for those already practicing in the medical field, as well as those who work in the justice system, offer hope for improvement, educating people earlier would be a good investment. As a recent article in the *Journal of Criminal Justice Education* noted, educating students "before they enter mental health and criminal justice professions could help increase addiction knowledge and reduce stigma among these professional groups."[23] Let's equip those who will work with people who use drugs with the knowledge to understand and help them rather than further stigmatizing those struggling with a serious and complex health challenge.

Meeting People Where They Are, But Not Leaving Them There

In the summer of 2018 in New York City, during one of my regular visits to check in on my elderly mother at that time who was still living in the apartment where I grew up, I met Andrew Tatarsky, a psychologist who ran a substance use disorder treatment center. We were introduced to each other by a mutual friend. When I visited him at his Center for

Optimal Living, he gave me his book, *Harm Reduction Psychotherapy: A New Treatment for Drugs and Alcohol.* Although it probably won't surprise you to say I love books about drug policy. I didn't start reading it right away. I hung on to the book and took it with me on a family vacation to Puerto Rico in 2019 during my kids Christmas break from school, determined to read it, sensing that this was something that could help me better understand what was going wrong with our country's response to the worsening opioid epidemic. Each morning, before the rest of the family woke up, I headed out to the beautiful San Juan beach to dive into the book. I wasn't disappointed.

There is a lot of confusion over the term harm reduction; it refers to an array of different approaches to addressing drug use. Some of these interventions long considered harm reduction have become very mainstream, including use of medications to treat opioid use disorder (methadone, buprenorphine, and naltrexone), and overdose reversal products (naloxone). Disease prevention methods such as syringe service programs, are widely supported by medical professionals since the health consequences and disease management costs for hepatitis and HIV are so significant, but are still opposed in some areas. Other harm reduction approaches, including safe injection facilities, providing a "safe supply" of drugs to those dependent on them, and legalizing drug use, remain, for understandable reasons, controversial. But the part of harm reduction which the health system must urgently adopt now is the philosophy of direct, no pre-conditions, flexible engagement with people who use drugs. Offering health and social services people need and want is a necessary first step toward engagement in some level of treatment and to reduce fatal overdoses.

For many years I was rather skeptical toward harm reduction because I perceived the advocacy movement for harm reduction as really a campaign for the legalization of hard drugs, which I do not support. But over time, as I watched fatal opioid overdoses continue to rise and met more families who had lost loved ones, I began to better understand that there were elements of harm reduction that were critical to helping us address the opioid epidemic. Still, I needed to learn more, and to see how some of these approaches could be better integrated into current drug policies.

Dr. Tatarsky's book has the virtue of bringing the reader, through in-depth case studies, into the therapy room, highlighting how, over time, harm reduction psychotherapy can transform lives. This wasn't the caricature of harm reduction enabling drug users to go on indefinitely misusing substances that were damaging their health and their spirit, but rather a method to help them find their own path and pace forward, guided and supported by a trained treatment expert.

In harm reduction psychotherapy, the client sets the goals and, in consultation with the therapist, establishes a timeline and a process for achieving them. Dr. Tatarsky highlights that the "cornerstone of all effective treatment is the therapeutic alliance between client and clinician around shared goals. Thus, the focus of therapy must be on the client's definition of the problem and goals."[24] In this environment the patient selects initial goals as a starting point, rather than looking to the therapist to instruct them on what he or she needs to do.

Even modest goals, such as reducing the frequency of drug or alcohol use, create positive momentum and build confidence. With the advice and coaching of the therapist on techniques and strategies that can help, the client initiates small changes in their relationship with addictive substances. As the client learns to gradually manage cravings and to cope with challenges without turning to drugs, they see and feel progress and gain confidence, often challenging themselves with more ambitious goals. Not every client achieves abstinence through this approach, but many do. Others reduce their risks and improve their health by cutting back their drug use and giving themselves more opportunities to undertake positive steps forward.

The takeaway for me from Andrew's book is that too many treatment programs were "high-threshold"—requiring immediate abstinence in a manner that deters people who use drugs from starting the program or causes them to drop out—or get kicked out—of the program after a relapse. Many drug users respond better to low-threshold approaches that facilitate a gradual effort to wean oneself from powerful addictive drugs and avoid excessive pre-conditions before treatment initiation. Harm reduction in this context should not be seen as facilitating indefinite substance use, but rather enabling those with a substance use disorder to gradually work toward reducing, and hopefully eliminating, their reliance on powerful, dangerous drugs.

Change is difficult for all of us, as our own life experiences and the popularity of self-help books attest. For people acclimated to coping with emotional pain through the daily routine and relief provided by powerful medications or drugs, ending drug use surfaces fears of: " . . . an unknown life where survival, either physical or emotional, is not guaranteed. We cannot work successfully with drug and alcohol use problems unless we understand this; if we do not, we just strengthen their resistance or drive it underground and create false compliance."[25]

Reconciling Traditional Treatment and Harm Reduction-Informed Approaches

What the country needs to do is build out a harm reduction-informed treatment system more fully. A decent foundation exists, but, like most programs for those impacted by a substance use disorder, not scaled to the country's enormous need. For many in the addiction field, including those who have benefited from twelve-step programs, the adoption of this type of approach is difficult. However, as all of us in the drug policy field struggle with the challenge of reducing overdoses and recognizing the lethality and complexity of today's drug supply, there has been a gradual increase in flexibility.

More programs are hiring people with recent lived experiences who understand the difficulty of quitting fentanyl. New pilot programs and initiatives are finding ways to integrate some harm reduction principles into their pre-existing programs. This is an encouraging trend. But just as those running traditional treatment programs need to adjust their philosophy and how they operate based on the reality that clients often need a more gradual approach on their journey to recovery, harm reduction programs must, when properly funded and staffed, increase their emphasis on facilitating voluntary treatment entry. There must not be a wall between harm reduction and mainstream approaches, rather there needs to be a bridge built to connect them.

Before exploring how harm reduction programs might be supplemented to further expand their capacity to transition people into treatment, it's important to highlight that such programs already have an impressive and widely underappreciated record in increasing treatment entry. The research on syringe service programs (SSPs), as summarized by former Surgeon General Jerome Adams, is quite compelling: "New users of SSPs are five times more likely to enter drug treatment and almost three times more likely to stop using drugs than persons who do not use SSPs. Nearly thirty years of research has shown that SSPs are safe, effective, and cost-saving and that they do not increase illegal drug use or crime."[26] These benefits are in addition to the highly cost-effective, life-saving impacts of reducing HIV and Hepatitis B infections, expanding access to naloxone and fentanyl test strips, and providing wound care, vaccinations, and other basic services that many SSPs offer.

Nonetheless, too many state and local authorities impose unnecessary and counterproductive restrictions on SSPs. Although in some places the urgency of the fentanyl crisis has eased some restrictions and expanded the legal protections offered to harm reduction workers performing lifesaving work, it remains true that "legal constraints in many places continue to hinder the prevention and reduction of drug-related harm."[27]

There is sometimes disagreement among those who work in harm reduction on how hard to promote treatment entry. This is partly based on some who, unfortunately, have a philosophical view that someone's drug use should not be viewed as a problem to be addressed, but their personal choice or their right. However, it is also a product of the incredible stress and lack of support for those who are out there on the street doing the heroic work of trying to keep people alive. The people harm reduction workers have been trying desperately to help often die. People are human, they grieve, they suffer. Further, the country has vastly under-supported outreach to drug users, making it hard for those who are out there in the streets to have the time, energy, and resources to educate people about available treatment and to encourage them to give it a try. These outreach workers, as they build rapport and trust with people who use drugs, need far greater access to doctors and nurse practioners that can prescribe buprenorphine, well equipped medical vans to offer mobile health services, and major staffing reinforcements—more recovery coaches and peer counselors—to reach far more people.

This type of work can be very difficult. Certainly, nobody does it for the money; this workforce is significantly underpaid. Most people work in harm reduction or street outreach as a calling—a deep personal commitment. Perhaps they have gone through their own difficult period of drug use and buried friends or family. These are our front-line people, the tip of the spear, it's time we gave them the backup they need. It's not right to ask harm reduction programs—understaffed, underpaid, and under-resourced—to do more than their core mission of keeping people alive if the country doesn't support them and fund them properly to offer additional services we want them to deliver.

It's important to get the balance right. There has been long-standing philosophical resistance to support harm reduction programs. This resistance has created obstacles to these programs' effectiveness and has prevented them from sufficiently emphasizing access to low-threshold treatment. Thus, harm reduction programs, operating on a shoestring budget, cannot do nearly as much as they would like to in terms of facilitating treatment entry. If they had better access to doctors and nurses who could prescribe medications on their teams, as well as more robust funding and core staffing, they could move beyond the desperate and vital battle to keep people alive.

We have been stuck in an unproductive "catch-22" in the sense that harm reduction programs are criticized for not sufficiently supporting treatment entry, but at the same time funders are not giving these programs the financial support and staffing they need to provide treatment to the patients they work with. Pilot programs indicate strong interest in treatment initiation with buprenorphine among those who utilize syringe service programs. One study round that overall, "participants expressed enthusiasm for onsite buprenorphine treatment at SSPs."[28] Another study identified some obstacles that needed to be worked through in initiating and sustaining buprenorphine treatment through an SSP but concluded that: "Expansion of low-threshold buprenorphine services is a promising strategy to address the opioid overdose epidemic."[29] A study of a program in New York State similarly highlighted strong interest and some operational challenges to be navigated.[30]

Unfortunately, the gradual initiation into treatment is just something our traditional drug policies have not supported. As one recent advocate for harm reduction wrote: "Our system has no holding space for people with addictions waiting for treatment or for whom treatment is inaccessible. And our system has no safety net for those that fall through the cracks of treatment because they dropped out, were discharged, could not continue to pay, or left for some other reason."[31]

Dr. Richard Frank, a health economist, noted, "There's no telling how many more people you could reach if you made the effort to identify and engage them. But as a system, we're terrible at outreach. Our entire paradigm is built on doctors sitting at their desks waiting for patients to come to them."[32] In an informative report based on focus groups of people who use drugs, called *Peers Speak Out*, it was clear that respondents wanted drug treatment services, but not necessarily in abstinence-based programs. The report found that focus group participants desired access to services that would "reduce substance use and harmful behaviors through harm reduction."[33] They are asking for a type of help that would keep them alive and launch them into formal drug treatment. It's time to give it to them.

Putting Lived Experience to Work—Why We Need Many More Recovery Coaches and Peers

When I first talked to recovery coaches directly, at the Providence Center in Rhode Island, while I was in town to participate in a National Governor's Association meeting, I felt the excitement of an idea whose time had come. Like many parts of the country impacted by the opioid epidemic, Providence was experiencing a concerning rise in fatal overdoses. They found that those whose overdoses were reversed and brought to the hospital often declined offers to enter treatment and, experiencing withdrawal, walked out of the hospital as soon as they could to seek drugs. As part of a plan to both encourage and facilitate treatment initiation, recovery coaches were dispatched to their bedside in the hospital. Sometimes the recovery coach was the first person the overdose survivor saw after they woke up. The message from the recovery coach with lived experience was always *both* about who they were and what they had to say. They were living, breathing, examples that recovery was possible. Sometimes, the recovery coaches in Providence told me, they were engaging with patients who were occupying literally the same hospital bed they were in after they overdosed. Their first prescription was a desperately needed dose of hope that recovery was possible.

Recovery coaches are people with lived experience who are in stable recovery, and who earn certification through formal training through at least a forty-hour program. It is also possible to serve as a peer counselor without training, but there has been a movement to standardize training requirements. SAMSHA has identified sixty-two core competencies[34] for peer workers which training programs are designed to provide.

The capacity of those with a history of addiction and current consumers to quickly forge a productive relationship is truly something powerful and important. The recovery coaches in Providence offer those new survivors of an overdose living, breathing proof that they, too can become free of a substance use disorder while dispensing practical advice on how to get started. Even when those they work with are not ready at that time to enter treatment, the recovery coaches get their phone number or address, follow up, and continue to serve as an advisor and friendly face encouraging treatment initiation.

There is a strong logic underpinning the impressive capacity for those with lived experience to spark hope in those struggling with addiction. In a book on how and why people change, the author, Damon Centola, writes: "When people need to be convinced that a new behavior or technology will be useful to them, the influential contacts are typically people who resemble them."[35] The peer counselors and recovery coaches with lived experience offer the type of social proof that can provide inspiration at moments when it is needed most.

A study of peer counselors within drug treatment courts noted that they offered benefits to clients due to their relatability, availability, and flexibility, by serving as a role model, listener, and explainer of what was happening in their case. However, it was also noted that drug treatment courts, like other programs adding recovery coaches, must think through the role peers should play in the overall program, ensure good communication among all the service providers, and prevent overlap in duties.[36] In this study, one program participant described their relationship with the peer:

> I felt like he understood. He knew where I was coming from, and I felt that he'd really been in most of the situations that me and him talked about. . . . I'm the type of person you can't tell me about my problems, or you can't say that you know what I am going through if you never had an addiction in life. I need somebody that's been down that road, that's clean.

The recovery coach movement has spread widely, with many training programs, both online and in person, available. All sorts of organizations are hiring them, treatment centers, Recovery Community Organizations, police departments, jails, hospitals, harm reduction organizations, etc. The training of recovery coaches behind bars, so they can support fellow inmates before their release and then transition to paid work in the community, also has great promise. Still, throughout the country, even with over 23 million people in recovery from drugs or alcohol, there are not nearly enough recovery coaches to meet the need.

Recovery coaches are not the only part of the workforce that is understaffed; a similar problem exists with every professional group who works in the field. As highlighted by the National Association of State Alcohol and Drug Agency Directors, "The implications of not effectively responding to the workforce crisis are vast. Staff shortages limit access to substance use services that save lives and reduce costs."[37] The country needs more addiction treatment doctors, psychiatrists, psychologists, social workers, and counselors. Recovery coaches and peer counselors cannot carry the whole weight of staffing treatment programs, there is no substitute for the years of training and education for those with graduate degrees in the medical or addiction-related fields. Prescribers, including doctors and nurse practioners, are particularly vital for getting people started on treatment medications. But training and utilizing recovery coaches are the quickest way to expand the workforce to meet the enormous need. The training is relatively brief and even if their pay increases, as it should, they are relatively inexpensive compared to the costs of a doctor. Most importantly, they are well-positioned to make rapid connections with those with a substance use disorder and offer sound advice and inspiration when it is needed most. Every person with a substance use disorder deserves access to a recovery coach or experienced peer counselor.

The Best of Both Worlds—A Treatment System That Works for All

Remember the old joke, "Why do people rob banks? That's where the money is." It's important for those working to improve the health and safety of people who use drugs to have convenient, regular access to the clients they want to help. This means structuring programs in ways that proactively remove obstacles to access, whether they are geographic, philosophical, financial or operational. This is relevant not just for outreach/low-threshold care initiatives, but for all kinds of treatment programs.

Having heard from families about the frustrating wait or the runaround they experience when trying to get a family member into treatment, I was blown away at one visit to a treatment center in Vermont. The executive director of the program told me that when someone calls seeking treatment for themselves or a family member, there was only one thing his staff was authorized to say: "When can you come in to see us?" Although generally not at a loss for words, I was momentarily stunned, having heard so many stories of backlogs and waiting lists. But when I asked how he managed to schedule patient access that way he explained that he built-in flexibility in his staffing to make sure someone could always come in to do an initial intake interview and start some programming. Wow, I thought, that makes a lot of sense. How come it doesn't always work that way?

Similarly, when I first heard about "bridge clinics" in hospital emergency departments initiating overdose survivors on buprenorphine before they left the hospitals and were transitioned to formal treatment programs, I realized that they should be standard practice everywhere. Too many people walk out of hospitals because they are entering withdrawal and go straight to purchase drugs. A dose of treatment medication that prevents painful withdrawal—and a connection to keep receiving it—literally alters life trajectories. Although the bridge clinics have only emerged over the past few years, "available data show promising rates of treatment initiation and retention."[38] Why isn't every hospital starting their own bridge clinic? The clinics, which now exist in some outpatient settings and even virtually, need to be accessible to everyone with an opioid use disorder everywhere who visits a hospital for any reason.

With drug overdoses still at historically elevated levels, it's time for the "kitchen sink" strategy. This means creating many more access points for treatment, including mobile facilities, twenty-four-hour access drop-in or stabilization centers, same-day treatment entry, including remote access via telemedicine—video and/or phone. During the pandemic, the system bent helpfully in this direction with good results. The country ought to sustain those reforms and build on them.

If, as I suggest, the objective should be for the health system to engage directly with all people who use drugs to both keep them safe and to provide a variety of voluntary pathways to low-threshold, no pre-conditions care, where to start should be clear. We should be asking those that consume drugs what type of addiction treatment and other health services and support they need and how they want to receive them. There is a lot we can learn from people who use drugs if we are willing to listen. Former Congressman Patrick Kennedy got it right when he wrote about those struggling with addiction and/or mental illness in the introduction of his 2024 book, that he "never stopped being amazed by how people can maintain such a high level of function and dysfunction"[39]—meaning they are often quite capable of working, taking care of their family and communicating clearly about the type of help they need regardless of their health challenges.

In addition to talking directly to those with a substance use disorder, it is also important to consult regularly with frontline staff who have valuable insight based on their daily work. The types of services provided and how they are delivered need to be regularly refined based on direct feedback. Available research indicates that these services should be available: low-threshold buprenorphine, mobile methadone, basic health care, wound care, clean syringes, naloxone, fentanyl and xylazine test strips, showers, laundry, food, housing or shelter access, transportation assistance, and help contacting a friend or family member, joining a faith community or social/sports/recreational group, and legal advice. What can be provided to drug consumers depends on federal and state laws, but getting them the support services they need and want will not only reduce addiction and overdose, but it will also reduce costs to society. Note that injection drug use has been decreasing, while smoking and snorting is increasing, thus the other items in the list above may become more important and syringes somewhat less so.

The country needs to greatly expand outreach to people who use drugs by facilitating the hiring of recovery coaches and others trained for this work. Everyone with a substance use disorder deserves regular access to an outreach worker who can offer a kind word, a friendly face, hope and well-informed advice, instead of the stigma and shame that too often confront those with a substance use disorder.

Of course, not everyone with a drug problem faces poverty or lacks resources. Those who have the means—on their own or via family or friends—to keep a roof over their head, access health insurance, and the ability to pay out of pocket for needed services and the basics of life have a big advantage. But those with socio-economic challenges can face enormous difficulties in starting and sustaining engagement in treatment. Part of supporting their recovery effectively requires the mitigation of economic barriers to their reintegration into society.

There is also much that can and should be done to reduce the stigma directed at those struggling with addiction. It is not just the medical and justice professionals who would benefit from education about the disease of addiction, the broader society also needs a deeper understanding. Those in recovery who are speaking up about their lived experience are providing a valuable public service. Unfortunately, it is a deeply embedded problem. Nobody can promise an easy fix. However, what the government can do is to fund a type of place where people who use drugs can count on receiving stigma free services, support and low-threshold treatment and care. A place of their own.

That's the concept behind the creation of dedicated, drop-in *Engagement and Support Centers*, described in the recommendations below. The establishment of 1,000 Engagement and Support Centers around the country will provide a safe space, a stigma-free zone, where people grappling with substance use and its consequences can walk in, any time, and meet with recovery coaches, peers, etc., and hopefully take a step toward recovery. The *Centers* can provide a range of low-threshold/no pre-conditions health and social service programs, including buprenorphine, and serve the function of sobering and stabilization centers which give people who use drugs or alcohol a safe place to rest when they are not feeling well. This one stop shopping for people who use drugs will provide a place where they can come forward and voluntarily seek the help they are ready to receive.

Overdose Prevention Centers Discussion

I don't want to leave this subject without discussing overdose prevention centers, also known as safe injection facilities. Those working in the two centers in New York City are motivated by compassion for people who use drugs and the life-threatening risks they face each day. I understand why some advocacy organizations want to see these sites expand. However, the debate on the centers can be a distraction from the pressing challenge to get those with a substance use disorder access to comprehensive health and social services, adequate housing, and low-threshold treatment with medications.

Since two centers are up and running and a couple more are in development, the country should try to learn from their experience. This research should be conducted by those with no involvement in running or advocating for the centers to ensure objective findings. In addition to tracking overdoses that are reversed, it would be critical for these centers to demonstrate the extent to which program participants access treatment and enter recovery.

There are a range of opinions on this question of the degree to which overdose prevention centers should emphasize treatment and recovery. I believe this objective needs to be *central* to all initiatives that provide health and social services to people who use drugs, including the existing overdose prevention centers. The centers in New York are facilitating treatment entry when clients ask for it.[40] Promoting treatment entry is, however, not a formal program goal—this has to change.

The trusted relationships built with program participants by the staff at these centers can be utilized to highlight the importance of treatment to drug consumers for both their short-term health and safety, as well as to their future hopes and dreams. If the centers are not working respectfully to help people initiate treatment then they are not providing what should be a core benefit of overdose prevention centers. Further, the lethal health risks daily fentanyl consumers face, even if they often utilize overdose prevention services, remain severe. Practically speaking, it is hard to imagine these centers ever becoming scaled beyond a few progressive urban areas without demonstrating that they are significantly increasing treatment entry and recovery of program participants.

I am not suggesting that a commitment to treatment be required for people to utilize the centers the first time they walk in. Rather, it should be an objective for the staff and management to encourage voluntary initiation in low-threshold or other treatment programs as they get to know their clients. Can the expert, compassionate staff, which includes many people with lived experience, proactively, but respectfully help clients learn about and utilize treatment and recovery opportunities in a manner that doesn't push them away from coming to the centers for the other health and social services offered? I believe they can and they should.

As drug policy experts and advocates debate this sensitive and controversial subject, I worry the country will lose sight of the huge, urgent need to ramp up the full range of health and social services for people who use drugs. As emphasized throughout this book, entire ecosystems of dedicated Support and Engagement Centers, recovery support programs, and justice reforms are needed urgnently now. These types of initiatives, although they face obstacles in terms of funding and implementation, already have significant political and public support and have the potential to reach far more people more quickly than overdose prevention centers.

Psychedelics—Minimizing Risks and Maximizing Therapeutic Benefits

The United States now knows the terrible costs of reckless expansion of access to medications and drugs that can be misused. We should recognize the risks that come with moving too quickly to legalize substances such as ketamine, MDMA, psilocybin, Ibogaine, Mescaline, LSD and other psychedelics (technically referred to as hallucinogens). But also, it's appropriate to take a hard look at the research on experimental use of these substances in their ability to treat mental health problems, such as post-traumatic stress disorder (PTSD), depression, and anxiety, as well as addiction. Sadly, 6,000 veterans commit suicide each year. In late 2023 legislation, supported both by Republican Dan Crenshaw from Texas, and Democrat Alexandria Ocasio-Cortez of New York the Veterans Administration, was signed into law to study the ability of psychedelics to help active-duty service members afflicted with PTSD or traumatic brain injuries.[41]

The possibility of utilizing psychedelics to treat substance use disorder (SUD) is tantalizing. Especially at a time when many people who use drugs are consuming not just powerful synthetic opioids such as fentanyl, but tough to treat drug combinations, any substance that could ease withdrawal and accelerate recovery is worthy of careful study. Nonetheless, the experience of the past advises caution. Further, the potential commercialization of psychedelics for treatment creates problematic incentives.

The emerging research does offer some hope that psychedelics combined with therapy could become a useful addiction treatment tool. An assessment of the research to date finds that additional studies are required to "evaluate the molecular basis of each psychedelic mechanism of action" and calls for "robust clinical studies with large samples to confirm the potential of psychedelics for SUD."[42] The same analysis noted that psychedelics might also one day be part of a therapeutic approach for those with co-occurring SUD and mental health disorders, including PTSD, depression, anxiety, and obsessive-compulsive disorder.

One recent summary of the psychedelics research concludes: "The exploration of the therapeutic potential of psychedelics has made significant strides, but several critical scientific questions remain unresolved, necessitating further research to gain a comprehensive understanding of their therapeutic use."[43] A study on post-traumatic stress disorder (PTSD) concluded that: "MDMA may be particularly effective for enhancing treatment efficacy by improving a range of problems with self-experience that are associated with treatment resistance."[44] This same study summarized the broader research on MDMA, beyond PTSD, as promoting a sense of interpersonal connectedness and openness, while enhancing positive "appraisal of favorable memories, while reducing negative evaluations of painful memories" and supporting the "extinction of fearful memories . . . and to promote social behavior."[45]

If the FDA had approved an application to treat PTSD by Lykos Therapeutics (formerly MAPS Public Benefit Corporation) it would have marked "the first instance of MDMA-assisted therapy and psychedelic-assisted therapy."[46] But in August of 2024 the FDA turned them down and asked the company "to conduct an additional clinical trial to assess whether the drug would be safe and effective."[47] The rejection was not a surprise, since earlier reports highlighted the difficulty of effectively studying MDMA since many of those in the research control groups clearly realize they did not receive the drug.[48] Policy makers must balance the potential benefits with the risks and ensure that decision-making relies on the highest quality independent research.

The research and practice of ketamine-assisted treatment raises some red flags. The substance has medical use as an anesthetic and has been used for recreational purposes. The FDA has approved ketamine hydrochloride (tradename: Ketalar) as a Schedule III controlled substance "as an intravenous or intramuscular injection solution for induction and maintenance of general anesthesia."[49] Ketamine is not formally approved for the treatment of any psychiatric disorder, but some psychiatrists prescribe it off-label to treat depressive disorders. In 2019, the FDA approved a similar product, esketamine, used as a nasal spray, for treatment-resistant depression.

Some prescribers customize a specific dose and form of ketamine through a compounding pharmacy to produce the drug for their patients. Only about 15 percent of the 56,000 community-based pharmacies in the United States offer compounding.[50] FDA has warned that they have "identified potential safety concerns associated with the use of compounded ketamine products through telemedicine platforms, including abuse and misuse, psychiatric events, increases in blood pressure, respiratory depression, and lower urinary tract and bladder symptoms. Home use of compounded ketamine products presents additional risk because onsite monitoring by a health care provider is *not* available."[51]

News report on the autopsy after the tragic death of "Friends" star Matthew Perry concluded that he died of the "acute effects of ketamine" that contributed to his drowning. He was taking the drug under a doctor's orders, but "the elevated concentrations of ketamine suggest high levels of use"[52]—meaning likely he was consuming more that his medically recommended amounts.

Psilocybin, which comes from certain types of mushrooms—sometimes referred to as magic mushrooms or "shrooms" is undergoing research supported by NIDA. They are seeking to understand the substance's impact on body and mind. NIDA supports "clinical investigations into psilocybin as a therapeutic substance. These include studies on its effectiveness and safety as a treatment for substance use disorders and to help people quit smoking."[53]

There are enough positive findings to offer encouragement for further research. Far be it for me to withhold significant potential benefits from suffering Americans, especially American veterans. However, the mass commercialization of these substances would raise concerns. Most of the research studies include rigorous supervision of the consumption of psychedelics during the entire time someone is under their effect and requires psychotherapy sessions to help the individuals process what they may have experienced. There is an issue of cost, access, and fairness with the psychotherapy and supervision, putting a potentially useful treatment out of reach for many Americans. Nonetheless, at this point it's right to go slow and carefully monitor the expansion of access. We should worry about "cash and carry" psychedelic clinics, like the pill mills that emerged after the release of OxyContin.

Microdosing, referenced in the first chapter as a Silicon Valley and celebrity trend, also does not yet have a record of effectiveness. Nonetheless, it is a subject worth further study. An analysis of the existing research on LSD microdosing finds mild effects on "mood, sleep, social cognition, reward response, and pain perception. Some of these effects might facilitate treatment of psychiatric disorders, but the findings need to be replicated and extended to clinical and more diverse populations."[54]

Researchers are experimenting with reducing the psychedelic side effects of LSD and ibogaine while maintaining the potential benefits. A science journalist wrote in late 2024 that "the hottest new psychedelic drugs might be the ones that feel as close to nothing as possible."[55] It remains to be seen if the full benefits can be retained with a reduced or eliminated psychedelic experience, but it's worth finding out. In a significant development, the state of Texas is partnering with private investors to fund ibogaine research, including clinical trials[56] focused on the acute needs of veterans impacted by war injuries, trauma, and addiction.

Hopefully, this expanding web of research will produce evidence-based medications for both addiction and mental health. This is a complex area, with many passionate true believers and advocates, a wide range of investment and research by private companies with strong commercial interests, and perhaps millions of Americans who are struggling with mental health and substance use disorders who are hoping for more options to assist them. A 2024 book, by journalist Ernesto Londono,[57] highlights both the potential benefits and the risks. Federal regulators should continue to move forward carefully and ensure that if these powerful substances are authorized for wider use independent researchers scrutinize the impact and track adverse consequences closely.

Enhancing the Quality and Duration of Treatment, Utilizing Technology and the Promise of Artificial Intelligence

Reality is complicated, but the road ahead is clear. Today's polydrug consumers often struggle with dependence not just on opioids, but also with methamphetamine or cocaine, or dangerous additives such as veterinary medications xylazine or medetomidine. They may also consume prescription medications, high potency marijuana and alcohol, and many have a co-occurring mental health disorder. A recent analysis emphasizes that "in clinical practice, patients who use more than one substance are still very common and a source of challenge in treatment and diagnosis."[58] These patients need a lot of help and support—most are not getting it. It is a relief that total annual fatal overdoses appear to have peaked, but it does not change the reality that the country still faces an enormous, complex, under-addressed addiction crisis.

The treatment system needs to find a way to provide the full suite of services and supports for a person who concurrently consumes multiple powerful drugs. Not as some kind of favor for these Americans, but because the evidence shows that such a wrap around, long-term approach is what is most effective. The full toolbox should be available so that counselors can individualize treatment plans. This chapter has explored many of the elements of a successful treatment program, but there are more. These include new devices based on acupuncture that are applied to the ear that "assist in opioid withdrawal and may increase initial treatment retention."[59] Research is also ongoing on wearable devices that utilize continuous, non-intrusive blood pressure monitoring for the early detection of heightened drug cravings.[60] Older techniques, such as eye movement desensitization and reprocessing therapy (EMDR) are underutilized. Research finds that when individuals engage in visual tasks unrelated to drug use while discussing their drug cravings "there is a significant decrease in both the frequency and intensity of these cravings."[61]

Also coming into view is the potential for artificial intelligence (AI) to identify new medications, or combinations of medications, that will both be more effective and more appealing to those who need them. AI, which experts in this rapidly emerging field, including Ray Kurzweil[62] and Dario Amodei[63] suggest will rapidly accelerate research and clinical trials for new medications. This capacity should be deployed to bolster the range of available addiction treatment medications. A 2025 assessment concluded that "AI-powered structure-based drug discovery is enabling researchers to analyze molecular interactions with unprecedented precision by combining machine learning with physics-based simulations. This integration facilitates the design of highly targeted and effective therapeutic compounds."[64]Although the AI assisted development of new treatment medications is just beginning, AI is already being integrated into a variety of treatment and recovery initiatives and products:

> From enhancing diagnostic accuracy through machine learning and natural language processing to enabling real-time monitoring via wearable technologies and smartphone applications, AI has expanded the scope and efficacy of mental health interventions. These advancements have made it possible to detect early warning signs of mental health conditions, predict treatment outcomes, and provide personalized therapeutic support. ...AI-powered predictive models and adaptive systems have improved long-term care by enabling proactive interventions and fostering better treatment adherence. AI aids in personalized recovery programs by predicting relapse risks, tailoring treatment plans, and facilitating behavioral modification through AI-powered therapy tools.[65]

Just as government, research organizations, and pharmaceutical companies search for better treatment for cancer, heart disease, and Alzheimer's, they need to invest in cutting-edge treatment for addiction.

Too often individuals impacted by addiction are too low a priority for medical research. This must not be the case as innovations driven by AI become increasingly possible over the next decade.

Recommendations

8. **Fund 1,000 *Support and Engagement Centers* to assist those with a substance use disorder**

   People who use drugs need dedicated, funded health centers where every time they walk in they know for certain that they will be treated with compassion and respect. Ideally, the first person they interact with would be a recovery coach or peer. These centers will offer low-threshold substance use disorder and mental health care, as well as access to a wide range of health and social services. Assistance provided would depend on state laws. Centers can be mobile or fixed sites. Grants should be provided directly to NGOs and health agencies, to establish a new facility, or for existing clinics to expand their current offerings to qualify as a *Support and Engagement Center*. To enable small organizations with less capacity to manage the grant application and paperwork, larger NGOs would have the ability to request funds to sub-contract with smaller organizations. CDC is well situated to administer this program due to its existing portfolio of drug-related work and long history of addiction-related projects. *Congress should establish the new Support and Engagement Centers program at CDC and provide a budget of $1.8 billion a year for this national initiative, with $15 million of these funds provided to establish a nongovernmnental Center of Excellence and $15 million for rapid research to assess and refine the Center's efforts to improve drug users' health and to foster the initiation of drug treatment.*
9. **Put lived experience to work by hiring 100,000 recovery coaches and peer counselors**

   The country has a troubling addiction workforce shortage. The fastest way to supplement it is to train and hire those in recovery. Famously, President Bill Clinton in 1994 pledged to hire 100,000 police officers to support the adoption of community policing. Similarly, the federal government needs to accelerate the widespread utilization of recovery coaches and peer counselors to staff the health system, and elements of the justice system—including police departments, courts, jails and prisons—by establishing a ten-year goal to add 100,000 people with lived experience to the addiction workforce. These new recovery coaches and peers are urgently needed to help those with a substance use disorder find their path towards recovery. *Congress should direct HHS to administer the program and fund it at $1 billion a year for a decade, with the money distributed to states based on need. This amount of money will cover the costs of training and paying 10,000 new recovery coaches or certified peer counselors each year and subsidizing their salaries in subsequent years. A non-governmental Center of Excellence to support the development of this vital but still new professional field should be funded at $10 million a year.*

10. **Conduct systematic surveys of drug users and first responders to identify the most effective strategies for increasing voluntary entry into addiction treatment**

Neither government nor treatment providers have been consistently seeking the perspectives of the people they are trying to help, but they need to. Asking people with substance use disorders what services they want, the best way to engage with them, and which mechanisms to initiate treatment they are most interested in is critical to strengthening treatment entry. This information will also update policymakers on drug consumption trends, such as the combination of substances used and route of administration (injection, smoking, or oral). HHS should develop an annual national survey through a contractor with the capacity to conduct this work. In addition to the survey, HHS should fund regular focus groups with people who use drugs and those that work with them to get their well-informed perspective and provide written summaries of their findings to policy makers and service providers. *Congress should appropriate $50 million a year for SAMHSA to fund surveys and focus groups to generate up-to-date information to facilitate successful treatment entry.*

11. **Increase access to medications for addiction, including long-acting injectibles, while investing in AI and studying the therapeutic use of psychedelics**

The addictive potential of today's drug supply is so serious that it is essential that those with substance use disorder have easy access to treatment medications at sufficient dosages. Increased access, via telehealth services piloted during the pandemic should be continued, with monitoring to ensure quality of service delivery. Weekly or monthly injections of FDA approved treatment medications, which offer important advantages over daily medications, should be far more easily available through a wide range of providers, including at local neighborhood pharmacies. There is a need to further expand low-threshold and mobile access to medications, including for those under criminal justice supervision. Psychedelics, which to various degrees are already being studied and piloted for mental health treatments, offer hope to those struggling with addiction. MDMA, psilocybin, ketamine, mescaline, and ibogaine should be assessed through rigorous, independent research to evaluate their safety and effectiveness and to see if the risks of utilizing these powerful substances can be managed. Important private sector research is already happening in this area but it would be prudent for the federal government to fund an NGO and an independent advisory council to help coordinate and monitor this sensitive work. *Congress should authorize the creation of a Center of Excellence on Addiction Treatment Medications and appropriate $5 million to run it and $95 million for HHS to host conferences, fund additional research and analysis, drive AI investments in addiction care and support the operation of an independent advisory council.*

Chapter Summary

6

Deep Recovery

Creating a Recovery-Friendly America

Chapter Introduction: Why Are Former Inmates Trying to Get Back to Their Jail?

Sheriff Karl Leonard of Chesterfield County, Virginia is doing something special in his jail. He has decided that anyone who comes into the jail who wants help with their drug addiction is going to get it. With that simple decision made, a lot of good things are happening. The Sheriff and a small staff, volunteers and a shoestring budget built a program, which is called Helping Addicts Recovery Progressively (HARP). The program started in 2016 and has continued to evolve. In 2020, a medication assisted treatment initiative, primarily providing the buprenorphine and naloxone combination (Suboxone)[1] was added to the program. Recently, in Sheriff Leonard's continued effort to improve the program, the Chesterfield Jail became the first one in the country to utilize a neuromodulation device to deliver electric pulses to the brain to ease withdrawal symptoms. Independent research has found that graduates of the HARP programs were significantly less likely to be arrested compared to those not in the program.[2]

HARP started just for men, but after word got out about the program, the sheriff was lobbied to open a women's program by families of woman inmates. During an afternoon visit when I was serving as Acting Drug Czar, I spoke separately with groups of forty male and female inmates, who grathered around me as I sat on a table in the center of a room at the jail. The program participants were eager to share their stories. Although some were in prison for repeated drug possession offenses, most committed more serious crimes to generate revenue to pay for their drug habit. The men, they explained, generally committed robbery and sold drugs while the women worked as prostitutes. Almost all the men raised their hand when I asked how many had survived an overdose.

Inmates in Chesterfield join a highly structured program of group therapy and peer support. Participants grapple directly with past traumas and abuses that led many to heavy use of drugs in the first place. They also study coping strategies to deal with normal stresses and frustrations without relapsing. Over the six months of the program, participants gradually learn about how to reconstruct a full life, without drugs.

Although there are costs involved, such as paying for counselors and some additional services, the additional costs over the $50,000 per year Virginia taxpayers already pay to keep someone behind bars are marginal. Thus, the Chesterfield taxpayers are already benefiting from huge savings due to reduced criminal justice costs from new arrests that have been avoided, and, thanks to the innovative program, living in a safer community.

A visitor to Chesterfield can't help but ask why every jail and prison in the country has not launched a similar program to support and encourage recovery. That is not to say that many jails and prisons do not have some excellent treatment recovery programs—sheriffs and jail and prison administrators across the country are piloting new initiatives, including providing medications for opioid use disorders. But so much more is needed since today our jails are full of Americans with a substance misuse history. Far more inmates in the United States have a drug problem than those who were arrested for drug selling or possession. An estimated 65 percent of the American prison population has a substance use disorder, and an additional 20 percent were under the influence of drugs or alcohol when they committed their crime.[3]

There are, of course practical questions about identifying resources and staffing to support treatment behind the walls, as well as the space to have program participants live together in a separate part of the prison. There are, nonetheless, solid hard-headed reasons why this is a good investment. Most prisoners will eventually return to the community—meaning they are not serving life sentences. Public safety is at severe risk if the underlying addiction, trauma, and mental health issues of inmates are not seriously addressed. Further, that transition from incarceration to freedom is a dangerous path, especially for those with a history of substance use who do not receive the quality treatment they need prior to their release.

I once thought that those who spent years behind bars without regular access to drugs would have essentially addressed their substance use disorder. Although it's true that drugs are, unfortunately, sometimes smuggled into prisons and jails, inmates cannot secure a predictable daily supply of their drug of choice behind bars. Most are fully detoxed soon after they arrive at jail, and after a surely unpleasant withdrawal period are unlikely to experience sustained cravings while behind bars in a highly controlled environment. However, the reality is that even those who are fully abstinent while in jail or prison are still at high risk of a return to drug use as soon as they are released. When former inmates leave prison and return to see familar people, places, and things their cravings often instantly return. If they have not developed the skills to effectively resist these cravings, through quality treatment programs and/or access to medications, the risks upon re-entry are very serious.[4] The high overdose death rate of returning prisoners should trouble us. These are men and women who have served their sentence, who now have earned a second chance.

It makes good sense for those who were opioid dependent prior to prison entry to be protected before they return to the community by a treatment medication, such as buprenorphine, methadone, or naltrexone. They also need a place to live and some minimal source of income. The idea that any state or the federal government would spend $50,000 a year to house an inmate but not at least a few thousand to ensure they are not sleeping on the street on their first night out doesn't make any sense.

Prisons and jails, whose most minimal baseline purpose is to protect public safety, should ensure a departing inmate with a history of addiction has short-term housing, some work or other income established, and access to a recovery coach or counselor set up before they are released. But there is one more thing they need, which is central to sustaining recovery from addiction—a community of friends they can count on. Everyone needs a social network. Former prisoners, especially those overcoming addiction, especially need a new community that will strengthen, not threaten, their recovery.

Sheriff Leonard's HARP graduates often come back to the jail through the front door to visit as welcomed guest speakers, to offer support and encouragement, to serve as inspiring examples of what is possible in a post-jail drug free life. But that's not the only reason they come back. When life on the outside gets them down and they need a welcoming, trusted community to provide emotional and spiritual support, the Sheriff bends the rules and allows graduates to return to the program informally, letting them enter through the back door.

These former inmates, who paid their debt to society and voluntarily entered and completed a jail treatment program, like others who have worked hard toward their recovery, deserve support upon release. They are fortunate that their former jail continues to help them out, but what about the millions of other Americans who have completed a prison sentence, a court-ordered substance use disorder treatment program, or a treatment program in the community? What and who is available to help strengthen their early, still fragile recovery? They, like everyone else who has battled addiction, deserve a place to visit, where they can come in through the front door to access support for their recovery.

Hard Lesson: Treatment and justice system initiatives are not sufficient to solve crisis; we also need a nationwide recovery support system

It's important, and urgent, for the country to continue to improve and expand its substance use disorder treatment system, but it's also critical to focus on what happens immediately after treatment. People do not go into treatment "broken" and come out "repaired." The accomplishment of transitioning from needing drugs to cope with daily life to living without them is huge and worthy of celebration. But it also represents just the tentative first steps of recovery. During active drug use all the core elements of life may have been damaged or destroyed. Further, people with a history of drug use face an ongoing sense of stigma and shame internally, and the many who have a felony conviction on their record for drug selling or other crimes face severe, ongoing obstacles in rebuilding their lives, particularly regarding work and housing. Fortunately, the field of recovery has flourished over the past two decades to ease this transition. There are about 23 million Americans[5] *already in recovery, and their ranks grow every year. Yet we are not doing enough to help them and the millions more eager to join them. It doesn't have to be this way.*

Social Determinants of Health and Recovery Capital

When someone successfully completes a treatment program, it is a critical moment in their journey to recovery, but it is not the end point. Many of those who experienced an extended time of active addiction lost a lot of the essentials all of us need. Their family relationships may be severely damaged, they may not have a home or a job, a viable source of transportation, childcare, legal services, a community of friends, or access to the basics of life. Such social and economic factors are referred to as the "social determinants of health" and these factors are estimated to be responsible for as "much as 80 percent of health outcomes."[6] Many of these services are not included in treatment or recovery programs, nor covered by health insurance, since they are considered ancillary services—they are nonetheless essential for reducing risks and enhancing recovery.

As people complete formal treatment, there is much work to be done to rebuild their lives and reintegrate into society. The extent to which individuals are set up to do that is their "recovery capital." The term refers to "all the internal and external resources that a person can access in support of their recovery process."[7] Thus, it includes not just health and social services, but also their personal motivation for recovery, the support of friends and family, the spiritual and fellowship benefits of a faith community, practical knowledge such as financial management,[8] and the ability to access services available near where they live. Paid work is also abosolutely essential for long-term recovery. The extent of someone's recovery capital can be measured through a screening tool—a series of questions that highlight gaps that need to be addressed. Such an assessment enables individuals who complete a treatment program to create a "to do" list for themselves and those seeking to help them. A gap in services or support can undermine progress made in treatment and increase risks of a relapse.

Back when I was learning about drug policy as a young Congressional staffer, I thought that stopping drug use via drug treatment was pretty much the whole process. But the reality is that the end of active drug use is the beginning of a just as critical recovery process. Early recovery, the first months, is critical. Experts view five years as the demarcation point when long-term, stable recovery is reached. Investing in support during this period is essential. There has never been a robustly funded recovery support system in the United States. The country needs to build one now.

There is one more important thing to highlight about recovery capital. Ultimately, just like every other person, those in recovery, freed from their dependence on drugs, need—in addition to the basics to survive—a driving purpose or passion in their life. Whether it's through work, family, faith, sports, artistic expression, or helping others find their own recovery, it's fundamental to their long-term well-being. As cultural anthropologist Ernest Becker wrote, all of us need to construct "a world of humanly created meaning"[9] to give us a rationale to organize our life, to feel like our existence makes a difference, and to leave behind a legacy. A strong recovery ecosystem can help those who have struggled with addiction find that purpose and move forward in their lives. Individuals are not on their own in finding new purpose, there are validated protocols such as recovery-oriented cognitive therapy, specifically designed to "build hope for the future through the development of personally meaningful and value-driven aspirations."[10] Absent finding that new purpose in their new, post-addiction life, those who have completed treatment successfully will find their hard-won sobriety at risk.

A New Home, A New Life

There is perhaps no more important foundation for recovery than access to safe, secure, and affordable housing. The obstacles to housing for current or former drug users, and those who have completed a prison sentence are immense. But the benefits of decent housing, whatever stage of recovery they are in, are also immense.

Before I dive more deeply into this issue, let me say explicitly that there is a much larger challenge regarding housing that the United States faces than just the one related to those in addiction recovery. Every American deserves safe, secure, and affordable housing. The fact that we have not been able to address this problem nationwide is highly troubling. I greatly admire the advocates and writers working on this issue and am appalled at the stories of the cruelties imposed on those whose rents are suddenly raised beyond their ability to pay or just cannot find affordable housing. Let me highly recommend the book *Evicted* by Matthew Desmond, which compellingly describes this broader challenge. Desmond writes: "Fewer and fewer families can afford a roof over their head. This is among the most urgent and pressing issues facing America today, and acknowledging the breadth and depth of the problem changes the way we look at poverty."[11]

There is a lot of blame to go around for this broader housing crisis. Too often: "Local governments decide what gets built and where, and they use that power to ban multifamily housing, entrench economic segregation, and perpetuate a national affordability crisis."[12] Encouragingly, as Ezra Klein and Derek Thompson highlight in their 2025 book, *Abundance*, some cities have figured out how to build affordable housing. They report that "it costs $17,000 to $19,000 to house a homeless resident of Houston,"[13] including the cost of supportive services, less than half of what it costs in San Francisco. Hopefully, more cities and states will figure out how to make housing affordable for all. The housing issue regarding addiction and recovery from substance misuse is just as serious, but narrower. I hope both problems can be addressed concurrently, but I will focus on the drug-related concerns.

It's fair to ask why someone who has used and perhaps sold drugs and committed other crimes "deserves" housing as much or more than someone who just needs a place to live. My answer is simple—the costs to society of not helping those in recovery rebuild their lives are enormous. Those weeks and months after completing a treatment program are pivotal. Putting those in early recovery either on the street or forcing them to re-enter a housing arrangement like what they utilized when they were actively consuming drugs will jeopardize their recovery and risk them returning to active drug use. It is essential that society assists those in early recovery to establish residence in a community not associated with their past drug use where they can form new bonds of friendship with neighbors and friends.

As the country moves forward towards finding more ways to support safe housing for those in recovery, including those re-entering society after leaving jail or prison and those participating in alternatives to incarceration programs, there are several critical factors to keep in mind.

First off, the corruption in some parts of the sober housing market has been a cruel and crushing blow to many families. Dave Aronberg, State Attorney from Palm Beach County, explained in Congressional testimony about the corruption and exploitation in Florida:

> We've had a surge of unscrupulous individuals enrich themselves by misusing well-intended Federal laws to prey on opioid addicts who are often willing to participate in patient brokering, illegal kickbacks, and insurance fraud, in exchange for illicit benefits, such as cash, free rent, transportation, and even drugs themselves. This is the Florida shuffle. This is the reality on the ground. Everyone's getting rich.[14]

It's important that West Palm Beach County has rid itself of such abusive practices and that Aronberg has described his experience in his 2025 book, *Fighting the Florida Shuffle*,[15] developed tools, and promulgated legislation that can serve as a model state law. Other parts of the country need to follow West Palm Beach's example, keep a much closer eye on sober housing corrupt practices, and ensure that when these sober living facilities are shut down those who lose access to their housing receive transitional support, so they don't end up on the street.

Secondly, some sober housing communities are rejecting the inclusion of those on medications for opioid use disorder. This ill-serves the growing percentage of people with opioid use disorder who are turning to these evidence-based medications for their recovery. One of the largest organizations in the country that supports sober living is Oxford House, a national NGO that does not accept government funds. They have been moving toward more acceptance of medications but have maintained their long-standing practice of enabling each of their group homes to self-govern and establish their own rules. I am not suggesting they change that practice of self-governance, but I would hope that their national organization and communities where these houses exist encourage inclusion of those on medications, since so many in recovery today are seeking to overcome years of fentanyl use and face a very difficult path without access to treatment medications.

Third, let me say a few words about supportive housing (often referred to as "Housing First"). This type of approach is designed to get people who are still consuming illegal drugs off the streets and into a stable living environment. The concept is that once people are in a safe home many will find their health improves, since the constant stress of being homeless, the risk of being robbed or attacked, and the need some feel to consume stimulants to stay awake at night for their own protection tends to worsen their condition. In these living arrangements there are a few rules—about limiting visitors, respecting your neighbors, keeping things quiet at night—but not a requirement for abstinence. Once established in a safe home those still using illegal substances have access to addiction and mental health services. The concern is that if abstinence is required many people will decline the housing and stay on the street.

I don't want to generalize about all Housing First programs, which vary in practice. The model was very much developed under what I would refer to as a harm reduction-informed approach and in reaction to the failure of housing programs that required immediate full abstinence from drugs and alcohol. "Repeatedly trying and failing discouraged many, and they eventually stopped trying, remained homeless, and withdrew into hopelessness."[16] Strong Housing First programs ensure that a "holistic package of support is built around each individual to develop his/her tenancy management skills"[17] and encourages gradual recovery from substance misuse with the support of peer counselors. However, as Housing First programs spread not every intervention maintained strong fidelity to the original model's commitment to strong staffing and robust services.

If the federal government increases funding for Housing First, as I am recommending, it's important that significant social services are connected to the housing and that beneficiaries be required to take some basic steps to improve their health. It's a tricky balance—ensuring people accept the housing and stay there—but also finding ways to improve the health and safety of these new residents who may have quite serious and complicated substance use disorders, a co-occurring mental health disorder, and other chronic health problems. It's important nonetheless that, even if the pace is slow, people make gradual progress—just as the harm reduction-informed programs described in chapter five seek to compassionately meet people where they are, but not leave them there.

One recent Housing First study concluded that the approach of starting with just housing and then adding services was effective. Once participants were settled in their home the program initiated "enhanced efforts to engage clients... in internal or external initiatives to improve mental and physical health, including substance use issues would increase program impact for quality of life, recovery"[18] and reduce the frequency of problematic behavior.

I believe federal funding must include clear guidance on the type of activities required of those who benefit from Housing First initiatives to ensure that participants will make progress regarding their substance use after moving in. Here is my view of what would be appropriate requirements, recognizing that this list needs to be refined based on research and the experience of those who have run successful Housing First programs:

1. Meet weekly with a recovery coach or peer counselor trained in harm reduction psychotherapy. The resident and recovery coach will work collaboratively. Goals for reduced drug use will be established by the resident with advice and support from the recovery coach.
2. Participate in a pro-social group activity: it could be an exercise program at a gym, hiking, biking, journal writing, listening to, or performing music, art projects or visits to museums, taking care of animals, attending a religious service, participating in a book club or meditation group, going to a sporting event, a museum, a park, or any other positive activity.
3. Volunteer for some type of work, even as simple as setting up chairs or making coffee for a group meeting, painting, or decorating the facility where they live, sweeping up common areas of their apartment building, or making some phone calls or running errands for the staff that they work with.
4. See a doctor or a nurse once a month to review and address any health problems.

These steps will help by repeatedly giving those in supportive housing encouragement to, at their own pace, develop a healthier lifestyle. The drug supply is just too dangerous, and the consequences of continued heavy drug use are too severe not to focus on movement toward recovery for those living in publicly subsidized housing.

Fourth, let me highlight that the federal Department of Housing and Urban Development (HUD) runs a "Continuum of Care" program budgeted at over $3.5 billion designed to prevent and reduce homelessness. The program provides funding for state and local governments and nonprofit groups to quickly rehouse homeless individuals and families. This is an important program that, although not designed specifically for those with a substance use disorder, surely helps many such individuals, when—as it should be—it is fully funded by Congress. HUD also has a much smaller, $25 million recovery housing program specifically to provide transitional housing for up to two years for those in recovery from a substance use disorder. This pilot provides about 25 grants a year. Although a tiny program for something that is a huge and urgent problem, it is important that HUD is gaining practical experience in this area which could inform the development of a far larger program, which I will propose below.

Finally, in wrapping up this discussion of the complicated and critical topic of housing for those with a substance use disorder, let me emphasize that although housing in general is expensive, facilitating access to recovery housing need not involve covering the entire cost of housing for an extended period. Most people who benefit from this assistance will be getting back to paid work and some are living in a group housing environment that makes their monthly rent more manageable. A modest amount of funds as a subsidy, or an advance to cover the security deposit and to help with the first month's rent, can make a big difference.

One study found that providing just an average of $1,256 enabled drug treatment court participants to be rapidly placed in housing, even for those with a criminal record.[19] Supportive housing, before people get to a point where they can work and contribute to the rent, will cost more. I understand that what I am proposing below will only meet a portion of the enormous unmet need, but it's a good start. Further, this increased effort will generate new information and research knowledge to guide best practices going forward.

My Hard Lesson about Homelessness, Addiction, and Mental Health

Growing up in New York City in the 1970s, I became familiar with homelessness at an early age. Like other kids walking to school in Manhattan's Lower East Side, I stepped around those sleeping on the street. My parents told my brother and me that we had to stop going to the closest park to my childhood apartment,Tompkins Square Park, when it became a frequent hangout for heroin consumers, alcoholics, and those with mental health issues. I didn't think about it much; it was just a fact of life we had to accept. Later, when I moved to Washington, D.C., to go to college, there was a similar challenge with homelessness. When I worked as a congressional intern in 1987, one day I was walking down the street right next to the Rayburn House Office Building heading to eat lunch with a friend near Washington's Botanic Garden. I never made it. Before I got there, I was surprised when someone who I didn't see coming rapidly crossed Independence Avenue and approached me. I felt a hard punch in the face that knocked me down. The next thing I remember, I was in the hospital. Hurt, but not severely. My memory is a bit blurry on the sequence of events, but I was later told by the Capitol Police officer, who had been the first to respond to the incident, that it was a local homeless person who hit me.

I am not suggesting that all, or even most people living on the street are dangerous. These days, I carry Narcan and an extra protein bar to give out to those I encounter when I am walking around downtown D.C. Still, I am wary. This is a complicated problem. We need to recognize how urgently those with behavioral health challenges need a safe place to sleep. Earlier in my career, when I conducted research on homelessness and street disorder, the focus was on justice system solutions. Those options should be available when absolutely necessary, but it's critical to start with a public health approach. Living on the street is not healthy or safe; it inevitably worsens physical and mental health and makes it hard to get decent sleep or nutrition. It certainly is not a good environment to reduce drug use, but neither is jail.

The best solution is for outreach workers, including recovery coaches and peers, to engage with people on the streets, to get to know them, and to encourage them to voluntarily accept treatment services, housing in shelters, or longer-term supportive or recovery housing. If repeated efforts fail to get them to voluntarily agree to other housing arrangements, I believe it is reasonable to bring them to a shelter or stabilization center in the least traumatic way feasible. To reiterate, I don't believe it's appropriate to remove someone who is not posing an immediate public safety threat without first trying to get them to voluntarily accept assistance. It's better for them, and for the public, if they are given an option they can accept on their own volition. A decent society has to work towards fair solutions, including taking earlier actions to help those before they end up on the street. To ignore the problem is wrong, as it is to carelessly drag human beings into jail. We need to do better.

Getting Back to Work

There are many millions of Americans who have overcome addiction, who have completed treatment, rebuilt their lives, and who are in stable recovery. They are our family members, friends, and neighbors. Many are looking for new employment opportunities. They deserve a fair shot at a good job.

When people complete treatment, they seek to establish new patterns of life that strengthen and support their recovery. This naturally includes finding a job. People in recovery, even with an extended period without drug use, often struggle to get jobs that are a match for their talents and capabilities. Like other Americans, people in recovery need work to pay their bills, to pursue their professional aspirations, and to develop the network of workplace colleagues and friends that are so critical to building a career and enjoying a full life.

Employers should consider what those in recovery bring with them to the workplace. They have overcome a huge life challenge. They will work hard, with gratitude and commitment, for those who are willing to give them a fair chance. They are not asking for special treatment, only for the same chance others receive to demonstrate what they have to offer.

I have met several business owners who actively recruit among the recovery community with great success. Sometimes particular employers, often restaurants, become known as a place that is recovery-friendly. One employee of a local pizzeria in Vermont told me that the restaurant owner not only gave her a way to pay her rent, a new group of friends, and a predictable routine, but it also helped rebuild her self-confidence and strengthen her recovery. She explained that one night the owner gave her the keys of the pizzeria to lock up and how that deep trust, after all she had been through during the time she was actively using drugs, moved her to tears and helped further strengthen her recovery.

Of course, it is understandable that employers would have questions about hiring those with a history of drug use and a past criminal record. Fortunately, there are ways companies can get the reassurance they need. First, treatment and recovery centers can vouch for the individuals they have known for an extended period. Secondly, Recovery Community Organizations are utilizing people in recovery as volunteers and/or paid employees, enabling these individuals to build a solid record of reliability. Third, there are several options for states or localities to provide tax benefits or grants to defray a portion of initial salary costs. Finally, employers or a treatment center can arrange for "check-ins" with peer counselors, or regular drug tests, to provide further reassurance. Employers willing to make the effort can find ways to address any concerns or questions they have.

Just as people in recovery often need some coaching and education about what is required in the workplace, employers can also benefit from education and training. Some employers may have the desire to hire people in recovery but not have a deep understanding of the addiction and recovery process. Recovery Community Organizations can provide that background and offer opportunities for potential employers to sit down for an in-depth discussion with someone in recovery. Such conversations can break down barriers, reduce misunderstandings, and set up both employer and employee for success.

Some companies are actively recruiting people in recovery. A website in Ann Arbor, Michigan lists recovery friendly employers. On the site is a letter from Phillis Engelbert, co-owner of a restaurant called The Lunch Room. She writes that not only are people in recovery reliable employees, but that there are also non-tangible benefits:

> Foremost is loyalty. I have found that if I take a chance on someone in recovery, they respond with a willingness to do anything the business needs. I have had crews of guys volunteer to come in and deep-clean the restaurant when we are closed. They also look out for each other and hold each other accountable. I have been surprised to see that if one person relapses and misses work, others will cover that person's shift. They demonstrate a great sense of responsibility to themselves, to each other, and to the business.[20]

As critical as it is to help those in early recovery to get and keep employment, it is just as important to ensure that those currently in the workplace receive the support they need if they are dealing with a substance use disorder problem.

There is, appropriately, a large focus in the addiction field on those with a substance use disorder who are homeless. However, we may forget what a small percentage of the total number of Americans with a substance use population are homeless. There are an estimated 771,480[21] homeless people in America. Estimates are that 26 percent of the homeless misuse drugs and 38 percent misuse alcohol, with some overlap, it is a reasonable to estimate that the number of homeless with a substance use disorder may be around 400,000. That's a large number, but it's small compared to the approximately 37 million Americans who misuse drugs other than marijuana each year—7.8 million who misuse opioids—and the estimated 28 million with an alcohol use disorder.[22] Where can we find all these Americans struggling with drugs and alcohol? In our communities and in our workplaces. They need help and support as well.

I did the best I could to get this message out about the importance of work, and workplaces, for those in recovery when I was serving as the ONDCP Director. In 2018 I organized with the D.C.-based think tank, CSIS, a forum with an impressive group of private sector, governmental, and NGO experts. This was my message to the group.

> Those of us in government need help and advice from the private sector. If there are tax changes or other incentives that would help, we want to have that conversation. The end-state we should pursue is clear. We want employees to receive the help and support they need when they ask for help with addiction issues. And we want those Americans who have struggled with addiction, who have been through treatment, and established a record of a stable recovery, to be able to get back to work. This

historic, catastrophic opioid crisis is an enormous challenge to the country, but it's also an opportunity to change our country for the better. We should, together, seize this opportunity.

Building Recovery-Friendly Workplaces

For those companies not ready to recruit and hire people in recovery, there is something else they should do—take a close look inside their own organizations. Most companies already have individuals that have been directly touched by addiction working for them. I can understand why some corporate leaders may not believe this, but their employees with addiction problems are often quite skilled at hiding it. Employees know they face severe risks to their career by sharing their past or present struggles. There is a tremendous stigma associated with addiction. But anything that keeps a problem hidden, which can discourage people from getting the support they need, is a problem.

Since companies have often invested a great deal of time and money in recruiting, hiring, and training current employees, retaining them clearly impacts their bottom line. Companies should find a way to reach out to employees and gather information through anonymous surveys. Some questions to ask their workforce include:

- Are there steps the company can take to provide a more supportive environment for people in recovery?
- Does the company's employee assistance program (EAP) function well to help those dealing with addiction issues, chronic pain, or mental health issues?
- Are managers ensuring that those who have family members affected by addiction receive the same type of workplace support for those dealing with cancer, surgeries, or other health issues?

The outcome of such a survey could enable companies to update their policies and programs. It would also allow companies to establish an advisory group, either virtual or in person, to consider necessary changes to company practices. Such a group could help companies, when they are ready, to set up recruitment and hiring programs for those in recovery, perhaps adding interviews conducted by those with knowledge of addiction and recovery.

Many employees have access to at least some benefits for substance use disorder services through their employer-provided health insurance or an EAP. These services, however, can be limited and even those who could benefit from them may worry that if their employer discovers their problem, they could lose their job. There are some great corporate leaders in the field that are proactively seeking ways to help their employees with a substance use disorder. One company, Belden, a manufacturer, launched a "Pathways to Employment" program in 2018, which offers employees who test positive for a drug screen treatment and a gradual road back to employment in safety sensitive positions.[23]

The research firm Fors Marsh conducts nationwide surveys on recovery in the workplace and publishes their findings, which are quite revealing, demonstrating important progress as well as continuing challenges.[24] One key theme was the importance of how messages on treatment and recovery from employers were communicated to employees. Survey respondents said that they were more likely to discuss issues with drugs or alcohol when *explicitly invited to do so* and to utilize resources from an EAP when it was *specifically highlighted* as an available resource for concerns about a substance use disorder.

Although half of companies that employed over 1,000 people had an EAP, that percentage drops to below 20 percent for companies under fifty employees. Flexible work schedules and return-to-work planning were offered by about a third of large companies, but by fewer smaller companies. Not many employers offered peer coaching or relapse prevention planning. The report also mentioned that employers are increasingly adopting "fair chance hiring policies" which ensure that applicants are not automatically disqualified for a job because of previous criminal convictions. Overall, the reports offer guidance to companies on how to support those impacted by SUD in a manner that promotes staff retention, improves productivity, and amplifies effective messaging to their employees that help is available for them, and they should utilize it. Despite recent progress, the Fors Marsh 2025 update highlights the need for: additional training on addiction and treatment for human resource professionals, stronger guarantees that employees' jobs will be protected if they seek treatment, and the reluctance of many companies to pursue an official "recovery-friendly workplace" designation.[25]

Although every workplace is impacted by addiction, there are clearly some that are particularly vulnerable. A report from the CDC found the highest rates of overdose deaths in the construction and mining fields and the second highest in food preparation and service.[26] Companies from these higher-risk industries need to increase their support for their employees and work to establish a culture that encourages people who need it to seek assistance.

Those in recovery should also be encouraged to share their achievement. Overcoming addiction is an enormous accomplishment, a triumph of the human spirit. They should be invited to discuss their experiences openly to help spread the word far and wide that recovery is possible for everyone. For too long senior managers in companies, and in government as well, have not embraced people in recovery. It's time for this to change.

Taking on Substance Use on College Campuses and in High Schools

Like many parents, I have been proud to send my children off to college. College life brings wonderful opportunities to engage in intellectual pursuits, meet new people, and to participate in a variety of activities. But like other moms and dads, I also know that college life includes peer pressure to try new things and new stresses to manage. Despite serious and well-intended efforts by school authorities and campus law enforcement officials, alcohol and drugs are widely available on or near college campuses. Many young people manage to navigate college life without risky alcohol and drug use, but not all.

College-age young adults have the highest rates of risky use of intoxicating substances in the United States. According to the National Survey on Drug Use and Health published in 2024,[27] 28 percent of young adults (ages 18–25) report binge drinking over the previous month (defined as more than five drinks on one occasion for a male and four for a female). Marijuana use among young adults has been increasing every year since 2008. The latest data finds that more than 25 percent of young adults (again, age 18–25) report monthly marijuana use. Misuse of opioids, pharmaceutical stimulants and sedatives are also a concern, but at much lower measured rates.

Many regular consumers of alcohol and drugs suffer academically, and some drop out and never complete their degrees. There is no denying the risks regular drug users face. The drug supply is extremely dangerous, and counterfeit prescription medications containing fentanyl pose an acute threat to young people who likely have very low tolerance for large doses of powerful synthetic opioids in today's black market pills. Not everyone survives their college years. Instead of planning graduation parties, some heartbroken parents are planning funerals. Having met many families who have lost a child due to a fatal drug overdose, I know they want to see all academic institutions do much more to prevent risky substance misuse and to rapidly get help to those who need it. Colleges and universities must adjust to today's very dangerous realities. They should make sure their institutions establish and support a collegiate recovery program (CRP).

These programs were initially designed to support students in recovery but have proven to be powerful in reshaping attitudes toward alcohol and drug use campus-wide. CRPs provide a sober gathering place for students in recovery where they can spend time together and meet with counselors. Students who have dropped out of school to receive treatment often need help to navigate their way back into college to complete their degrees—CRPs help them in this process—serving as an intermediary and advocate with college administrators.

CRPs offer a range of alcohol and drug-free events open to all students, including parties, movie nights and football game tailgates. They are visibly showing all students that alcohol and drugs are not required for a fun and fulfilling social life on campus. Some schools have also established alcohol and drug free dorms open to all interested students. Many young people today, including those who never had a drug or alcohol problem, just don't want to live with a roommate who is regularly intoxicated.

CRPs are generally funded with a modest amount of money from colleges and support from alumni. There are approximately 180 colleges and graduate schools that have stood up a CRP. These schools report significant positive outcomes for students in recovery, including improved retention rates, higher average GPA, and better graduation rates when compared to the rest of their institution's population.

The visible presence and vocal leadership of students participating in CRPs are helping to transform the culture surrounding substance use on campuses all over America. Every college should have a CRP. Students in recovery deserve the support, and every student needs to see and hear that risky substance use threatens their hopes and dreams. Proud, but worried parents across our country are counting on colleges to do all they can to keep our children safe.

Younger children also need assistance. Recovery High Schools have sprung up around the country, serving kids who are already grappling with a substance use disorder and providing the structured support they need and deserve. To date, there are about forty Recovery High Schools in the country. These schools are designed to help students in recovery from a substance use disorder complete their high school education while working on and strengthening their sobriety. Clearly there is a need for more Recovery High Schools.

Funding for these schools is often difficult to cobble together considering the many other demands on school budgets. Direct federal funding for starting and sustaining Recovery High Schools can help fill this growing need. The Association of Recovery Schools has collected lessons learned and other resources on how these schools support students.[28] High school-age children struggling with addiction are at tremendous risk. The federal government should do more to help both those already in recovery who need a dedicated school and everyone else at risk. It is another investment that will pay dividends in both lives and costs saved.

Rebuilding Lives After Treatment—The Vital Role of Recovery Community Organizations

Recovery is a process and a journey. Understandably, the government focuses on the urgent needs associated with preventing and responding to drug overdoses and supporting a wide range of drug treatment programs. These are critical priorities. Nonetheless, those investments in getting people into and successfully through treatment programs, whether in the community a court supervised drug treatment program, or behind the walls in jail or prisons, need to be protected and reinforced *after* treatment is completed. Many treatment programs do provide continued support, however that is not their primary purpose. In contrast, Recovery Community Organizations (RCOs) are established specifically to support, assist, and advise people in recovery. There are over 16,000 substance use disorder treatment centers in the country, but only around 170 RCOs. That's not nearly enough.

RCOs are a great place for people who have completed treatment to visit. They host all types of meetings and skill development programs for those working to rebuild their lives. Individuals can attend group therapy sessions, use the computers and the help of RCO staff to write a resume, receive appropriate clothes for job interviews, and get connected to a voluntary peer or recovery coach for advice and support. I visited two RCOs when I was Acting Drug Czar, The Door in Atlanta and Pro-Act in Philadelphia. Both were vibrant, busy centers of activity. In Philadelphia, I saw the kitchen they used to give people cooking lessons and nutrition advice and heard about in Philadelphia how Pro-Act gets participants involved in voluntary and paid work at the center to build up their confidence when re-entering the workplace. Even if their tasks are simple, it provides work experience to those who may not have been regularly employed for a while.

In Atlanta, I was told how when people stop by to visit the first thing the staff asks them is "how can we help you today." Whether it's connecting them to a counselor, helping with accessing health insurance, getting a state identification card, finding a job, a place to live, or a welcoming faith community, the experts at The Door know how to help or who to call.

Pro-Act has on their website a great description of RCOs. An RCO, they explain, "promotes improving quality of life, preventing relapse and sustaining recovery. It is not a clubhouse. It is a place where life's challenges are faced with solutions and guidance. It is a place where skills are shared and learned. It is a place where isolation becomes inclusion and strangers become friends." Local RCOs know their communities and adapt their programs to the need. They are welcoming places for people who are starting over, seeking practical help, as well as friends, social activities, and renewed purpose in their lives. Many choose to give back to these centers by sharing their lived experience via volunteering as a peer or coming back as a trained recovery coach.

The development of RCOs is relatively new, but the early academic analysis is positive. A 2020 study concluded that the centers: "appear to play a valued role in facilitating the accrual of social, employment, housing, and other recovery capital" and calls for more research to "determine their broader impact in initiating and sustaining remission and cost-effectiveness."[29] Like many innovations, this one shows enormous promise and potential. The federal government should fund their expansion, while also supporting research on their effectiveness and identifying best practices for the centers.[30]

Just as Sheriff Leonard allows people to come back and visit friends from the program they run in the Chesterfield jail, other programs are stepping forward to extend connectivity and support. Whether these initiatives are through brick-and-mortar RCOs, online alumni networks such as Facebook Groups, job training and placement programs, extended aftercare or check-ins with recovery coaches coordinated by treatment programs, they are collectively moving us toward the expanded recovery system we need.

Recommendations

12. **Build a recovery-friendly America in communities, colleges, and workplaces**

    The first five years after successful drug treatment can be challenging. The United States needs dedicated funding for local Recovery Community Organizations (RCOs), as well as collegiate and high school recovery initiatives. The country also needs to foster a better environment in the workplace and the community for people seeking to rebuild their lives after completing treatment. The 23 million Americans in recovery need access to services and support to sustain the progress they have made and to reintegrate themselves fully into society. *Congress should authorize HHS to provide renewable three-year grants directly to RCOs, collegiate recovery programs, and Recovery High Schools, accepting proposals from both existing and newly* *proposed programs. Congress should appropriate $500 million a year to support this program, including $10 million annually for a Center of Excellence on Recovery to spread knowledge of what is working, and what isn't, in terms of sustaining recovery.*

13. **Increase the availability of recovery and supportive housing**

The need is huge, and the issue is complex. However, the entire treatment and recovery enterprise is undermined by the difficulty in getting people with substance use disorder reliable access to the housing they require at different stages of their treatment and recovery. HUD needs to build out a housing initiative that provides cities and county public housing authorities funds to support access to housing for people impacted by addiction. Grant recipients could use the funds for supportive housing to reduce homelessness if they commit to incorporating, according to the original model, robust health and social services and require adherence to reasonable behavioral requirements by residents designed to gradually reduce substance misuse. Note that these funds are not intended to pay for housing for those in recovery indefinitely, but to assist them early in their recovery when they are most vulnerable to relapse and financial challenges. *Congress should authorize a new program at HUD focused squarely on reducing homelessness among those impacted by addiction and mental health challenges and appropriate $2 billion a year for this initiative, including $15 million annually for a nongovermental Center of Excellence on Recovery and Supportive Housing.*

Chapter Summary

7

Precision Impact

Controlling Retail Drug Markets without Mass Incarceration or Racial Bias

Chapter Introduction: When Reality Hits You in the Face

I have been to a lot of conferences, briefings, and speeches on drug policy throughout my career. But when I heard in 1995 a deeply disturbing presentation on the severity of the racial implications of the sentencing for drug offenders, I still remember exactly how I felt: not good.

Nearly "one in three (32.2 percent) young African Americans in the entire country is under criminal justice supervision on any given day."[1] Wait, what? My face burned. This wasn't the first report of the Sentencing Project on the racial implications of the War on Drugs, which was five years earlier, but this is the one that hit me like a ton of bricks.

At this time, I was between government jobs. I had left Congress in 1993 when the House Select Committee on Narcotics Abuse and Control was abolished and was doing some writing and research, before later starting at ONDCP in 1997. For a while I was editing/publishing two newsletters called *Drug Policy Report* and *Crime and Drug Report,* so I was covering as a journalist drug and crime policy conferences and media events. That was back in the day when the internet was rudimentary, so everything was in person. Also, that day in 1995, having left the hothouse political environment of Capitol Hill, I was more open to new information. As a journalist, I was also always on the lookout for an important, under-appreciated story.

For many readers, it may be hard to put one's mind back before the racial implications of drug sentencing were widely discussed and a major public policy issue. But during the cocaine era when I worked on Capitol Hill and played a small role in working on the Anti-Drug Abuse Act of 1988, it was generally believed that long sentences and a "tough on drugs" approach was sound policy. The staff at the Narcotics Committee, on both the Democratic side that worked for Democrat Charlie Rangel, from New York City, and on the Republican side, where I worked for moderate Ben Gilman, from upstate New York, were working together on the legislation.

At the Committee, from our perch on Capitol Hill, we believed this aggressive approach was helping hard-hit minority neighborhoods struggling with drugs. I clearly remember what I thought about arresting and incarcerating crack dealers—we would be making neighborhoods safer so kids could go to school and play outside, and adults could go to work, visit family and friends, and participate in community life. The Sentencing Project data told a starkly different story. The over-reliance on incarceration was devasting communities by locking up such a high percentage of its youth.

I had been a firm believer in the "bad apple" theory, meaning one rotten apple destroys the whole barrel. Remove the one bad apple and the rest are good. I had not grasped that the scale of arrests had gone so far beyond removing from a community a handful of bad apples. States and localities, supported by the federal government, had built a relentless incarceration machine that was inflicting severe damage on communities. The individuals arrested, besides receiving long sentences, were burdened with a felony criminal record for the rest of their lives. Arrestees addicted to drugs rarely received treatment.

At the 1995 conference, belatedly, but suddenly, I got it. As summarized by the Sentencing Project in 2023, over thirty years later, such high levels of incarceration "destabilizes entire communities."[2] This was a disaster I, like others working in government during the crack epidemic, had contributed to.

I realize I am not the first white person who thought that my actions were helping people of color when in fact I was making things worse. But at the time I realized this, I just felt bad. As mentioned earlier, I grew up in a high-rise apartment building in the Lower East Side of Manhattan well before the neighborhood became the trendy East Greenwich Village. My neighborhood and schools were diverse, and my parents were strongly supportive of the civil rights movement. Although I never met him, a cousin on my father's side, Andrew Goodman, also from New York City, was murdered in Mississippi in 1964, along with Michael Schwerner and James Chaney. The 1988 film, Mississippi Burning tells their story. The three were members of the Congress of Racial Equality (CORE) who were training volunteers to register African Americans to vote in Mississippi. They had traveled to Philadelphia, Mississippi to investigate the burning down by the Ku Klux Klan (KKK) of a church utilized for voter registration efforts when they were pulled over by the local sheriff and arrested. After their release, when they were driving back to CORE's regional base in Ohio, they were ambushed by the KKK, captured, and subsequently shot to death.[3]

Andrew Goodman was killed the year before I was born. My parents went to the funeral and later, when I was in elementary school, they gave me the program from his memorial service, which I read through carefully and learned about his short but consequential life. I kept the program in my room during my childhood. The courage he showed was hard for me to fathom, his sacrifice heartbreaking. To me he was a hero, a role model, someone who I aspired to be like. In 1995 it didn't look like I was doing too well.

Hard Lesson: Mass incarceration damages communities—to combat drugs police must rebuild frayed relationships and adopt a much more targeted approach

The question drug policy reformers often ask is why we don't just stop arresting people caught with small, personal possession amounts of drugs, and focus on a public health approach. It's a fair question. The answer is yes, most of these minor offenders do not need to be arrested and incarcerated. This is already the case in many places, but not everywhere. However, there is another question that is more difficult to answer: what do we do with people that sell drugs? A progressive drug reformer might suggest we just legalize all drugs and have government health officials control distribution of hard drugs. This type of "safe supply" drug distribution approach has no chance of enactment in the United States and is highly risky with today's potent synthetic drugs. Such an approach is much more controversial than Oregon's overturned drug decriminalization effort and more radical than Portugal's national decriminalization.

We are left with the dilemma that people are selling dangerous drugs across the country, and every community wants it to stop, but the public now rightly, also opposes mass arrests. Drug selling obviously poses a threat to the public's health and safety. But we can't save communities by destroying them. What we need is another approach—a way to combat drug markets seriously, but in a manner that minimizes arrests, maximizes protection of public safety, improves community/police relationships, and permanently reduces drug sales.

Grappling Honestly with Race and Drugs

To be honest, with my long personal history working inside America's War on Drugs, Michelle Alexander's *The New Jim Crow* was a tough read for me. It's an important book. In a nutshell Alexander's argument is that just as Jim Crow laws were instituted after the Civil War ended slavery to restrict voting rights and equal treatment in society for African Americans, mass incarceration was put into place to undermine implementation of civil rights laws enacted in the 1960s. What was difficult for me was not her detailed description of the practical impact of the drug war, especially in the crack cocaine era. As highlighted earlier in the book, that reality became apparent to me some time ago. What was tough for me to absorb was the implication that the tough drug laws were intentionally racially motivated.

Did the near universal support for tough drug laws considering the explosion of crack consumption, sales, and violence reflect a racist intent? Did it matter that most African American leaders, including the then chairman of the House Select Committee on Narcotics Abuse and Control,

Charles B. Rangel, Democrat of Harlem, and virtually the entire black caucus voted for the legislation?

Before attempting to answer those questions, let me share some additional highlights from Alexander's 2010 book that are important for people to know. These are all quotations directly from the text.[4]

- More African American adults are under correctional control today—in prison or jail, on probation or parole—then were enslaved in 1850, a decade before the civil war began.
- Hundreds of thousands of black men are unable to be good fathers for their children, not because of a lack of commitment or desire but because they are warehoused in prisons, locked in cages.
- Fully 70 percent of men between the ages of eighteen and forty-five in the impoverished and overwhelmingly black North Lawndale neighborhood on Chicago's West Side are ex-offenders, saddled for life with a criminal record.
- Young black men are more likely to go to prison than to college.
- Prisoners are kept behind bars, typically more than a hundred miles from home.
- In the era of mass incarceration, poor African Americans are not offered the option of great schools, community investment, and job training. Instead, they are offered police and prisons.

Back to my question. For me, upon reflection, I have come to believe that it shouldn't matter that tough drug sentencing laws had near universal support at the time of enactment, or whether those supportive of the tough sentencing laws had good intentions or not. As evidence emerged of the impact of mass incarceration, the laws and the whole approach should have been adjusted far more rapidly. However, this doesn't mean that political leaders and government officials are not responsible for failing to take a closer look at the severe consequences of excessive drug sentences. We should have acted much sooner.

Returning to the issue at hand, of course Alexander is not the only author or activist to call for an end to the War on Drugs to end mass incarceration and the racial consequences of drug enforcement. That phrase, *ending the failed War on Drugs*, is thrown around a lot, but decoding its meaning in a useful way and laying out the steps to change our current expansive set of federal and state drug policies to something else, something much better, while also still seeking to protect the country from the many harms associated with drugs is complicated, both practically and politically.

As a veteran practitioner of drug policy, let me state plainly that there is no lever available to turn off the drug war. Nobody can snap their fingers in a huge country like ours with fifty states and 3,000 counties with broadly distributed decision-making and instantly change everything. Even if we could, what would we replace it with? Legalization, even if it were politically viable, won't make drug problems go away, as we see from the continued very high levels of death and suffering caused by alcohol and powerful prescription medications. However, that doesn't mean a series of policy, program, legal, and funding changes cannot be launched which will add up to a *transformation* of today's drug war to something that is far more effective and more widely supported throughout the country. A transformation is what we need and what I am calling for.

In these pages I highlight the views of many articulate critics of the War on Drugs. Their insights are important and useful in drawing focus on real problems that require focused attention. Their surfacing of alternative policies can be catalytic in creating an environment receptive to changes. I say to scholars, community activists, and reform-oriented NGOs, keep it coming. Our drug policies, and our drug problem, are hugely consequential and require rigorous review. Still, I worry that the country, and our elected officials at every level, can get stuck in opposing camps that impede progress rather than fostering it. It is important for our debate and political processes not to be paralyzed in a futile search for a simple solution to make the drug problem, and the collateral consequences of drug policies, just go away. We must directly confront these failures and weaknesses and systematically address them.

As I have highlighted, some of these are hard lessons we must take to heart, but heeding the hard lessons should also mean getting to work on fixing problems, rather than waiting for the country to find the non-existent easy "end the drug war lever." It doesn't exist and we won't find it. But there is a pathway toward a transformation that would be a huge improvement over the status quo. It is time to get moving.

Some important reforms have been accomplished in recent years, due to the waning of the crack epidemic and the shocking toll of today's opioid epidemic. But many more changes are needed. I will lay out steps to accelerate progress on that path toward an approach that lifts people up instead of holding them back and which fosters reconciliation and partnership between communities and law enforcement instead of division. Further, I will below identify ways to disrupt the lethal drug trade without imposing unfair collateral consequences on our own citizens.

Rethinking Drug Sentencing

Sentencing for drug crimes has long been tied to the weight of drugs an individual is caught with, along with whether it is a first, second, or third offense. As discussed earlier regarding the crack/powder cocaine disparity, the intent is that those caught with a distribution amount of narcotics face a longer sentence, while those with personal use amounts face a lower sentence. However, there are problems with this approach. The leader of a city's biggest drug dealing operation may be careful to never have narcotics on him, while a low-level "user-dealer" or courier may have no significant role in managing the organization but is tasked with transporting or holding significant amounts of drugs. Also, regardless of the weight of drugs someone is caught with, not every drug dealer is the same. Some are instigating violence and undermining community safety; others avoid conflict or violent behavior of any kind. Why should everyone be treated the same? They shouldn't be.

Long sentences, ten years or more, should be reserved for those who have earned them through either their top-level leadership role in an organization or their reckless, violent behavior. Lesser drug dealers are still committing serious crimes and should pay a price for their behavior, but they do not need to serve as long. It's a waste of resources, contributes to excessive, expensive incarceration in the United States. Also, as the late, great, Mark Kleiman and other drug policy experts have explained, long prison sentences are of questionable effectiveness in terms of serving as a deterrent to others or in facilitating rehabilitation. More effective are swiftly applied shorter sentences, Dr. Kleiman wrote in his book, *When Brute Force Fails* that: "Theory and evidence agree swift and certain punishment, even if not severe will control the vast bulk of offending behavior."[5]

Tough "drug-induced homicide" laws with lengthy sentences have been adopted by thirty states. It is a quite serious matter when a fatal overdose occurs, and it is easy to understand why many parents want to see the person who sold their son or daughter the drugs that killed them severely punished. As a dad, I can't say I would feel any different in their situation. However, it remains true that prison sentences are best assessed by the circumstances of the case. In recovery advocate Ryan Hampton's latest book, he shares anecdotes of sentences in these cases exceeding twenty years in cases when the drug seller was a friend of the deceased who used drugs together. Hampton concludes that drug-induced homicide laws "not only stretch the definition of a drug dealer beyond recognition, but they also ignore the basic facts of any accident—including the fact that people who are scared to be charged as killers simply won't call 911 when their friend is in danger."[6]

I won't pre-judge individual cases and would emphasize that it's important for the impact statement of families who have lost a loved one to be heard. However, when the drug seller is a user-dealer and a friend of the deceased, rather than a decade or more in prison they should be sentenced to a modest amount of time behind bars followed by intensive court-supervised treatment with five years of further probation monitoring including regular drug testing. This would balance the need to impose real consequences for the loss of a life, while protecting the effectiveness of "Good Samaritan" laws, which, as Hampton notes, are critical in ensuring individuals don't risk decades in jail for calling the police when they witness an overdose and are trying to save a life.

A justice policy group, the Criminal Justice Council, has come out with a series of recommendations from their bipartisan task force of experts chaired by former republican Congressman Trey Gowdy and former democratic Deputy Attorney General Sally Yates on long prison sentences. They note in their report that long sentences have "no statistically significant relationship between state drug imprisonment rates and three indicators of state drug problems: self-reported drug use, drug overdose deaths, and drug arrests."[7] They also highlight that long sentences are especially ineffective in helping those impacted by either a substance use or mental health disorder and that such sentences should be preserved for leaders of drug trafficking organizations. Their recommendation to focus on behavior rather than drug amounts is logical and I strongly endorse it. Both the federal government and state governments should move forward to implement it—it's long overdue.

Rightsizing sentences for drug offenders would take a large bite out of mass incarceration for all drug offenses. As the President of the Vera Institute of Justice, Nicholas Turner concludes, the United States continues to rely on mandatory minimums, "three strikes laws and additional sentencing enhancement. And yet evidence to support our retributive, punitive approach is limited. In fact, we know this approach doesn't make our communities safer in the way proponents claim and the public assumes, causes more damage than they are willing to admit, and does not repair harm."[8]

Before moving on to two issues impacting drug-related arrests, marijuana and dismantling retail drug markets, it's important to highlight that who is serving time behind bars for drug offenses is a more complex issue than one might think. Drugs, especially during the crack cocaine epidemic, have played an important role in increasing incarceration, but there are other factors.

As John Pfaff skillfully writes in his book, *Locked In: The True Causes of Mass Incarceration and How to Achieve Real Reform*, the percentage of state prisoners serving a drug sentence increased from 6.5 percent to 22 percent between 1980 and 1990. That's an increase from 20,000 to 150,000 during the same period, and up to 250,000 by 2010. But there were also many people arrested for *non-drug* violent crimes. Pfaff explains that between 1980 and 2009, states added over 1 million people with "over half that growth coming from locking up more people convicted of violence compared to only about 20 percent due to" drug offenses.[9]

Nonetheless, the impact of drugs on criminal behavior and the justice system is still substantial. Many people who commit non-drug violent crimes are consuming drugs or alcohol, including when they commit their crimes. Many non-drug crimes, such as robbery, fraud, and identity theft, are often directly associated with drug use. The vast majority of those in prison and jail have a substance misuse problem regardless of the crime they committed.[10] Reducing sentences for drug offenses and sharply increasing access to alternatives to incarceration for those with substance use problems will not solve the whole mass incarceration crisis itself. However, it remains an excellent place to start. In addition, it will reduce the number of Americans who are living with a felony conviction. Let me say a bit more about this subject.

The lifetime burden on those trying to rebuild one's life after completing a prison sentence for a felony conviction remains an underappreciated issue. The country, specifically Congress and state legislatures, needs to find a way to reduce that heavy weight people are forced to carry around the rest of their lives. It's important to spotlight what should be obvious—asking people to successfully re-enter society, get a job, find a place to live, and reconnect to their family is a big enough challenge for anyone who has been out of circulation and locked up for multiple years. Add to that the scrutiny, restrictions, and stigma associated with having to reveal to a potential employer or landlord their criminal history makes everything harder. Reuben Jonathan Miller writes about this topic eloquently in his 2021 book, *Halfway Home: Race, Punishment and the Afterlife of Mass Incarceration:*

> Today, 19.6 million people live with a felony record, four times the size of the population on probation and parole, and ten times the size of the American prison census. Almost all of these people lived in dire poverty before they entered a cage, and they return to these same conditions on the day of their release. One-third are black; one in three currently living black American men have felony records.... In most states, this means that people with criminal records may not hold public office or live in public housing. They can be fired from their jobs on the whim of their employers or have their applications for apartments denied, even when they have the jobs, the credit scores, and the references to qualify otherwise.[11]

Felony arrests are not the only area where racial bias persists. Misdemeanor arrests in certain states can result in lengthy sentences and are concentrated in heavily policed minority neighborhoods, often reflect racial bias. Plea bargains, which are how the overwhelming majority of cases are resolved, also reflect a disproportionate impact on African Americans. One recent study concluded that the "structure and process of plea bargaining makes it more likely that the historical racial bias that exists against African American male defendants will taint the negotiation process and justice outcomes."[12]

As referenced in chapter two, community drug stops disproportionately impacted minorities. From 2002 to 2019, "the New York City Police Department (NYPD) conducted over five million pedestrian stops. Approximately 85 percent of those stops were initiated against blacks and Latinos."[13] For many years political leadership in New York assumed that stop and frisk policies were essential for reducing crime. However, as referenced in chapter 2, when stop and frisks were reduced from 685,724 in 2011 to 11,629 in 2017[14] crime went down.[15]

There is, of course some complexity underlying this data, such as the type of crime threat in a neighborhood, the police-community relationship, and the pressure for concrete action imposed on law enforcement. However, this natural experiment on stop and frisk shows that quite consequential changes in the daily activities of police can be made to reduce repeated confrontations between police and local citizens without a negative impact on the crime rate.

Racial bias in the justice system, as well as the consequences on an individual's life of having a criminal record, are important problems that need to be addressed. A significant portion of racial bias is implicit or unconscious, meaning that "the individual is likely not aware of the biased association. Implicit racial bias can cause individuals to unknowingly act in discriminatory ways."[16] The scholarship on this subject shows that a modest updating of procedural practices that allow arrestees to be treated as individuals can have a large impact. This can include encouraging justice system decision makers take the "Implicit Association Test" to confidentially surface subconscious bias. It also makes sense to collect data to reveal sentencing trends, facilitate broader exposure to minority communities outside the courtroom by prosecutors and judges, and to mute racial cues in pre-trial court records and reports "such as names, addresses, and race identifying information that may contribute to race-influenced decision making"[17]

A 2024 book on how the brain reacts to information highlights both how one's upbringing or environment can lead to unconscious bias, including on race and gender issues, and how that bias can be addressed:

> The roots of discrimination and bias are without doubt complex. They are spurred by history, economics, politics, and religion. But many of the roots can be traced back to the basic rules of how our brains work. Those rules that govern what we see and what we miss. What we expect and what surprises us. Once we become aware of the rules we can make seen what should be salient but is not, and perhaps make less salient of what should be of no importance.[18]

The Tragedy of Re-Entry from Prison During the Opioid Epidemic

There is much that can be said about jails and prisons in the United States, about the cruelty of solitary confinement, about the difficulties most inmates have in sustaining reasonable access to their families, and about the failure to focus on the task of ensuring that the 95 percent[19] of all inmates who will eventually return to the community receive opportunities to develop the employment and life skills needed to avoid recidivism. But in terms of access to quality evidence-based treatment, or mental health care for the many who have a co-occurring mental health and substance use disorder, jail and prisons are a particularly difficult environment.

Most jails and prisons are not well-situated to provide quality behavioral care. Even worse, as Victoria Law writes in her book about incarceration myths, "prison practices frequently replicate past experiences of trauma and violence, which are often underlying causes" of addiction.[20] For this reason it is critical that jails and prisons take serious precautions when individuals with untreated substance use disorders are preparing for release, as they will face an illicit drug market that poses an acute threat to their survival.

It's a strange thing that state taxpayers pay the bill to keep someone locked up to protect public safety at the rate of about $50,000 a year, but often can't come up with a way to provide decent addiction treatment behind bars and to ensure a safe reentry. Whether or not one believes that prison serves as a deterrent, an opportunity for rehabilitation, or a method of incapacitating criminals, surely it shouldn't be a radical idea that the first few days and weeks after prison are critically important, both for the individual's future and the risks of recidivism. This is not a new problem, but the costs are mounting at this stage of the opioid epidemic when those with an untreated substance use disorder return to the community. A single use of an illicit drug containing fentanyl can be fatal to anyone, but especially someone whose tolerance has been reduced from being behind bars for an extended period.

The Vera Institute of Justice notes a study in Washington State found that, in the two weeks following their release, "people who had been incarcerated in state prisons were 129 times more likely to die from an overdose compared to the general public"[21] while North Carolina study found that upon re-entry state prisoners were forty times more likely to die from a fatal opioid overdose two weeks post-release[22] compared to other state residents. These studies were done before synthetic opioids were more widely integrated with stimulants, so current overdose rates could even be higher. Regardless of the exact rate, it is horrifically high and ought to be a major priority to address through multiple mechanisms.

Mark Kleiman wrote prophetically, before the fentanyl epidemic, about the need to develop a credible performance-measurement system to "hold wardens accountable for performance, as measured by the post-release welfare and criminal activity of the prisoners."[23] Some basic data can and should be collected for each jail and prison, including new arrests of former inmates, employment, housing status, access to overdose prevention information, and health care. Ensuring that a warden's continued employment and potential bonuses, along with other senior prison administrators, are tied directly to the actual results of what happens once prisoners leave incarceration would motivate better information collection and follow up. Further, if prisons find their budget squeezed by spending a few percent of the annual cost of keeping someone behind bars to provide treatment and support safe re-entry, they can add their voices to others who are advocating for greater investment in these programs.

It's important to remember the words of wisdom from the classic book *The 7 Habits of Highly Effective People—begin with the end in mind* (habit two). The objective of incarceration for all those who are destined to return to the community is, through a mix of punishment and rehabilitation, to ensure that former inmates no longer pose a public safety risk and can be productive members of society. Setting up those released for success, not failure, must be integrated into the operations of jails and prisons. If it's not working, administrators need to change their practices. Further, if they are not tracking outcomes, they are flying blind and the performance of these facilities and their managers cannot be properly assessed.

In fairness, this poor state of affairs is not just the responsibility of wardens, who have very difficult jobs. Their managers at state departments of corrections and senior state officials should change the rules of the game, make it clear what results are expected, and provide the additional resources necessary. Also, I do not mean to over generalize. There are good re-entry programs that help people transition, provide resources, and partner with other agencies and organizations to reduce risks. There are initiatives to arrange for housing, paid work, and health services prior to inmates leaving prison. But by no means are current efforts sufficient.

The federal government should help by providing additional training and technical assistance in supporting re-entry, funding evidence-based substance use disorder treatment behind bars, and drafting a model performance system for holding prison management accountable for post-release results. The enactment of the bipartisan Re-entry Act proposed by Senators Tammy Baldwin (W-WI) and Mike Braun (R-IN) would be an excellent place to start. This legislation would restart benefits for Medicaid-eligible individuals thirty days prior to release, make it easier for states to provide effective substance use disorder treatment and services, and helps ensure warm handoffs upon release.[24] Already some states with Medicaid expansion are utilizing what are called "Section 1115 Demonstrations" to sign people up to receive health care before they leave prison.[25] These Section 1115 Demonstrations should continue to be supported.

Even more, as I outline below, can and should be done. Getting released from jail or prison should not be a death sentence. Every inmate with a history of drug use must have a carefully prepared and supported discharge plan. Sending people back to the community without the resources and support to survive will surely increase recidivism and potentially pose a risk to public safety. It's shortsighted, unfair, and cruel.

Case Managers and "Warm Handoffs" for the Justice-Involved Population

Let me say a bit more about "warm handoffs." Navigating the justice and health systems upon completion of a jail sentence can be hard enough for anyone, but when you add the complexity associated with court mandates, it can be hard to keep up. Sometimes people just lose track of where they need to be when. For this reason, the justice-involved population is often assigned a caseworker who helps the client manage their obligations. The organization that developed *Specialized Case Management* was created by the federal government in the 1970s under the name *Treatment Alternatives to Street Crime* (TASC) specifically to direct nonviolent arrestees with drug problems to treatment. TASC, based in Chicago, still provides case management services around the country, but now goes by the name *Treatment Alternatives for Safe Communities*. Case managers ensure that engagements with the justice system (e.g., meeting with their probation officer) and the health system (e.g., attending counseling sessions) are not forgotten or skipped and provide much needed support for those re-integrating into the community. There is now a widespread recognition that those who have just completed a time behind bars should not be left on their own in navigating their continuing obligations.

The warm handoffs approach is also used to highlight that giving someone with a drug problem a brochure or a contact phone number about treatment is usually not sufficient to get them there. It's far more effective, especially when someone survives an overdose and expresses interest in treatment, to drive them directly to the treatment center and facilitate their entry process. The concepts of warm handoffs and case management are now widely accepted, but once, when I was speaking at a town hall in Pennsylvania in 2017, I was heckled by a local district attorney who mocked my comments on this issue and called for "hard handoffs." I pushed back pretty hard—the exchange made for a good soundbite on local TV news. Today there is a much better understanding of the necessity of providing more support to keep people on track, especially those with substance use disorders facing a serious risk of a fatal drug overdose.

Addressing the Collateral Consequences Imposed on those with a Substance Use Disorder

Taking concrete steps to mitigate the heavy collateral consequences imposed on those who have successfully completed a sentence for a felony or misdemeanor conviction is vital. We can't have it both ways: asking people to rebuild their lives while avoiding a return to illegal drug consumption and then make it extremely difficult to do so. In fact, it would be better not just for the returning inmate, but for public safety, if the former prisoner's past convictions were largely removed from public records through the limited expungement of their convictions upon release. They could still be required to reveal their criminal record when seeking to purchase a gun or when seeking employment in certain sensitive fields, such as law enforcement or private security, but otherwise be legally authorized to *not* "check the box" on job applications or rental/home purchase agreements that they had a conviction in their past. Those convicted of murder or sexual violence should not be eligible.

To zero in more precisely on collateral consequences linked directly to addiction, let me reiterate, as highlighted above, how common it has become for those with a history of untreated drug addiction to suffer a fatal overdose after a long-awaited release from prison. Addressing this problem requires that every inmate receive treatment while still behind bars and be connected to an outside treatment or recovery provider at least ninety days before re-entry. Although today some prisons are providing quality treatment and conducting serious re-entry planning, these efforts would be greatly advanced by the long overdue end of the Medicaid inmate exclusion, the federal law which prohibits the use of Medicaid funds to pay for health service to those who are incarcerated."[26] This would allow prisons to be reimbursed for health services and greatly simplify their efforts to provide quality treatment and recovery services to those who could benefit from them.

The excessive collateral consequences imposed on those with a diagnosed substance use disorder that hamper reintegration into society must be removed by changes in federal and state laws. The cruelty of sending someone back out into community, after they have paid their debt to society, without ensuring the basic minimal requirements to re-start their lives is morally unacceptable and so clearly not in the interests of minimizing recidivism and protecting public safety.

I believe the stakes are too high to continue to impose such potentially severe consequences on those with a history of a substance use disorder to leave incarceration without a greater effort to set them up for success. The costs of impeding access to work and housing are unacceptable. A fair solution would: (1) ensure intake processes identify those with a substance use disorder when they begin their sentence; (2) provide treatment and counseling in prison; (3) require an outgoing inmate to connect and stay in regular touch with a treatment or recovery program in the community; (4) authorize via state and federal law the limited expungement for felony and misdemeanor convictions for these inmates as long as they maintain continuous engagement with the treatment/recovery provider and avoid new convictions for five years; (5) allow full access to public benefits such as food stamps for those enrolled in this expungement program; and (6) require monitoring of these former inmates by state or federal probation programs and ensure felony records are available to law enforcement if there are new arrests of the individual.

This approach aligns the interests of the individual and society by incentivizing a sustained recovery of those leaving incarceration with a history of addiction. More can be done to help outgoing inmates and their potential employers and housing providers reduce risk, but giving former prisoners a fair shot to transition to a safe place to live and the practical ability to get work would vastly increase their ability to survive this very dangerous transition.

Thinking Through How to Deal with Marijuana in Today's America

Marijuana has long played a significant role in mass incarceration. The number of marijuana arrests in the United States has been quite consequential. For many years marijuana arrests constituted over half of all drug-related arrests, peaking at 858,408 in 2009, according to the FBI. Although many of the sentences for marijuana possession may have been brief, that doesn't mean the impact on the individuals arrested is insignificant. Being stopped and frisked in the search for drugs and arrested if caught with a single joint on your person, can be a very traumatizing and stigmatizing experience for a young person. In some communities such experiences can happen repeatedly. It's not good and on balance harms rather than helps public safety.

On the one hand, the threat posed by marijuana has historically been exaggerated by politicians, while research showed that the substance posed only a minor health risk. Harry Anslinger utilized outlandish rhetoric about marijuana to help maintain support for his Federal Bureau of Narcotics at the Treasury Department. A study requested by the Nixon Administration, the 1972 report of the National Commission on Marijuana and Drug Abuse chaired by Pennsylvania Governor Raymond Shafer, *Marijuana: A Signal of Misunderstanding*,[27] concluded that all criminal penalties for the possession and private use of marijuana be eliminated. President Nixon rejected the Commission's recommendation and communicated clearly that his administration would not decriminalize marijuana.

Much of the public now agrees with the Schaefer Commission, with polls showing two-thirds of Americans supporting marijuana legalization. As of this writing in late 2025, twenty-four states and Washington D.C. have legalized adult use of marijuana. Most states—thirty-nine—have some form of medical marijuana access. There is a lot that could be said about the results of marijuana legalization to date. The extent to which marijuana arrests have already declined is impressive, to around 200,000 today. That change has been a significant contributor to the reduction in overall drug arrests.

On the other hand, legal marijuana in half the country has had quite a few negative and troubling consequences. The expectations of marijuana reformers that legal marijuana would result in the elimination of black market sales of marijuana have proven not to be true.[28] Due to a variety of factors, including the high tax rates in some states and a permissive environment for illegal production and sale, drug gangs, including Chinese criminal groups and Mexican drug cartels operating in the United States, are significantly involved in marijuana production and trafficking.[29] This marijuana, often produced with unsafe pesticides, ends up in both the illicit and licit supply. Further, the country, regardless of marijuana's legal status, still must grapple far more effectively with the concerning health consequences of marijuana consumption, especially for the increasing number of high volume/high potency users and those who consume marijuana every day.

It's another hard lesson of the drug war that substances change over time as entrepreneurial drug sellers experiment with new products. This was the case with opioids, which began with the smoking of raw opium, then due to advances in chemistry, evolved to morphine, heroin, powerful prescription opioids, and now to fentanyl and other even more potent synthetic opioids. Before 1995, according to the DEA, marijuana seizures averaged less than 4 percent THC in 1995. Today it averages over 15 percent[30] and marijuana measuring around 20 percent THC is widely available. These days marijuana can be smoked not just in joints and blunts, but also in slick vape pens. High potency concentrates called wax or butter, which can be 40–80 percent THC, are consumed via smoking, vaping or dabbing. Further, private sector markets are offering a bonanza of edibles, including not just gummies and brownies, but cookies, candies, and drinks. The type of marijuana and the potency in these consumables vary but are often quite high.

Among drug policy experts, there has been debate on how people may adjust or "titrate" their use of marijuana when it is of higher potency. Often consumers of drugs and alcohol are seeking a certain level of intoxication they find enjoyable, slowing or stopping their consumption when they feel like they have had too much. Younger people who have initiated marijuana use with higher potency products appear to have become acclimated to a higher level of intoxication. Today, in terms of health consequences, the risks are rising.[31]

There have been a lot of myths thrown around about marijuana, but it's quite unfortunate that there is a widespread perception of marijuana as non-addictive or always low risk. According to recent research, about 20 percent[32] of those that are regular consumers of marijuana develop a dependence, with the risks much greater for those who start using earlier[33] and for higher potency consumers.[34] There is compelling reporting showing an association between marijuana consumption and psychosis for those with certain genetic risk factors."[35] There have also been a number of anecdotal reports about regular marijuana users going to the emergency room with the odd combination of screaming and vomiting[36]—dubbed "scromiting" which is a disturbing trend.

In late 2024, *The New York Times* noted the rise in reports of "cannabinoid hyperemesis syndrome" a condition caused by heavy cannabis use and resulting in disturbing symptoms such as seizures, kidney failure and cardiac arrest, in addition to nausea and vomiting. Overall, they noted that:

> nearly a third of all users ages 18 and up have reported symptoms of cannabis use disorder, according to estimates from a unique data analysis conducted for *The Times* by a Columbia University epidemiologist. That would mean they continue to use the drug despite significant negative effects on their lives. "almost everybody that uses it every day is reporting problems with it," said Dr. Wilson Compton, deputy director of the National Institute on Drug Abuse, who was not involved in the analysis.[37]

The country seems to be on a steady course of increased legal access to marijuana, with some people consuming it relatively safely, just as many drink alcohol without developing a problem. At the same time, again, like alcohol, a significant minority is developing problems with their marijuana use. The question then is what to do now regarding marijuana policy. States that have legalized marijuana have no interest in reversing course, while the federal government has not taken action to address the situtation. There is an increasingly obvious need for better oversight on a national level of state implementation of their production, sales, and marketing of marijuana.

The attention paid to the safety of marijuana sold in legal state markets leaves a lot to be desired. There are no "national standards for testing marijuana for possible contaminants such as pesticides, solvents, fungi and bacteria. Nor is there a federal agency providing oversight."[38]

I believe Congress should enact a compromise federal law that would allow states to continue to make their own decisions on legal sales of marijuana to adults but would better take into account the significant public health risks of regular high potency marijuana use today, especially for youth. Here's are what I believe are the key principles for Congress to utilize when considering national marijuana policy reform.

1. Focus on protecting youth under twenty-one, supporting the enforcement of state age limits on dispensaries, while funding the Surgeon General to establish a national youth education campaign on potential health consequences of marijuana.
2. Authorize and fund FDA to establish and monitor federal standards for marijuana sales in states where it is legal, ensuring strict adherence to safety requirements and ethical marketing practices.
3. Support an intensified study of state marijuana programs to assess further reforms, including the possible establishment of a national marijuana potency cap, the removal of the highest potency products from the market, and other steps to increase the emphasis on protecting public health and reduce the focus on profits.
4. Expand funding for evidence-based treatment for marijuana use disorder and research on the consequences of consumption of high-potency marijuana.[39]
5. Accelerate research on the effectiveness of marijuana roadside tests to better enforce "drugged driving" laws.
6. Continue to enforce federal and state laws against illicit production and trafficking, especially targeting foreign drug cartel operations, while approving federal legislation decriminalizing marijuana possession to

help further reduce the utilization of law enforcement searches and arrests specifically for possession of personal use amounts.

Of course, this approach isn't perfect, but it's a serious path forward that will help the country continue to reduce marijuana arrests while better protecting youth who are most vulnerable to developing a serious marijuana problem. Federal decriminalization of marijuana possession will send a message to non-legal states that arrests are not the best way to address marijuana consumption, while reserving federal authorities to deal with large-scale black market marijuana trafficking which is now a mounting threat.

Much of the country wants legal access to marijuana, and law enforcement has their hands full with the lethal opioid crisis, which as I outline below, requires an even greater level of law enforcement time, energy, and focus. Significant state and local drug enforcement reforms are necessary to better combat today's dangerous drug markets.

A Hard Look at Retail Drug Markets

There is a simple reality about drug markets that explains why they are so difficult to eliminate. Drug markets consist of a series of *consensual transactions* between a seller and a buyer. There is no victim in the conventional sense. Nobody has broken into someone's home, or been attacked on the street, or is robbed of their personal property. This makes policing drug markets difficult. Law enforcement must get in between these consensual buyers and sellers. They do this through "buy and bust" operations—with an undercover officer who can testify about the crime. Law enforcement can also conduct surveillance of drug markets, capture drug sales on video and use that evidence in court. This is easier to do in overt, public drug markets, more difficult in covert drug sales where a drug seller and buyer are meeting very briefly in a discrete specific location—agreed to via smart phone messaging applications—that vary from purchase to purchase.[40]

Communities, for understandable reasons, are not happy about drug markets in their neighborhood, even if they are covert. Residents often call and complain to the police about drug sales, and the police attempt to respond. Running such drug enforcement operations always poses real risks to the safety of officers since dealers often carry weapons. Nonetheless, even when drug dealers are arrested and drug markets are disrupted, the relief is often temporary. Drug markets usually reconstitute. Buyers are still plentiful, and even in the unlikely event that a drug enforcement operation literally arrests all active sellers in a neighborhood, drug dealers are easily replaced. Both the police and the community are frustrated by the outcome.

It won't be unusual for the community, seeing drug markets continue to endure even after repeated drug enforcement operations, to believe that the police are not trying hard to shut down drug markets. Meanwhile, the police are also frustrated. They may believe, falsely, that many in the community do not really care about drug sales in their neighborhoods and are not trying hard enough to control their family members involved in drug markets as buyers or sellers. High-crime communities desperately want to see violence, crime, and drug sales reduced. The police want the same result. New approaches are necessary to get us there.

As highlighted above, I don't believe that legalization or some other way of providing a "safe supply" of drugs such as fentanyl, heroin, methamphetamine, or cocaine is either politically feasible or wise, considering the severe health risks associated with these drugs. So, the cat and mouse game of catching drug sellers continues, without the results that everyone wants. Is there a way out of the dilemma? I will argue that there is, but it does require a change in the way the problem is addressed, by both the police and the community.

When law enforcement seeks to disrupt drug markets, they, understandably, with their many responsibilities and the difficulty of the task, tend to go after the easiest targets to identify. They make some drug buys, acquire informants, conduct surveillance, record videos of drug sales if they can, and ensure that they have a good case that would satisfy a prosecutor, and make arrests. However, an expert on drug markets, David Kennedy, has been making a strong argument, not just through research and writing, but also via successful pilot programs, that there is a better way to control drug markets. It requires careful study of specific markets to identify all the drug sellers involved and building an understanding of everyone's role in the organization, their level of violence, and the threat they pose to the community. The program is referred to as Drug Market Intervention (DMI).

Not every drug dealer is the same. Some are drug-dependent individuals who may be running errands for dealers but have no significant responsibilities in terms of managing the criminal organization nor are they committing violent acts or profiting significantly from their role. On the other hand, some dealers instigate violence or serve in a leadership role in the organization. A careful mapping of a whole drug market—to understand the entire set of personnel and processes drug markets utilize—will enable law enforcement to differentiate between participants' specific roles. The most dangerous drug dealers, and the organization's leaders should be arrested and prosecuted. This, after a thorough analysis—turns out to be a much smaller group than expected—no more than one-third of all drug dealers.[41] For everyone else that is not identified as particularly dangerous or senior in terms of leadership—especially user-dealers—there is a different approach.

Those minor players can be leveraged out of the business of drug selling through the combination of (1) a very specific and credible threat of future arrest for any continued drug selling; (2) offers of social and health services; and (3) a clear message from local community members about the need to change their behavior. So that's the concept—target for arrest the most dangerous, problematic drug dealers and make an example of them. Learn what everyone else is doing in the drug market and incentivize them through a variety of options they can select from, and under the threat of arrest, to stop selling drugs. Let's go deeper into how this works.

Dismantling Drug Markets without Mass Incarceration

Once a drug market has been mapped, and those identified as most dangerous have been arrested, it is time to focus on the remaining dealers. If you are wondering how to get a drug dealer, presumably making some decent cash selling narcotics to just give up on selling drugs because someone asks them to, you're asking yourself the right question. But before attempting to answer that, let me highlight that most drug dealers are not making as much money as one might think. The research indicates that most are earning minimum wage and often living with their mom.[42]

The organizational leadership does much better, but they represent a very small percentage of the total drug dealing workforce.

There is an important aspect of police work that is useful to highlight at this point. Most crime control occurs through social control and implicit disapproval of society for committing criminal acts. Informal influences of family, friends, and one's social network, along with community norms, stops most people from committing crimes. Yes, repeat criminals, especially violent ones, will eventually face arrest, but the odds of an individual getting arrested, prosecuted, and incarcerated for each individual crime they commit is quite low. For someone not involved in regularly committing crimes, one might think the risks and consequences of getting caught appear substantial. Sure, it's true, for someone with a conventional job, even a low percentage risk can be a very effective deterrent to taking a chance on committing a crime. However, it's a different calculus for those with few opportunities in the mainstream economy and more experience in illicit activities.

When drug researchers analyzed the chances of ending up in prison for selling cocaine, they came up with an estimate of one in fifteen thousand chance per each transaction."[43] That's some amazingly low odds and explains why so many with limited employment options are tempted by the seemingly easy money of selling drugs.

However, there is a clever, but little-used way to increase those odds of arrest to nearly 100 percent. Police can work cases, capture video of individuals selling drugs, then "bank" the case, meaning don't go forward with the arrest, but use the information as a very specific deterrent for that individual. This approach has a lot of potential. Of course, it only works to change behavior if the offender is very much aware of the imminent threat he is under for potential arrest.

Right now, drug dealers have a very low, but from their perspective, unpredictable chance of a future arrest each day selling drugs. Bringing that deterrent front and center in their minds, and empowering police to follow through, is critical to this approach. Figuring out the right way to inform them to maximize the possibility of getting drug dealers to walk away from selling drugs is a central part of the intervention.

This is ideally done in person, at a community meeting in a local recreational center or church. David Kennedy refers to these meetings as "call-ins." Those drug dealers for whom police have banked cases are contacted by letter. They are invited to the community meeting, told they will not be arrested, and are encouraged to bring a family member or friend. At the call-in meeting, video monitors are set up so invitees can watch videos of themselves committing a felony. A police leader or prosecutor explains the situation to the drug dealers and guests, stating plainly that if they continue selling drugs, they 100 percent will be arrested—their case is all ready to go. Ideally the law enforcement official also speaks with some humility, explaining how they care about each of the individuals, do not want to arrest them if they don't have to, and acknowledging that past tactics police utilized to address drug markets have not been effective and that they intend do better through closer collaboration with community partners. Videos of some of these call-ins can be found online.

The police send the clear message that they want to give everyone who was invited to the call-in a fair chance to get out of the drug business before they arrest them. This *highly specific* warning ensures the participants understand their real legal risks and makes the deterrent extremely effective, far different from the rare and unpredictable risks of arrests they typically face. Further, a concrete warning in an open community forum creates increased legitimacy and a sense of fairness that is often missing in traditional drug enforcement operations (from the perspective of the community).

Key is integrating community pressure with police pressure. Other speakers at the call-ins include community leaders, pastors, and mothers or grandmothers who have had children arrested or who overdosed on drugs. Former convicts arrested for drug crimes also advise the younger dealers to take the opportunity given to them and share their stories of transitioning from drug dealing to lawful employment. Present at the call-ins are also local officials and NGOs that can offer a range of services. The idea is not just that the drug dealers will be leveraged into stopping their drug use just out of fear of arrest, but that they will also see, hear, and feel the authentic voice of the community asking them to change their behavior. These community members, and the social and health service providers, will explain that they want to help them to move their lives on to a better, safer, healthier path.

This type of intervention cannot work with the police acting alone. Law enforcement officials, including leadership, need to lay the groundwork for the intervention by first meeting and talking honestly with the community. By providing opportunities for dialogue, listening to community members' views, sharing the concept for the new initiative, and responding to questions, the police can build support and rapport. These efforts create an opportunity for the police and community to act together to dismantle drug markets that both are worried about.

Prospects for Expansion of Police/ Community Drug Market Interventions

Will this work? It has, famously in High Point, North Carolina[44] as well in other communities nearby, sharply reducing drug dealing.[45] There have been other replications around the country, including in Nashville, Tennessee which reduced drug crimes by over half in the targeted area.[46] Drug markets have been dismantled, and when police commit to a ongoing maintenance of the intervention to prevent the drug market from returning, the results can be sustained. However, it is important to highlight that not every intervention utilizing this model has been as effective as the one in High Point. The mixed results of some federally funded replications under the Department of Justice's *Project Safe Neighborhood* program, nonetheless, offer important insights into how to improve the model. The mix of social and health programs offered had to be fine-tuned, and the role of the police in following up and maintaining gains must be prioritized.

David Kennedy argues convincingly that the challenges that surfaced can be addressed: "The apparent failure of the social service outreach has led to the development of a broader portfolio of offerings that may be more relevant to the immediate needs of this very high-risk population."[47] Newer iterations of the intervention utilize efforts to: relocate former dealers so they can better avoid intimidation; help them to access identification documents; offers assistance managing issues associated with previous criminal justice contacts—such as outstanding warrants and fines. As highlighted throughout this book, there is no better way to get people to accept help than talking to the individuals involved about what they want and need and how they want to receive it.

Too often, rather than learning important lessons from the implementation of each intervention and pushing that knowledge into future interventions to create a continuous improvement loop, funders or local officials walk away when challenges arise. This is difficult work, but when research demonstrates that an intervention can both get drug dealers to voluntarily stop their illegal activities and help to rebuild trust between law enforcement and the community, it represents the foundation of a new, better way, to conduct drug enforcement operations. It also can get a virtual cycle going in these communities to improve public safety.

When people get to know the officers working in their neighborhood, as well as their chief down at headquarters, they are much more likely to share actionable leads about exactly who is committing crimes, when, and where. This improved partnership further enables innovative police chiefs and sheriffs, as well as the researchers and community activists they work with, to collaborate not just on addressing drug markets, but also, as highlighted in the next chapter, on facilitating access to health services for those with a substance use disorder.

As pointed out in a 2024 Manhattan Institute report on *Drug Policing in the 21st Century*, approaches such as drug market intervention crackdowns hold promise compared to traditional retail drug enforcement. "Reactive drug policing is easy; see a dealer, lock him up. Crackdowns require planning, surveillance, interagency coordination, and coordination with community stakeholders. In other words, they are easy to get wrong."[48] Fair point, but with some federal support and a strong police/community partnership, odds of success increase considerably and the potential benefits make it worth the effort.

Combating Covert Drug Markets that Use Social Media and the Internet

As drug markets evolve, interventions such as this drug market intervention model must be tested in the new environment. Drug markets in the fentanyl era have significantly changed. There is a much-reduced reliance on the classic open-air markets for which the program was originally designed. Instead, drug dealers often reach their customers via text or social media where a deal is set up and the buyer and seller agree on a place to meet for a quick single transaction. These covert markets, as it turns out, appear to have commonalities with more traditional markets. There has been one recent DMI effort to address a covert drug market in Rutland, Vermont.

Rutland, a city of about 16,000 residents, had become a regional drug hub and was contributing to overdoses and drug-related crime and disorder. When local police, with federal and state support, mapped the market, they found—like in other drug markets analyzed—a small group of key actors and connectors who brough in the opioids from Brooklyn, New York. The sales force was made up of user-dealers who knew local heroin buyers. Although there was not a fixed location for open drug dealers, out of town visitors could easily locate the popular drug houses and get hooked up with a drug seller.

The drug enforcement team moved forward with a DMI-type approach, arresting around twenty out of state drug distributors and holding a call-in with the user-dealers. In this example there was a greater reliance on court supervised drug treatment with some of the sellers offered an opportunity to plead to a reduced sentence, including enrollment in treatment programs and supervision conditions. The results were encouraging, with reductions in thefts, disorderly conduct, vandalism, and reports of an overall improvement of the city."[49]

One should never become overconfident that there is a single approach to disrupting and dismantling drug markets that can be applied everywhere, because there is wide variation in how markets operate, and the drug markets continue to change. Nonetheless, the principles of mapping a whole market to selectively focus for arrest on the key dealers, leveraging minor players out of the drug business with a mix of carrots and sticks, strengthening community/police relations, and a long-term maintenance effort to prevent the market from reconstituting is a logical approach. A much larger scale federally funded effort is needed to support police more systematically in these types of operations along with an ongoing research and technical assistance program to ensure continued refining of the intervention.

At the same time, an intensified focus is required on covert, internet, and social media assisted drug markets. As DEA concluded in their 2024 National Drug Threat Assessment:

> Social media platforms and encrypted apps extend the cartels' reach into every community in the United States and across nearly 50 countries worldwide. Drug traffickers and their associates use technology to advertise and sell their products, collect payment, recruit and train couriers, and deliver drugs to customers without having to meet face-to-face. This new age of digital drug dealing has pushed the peddling of drugs off the streets of America and into our pockets and purses.[50]

In the recommendations section, I will call on Congress to authorize and fund DEA to establish a new covert drug markets division that will squarely focus on the kinds of drug markets that are utilizing high-tech approaches to attempt to evade law enforcement.

Deeper Partnerships between Community Groups and Police

Any effort to establish and maintain safer neighborhoods with reduced drug sales, violence, and disorder will require strong, trusted relationships between police and community groups. Where that relationship has been damaged, for whatever reason, it must be repaired. The police need the community for accurate information on crimes such as drug selling and to testify in court. The community needs the police both to respond effectively to crime and to ensure that people have a sufficient sense of safety and security to lead their lives. The police have a tough job, but they should not try to go it alone. Community groups often want to help but lack rudimentary staffing and resources to sustain their organizations and expand their reach and impact. But if one looks at examples where community/police partnerships have worked well and imagine what would be possible with both a deeper partnership with police and more capacity among the community groups it is possible to see opportunities for real progress.

Community groups can do a lot more than show up at meetings or call-ins organized by law enforcement described above. They can act on their own, or in coordination with police—especially regarding youth who may be at risk of involvement in drug sales or violence—before these young people get arrested and face the cascading consequences of becoming justice-involved. Although this book is focused squarely on drug-related issues, other police-community partnerships also have great potential to build community capacity, reduce the reliance on arrests, and strengthen public safety more broadly.

In one example, community groups have supplemented police work as violence interrupters, serving as the first responders to 911 calls about local disturbances. In Brooklyn, New York the Brownsville Safety Alliance, which include a coalition of groups, police, and the local district attorney's office, is working together to "ensure that fewer people are arrested and entangled in the criminal justice system."[51] They are not a replacement for police, since plainclothes police officers deploy with them to assist as needed, but a group of citizens experienced in violence interruption have managed to defuse potentially dangerous situations without arrest. They have persuaded individuals to turn in weapons voluntarily, prevented shoplifting, and stopped domestic arguments from turning to violence.

Growing trust and collaboration between police and the community is going to be critical in promoting community safety and addressing difficult problems often linked to the drug trade. These efforts require a dedicated, significant funding stream to build national momentum. How to do this is described in the recommendations below. A *Washington Post* article in 2025 noted that there can be some tension between police and civilian intervenors because of their past criminal history, but former Los Angeles police chief Charlie Beck explained that the partnership can be quite useful. "A lot of the reason that communities mistrust police, particularly communities of color that live in violent environments, is that they tend to see us as an outside force, as somebody that is just there to remove people from their community and is not really interested in the solution. So when they see you working with these nontraditional partnerships …we increase community trust. Then you're able to reduce violence."[52]

Let me also highlight that many writers and advocates have highlighted the need to emphasize alternatives to police. Alex Vitale calls for "redirecting resources from policing, courts and jails" particularly to address youth crime and violence more effectively.[53] Alternatives are absolutely needed and are long overdue, but the reality is these new approaches must be done as a collaboration and partnership with law enforcement. Any effort to "defund" the police is both substantively and politically reckless. Rather than utilizing funding mechanisms that create divisions between police and community, government at every level must utilize funding streams to ensure that these critical partnerships flourish. It is not either or, but both, working together. The recommendations below take this approach.

Oregon Decriminalization: Some More Hard Lessons

The drug policy world was understandably fascinated by the experiment in the state of Oregon. This book emphasizes the importance of creating a wide variety of voluntary, low-threshold paths into care while altering law enforcement's role to one that is collaborative with the health system rather than focused primarily on arrest, prosecution, punishment, and incarceration. Would the decriminalization of hard drugs, such as fentanyl, heroin, methamphetamine, and cocaine, create a better, safer environment that would enable people who use drugs to find a healthier path forward in their lives?

I tried not to be too quick to judge, because even struggling initiatives can sometimes make adjustments and right themselves with experience and a commitment to evidence-based outcomes. Surely, a single state experimenting with such a significant policy change is far better than the entire country moving forward with something so consequential. If Purdue Pharma tested use and misuse patterns of OxyContin consumption in just a single county or state before unleashing their marketing army on the entire country, we would all be so much better off.

Oregon's experiment, launched via ballot measure 110, was approved by 58 percent of voters in 2020. The experiment was ended by the state legislature and the governor in March 2024. What can the country take away from Oregon's experience? Here is my assessment.

First, the hopes of supporters of the decriminalization law that the complete removal of the threat of arrest for drug possession would cause a surge in treatment entry were disappointed. Perhaps their results would have been better if the state had massively expanded low-threshold treatment, mobile care, and street outreach capacity before decriminalization took effect. They didn't. Regardless, existing treatment centers were not overwhelmed with requests for services. Unfortunately, the architects of the reform were unable to create an environment conducive to people seeking and receiving increased help. Fatal overdoses also increased sharply—43.8 percent in the twelve months between October 2022 and 2023—the highest rate in the nation.[54] Surely there were more factors than just the decriminalization policy contributing to this increase, including the continuing impact of the COVID-19 epidemic, homelessness, and the incredible lethality of the drug supply. Still, it's not a result decriminalization supporters would have anticipated.

Secondly, the implementation of the proposed civil sanction—a $100 ticket—which could be waived if someone called a counseling phone line and went through an assessment for substance use disorder, was a failure. According to a state audit, during the first fifteen months of the decriminalization hotline's operation, just 119 calls were received, at a program cost of $7,000 per call. Only twenty-seven individuals expressed interest in treatment.[55] I believe it would be fair to say that the Oregon decriminalization supporters sought to provide the most modest, least confrontational enforcement incentive to encourage people who use drugs to pursue options for some type of care. It wasn't sufficient.

Third, the justice/health cooperation, so clearly needed for the initiative to produce results, was not established. There was not a formal, organized, funded police-facilitated diversion program that would have created a pathway into treatment. One 2024 analysis found that the decriminalization law intended to establish a new role for the police to help implement the law, but it was never developed:

> The failure to turn police encounters into successful on-ramps to rehab has been cited by critics as prime evidence the measure isn't working.... The Legislature, the court system and the bureaucracy under two governors ignored or rejected proposed solutions as seemingly straightforward as designing a specialized ticket to highlight treatment information. They declined to fund a proposed $50,000 online course that would have instructed cops how to better use the new law. They took no action on recommendations to get police, whose leaders campaigned against the ballot measure, talking with treatment providers after decriminalization passed.[56]

These are important, useful lessons. In fact, the Oregon experiment reinforces the principle highlighted in this chapter, and even more so in the next one, that law enforcement and public health officials need to collaborate closely on solutions to address drug problems. As two drug policy veterans point out, Oregon, before decriminalization, already had relatively light criminal sanctions for drug users, while many states still rely far too heavily on drug enforcement sanctions. If these more hardline states "could be persuaded to dial down their criminal-justice approach to approximate what Oregon had before Measure 110, except with adequately funded, evidence-based prevention and treatment, substantial gains in public health and safety would likely follow."[57]

The path to effective drug policy does require significant reforms to drug enforcement efforts around the country, but it still very much needs the justice system as an informed and engaged partner in getting help to people who need it. Those with substance use disorder struggle with a difficult, often fatal condition. They need everyone to pull together to open new paths to a brighter, healthier future for them and those who love them.

Recommendations

14. **Combat illicit drug markets—without mass incarceration—by targeting the most dangerous dealers**

    Communities should not tolerate drug dealing, but that doesn't mean that all those involved in a drug market must be locked up, or that mass arrests are the best way to permanently eliminate drug markets. A more strategic approach is required. Minor players in drug markets such as user-dealers can be leveraged out of drug markets via combined community/law enforcement pressure and opportunities for addiction treatment, other services and support, and/or paid work. This type of drug enforcement requires the careful mapping of drug markets, with the support of skilled researchers and/or training of police officers, rather than just arresting easy targets of opportunity. Law enforcement agencies could hire expert civilian staff or researchers, either as in-house employees or contractors, to help them do this work. They also need resources to support community collaboration in this effort. *Congress should enact legislation to provide $500 million a year for DOJ to fund states specifically for Drug Market Intervention programs. States must utilize 25 percent of these funds to support community groups to partner with police to address drug problems. Ten million dollars should be provided for a non-governmental Center of Excellence to study and promote continuous improvement of the initiative.*

15. **Establish at DEA a *Covert Drug Markets Division* to disrupt social media and internet drug sales**

Covert drug markets, including those that sell illegal drugs to youth via social media, require specialized focus. Federal, state and local drug enforcement task task forces would benefit from technical assistance, expertise, and operational support in disrupting and dismantling these discrete covert markets. Investigating covert drug markets, identifying roles and responsibilities within organizations, and making undercover buys is more challenging than monitoring and responding to open-air drug markets, such as the crack cocaine markets described in chapter 2. DEA, through their field offices, task force officers, and expertise and analysis at headquarters should provide more assistance to states and localities in this area. *Congress should enact legislation to establish and fund the new division, increasing DEA's budget by $200 million for this purpose.*

16. **Sentence drug offenders based on behavior, not by the weight of drugs**

Major traffickers and violent offenders deserve a long criminal sentence, while low-level drug dealers and drug couriers should receive a sentence aligned with their criminal acts and role in the organization's power structure. If someone's actual crime is only drug possession, absent unusual circumstances that pose a serious threat to public safety, they should be diverted to community treatment. It is important to appreciate that many of those today charged with drug possession were arrested for distribution but pleaded down to a possession offense, and depending on their role in a drug dealing organization may deserve a more serious sentence than for actual possession. To avoid this confusion, an alternative lower-level drug distribution charge, with a reduced sentence compared to organizational leaders, must also be created. A new federal "drug-induced homicide" law, and model state law, is also needed to allow for the sentencing of drug-dependent offenders to extended court supervised treatment and five years of probation supervision to ensure there are real, but fair consequences when an overdose death occurs. *Congress should enact legislation to overhaul federal drug sentencing guidelines shifting the entire approach to a reliance on an offender's role in a drug organization and the threat they pose to public safety, rather than the volume of drugs they are caught with. DOJ should formulate a state model law to assist states in taking the same approach.*

17. **Enact limited expungement of convictions for those with a diagnosed substance use disorder upon their release to facilitate their successful reentry**

    A felony conviction, and many misdemeanor convictions, often result in not just a significant prison sentence but also a range of restrictions on the former inmates' lives once released. Those who complete their sentences should receive relief from the collateral consequences associated with their past convictions if they continue to work on their addiction recovery. New federal and state laws should guarantee that such paroled inmates have opportunities for work, housing, and public benefits, such as health care, while requiring them to disclose their criminal history if they seek to purchase a gun or work in law enforcement or private security. Their past criminal records should be accessible to justice officials upon a new arrest. Those convicted of murder or sexual violence should be excluded. *Congress and states should enact legislation providing expungement opportunities for felony and misdemeanor convicts who have been diagnosed with a substance use disorder. Legislation should require treatment behind bars, sustained connection to a treatment or recovery center, monitored by probation programs, and exclude those convicted of new crimes. The Department of Justice should develop a state model law and dedicate $10 million a year for a nongovernmental Center of Excellence on this subject.*

18. **Restrict reckless marijuana marketing, educate the public about the serious health risks of regular use *and* federally decriminalize marijuana possession**

    So many states have now voted to legalize high potency marijuana for recreational and medical use, that problematic use and addiction are increasing, especially among young adults. It's time for the FDA to be empowered to monitor the industry nationally to reinforce state efforts to manage the growing national market by setting and enforcing standards to protect the public. Health officials must also substantially increase their efforts to educate Americans, especially youth, about the real risks of regular marijuana consumption and the serious potential harms posed by very high potency products. At the same time, the country, by a large majority, does not support the arrest of marijuana consumers, thus making federal decriminalization of marijuana possession a reasonable step. *Congress should enact legislation which authorizes and funds FDA at $50 million a year to set and monitor implementation of federal standards for state marijuana programs, while decriminalizing marijuana possession on the federal level. Congress should also provide $50 million a year for the US Surgeon General to educate the public about the risks of marijuana consumption through a dedicated website, and use of social media platforms to reach youth and others with high rates of marijuana use.*

Chapter Summary

8

True Justice

Combating Drug-Related Crime and Illicit Drug Use Effectively Requires Much Closer Collaboration Between Justice and Health Agencies

Chapter Introduction: Catching Fire—Police Facilitated Treatment Entry

My skin was tingling. As John Rosenthal, chair and co-founder of the Police Assisted Addiction and Recovery Initiative (PAARI), described a new initiative where people seeking treatment for substance use—active drug consumers—were voluntarily walking into police precincts, asking for help and immediately receiving it, I couldn't help but feel a wave of excitement. Finally, people were able to access treatment on demand, no insurance coverage or payments required, no extensive application process, delays, waiting lists or other bureaucracy. All those with a serious drug problem had to do was walk straight into a police precinct.

The program was simple: the police got the word out that they had an initiative to help people with a substance use disorder receive care and interested individuals would walk into a participating precinct, work through a short screening process and an interview with a clinician (sometimes over the phone) to confirm their eligibility. Then, if they had no warrants out for their arrest for a significant crime, an officer would find a treatment slot, arrange for the individual to be accepted into a program, and then drive them right over. Someone seeking treatment could go from walking into a precinct to sitting in a police cruiser, in the front seat next to an officer, driving straight to treatment in an hour or so.

The program was launched in June 2015 when the Gloucester Police Department in Massachusetts established what they referred to as the Angel Program with the mission to create "a simple, stigma-free entry point to treatment on demand and reframed addiction as a disease, not a crime."[1] PAARI was set up as a nonprofit organization to assist law enforcement agencies to similarly create programs that would facilitate pre-arrest access to treatment services. Through technical assistance, training, and other resources—including recovery coaches funded by AmeriCorps—versions of the program now exist in about 800 police departments across forty-six states. PAARI helps police departments and sheriffs' offices gain access to fully funded drug treatment slots while also promoting distribution of naloxone. Officers can also facilitate treatment entry to those they encounter in their daily work or when citizens ask them for help accessing treatment for a family member or friend.

When I first heard about the initiative and visited several of the PAARI programs, it was clear that they were on to something important. Further, the fact that so many people with serious drug problems would voluntarily walk into a police precinct to get help, when active drug consumers generally work hard to avoid police interactions, tells us something important about gaps in our treatment system.

So, why does it make sense for those who consume illegal drugs to walk into a police station and ask them to refer you to treatment? Well, the short answer is the program makes it easy. They invite people in, offer to help, no shame or stigma, no waiting lists, no private health insurance required. The longer answer, about how this program could spread rapidly from a handful of pilots in Massachusetts to a nationwide program, shows that the treatment system still has not made its services as accessible as they need to be. It also tells us that the two options for police when they encounter drug consumers—either arrest or a warning—are insufficient. This third option, now referred to as "deflection" (to distinguish it from post-arrest diversion to court-ordered treatment) is what PAARI and other similar programs do to fill this gap. It is a welcome development both for officers looking for more options and for people or use drugs who want a far more navigable path into treatment.

The term was first introduced by Jac Charlier in a 2015 *Police Chief* article.[2] In deflection there is no arrest involved and the decision to work with police to access treatment is voluntary. Deflection has become a vital new entry point for treatment that, prior to the fentanyl overdose crisis, did not exist. The development of deflection provides an appealing alternative to over reliance on arrests in minority and impoverished communities. It is also a good fit under the philosophy of community policing, which emphasizes the need for local officers to get out of their cars and to get to know the people in the neighborhoods they are charged to serve and protect. Deflection—now a decade old—is a key innovation.

Deflection for nonviolent drug consumers has significant advantages over arrest. When someone is arrested, it has lasting consequences—socially, economically, and psychologically. The experience of being handcuffed, placed in a police car, booked in a police station, spending a night in jail, needing to engage with a lawyer and a judge, facing a potential criminal sentence, missing work without notice, and failing to meet family responsibilities is emotionally difficult and disruptive to one's life. It also can create or worsen shame and stigma. Though sometimes it is necessary to arrest drug consumers involved in significant criminal activity, if it can be avoided, it should be.

Deflection does not impose the collateral consequences of arrest and incarceration. It is a valuable new tool that should be available everywhere, while it is concurrently studied to assess and improve its effectiveness. Below, we will look more closely at how this deflection movement has grown since PAARI launched in 2015 and explore what other justice/health collaborations are currently available to increase voluntary access to treatment and what it would take to vastly expand the availability of such valuable services.

Hard Lesson: Police, courts, and jails can only reduce chronic drug use and overdoses through coordinated initiatives with health agencies

Drug enforcement is important, difficult, and dangerous work. When drug markets are permanently disrupted and dismantled, it improves neighborhood safety and reduces the opportunity for young people to initiate drug use. However, drug enforcement impacts chronic drug consumers differently. Locking up their drug dealer or disrupting their local drug supply throw drug users into a crisis. Although I had long believed that interruption in a steady drug supply would cause illicit drug consumers to re-think their behavior and seek treatment, the evidence suggests that although this sometimes happens, not nearly as often as one might think.[3] *Most drug users, fearing the painful effects of withdrawal, seek a different supplier and often end up consuming drugs at unpredictable potency with unknown additives. This sudden change is risky and can lead to a fatal overdose. However, it doesn't have to be this way.*

It's possible for police to help get many more drug users to enter treatment. They can give health authorities a heads up before a major drug enforcement operation so that they are ready to deploy outreach workers to offer immediate low-threshold treatment options. Further, there are an array of other ways in which police and public health authorities can collaborate more effectively. There are deflection opportunities to get people started in treatment without an arrest and new drug courts that are "front-loading" treatment services right after arrest. This flourishing of new initiatives reflects a great opportunity to help many more people.

Why People with Substance Use Disorders Can Still Pursue Recovery

A good deal of this book emphasizes the need to understand how difficult it is for chronic drug consumers to stop their use and to urge society to have empathy for their struggles and reduce stigma directed at them. However, addiction isn't like cancer; people can still make choices that will enable them to get better. Just because it's not easy, it doesn't mean it doesn't happen. Clearly many people take steps on their own to reduce or end their drug use, often through pressure from their worried spouse, parents, or children, or when they risk losing their jobs or fear a potential arrest. It's true, as Dr. Sally Satel writes:

> People who are addicted can respond to carrots and sticks, incentives and sanctions. They have the capacity to make different decisions when the stakes change. There is a great deal of evidence to substantiate faith in the agency of addicts. Acknowledging it is not tantamount to blaming the victim; it is, much more positively, a recognition of their potential.[4]

Getting this balance right is tricky. It's important to appreciate that addiction is often an extremely difficult condition to deal with and that there is a long, ugly history of mistreating those who struggle to overcome it. I have emphasized the importance of reducing stigma because it deters people from coming forward voluntarily for treatment. However, it's appropriate, as highlighted by Hanna Pickard, to recognize and "mobilize a sense of agency and empowerment in addicts, avoiding blame not through conceiving them as helpless victims of disease, but through acknowledging and working with their agency without adopting moralizing or stigmatizing attitudes and practices."[5] Well run justice interventions can give those with a drug problem the opportunity to choose a pathway that can improve their health and avoid negative consequences. Many are making that choice today.

How to "Deflect" More People Away from Arrest and Into Treatment

There are those who argue police should not play such a large role in determining who gets access to drug treatment services, but rather that public health organizations and community groups should have these resources. This is an important point. But rather seeing this as a zero-sum game where limited resources should be designated primarily to one group or the other, we should be looking to increase the points of access to treatment more broadly while also assessing the effectiveness of each of these paths.

Just as increasingly individual police officers are empowered to offer people in need a simple pathway into drug treatment, others who encounter and get to know troubled drug consumers should have that capacity. This should include school nurses and counselors, sports coaches, faith leaders, and local community groups. Already, police are not the only ones who do deflection-type work. There are also efforts by emergency medical services (EMS) and fire departments to utilize deflection. For communities where distrust of the police is high this approach offers an alternative deflection workforce. Further, there are deflection efforts that do not involve any first responders, but rather outreach workers or counselors "working the streets" to communicate to people who use drugs about treatment opportunities.

But let's not slow down the expansion of police departments and sheriff offices in facilitating treatment entry; they are on to something good. Their efforts are evolving and spreading, giving people access points to care that previously never existed. Also, deflection, because it is not a response to an arrest or overdose, often brings health services to individuals *before* they face an acute crisis. At the same time, deflection, since it avoids arrests, can reduce the burden on police and enable them to serve the community in a new and important way.

Deflection programs demonstrate a significant advance in how police interact with people who use drugs. There is something important happening with those police officers who are seeing the country's overdose catastrophe up close and personal and finding ways to make a difference without an arrest. The officers are the ones often called to the scene of an overdose, interacting with terrified families, and engaging with homeless individuals impacted by substance use and mental health issues. These experiences have motivated many police officers and their leaders to become influential advocates for additional treatment resources.

Remember, it wasn't too long ago when the idea of police officers carrying naloxone was controversial, now its commonplace. Many officers, whose quick actions save lives, walk away from that experience with a new perspective on addiction. Consider this conclusion from a recent study of deflection:

> The role of overdoses and overdose deaths in the origin and development of deflection initiatives—particularly the large share of programs founded and led by law enforcement entities—illustrates the impact of the opioid

> crisis on how many police and first responder agencies have come to view their roles. This marks a shift from an enforcement/arrest approach to one that emphasizes, in many cases, treatment and recovery.[6]

New deflection programs have been increasingly launched by police chiefs and sheriffs in response to the devastation wreaked by opioids, some modeled on the PAARI approach and others that utilize different pathways for police-facilitated treatment entry. Since individual officers, even when working with social workers, recovery coaches, and clinicians, do have an important role in identifying people to participate in these treatment entry pathways, it is critical that the officers are educated about addiction and how the treatment and recovery process works. Many are learning on the job, working closely with public health colleagues, and receiving additional training.

However, the fact that deflection programs are thriving does not mean every police officer is supportive of the approach. Police chiefs and sheriffs do not randomly assign officers to initiate a deflection program; rather, they seek out volunteers who are frustrated with the status quo and want to be part of an alternative approach. In this way a cadre of reform-oriented, pro-treatment officers develops within departments. This group of officers, working directly to help people who use drugs access treatment, can foster a broader transformation of how the wider police force perceives consumers of illegal drugs. These champions of reform build legitimacy within departments to move away from over-reliance on arrest and incarceration and towards supporting health interventions.

Those with a public health background might fairly wonder if a police officer is sufficiently qualified to make these difficult decisions on who gets treatment and who doesn't. Fortunately, as deflection matures, law enforcement's approach has become more comprehensive. Police are increasingly relying on "research-validated, evidence-based risk-need screening tools to make a referral to behavioral health treatment so individuals who pose a risk to community are placed in custody and those who do not are deflected away from the involvement in the justice system and into treatment."[7] These assessment tools have been adapted from other components of the justice system and require further testing and refinement when utilized for deflection. In addition, police departments can develop a standard written protocol to promote fair and consistent utilization of deflection and reduce the potential for bias.

Research has found that some officers, like the rest of the public, can hold stigmatizing views toward those with a substance use disorder[8] and that deflection programs may not sufficiently support treatment programs incorporating medications, utilize options to engage with harm reduction, or excessively limit participation in deflection.[9] Like any intervention, deflection should be scrutinized so that the programs can improve and evolve. Rapid research programs should identify weaknesses and propose ways to integrate findings into a continuous improvement cycle as deflection programs expand. Updated training on addiction is likely appropriate for officers making these important decisions.

Another important question is where the treatment capacity utilized by deflection programs comes from and who is paying for it. In my visits to these programs, it appeared as if police leaders, by calling around to treatment centers and asking for help, were often receiving donated treatment slots. This says a lot about the authority of police chiefs and sheriffs in communities, and it's a credit to those who have donated the slots for the benefit of the people police have identified. Nonetheless, for these deflection programs to continue to expand, the total availability of treatment slots must grow.

Especially for inpatient treatment programs, there is often limited capacity. More funding to pay for treatment required by deflection programs should increase total capacity, rather than just shift it among different programs. This is easier in Medicaid expansion states that provide addiction coverage, which tend to have more deflection sites,[10] but not everyone is eligible for this care. Deflection originated in the northeast, which was hit first by fentanyl, but now overdoses from synthetic opioids, including when combined with methamphetamine and cocaine, are occurring nationwide. Many areas of the country, including southern states and rural areas, would greatly benefit from more funding for deflection and associated evidence-based substance use disorder treatment.

Further, it is not just law enforcement agencies that can benefit from education and training. Public health agencies may not have a history of working directly with police officers, but for deflection to continue to thrive, they need to. I believe that these barriers between public health agencies and police are eroding, as evidenced by the growing array of health/justice collaborations, but to ensure that health officials are open to collaborating with police efforts should be made to increase exchanges, dialogue, and information dissemination to health officials about police collaborations. It also will require a broader array of treatment centers to be able to receive admissions twenty-four hours a day and to respond to requests for assistance on short-term notice. All of those in the addiction/drug policy workforce must be willing to evolve their beliefs and work habits based on the daunting crisis the country is facing.

These deflection programs were built as an emergency response to the rapid increase in fentanyl-related overdose deaths and the research base to assess the program is still emerging. Importantly, best practices and lessons learned from the field are now being more systematically shared through the Police, Treatment, and Community Collaborative (PTACC), which serves as the voice of the deflection movement. As in other fields, a dedicated nonprofit organization can be an important guide in policy, practice and in advocating for research to refine the intervention. PTACC has promulgated several helpful documents for police departments considering setting up a deflection program, or for anyone interested in learning how they work. They note that: "the variety of operational characteristics creates nearly unlimited possibilities for the final program design, some common themes can be observed in deflection programs currently operating."[11] They have usefully distinguished between different deflection pathways to treatment as follows.

1. **Naloxone Plus:** Engagement with treatment occurs following an overdose response, and crisis-level treatment is readily available.
2. **Active Outreach:** Participants are identified by law enforcement but are engaged primarily by a treatment expert who actively contacts them and motivates them to engage in treatment.
3. **Citizen Self-Referral:** Drug-involved individuals are encouraged to initiate engagement with law enforcement without fear of arrest, and an immediate treatment referral is made.
4. **Officer Prevention Referral:** Law enforcement initiates the treatment engagement, but no charges are filed.
5. **Officer Intervention Referral:** Law enforcement initiates the treatment engagement, and charges are held in abeyance or citations issued.
6. **Community Response:** A form of deflection that does not rely on first responders but rather utilizes peers and people in recovery to engage directly with drug users to provide a referral to treatment or other health services.[12]

What we are seeing across the country is a rapidly growing and evolving intervention, which, like when PAARI emerged a decade ago, represents a ground level, innovative, and promising response to a crisis. Now, with the strong support of not just PTACC, but the also the National Sheriff's Association and the International Association of Chiefs of Police, it's time to supercharge deflection so this option can be available to everyone who could benefit from it, at the same time as the programs are assessed and refined, and an effort is made to involve a wider array of community actors in creating new facilitated pathways into treatment. Further, the immediacy of the provision of medications for those dependent on opioids must be accelerated. EMS are already piloting the initiation of buprenorphine after an overdose response.[13] Police, through connecting to clinicians called to the scene or via telemedicine connection with a prescriber, should similarly develop a direct, immediate access to medication approach. There is no time to waste.

Front Loading Life-Saving Treatment at Drug Courts

When you sit in a drug court on a morning when new potential program participants first meet the judge, there is a lot to take in. First off, it's a formal courtroom setting, with the judge presiding, the prosecutor and defense attorney at their respective tables, and the drug court staff on the side, with any guests or visitors. It's a secure environment, with armed guards. But what was so striking to me that day when I was visiting the court in Buffalo was the arrestees, walking tentatively into the courtroom, and standing to speak to the judge. Those appearing at the court that day were experiencing one of the worst days of their lives. They had been locked up and spent the night in jail, and they weren't sure what was going to happen to them. Perhaps they were planning to be somewhere, either at work or taking a kid to school. Their whole life had been disrupted. Worst of all, they were likely in, or about to be in, severe withdrawal from whatever drug or combination of drugs they were dependent on. Would they be sent to jail, for how long, where, what would their family think? It was clear from their body language; they were not feeling good.

Drug courts are not new. In fact, they are the original alternative to incarceration. Treatment courts were developed as a response to the surge of arrests during the crack cocaine epidemic in the 1980s and growing concern over excessive criminalization and racial bias. In 1989, the chief judge of Florida's 11th judicial circuit set the first drug court in motion.[14] The concept was to bring drug treatment into the justice system as an alternative to a jail sentence. Based on the effort and progress of program participants in treatment and other program requirements, the judge, along with the prosecutor, could agree that all obligations for justice had been accomplished and avoid sentencing the participants to jail. One of the key original supporters of drug treatment drug courts in Florida, Janet Reno, then the State's Attorney for Dade County, Florida, later became President Bill Clinton's Attorney General and an advocate for reduced drug sentencing in the 1990s.

Drug courts have long been the most well-known and politically supported alternatives to incarceration. Comprehensive research assessments have also been quite positive, with studies showing that drug treatment courts reduce drug use and crime and improve the well-being of participants.[15] But support has not been universal. In 2014 the Drug Policy Alliance, in their report, *Moving Away from Drug Courts: Toward a Health-Centered Approach to Drug Use,* charged that drug courts " . . . do not reduce imprisonment, do not save money or improve public safety, and fail to help those struggling with drug problems."[16] Others have questioned drug treatment court's use of jail as a sanction for a positive drug test, whether some offenders are sentenced to drug courts who do not need substance use disorder treatment, and if evidence-based medications for opioid use disorder, such as buprenorphine and methadone, was being offered to all program participants who could benefit from them.[17]

By no means am I suggesting that this criticism be ignored—rather it should be utilized to improve those courts that are falling short. Every program, especially in a rapidly evolving drug supply environment and with new research on effectiveness constantly coming out, should be looking to improve. However, as Maia Szalavitz points out, some criticism of drug courts is misplaced, especially regarding who is enrolled in drug court programs. She notes that: "There's a common assumption that drug courts focus on possession cases. . . . But these courts overwhelmingly deal with more serious addiction-driven offenses, like drug dealing and property crime—and research finds that they are more likely to be effective for these higher-risk cases."[18] Nonetheless, review of drug treatment courts are appropriate. With about 4,000 such courts in existence it shouldn't be a surprise that there are individual drug treatment courts under-performing, or system-wide areas where improvements can be made.

In an effort to improve the effectiveness of drug treatment groups, the movement's national association, All Rise, has sought to foster best practices through the publication of its research-based new *Standards* document released in 2025.[19] As Doug Marlowe, who helped develop the guidance, points out, "criminal justice professionals must check their gut instincts at the door and pay studious attention to these science-based principles if they wish to achieve rehabilitation goals." Services provided have to be evidenced-based, individualized based on clients risks and needs, implemented in appropriate phases, and supervised by a trained clinical case manager. All Rise, through a variety of training programs and reports, has sought to encourage all drug treatment courts to ensure that treatment decisions are made by clinicians, not judges; incorporate the use of medications for opioid use disorders; reduce the use of jail sanctions, especially with regard to relapses in the initial phases of the program; provide sober housing; integrate peer counselors into their staffing; and provide sufficient time in treatment, generally 12-18 months. Most revolutionary, a growing number of courts, starting with the one in Buffalo, began to formulate a new type of program built on drug court principles, which frontloaded treatment services for new program participants. When I was appointed Acting Drug Czar I was eager to travel to Buffalo to see firsthand how the country's first *Opioid Intervention Court* was working.

Judge Craig Hannah, a New York State Supreme Court Justice and former Chief Judge of the Buffalo City Court, found that the standard practice of delaying formal sentencing and the initiation of drug treatment for a month or two after new participants were admitted to the program had a serious flaw. Due to the growing presence of fentanyl in the local drug supply, clients were not making it back to start the program. People were overdosing and dying before they even were formally enrolled in his drug court. Judge Hannah decided to change the program. Treatment would start immediately, and sentencing was delayed 90–180 days, to make sure the participants were getting the help they needed first. Charging decisions were held in abeyance until after the initial treatment period was completed.

Judge Hannah's *Opioid Intervention Court* launched in 2017 with the mission of saving lives. Clients who agreed to participate in the program would immediately gain access to medications for opioid use disorder, cognitive behavioral therapy, peer support, intensive case management, and meet regularly with the judge. Although the program has similarities with traditional drug courts, it differs in conducting a clinical screening of the client on the day of the arrest and in requiring an immediate assessment for initiation of buprenorphine, methadone, or naltrexone by a physician. The first evaluation of this new iteration of drug treatment courts was quite encouraging. Participants were "one-third as likely to die in the first six months of the program, and half as likely to die within one-year."[20]

The program participants were not promised any leniency in sentencing, just a delay in the formal adjudication process of their case. They would start treatment immediately and would return to receive the sentence for the crime they were arrested for. Future research will have to gauge whether the sentences vary for those who go through these "pre-plea drug treatment courts" compared to more traditional treatment court participants. However, I think it is likely that a program participant, who, rather than receiving their sentence on that first difficult morning after arrest, presents themselves several months later after benefiting from treatment, would have a better experience at sentencing. They would be able to speak about their progress, share their reflections, and articulate plans for their future. This strikes me as likely to not only result in a more appropriate sentence, but also as a much fairer process. It's hard for anyone to navigate these important moments in their life while suffering through painful withdrawal from powerful narcotics.

This new approach by drug courts is spreading.[21] It is a welcome step forward, and something that could be accelerated through more direct federal assistance. No court supervised program, or treatment program for that matter, can help a client who experiences a fatal drug overdose. Drug interventions across the board, not just drug courts, must adapt to this harsh new reality and front-load assistance and support to those who require it.

How Police and Health Agencies Can Work Together to Reduce Overdoses After Drug Enforcement Operations

Drug enforcement is important work. As highlighted in the previous chapter, there are ways to better focus such efforts to minimize mass incarceration and more tightly target arrests on those that pose the most severe threat to the community. But in addition to a more disciplined approach to arrests, to limit both the huge financial costs of incarceration and the damage done to individuals, families, and communities from excessive incarceration, it is also important to mitigate the short-term impact of drug enforcement on people who use drugs.

Many of those working in of drug policy, including me, have long believed that enforcement and supply reduction would not only bring justice to violent drug traffickers and major dealers, but also would have a positive impact on promoting treatment entry. As referenced above, the way I used to look at it was that when drug distribution networks were disrupted and destabilized it would create an action-forcing mechanism for regular retail drug buyers who lost reliable access to their drug supply. Even if drug markets reconstitute relatively quickly, as they often do, a several-day interruption could compel a drug consumer, facing withdrawal, to proactively seek treatment entry. However, based on available research, that appears not to be the case. It is a question that needs further study, but until a stronger case can be made that drug enforcement operations trigger more than a rather modest increase in treatment demand among active drug consumers, it would be wrong to assume that it does.

Further, emerging research on today's drug markets offers some disturbing evidence that major drug interdiction operations appear to increase fatal drug overdoses.[22] It seems, in yet another example of the real world not operating the way one hopes it would, anxious drug consumers facing withdrawal from fentanyl and other powerful drugs tend to seek out a new dealer offering a different product or product mix. The sudden change in the potency of the drug or drugs consumed increases the risk of overdose. Thus, it appears to be the case that successful drug enforcement operations, although likely protective of those who do not purchase drugs regularly and potential future drug consumers, put current chronic drug consumers at greater risk. Something must change. Fortunately, there is an approach that can save lives *and* protect public safety.

In a 2013 research study entitled "Does robust drug enforcement lead to an increase in drug users coming forward for treatment?" Neil McKeganey and Joe McGallagly explored how drug enforcement operations in the United Kingdom impacted treatment seeking behavior. They concluded that there was some increase in entry into methadone programs after police operations but highlighted the potential for a much larger impact: "The fact that drug enforcement can clearly act as a stimulus to drug treatment suggests the value of including drug treatment services within the planning of major drug enforcement operations in order to ensure that treatment services are able to respond appropriately to any increase in demand following the police operations."[23] Well, that's a hell of an idea.

The hard and often risky work of drug enforcement does create a window for action. It generates a crisis in the life of a person dependent on illegal drugs where a change in their daily routine is forced upon them. What if on the same day as a drug enforcement operation public health experts, harm reduction organizations, and first responders deployed to the geographic areas of a city or town most directly impacted by a drug enforcement operation? Outreach workers, operating in mobile vans, could interact directly with people seeking to buy drugs and offer them immediate assistance. Just providing them with naloxone at this time could potentially save their lives, but even better would be offering immediate access to buprenorphine, which would enable opioid consumers to avoid withdrawal and provide a real window to transition them into a treatment program.

Today we are too often wasting this valuable window, earned through the hard work of police, and failing to accrue a critical societal benefit made possible by drug enforcement operations. How many more people would eventually access some level of treatment and avoid overdoses if police and health agencies were committed to surging treatment outreach capacity right after a drug enforcement operation? We don't know, but we should work in earnest to find out through pilot programs. It's a reasonable assumption that this type of effort will produce a net increase in treatment entry, as well as a net decline in drug overdoses.

How would this work? The first step is simple: police and public health authorities must get to know each other. Depending on the community, this may already be happening, but if it hasn't occurred yet it needs to. Although precisely who the public health contact in any specific area can vary, the right place to start is for a police leader to get in touch with the city, town or county local health agency and get together. They should establish a mechanism for police to provide a heads up when and approximately where a drug enforcement operation is going to happen. The public health officials do not need any sensitive details of the operation, nor do they necessarily require a lot of time to prepare once they have an established relationship with the police department or sheriff's office.

This idea is ripe for further action. As I continued to update my Georgetown University graduate class on drug policy to incorporate the worsening opioid epidemic several years ago, I started displaying to the students the visceral images of pill mills getting shut down by drug enforcement and the doctors in their white medical coats handcuffed and arrested. No doubt many of these doctors deserved to be punished and to lose their medical licenses—a warranted sanction for these corrupt cash drug businesses. But what happened to the patients? As explored in the context of prescription drug monitoring programs in chapter four, it wasn't good.

The reality is that in most cases, these drug consumers either had a substance use disorder or were pain patients who had lost their other sources of supply for opioid painkillers. Regardless, what these patients needed were careful, serious referrals to either addiction treatment or legitimate pain care. Instead, they were abandoned and left to fend for themselves. When they showed up at their clinic, they would see the police tape and a notice nailed to the door that the clinic had been closed with a phone number on how they could get their medical records. Most of the customers of these pill mills were not offered any help and many turned to the illicit drug market where they faced an increasingly lethal drug supply. Surely some overdosed and died.

Back in 2018, an initiative was launched in six states to try to connect pain patients to care when their doctor was arrested and later expanded with the support of the CDC into the federal *Opioid Rapid Response Program*[24] over time. A very worthy effort run by dedicated, hardworking professionals tightly focused on disruption in medical services to those who had been receiving pain medications. However, today the most urgent need is to assist people when illicit drug markets are disrupted. Such critical, lifesaving work should be funded on a national level so that drug users who discover that their dealer has been arrested can immediately, before they are faced with painful withdrawal, gain access to low-threshold treatment. This doesn't happen today, but with a modest amount of coordination and pre-planning by police and health agencies, it could, and it should.

Drug Enforcement Agencies Rely on Task Forces—Why Not Create New Ones to Coordinate Treatment and Recovery Efforts?

As highlighted in the introduction, the existing government infrastructure to combat the continuing acute opioid epidemic is insufficient. Most of the new funding initiatives proposed in this book are designed to address those gaps and build up capacity and funding streams that will strengthen the overall effort nationwide. However, not every community or region is impacted the same. Some are experiencing such a disturbing loss of life and high rate of addiction that they need a coordinated task force to get them the help they require now.

This is what federally funded law enforcement task forces do when a region is at acute risk from a crime threat, whether related to drugs or something else. However, no comparable task forces exist that focus squarely on strengthening drug-treatment capacity by bringing together leadership, expertise and resources from the federal government, states, and localities—but there should be. Just as jurisdictional lines can make drug enforcement inefficient and create coordination and information sharing barriers, the need for treatment and related health services overlaps among counties, health agencies, treatment centers and providers, hospitals, and NGOs that offer health services directly to drug users.

As outlined below in the recommendation, a program to establish *Treatment Coordination Task Forces* is proposed to bring together government organizations and health service providers in fifty of the areas of the country's hardest hit by the opioid epidemic. The way it would work is a group of neighboring counties and cities would band together to submit a grant proposal to ONDCP, with support from the state Governor's office and Members of Congress from the area. They would be required to provide a regional needs assessment, a proposed board of directors and a plan to set up the program if they win the grant.

ONDCP can apply lessons learned from its long experience running the HIDTA drug enforcement task force grant program to quickly build out the new program. I know how valuable it is for the Drug Czar to receive timely insights from the talented HIDTA Directors embedded in thirty-three regions around the country. Advice from a new set of *Treatment Coordination Task Force* Directors will similarly provide expert insight on local conditions.

Although this task force is primarily to provide regional leadership and coordination, some funds would be available to supplement the region's priority needs and could support: inpatient treatment; outpatient programs; mobile treatment—including the purchasing and outfitting of mobile medical units—medications such as buprenorphine, methadone, and naltrexone; sober and transitional housing; syringe service programs; hospital-based treatment programs; diversion and deflection initiatives; probation, parole, and in-jail and prison services, etc. The only limitations would be state laws—meaning, for example, if a state or region does not allow a syringe service program, the new task force would be obligated not to establish one, but could urge the state to reconsider if that's what the board believed.

There is an additional advantage to making this type of investment in fifty of the country's most severely impacted by addiction: it would allow for the consistent collection of data, the sharing and exchanging of information and experiences among hard hit regions and serve as an ideal test bed to pilot and study new initiatives. This on-the-ground experience and the pipeline of information back to the national government will educate and inform policymakers in Washington about what is happening, what is working, what is not, and where additional resources should be focused. This knowledge can help Washington avoid mistakes and focus on what else must be done to increase the effectiveness of drug treatment programs, not just in these fifty task force regions, but everywhere.

The country has had a great deal of experience and some important successes with law enforcement task forces. Congress has invested many billions of dollars in supplementing state and local law enforcement funding with such programs. Public health agencies can benefit from their experience and adapt their models of leadership and coordination to the acute drug treatment challenges regions face today. Congress, just as it has funded a significant expansion of federal law enforcement task forces over the years, should see the wisdom of financing a similar approach on the public health side.

Recommendations

19. **Bring police, health agencies, and NGOs together to "deflect" minor drug offenders to treatment without an arrest**

    It is time to bring deflection programs everywhere across the country while facilitating much closer collaboration between local police and local health service providers. Already DOJ is providing grants to support deflection. These efforts should be vastly expanded through a dedicated DOJ program to provide financial support to every state law enforcement agency, who will distribute funds to local police forces in the areas of highest need. Half of the local funds would be subcontracted to public health agencies and NGOs to provide deflection-related health support services, including treatment, emergency response, medications for opioid use disorder, housing, employment, and transportation assistance, and to hire staff, such as recovery coaches and social workers. A portion of these funds must be used to finance treatment vouchers for use by college and high school health officials, coaches, faith leaders and appropriate community groups. This funding can also be used to support treatment capacity surges to facilitate access to care for those impacted by drug enforcement operations that would result in a sudden disruption of the drug supply. Decision-making for the public health/community half of the funds should be made by a co-chaired local board with equal representation of police and health officials to ensure effective coordination. The police departments can utilize their half of the funds to train police officers in deflection and on the disease of addiction, to hire officers and civilians specifically to support these efforts, and to pay for deflection specific overtime. *A total budget of $1 billion is proposed per year for these deflection initiatives. Fifteen million should be used to provide an annual grant to establish a deflection Center of Excellence outside of government.*

20. **Create 500 *Treatment First Drug Courts* Throughout the Country**

 The drug supply is too dangerous for arrestees with an active substance use disorder to wait for court-ordered treatment to begin. More drug courts should hold arrestees' sentencing in abeyance while they immediately initiate drug treatment for at least ninety days. These types of courts are gradually expanding, but not quickly enough. DOJ should administer this program, distributing the funds to the state judicial systems to either create new pre-plea, treatment first courts, or to convert existing courts into health centered treatment first courts. *A budget of $250 million is proposed to directly finance the development of treatment first drug courts. Five million should be used by DOJ to provide an annual grant to establish a Center of Excellence outside of government to provide technical assistance and training to the new courts and to evaluate their effectiveness.*

21. **Establish *Treatment Coordination Task Forces* in the fifty areas of greatest need**

 The fifty regions of the country with the most severe drug overdose and addiction rates require federal support to facilitate increased collaboration between health care providers, NGOs, police, and other agencies. Each program, adapting ONDCP's HIDTA task force model to the demand reduction side, will be led by a director with a public health background and a deputy director with a justice background who will work under the supervision of a board of directors that includes regional federal officials, state authorities, local county and city authorities and treatment and recovery service providers. Neighboring counties would join together to apply for a grant. Like law enforcement task forces, these new treatment task forces will ensure the integration of federal, state, and local officials into a coordinated team, with the ability to pool resources and share information, cut through bureaucratic obstacles, improve collaboration, and empower key regions with the supplemental resources and focused leadership they need to serve their residents. Each region would develop a strategy, brief political leaders on their activities, and keep NGOs, and the public informed on what is happening in their area regarding expanding treatment access. *ONDCP should be directed by Congress to establish a program support office to manage the grant, ensure data collection and facilitate the use of shared software platforms to foster collaboration between different regional Treatment Coordination Task Forces. Congress should appropriate $250 million for this effort, with $2 million designated for ONDCP's administration of the initiative.*

Chapter Summary

9

Defense in Depth

Smart Border Security and International Supply Control for Today's Synthetic Drug Era

Chapter Introduction: In Deep

I took another slippery step. I must have been more than halfway down but couldn't yet see the bottom. All I kept asking myself was, "how deep is this damn hole?" A nasty odor wafted up as I kept moving gingerly down the rough-hewn ladder. There was no chance of me falling since I was hooked to a harness and had United States Border Patrol officers above and below looking after the safety of America's Acting Drug Czar. Still, slipping off the ladder, dangling in the air with my legs and arms flailing and looking like an idiot was definitely a possibility. There was no turning back now. I kept going down, determined to step foot in a drug cartel tunnel.

We were literally on, or under, the Southwest Border with Mexico, in Otay Mesa, San Diego. On the surface, just a few yards separated Mexico and the United States. The 70-foot hole I was trying to get to the bottom of was engineered by drug traffickers to connect San Diego, California and Tijuana, Mexico. This tunnel had ventilation, lighting, and a rail system.

This was not dug by a few guys with shovels. They had used trained engineers, excavating equipment, and a team of skilled workmen.[1] They also had enough friends on the Mexican side to build the tunnel and to move and dispose of tons of dirt without anyone snooping around.

When I finally got to the bottom of the hole and stepped on to the wood planks placed to protect visitors from the muddy, puddle-soaked ground, I saw a portion of the actual tunnel. It was about six feet high and four feet wide. As the Border Patrol agent was briefing how the traffickers built the tunnel I stole a glance down at my now muddy black dress shoes—they were going to need some work when I made it back up to the surface. As the Border Patrol agents showed me around the cramped space, I tried not to think about whatever was rotting in the soupy goop beneath my feet.

This tunnel was one of hundreds dug by drug traffickers and discovered by US law enforcement. There is a very dedicated and talented team of Border Patrol experts, known as the Tunnel Rats, who search for tunnels and shut them down. The technology to detect them is still imperfect—usually, tunnels are located through old-fashioned police work or on a tip from an informant.

Since 1990, US authorities have found over 220[2] tunnels under the Southwest Border. Many of these are rudimentary, but around fifteen sophisticated tunnels like the one I saw have been discovered. Just a handful of tunnels, operating at night, can deliver a large volume of illegal drugs directly into the United States. Public officials want to know when the United States Government is going to be able to shut down all these tunnels. But as is the case for all our efforts to block drug traffickers from trafficking illicit drugs into our country, the answer isn't great. In the case of drug tunnels, we only know about the ones we have found; we don't know what we don't know.

Our hard-working United States Border Patrol agents and other agency partners are out there looking for tunnels every day, day after day, often in extremely hot and unpleasant conditions. They have a tough job that they take very seriously. Yet it's impossible to believe we have discovered and sealed all the tunnels under the Southwest Border. In drug control, nobody catches everything.

These tunnels pose a serious threat to US national security because, even though they were designed to move narcotics, once built they can also transport weapons of mass destruction, terrorists, and criminal operatives into the United States. The Tunnel Rats are not going out of business any time soon. I climbed out of the hole and headed to the rest of my Southwest Border tour, worrying about how many drug tunnels were operating that very moment somewhere else along the border.

Hard Lesson: Supply control is wickedly difficult—a disciplined focus is needed on the most dangerous drug threats

International drug supply control is the original anti-drug program envisioned by international diplomats and policymakers as the primary way to address the drug problem. We have been at it for a century and today face a larger and more dangerous drug supply than ever before. What should we do about that painful reality? It's a simple question, but unfortunately the answer has gotten caught in the crossfire between two camps on drug policy. One side wants to legalize drug production or just stop investing significant resources in trying to accomplish what they describe as a mission impossible. The other side argues that the key to addressing America's drug problem is to focus on the international production and trafficking of the drugs that are killing so many of our citizens and to "seal the border."

The debate over the supply-side, among partisans on both sides, has clouded the challenging realities of restricting the supply. Having written so many drug policy speeches and given more than a few over my long career, I understand the appeal of a simple message. The supply control rhetoric is easy to write and pleasing to deliver. However, to make a credible case to continue significant investments in a supply-side strategy, one must grapple with the reality of decades of over-promising what can be accomplished. In this chapter I intend to candidly dive into this difficult challenge and lay out a path forward firmly grounded in experience and current threats. It will involve the border but will require the country to go much deeper—to work throughout the global drug supply chain to precisely target the operations of the most dangerous traffickers to better protect Americans from the lethal drug supply.

The Border Battle—It's One Thing After Another

Customs and Border Protection (CBP) agents are very skilled at their jobs, and they seize a lot of drugs on the border, especially considering they only have about forty-five seconds per vehicle to decide if they are going to send the car or truck to secondary inspection or let it enter the United States. They can't allow that long line of cars to back up too far. Most of the people moving across the border have legitimate business to conduct in the United States. Some are hauling edible cargo with an expiration date, or manufacturing parts that are a critical part of the US industrial supply chain. We wouldn't want the Mexican avocados to rot in the sun. Agents, of course, are looking for more than drugs. They are worried about illegal immigrants, wanted criminals, weapons of all kinds, unapproved animals and plants, counterfeit products, etc.

There are countless businesses depending on a reliable flow across the border. The United States imports well over a billion dollars a day worth of licit goods from Mexico.[3] Every truck of fresh fruit or auto parts has one or more company counting on timely delivery. When they don't get their products on time business owners complain, not just to Customs and Border Protection, but to their local member of Congress. Once, when I was providing a briefing on a new government Southwest Border counternarcotics strategy on Capitol Hill that I put together at ONDCP with the National Security Council and the Department of Homeland Security, I received a hostile question from a Texas Congressman representing a border district. He asked about the new strategy, "will this slow things down?" It took me a few seconds to grasp what he was getting at. But I got his point. He didn't want to get angry phone calls from businesses about some new drug interdiction plan that was messing with the legitimate flow of goods to companies in his district. I told him not to worry, but also, I got the message—licit border trade had to keep moving.

It is clear to all who worked on border issues that the only way to increase border drug seizures was to find ways to rapidly sort through the enormous flow of vehicles and pedestrians by identifying those who were higher-risk travelers ahead of time. Speed is critical. Although electronic screening of vehicles is improving, and cameras now capture license plates and other useful data to provide information to border agents, the pace is relentless. US agents must carefully select which vehicles to send to secondary and literally take apart based on the latest analysis of trafficker tactics, as well as their own instincts. Absent a specific tip, a hit on the plate or a passport from the electronic databases used by CBP, an extremely nervous driver, or a sloppy job on a hidden compartment, most vehicles are allowed into our country.

Detecting a kilo or two of narcotics carefully hidden in a car is not easy. There is a whole industry in Mexico of skilled mechanics who create ingenious ways to disguise the contraband in hidden compartments. These cartels, the fifth largest employer in Mexico, with an estimated 175,000 members,[4] have a lot of people working to smuggle drugs across the border into the United States. "Many organized crime groups specialize in moving things across the southwestern border."[5] Specially manufactured compartments can be anywhere in the car, buried under carpeting, metal, and other personal belongings or commercial cargo. The latest United Nations estimate that Colombia produced in 2023 enough coca to manufacture 3,708 metric tons[6] of cocaine a year, the most ever.[7] Although precise estimates are hard to come by, it would be reasonable to believe that at least 1,000 metric tons of cocaine enter the United States each year, that's one million kilos. By the time this cocaine reaches Mexico's northern border it has been broken down into small shipments—a few kilos or less. These small packages are split up among many vehicles, each with its own specially designed compartment for narcotics. The same method of operations by the traffickers is used for Mexican-produced heroin, fentanyl, and methamphetamine.

That's not to say that CBP doesn't seize a lot of drugs. It's great to see, as I did on my border tour, a drug trafficking car ripped apart and the narcotics found and removed. But while Team U.S.A. is doing the necessary follow-up work on such seizures, arresting and processing the drivers, sending the drugs out to the lab for testing, making sure every ounce of drugs is found in the seized vehicle, and understandably feeling good about their hard day's work, traffickers are not breaking a sweat. They can easily afford to lose ten to twenty cars seized for every hundred they send north.

Two contradictory things can be true at the same time. Drug agents should have a sense of accomplishment for any seizure that takes dangerous drugs off the streets. At the same time, back at drug cartel headquarters on the other side of the border, the bad guys are not feeling much pain just from border seizures. The loss of a couple of vehicles and some low-level operatives, perhaps impoverished Mexicans trying to feed their family, or more frequently these days Americans[8] recruited for a big payday, pose no real threat to their highly lucrative business model. Even when they take some losses, they are still making a killing.

Each year, Customs and Border Protection gets new technology to detect drugs. They need to have the best, including the increasingly effective non-intrusive inspection technology. But the traffickers have technology too, as well as vast financial resources, a powerful economic incentive, and a virtually unlimited labor force to replace those captured by the United States or killed by rival cartels. The truth is, those of us who work in drug control understand that border drug interdiction is a game with tough odds. There's just too much volume of legitimate commerce mixed into the flow. The tons of drugs coming across in tiny packages are needles in a haystack. Customs and Border Protection reports that 868,867 people enter the country each year—this includes 226,589 vehicles and almost 100,000 truck, rail, and sea containers.[9] Just .02 percent of people arrested for an illegal crossing were found with fentanyl.[10] Further, traffickers are creative and flexible, adjusting their tactics and experimenting with new ways to supply the lucrative American drug market.

As CBP's legendary senior agent, and my occasional guide on Southwest Border visits, the late Rick Davis put it, "there are as many mediums to smuggle the illegal wares as the human mind can imagine."[11] I will return to the subject of border drug control below and articulate why, despite the difficulties involved, it still plays a critical role in a sound approach to international drug control. But first let's turn to the challenge of source country drug control.

Going to the Source—International Supply Reduction and Colombia

As a city kid who grew up in a high-rise apartment, I was not known for my skills in yard work. Even now, when I live in the leafy suburbs of Falls Church, Virginia, not much has changed. The first time I tried to cut my own lawn I wrecked my shiny new mower. My wife made the sound family decision to outsource our lawn care. Still, despite my limited skills, I was not going to pass up the chance to personally eradicate a coca plant.

I was standing in the middle of a Colombian coca field, surrounded by the Colombian military and a team of army eradicators. The Colombians had helicoptered us in from a military base to the coca field after flying out of Bogota early in the morning. Following instructions, we had to write our blood type on our shoes in case the helicopter crashed or was shot down. I couldn't remember mine and guessed, hoping they wouldn't really need the information.

When we got safely to the field and waded into the sea of coca bushes, I looked down at one coca plant I was determined to eradicate. The coca bush grows about waste high. The manual eradication of the plant seemed relatively straightforward, even for a city boy. You push deep under the plant with a kind of claw-type tool and dig up the entire coca bush, roots and all. It was hot, and I strained trying to get it all the way out of the ground. But after some effort, I pulled it out and pushed it aside. It felt good. That was one less coca plant the traffickers would have to feed into their cocaine manufacturing machine.

Unfortunately, that was just a single plant in one field. Colombia has about 200,000 individual coca fields. From a distance, eradicating coca bushes or opium poppies in the field seems like a straightforward endeavor. The reality is more complex. There are two ways to eradicate drug crops: you can spray them from the air, or you can cut them down by hand, as I so skillfully demonstrated in Colombia.

The objective is to get enough capacity of either or both aerial and manual eradication to overwhelm and frustrate the many thousands of small-scale farmers who grow the drug crops. If coca and opium poppy farmers repeatedly lose the bulk of their drug crops due to forced eradication, the logic goes they would eventually move on to another line of work. With the United States taxpayers footing the bulk of the bill for spray planes and weed killer for aerial eradication, and labor costs for manual eradication, it should just be a matter of inputs and outputs, and presto, no more drug crops. Unfortunately, the reality on the ground is much more complex than it seems from a distance.

The biggest difficulty with eradication is that every time a field is eradicated, it creates a very unhappy coca or opium farmer. In communities where producing drug crops is the primary source of income farmers push back hard against government eradication. They protest, they march, they physically block manual eradicators from entering their fields. In more extreme cases they turn to violence. Drug crop farmers shoot at spray planes and mine the fields with improvised explosive devices (IEDs), like the ones used in Afghanistan and Iraq. These IEDs have killed or maimed Colombian manual coca eradicators. Crop eradication efforts are only accomplished with significant risk to personnel and often under difficult conditions.

Colombia continues to make efforts to constrain the growth of their drug production through manual eradication, as well as through alternative development projects that seek to persuade coca farmers to switch to licit crops. The United States continues to encourage more systematic and sustained efforts to drive down the production of coca. However, according to United Nations data, Colombian coca production has sharply increased from around 50,000 hectares in 2013 to around 253,000 hectares in 2023, a disturbing trend line.[12]

There was a time, not so long ago, during the administration of Colombian President Alvaro Uribe (2002–2010) when a sustained aerial eradication campaign sharply reduced net coca production in Colombia and contributed to reduced cocaine consumption in the United States. This effort, part of the two-decade Plan Colombia initiative, which was developed in 1999 and was continued by multiple administrations in both countries, did have a significant impact, both abroad and at home. Cocaine overdoses in the United States declined in line with the reduced production. However, President Uribe's successor in Colombia, Francisco Santos, ended aerial eradication and questioned the usefulness of anti-drug efforts he had once led as Defense Minister under President Uribe.

President Santos' focus was on achieving an important peace deal with the FARC guerrilla group. The FARC, which received a large portion of its funding from taxing and controlling the drug trade, sought to end aerial eradication, which was imposing increased costs on them and their coca-growing partners. Although the official reason given when aerial spraying ended in 2015 was health concerns raised by the World Health Organization over the use of the weed killer Roundup (glyphosate) to spray coca, absent the peace negotiations, spraying likely would have continued. Over the next several years, the hard-fought gains in reducing the total Colombian coca crop, were reversed. Today, there are record levels of cocaine production in Colombia and there are indications of more Americans consuming and overdosing on cocaine.[13] It's important to note that many of today's cocaine overdoses result from the combined use of cocaine and fentanyl.

It was bitterly painful for those who worked on drug control to watch the gains of Plan Colombia melt away. This was *the* model drug control program—it showed that eradication and interdiction could work to sharply reduce production and consumption in the United States. But looking back now, it's clear that keeping these efforts going at a high operational tempo over the long term is extremely difficult. Anti-drug efforts can only be sustained if drug-producing nations are fully committed, year after year. The reality is that although producing nations also have consumption problems, it is generally not among their top priorities when also trying to address poverty, violence, and other national interests. When the level of drug control effort is reduced, drug markets quickly recover. It's a lot like mowing the grass; unless someone is out there every week cutting, the grass keeps growing.

Of course, today, the United States faces a much more complex array of drugs than just cocaine. At least with organic drugs like cocaine and heroin, there is a crop in the field that can be found and targeted. With synthetic drugs, such as methamphetamine and fentanyl, the challenge is even greater.

Breaking Bad—Taking on Methamphetamine

One of the most painful things for me to hear is when experts or officials brag about how much drugs are being seized. Too many times I have read or heard expressions of sheer joy when seizures go up, with agency leaders saying how great they are doing. Of course, it is good when drugs are stopped from reaching American communities, but seizures do not occur in a vacuum. If seizures double from year to year, it should not be interpreted as a sign of success. Our agents don't get twice as good from one year to the next. Major increases in methamphetamine seizures are a tell-tale sign that there was a far higher total volume of drugs being manufactured and getting into the country. The fact is US border methamphetamine seizures increased from just under 20,000 pounds in 2012 to 180,000 pounds[14] in 2021, a 900 percent increase—is not anything to write home about. Rather this indicates a massive supply increase of Mexican produced methamphetamine flooding into our country.

Looking at all the publicly available data, it is clear we were not winning; we were getting our asses kicked. It became even clearer over time, as meth prices reached record lows and purity reached record highs—stark indicators that the market was saturated with supply. During the initial methamphetamine crisis in the United States in the early 2000s much of the drug was produced in the United States. Methamphetamine, especially if you are not aiming for the highest quality product, is not that hard to make. All you need are some chemicals that can be purchased inside the United States, glassware, a recipe off the internet, and a place to cook. You also don't have to be a skilled chemist like Walter White from *Breaking Bad*. Most small toxic meth labs in the United States manufacture just 2 ounces or less of product at a time. This is enough for a few regular consumers to share or to sell for some cash.

In 2004, there were 23,929 methamphetamine lab incidents and dumpsites[15] found by US law enforcement. By 2014, the number of lab sites dropped to below 10,000 and then continued to fall. That represents an important victory for US drug enforcement. It was the result of great work by state and local law enforcement, and legislative changes in key states and later, nationally, to regulate the sale of the cold medicine pseudoephedrine, a critical ingredient to manufacture meth. Before state and federal retail pseudoephedrine purchase limits were imposed, meth manufacturers were buying large quantities of it. But as the tighter per purchase and per month limits kicked in, especially in some of the early acting states like Oregon who made pseudoephedrine prescription only, the number of small toxic lab sites dropped like a rock.

So, for those readers who wonder why in many states cold medications are behind the pharmacy counter, now you have the answer. Every time one of my kids caught a cold, my wife got annoyed at me yet again for the extra time we had to stand on a line at the pharmacy to buy the product. But the strategy of restricting pseudoephedrine access worked. My colleagues and I in the federal, state, and local government that supported the restrictions are proud of this accomplishment. It made our country safer by reducing the number of small user labs that became toxic waste sites after the meth was produced. For a time, the new restrictions also seemed to drive down meth consumption in the United States. Unfortunately, it didn't last.

As often happens in the drug business, the market adapted to successful controls. Production shifted to Mexico. Mexican traffickers now produce methamphetamine on a large scale, at low cost and high purity.[16] They and their business partners inside the United States are working to expand the meth market, moving beyond traditional areas of use in the Western United States to target the East Coast. Methamphetamine moves across the Southwest Border, just like heroin and cocaine, in hidden vehicular compartments, as well as via commercial shipping by truck, train, boat, and air.

Further, it's not just white powder that our agents are looking for when searching for meth. Traffickers can also liquefy methamphetamine and smuggle it in gas tanks or bottles. Back in 2016 at the San Ysidro, a Mexican teen attempted to carry across a couple of single serving bottles of a viscous liquid marked juice and tea. The border agents were suspicious and asked the boy what was in the two bottles. When he insisted it was apple juice, they suggested he drink the liquid to prove it. He did. Unfortunately, since it was liquefied crystal methamphetamine, he died shortly thereafter from a fatal overdose. According to news reports, his heart rate was measured at 220 beats per minute before he died.[17]

The scope of Mexican drug trafficker operations within the United States is vast, and they are adept at expanding distribution to reach new users. Their tactics, not just for methamphetamine, but for other drugs as well, include providing free samples, targeting areas near drug treatment centers, and embedding operatives inside communities to build an informal friends and family network to reach more potential drug consumers.

Disrupting the methamphetamine supply is even tougher to stop than cocaine or heroin. Not only is there no crop to eradicate, but the drug also only needs to move across one land border to reach its market—there are no large shipments moving north by boat from Colombia to interdict on the high seas. There are only a few options for law enforcement. US agencies and international partners can target the precursor chemicals coming in from China to ports in Central America or Mexico, mixed in with many other licit shipments. Because most of these chemicals also have legitimate uses, it is not feasible to ban them. Another option is trying to find and destroy the labs inside Mexico. Or they can hope Customs and Border Protection catches the ant army moving it across the border. This is a hugely challenging task, as is combating an even more concentrated and deadly synthetic drug—fentanyl.

The Global Battle to Disrupt the Fentanyl Supply Chain from China

The seventy-five-year-old JFK airport in New York City became, surprisingly, a critical new front for the War on Drugs. Initially, drug traffickers transshipped large quantities of the powerful painkiller fentanyl, the elephant tranquilizer carfentanil, or other synthetic opioids into our country straight through the mail. These synthetic opioids were produced in China and sent either directly to the United States or moved through a third country to throw US authorities off the trail. These synthetics were further distributed through the US mail and private parcel-delivery companies.

Interdicting fentanyl is a frustrating challenge. Although multiple kilos are also shipped through the US postal system or through express consignment commercial shippers, often the product is mailed in small packets of 10mg or so. That much Fentanyl barely fills a tiny plastic baggy with the white powder. The baggy is small enough to fit into a business-sized envelope or to be wedged inside a greeting card. These little packets are often hidden inside a larger package.

It is hard to believe how quickly drug markets have changed, but before 2013, fentanyl barely showed up as a significant cause of fatal drug overdoses. By 2016, it was the number one cause of drug overdoses in the United States, topping 20,000. As of this writing there are just under 80,000 estimated total fatal overdoses per the previous twelve months for which data is available, with almost 44,000 involving synthetic opioids such as fentanyl. That dramatic escalation between 2013 and today is very unusual in the drug business, and quite scary. The interdiction challenge is also scary. Catching these small shipments among the over 100,000 small packages that come through JFK each day makes the Southwest Border challenge look easy.

There are a few tools US authorities use to target fentanyl. They increasingly use advanced electronic data to look for suspicious addresses or shipping patterns associated with incoming packages, and they can run the package by some of the hardest working drug dogs in the world. It is amazing that even with all the high-tech detectors manufactured by US industry today (which they also use at JFK), dogs are still such an important part of the drug control effort. When Fentanyl first emerged, we didn't even know if synthetic opioids had a smell, and if they did, if drug dogs could be trained to detect it. Turns out, the answer was yes on both counts.

Giant sacks of packages and an enthusiastic canine were great eye candy for the TV cameras when government officials visit JFK with journalists in tow. I enjoyed my media friendly walk and talk through the facility with CNN's Dr. Sanjay Gupta when I was leading ONDCP. It was another opportunity to highlight the severe health risks from fentanyl and show how hard government officials were working to stem the tide. Unfortunately, all kinds of people in the United States were ordering fentanyl from China—on their smartphones or computers—for delivery to their homes, or a P.O. box in the United States. Some were individual consumers, others were professional drug dealers, perhaps trying to break into an extremely lucrative business for the first time.

There is no illegal activity that is more profitable than importing and selling fentanyl or other synthetic opioids. According to a news report quoting the DEA, profits from a $50,000 kilo of heroin were around $200,000. However, a kilogram of Fentanyl purchased from China for $3,800 can generate up to $30 million in sales on the street.[18] It is that stunning profit margin that has drawn in more criminals willing to take the risk of getting caught for the huge potential profits. Now that the fentanyl market is more mature, the profit margins, although still considerable, are surely reduced.

This is the new drug war. And like the old one, the odds of stopping each individual shipment are not good. When a synthetic opioid seizure is made, US authorities send the sample out for further testing and often follow up on both the recipient's and senders mailing addresses. However, many of these small shipments never result in prosecution. Even though one gram of Fentanyl can be broken down into well over one thousand doses, it is still usually small potatoes to prosecutors looking for multiple kilo seizures to justify the time and trouble of working the case. Unfortunately, too many of the synthetic opioid shipments, although containing a deadly substance, do not result in an investigation or a controlled delivery. As I walked through the JFK cavernous mail facility I imagined the mounting seized packages piling up in a giant government warehouse like the one shown at the end of the film Raiders of the Lost Ark.

Still, after a lot of brilliant work by US agencies, a good bit of progress has been made in reducing the threat from fentanyl in the international mail. Controlling this mail flow of Fentanyl in the United States has, to a significant degree been accomplished due to major law enforcement and diplomatic efforts. An FBI led investigation shut down AlphaBay, at one time the largest dark web marketplace for synthetic opioids. The Chinese government banned, at US and international urging, many of the synthetic opioids that were being transshipped directly to the United States. This was important progress. Unfortunately, this significant tactical success did not lead to enduring success at the strategic level. Rather than small shipments of finished Fentanyl coming directly from China, the precursor chemicals needed to manufacture Fentanyl are now transshipped to Mexico. Mexican traffickers finish the manufacturing and are now the major source for most of the supply of synthetic opioids into the United States.

Nonetheless, just as the traffickers adapted, so have federal agencies by targeting the illicit manufacturing and trafficking of precursor chemicals and continuing to press China to permanently shut down corrupt chemical manufacturers, ban the new generation of fentanyl analogues and precursors, and impose financial sanctions on individuals and companies. These efforts are making a difference.

US agencies continue to innovate. The Department of Homeland Security announced in 2024 that it would launch pilot projects utilizing artificial intelligence, including one through Homeland Security Investigations to detect fentanyl. Investing in new cutting-edge tools will be critical to any effort to better combat fentanyl smuggling across the border—the top drug threat to the country.[19]

There is more that must be done to try to address this difficult challenge, and as referenced in the introduction, the apparent decline in retail level fentanyl potency is an encouraging sign. Nonetheless, as Vanda Felbab-Brown rightly observed in her study of *China and Synthetic Drug Control*, the structural "characteristics of synthetic drugs, including the ease of developing similar, but not scheduled synthetic drugs and their new precursors . . . pose immense structural obstacles to controlling supply, irrespective of political will to prohibit and regulate their use and enforce the regulations."[20] The rapid pace of substitution of synthetic chemicals or their precursors, once they are banned with slightly different chemical variants, is outpacing the ability of the United Nations to keep up. None of the three existing United Nations drug treaties was written with today's situation in mind. It is time that a fourth drug treaty be established, focused squarely on the rapid banning of new synthetic drugs and designer precursors that enable the production and sale of dangerous new opioids and other drugs of misuse. See recommendations below.

What's particularly troubling about the phenomenon of synthetic opioids is that drug traffickers and street dealers are now not just mixing fentanyl into heroin. They are reaching a larger market by utilizing fentanyl to manufacture fraudulent prescription drugs and adding it to cocaine and methamphetamine packets for retail sale. Although traffickers and drug dealers are killing many of their customers, there is a cruel economic logic to these tactics. Traffickers are adding fentanyl to more of their drug product line to further increase the intensity of the high and the addictive potential of these substances—creating many more repeat customers each day. This approach is particularly dangerous for drug consumers buying cocaine or methamphetamine who may be opiate naïve, as well as for injection drug users at risk for disease transmission. This means even a very small amount of fentanyl, something which a regular opioid user's body could safely handle, is enough to cause an overdose in a new fentanyl consumer. That's the new drug war. I would say it's the future, but it's already here.

Hard Lessons from the Supply-Side

I have painted a somewhat bleak picture. Unfortunately, the drug supply problem is wickedly complex. It would be understandable if someone read this chapter and concluded that drug enforcement programs don't make any difference. But that is not the argument I am making. Yes, the difficult economics of the drug trade, in most circumstances, make it hard to sharply curtail drug use inside the United States primarily through reducing the drug supply abroad. But that doesn't mean drug control has no impact and should be discontinued. Rather, there is a need to focus, enhance, and improve drug supply control, not with the unrealistic expectation that such efforts will eliminate the entire drug problem easily, but with the hard-headed understanding that ending such efforts would make a very difficult drug problem even worse.

We clearly need both supply and demand reduction efforts. Imagine a world where drugs like heroin, fentanyl, cocaine, and methamphetamine are legal and either commercially sold, or regulated by the government in a manner sufficient to end most black market drug sales. It would be worse than the status quo, likely much worse. The entire supply reduction and drug enforcement enterprise imposes costs on traffickers and elevates retail drug prices—sometimes significantly—depending on the drug. Ordering a small wholesale amount of Colombian coffee for delivery to your home costs around $18 a kilo.[21] Compare that to the cost of cocaine on the street today, which hovers around $25,000[22] per kilo. If there were no significant risks of arrest or prosecution for traffickers, the cost of cocaine would drop like a rock, not down to what coffee costs, but far lower than street prices today.

It's true that drug prices have been declining in recent years. Critics of drug enforcement and drug legalization advocates point this out, suggesting supply-side controls are failing. They are right about the prices declining, but they are wrong about drug enforcement and the illicit status of drugs not being useful in keeping prices higher than they would otherwise be. Also, it is not correct that most drug buyers will pay any price for a drug. Drug users are influenced by the price and availability of drugs. They buy more when prices are lower. They consume more when availability becomes easier.

For example, in 2016 there were over a million Americans who tried cocaine for the first time. It was no coincidence that this surge of new cocaine users came on the heels of record-breaking Colombian cocaine production. Price is especially important for young people, who generally don't work full time and have a hard time financing an expensive drug habit. Yes, some people, especially after they become dependent on a specific substance, will sell drugs, steal, or conduct other illegal activities to finance their drug use. But higher prices can still be an obstacle for new drug consumers. These drug market dynamics evolve, so it's worth continued data collection, analysis, and discussion with drug consumers through surveys and focus groups. Even regarding synthetic drugs such as fentanyl and methamphetamine, for which the price declines have been rather significant, prices would be even further reduced if the product were legalized.

Let me say that I do appreciate the scholarship around the concept of "The Iron Law of Prohibition"—which is a term coined by a cannabis advocate and adopted by many drug war writers and researchers.[23] The idea is that efforts to criminalize and control any illicit substance will result in that substance becoming more concentrated, potent, and dangerous. Certainly, the trend line of drugs such as opioids, methamphetamine, and marijuana suggests that these drugs are getting more potent over time, and drug control efforts may have an association with those changes. The reports of the very low cost of fentanyl pills are disturbing. On the other hand, the concept that the illicit status of drugs is the key driver of changes in drug products is not compelling.

It seems quite unlikely that allowing legal production, trafficking, and sale of illicit substances would result in drugs becoming less dangerous, or stop drug sellers from experimenting with different, stronger variants of their products. It is just as likely that licit drug markets, as we are seeing with marijuana, would result in more concentrated and dangerous substances. The private sector unleashes powerful financial motivations. Mobile phone companies did not need law enforcement scrutiny to incentivize them to, through research and innovation, turn large 1980s car phones into today's pocket-sized smartphones. Drug markets will continue to evolve, whether illegal or legal. Although the large reduction in marijuana possession arrests is an important achievement, we do otherwise seem to be getting the worst of all worlds regarding marijuana, with illicit Chinese and Mexican producers exploiting the legal market while private sector companies are developing more potent and risky products.

I have argued throughout these pages for a major increase in resources for evidence-based prevention, treatment, and recovery support programs. This is overdue, and I agree with the wide range of drug policy experts who also see a need for such investments. But it's important to recognize that the supply-side programs should not be seen as a "bill-payer" for such important public health investments. The Department of Homeland Security is still going to need to monitor everything that comes through points of entry, whether it's drugs, invasive species, weapons of mass destruction, or other illicit contraband. The Tunnel Rats still must find and disable border tunnels that pose a terrorist as well as a drug trafficking risk, and the Coast Guard still requires patrol boats for search and rescue and its many other missions.

I have tried to very directly describe the enormous need for more public health programs and have proposed a source for those funds. But the concept that money for demand reduction can be found by shifting resources from interdiction and enforcement agencies is unworkable, impractical, and is also counterproductive in terms of fostering needed public safety/public health collaborations. This problem is too big and too complicated for any one sector of society to solve on its own.

Let me turn to some practical suggestions to improve supply-side results. I also want to reiterate that supply-side programs, like other taxpayer-financed programs, are not above scrutiny, and should be rigorously assessed to improve them and to encourage investment in new initiatives that show the most promise.

A Way Forward on Border and International Drug Control

What needs to change?

First, as I have outlined throughout this chapter, there is greater candor needed about the challenge in sharply reducing the international drug supply. Similarly, it is time to move away from the simple story that it is somehow easy to separate profit-driven sellers and addiction-driven buyers from sustaining an illicit drug market that consists of hundreds of millions of private, consensual transactions each year. However, that doesn't mean we should give up on supply control.

The United States has the capability to disrupt and dismantle major drug trafficking organizations through complex international investigations—connecting various parts of an organization together through network analysis and a range of other investigatory techniques. This effort is often assisted by our international partners. Such efforts lead to federal indictments and, if we can arrest suspects in the United States, or in a country with which we have an extradition treaty, they can be brought to justice.

There are a wide range of bilateral tools that US agencies utilize with some notable successes. These include joint interdiction operations at ports, vetted sensitive investigative units based abroad, economic sanctions, high-level strategic dialogues, international investigatory and operational training, intelligence sharing, equipment, and technology support. There is also a range of bilateral programs run by the Department of State's Bureau of International Narcotics and Law Enforcement that help build capacity in partner nations. It is critical that as agencies employ these tools while they continually assess results and tailor approaches to evolving drug threats and the specific dynamics within each partner nation. Relatively inexpensive international demand reduction and justice reform programs that help anti-drug partners address their own domestic drug problems, build good will, and deepen partnerships. They are also worthy of continued support. Congress should restore recent cuts in this area.

The courageous men and women out there every day trying to slow the flow of drugs into this country, whether based abroad or at the border, are helping to limit the scale and scope of the drug problem. Restricting the supply and availability of drugs, even partially, benefits the country. On their own, these efforts cannot solve the enormous drug problem we have. But that doesn't mean they are not important. Drug supply control efforts shed light on what drugs are being produced and consumed within the United States, are critical to bringing the most dangerous drug traffickers to justice, and to generating knowledge of traffickers' techniques not just for moving drugs, but also managing illicit proceeds, and corrupting officials abroad and in the United States.

One valuable tool that has been underutilized is the *Counter Narcotics Trafficking Sanctions* program run by the Treasury's Office of Foreign Assets Control (OFAC). This program enables the United States to impose consequences on individuals in China and other countries involved in drug crimes, even if they cannot be brought to the United States to face justice. It should be expanded, as should the *Narcotics Rewards* and *Visa Sanctions* programs run by the State Department that prevents traffickers and their family members from visiting the United States (see recommendations below). However, as much as these tools are essential, it's important to conduct after-action reports to ensure we understand the impact sanctions and rewards have.

It would be wise to test and assess whether utilizing the leverage of a threatened potential sanction might be more useful than executing that sanction. If China could be pressured to arrest and prosecute a significant chemical producing or trafficking organization in exchange for avoiding the embarrassment of a publicly announced sanction, which greatly irritates the Chinese government, it might be worth suspending the sanction. This is an approach that is utilized in drug enforcement cases at home (see chapter 7's discussion of "banking cases" targeting drug dealers), and it could be done internationally as well. The US must keep in mind that the goal is not to enact as many sanctions as possible, but to reduce the trafficking of dangerous drugs and chemicals to the United States and to save American lives. The government must focus on results, even if it means making changes in a popular, important, and longstanding program.

Finally, I want to emphasize the two key fronts in the global fight against drugs that require the most focused attention—these are in Mexico and in China. Both are challenging. Mexico and the United States, as neighbors that share a long border, have a linked destiny. Just because it is hard doesn't mean that both countries cannot find ways to collaborate more effectively. Below I propose a large new foreign assistance program to Mexico aimed at strengthening its judicial system, their port controls, and otherwise assist them in building their capacity to take on the violent drug cartels based in their country. Such an aid package must be negotiated with the Government of Mexico and formally accepted by them as part of a bilateral agreement.

China is a different type of challenge. Unfortunately, the counternarcotics relationship is entangled with the larger geopolitical situation. Nonetheless, US officials should continue to look for opportunities to strengthen bilateral cooperation, while in the interim also collaborating with other countries to jointly pressure China over their companies uncontrolled precursor chemical sales. Europe, Canada, Australia and other countries are acutely concerned with China's contribution to their drug problem as well. Efforts to get China to modernize its money laundering laws and to get its chemical companies to adopt global "know your customer" standards are worth pursuing.[24] Surely, any large-scale sale of fentanyl precursor chemicals to Mexico should automatically raise suspicions.

It's disturbing that China has not stopped such massive chemical shipments from reaching the Mexican drug cartels. The United States must continue to ensure that drug and chemical sellers know there is a price to be paid for supporting the manufacture of synthetic drugs in

Mexico that are killing Americans. Global efforts to tighten control of high-speed pill presses used to produce fentanyl pills and work with the United Nations and the International Narcotics Control Board to combat diversion of precursor chemicals are also important elements of addressing the drug threats emanating from Asia.

As I close this chapter, I want to say a word about the many thousands of dedicated Americans who work on the supply-side, including internationally, on our borders, and domestically. I support reforms, but I don't doubt for a moment the courage and commitment of those who perform this difficult, dangerous, and important work. Over my long career I have met many, whether in the field or in briefings in Washington. They are doing their level best to protect their country against a relentless onslaught of illicit narcotics headed our way and often face serious threats from violent trafficking organizations. These agents and officers have families that worry about them. Let me quote from Jack Riley's memoir. Riley is a legendary drug cop who rose to the position of Deputy Administrator of the DEA and spent much of his career chasing down drug kingpin El Chapo. Riley, said about his wife:

> She never complained, but she didn't stop worrying. She knew my job was dangerous. She knew I had been in fistfights with bad guys in dark alleys. She knew I had been jumped by gun-toting drug dealers. She was afraid of that call in the middle of the night, the summons to a hospital, the nightmare of every spouse of every cop and soldier and warrior in the world.[25]

Recommendations

22. **Reinforce DHS's ability to partner with other agencies to conduct complex drug cartel investigations**

    This is a tough mission; our agents need every tool while we work at home to reduce drug demand. There is a range of new and under development non-intrusive inspection equipment that will enable US agencies to better detect drugs at the border. However, the goal should not just be to pile up seizures, we must recognize that drug seizures on their own have only a modest impact. Far more important is to utilize border drug enforcement operations to gain intelligence about trafficker operations and to strengthen international investigations to dismantle or disrupt entire trafficking organizations. That means conducting controlled deliveries, turning smugglers into sources, gaining insight into trafficking routes, finding the location of stash houses and key operatives, and understanding traffickers' management of illicit proceeds from drug sales. The information that DHS agents collect from seizures, arrests, and follow-up operations, on their own or through partnerships with other agencies, can provide a valuable piece of the puzzle. That's the real value of the enormous effort the United States puts into border drug control. *Congress should appropriate $200 million specifically to supplement DHS's capacity to collaborate with other agencies to conduct controlled deliveries, recruit informants, and to support other investigatory efforts focused on disrupting Mexican-based drug cartels.*

23. **Target trafficker vulnerabilities through financial sanctions**

Under the Treasury Department's leadership, the United States must intensify efforts to identify and target international traffickers through economic sanctions to punish those that sell synthetic drugs and precursor chemicals to Mexican drug cartels. Chinese companies should know they won't be able to access the vast US banking system if they choose to continue to sell fentanyl and methamphetamine precursors to Mexican drug cartels, nor will they or their families be able to get a visa to travel to the United States to purchase real estate, shop for US companies to invest in, send their kids to elite American universities, or visit Las Vegas, Disney World, New York City, or other popular tourist sites across the country. *Congress should quadruple the budget for the Office of Financial Asset Control's narcotics sanction program to $5 million and double the State Department's $25 million Narcotics Rewards Program to $50 million. An additional $10 million should be provided to the State Department's Office of Economic Sanctions Policy and Implementation to study lessons learned from previous sanctions and $10 million should be appropriated to fund a Center of Excellence, housed in a think tank or a university, that can conduct research and host international conferences and meetings and propose refinements of drug sanctions programs.*

24. **Fund a ten-year bilateral anti-drug partnership with Mexico**

Our southern neighbor is the entrenched base for the world's most dangerous drug cartels. Helping them requires a long-term commitment of aid, training, and support. It is strongly in the US interest to increase a wide range of assistance to Mexico. Such spending should be on the scale of Plan Colombia. Just as aid to Colombia advanced that country's drug enforcement, interdiction, and its capabilities to conduct complex operations and to capture dangerous drug traffickers, Mexico's capacity will improve with US help. Judicial training, vetted law enforcement units, anti-corruption programs, port management, jail and broader justice reform hold promise if implemented at a large enough scale over an extended period. Although in the case of Colombia the United States delivered training directly, if Mexico prefers assistance can be provided via a third country, such as Colombia or Canada, or through a organization, such as the United Nations. *An increase of $500 million over current efforts should be negotiated by the executive branch with the Government of Mexico and funded by Congress.*

25. **Negotiate a new international drug treaty to more rapidly ban new synthetic drugs and chemicals used by traffickers**

As is the case for domestic laws, when international laws fall short of the need, they need to be updated. The most recent of the three global drug conventions was completed almost forty years ago. We need a new one for the opioid crisis/synthetic drug era we are living in today. Annual processes for international scheduling established in the previous international drug conventions cannot keep pace with the frequent emergence of new synthetic drugs, designer precursor chemicals and dangerous adulterants developed, through repeated minor changes in the chemical structure, to replace ones internationally banned. Although the DEA can act quickly to temporarily ban substances from entering the United States, most foreign producers who supply the cartels in Mexico wait for the U.N. to act. Governments should not be sitting around for a once-a-year opportunity to ban substances that are killing their citizens, but must establish mechanisms to ban dangerous substances as they are identified. Traffickers are resourceful, as are the manufacturers of drugs and chemicals. DEA's *2025 Drug Threat Assessment* noted, as just one example of the constant churn in global drug markets, that seventeen different nitazenes, an opioid widely misused internationally, have been identified to date, with new ones released to the market soon after older ones are banned.[26] With current reality in mind, whole class scheduling should be included to get out front of the traffickers, with safeguards to ensure that scientists have access to research any product that has potential as a medication. Existing international controls on pill presses should also be tightened. It is time for a new U.N. Convention to squarely focus on today's acute and rapidly evolving synthetic drug threats. *The State Department should take the lead in drafting a new treaty and engaging with global partners to pursue its enactment on an urgent basis.*

Chapter Summary

10

Maximizing Impact

Achieving Better Results from Investments in Anti-Drug Initiatives

Chapter Introduction: *Deserve to Win* the Fight for More Resources

When you walk into the Drug Czar's Office, not just into the building, but into the inner sanctum, where the Director has their personal office, it can be a stressful experience. Any staff member wants to make a good impression, get their facts right, and deliver responses to questions skillfully. Even the most polite Director can, due to their position and their ability to impact one's future role in the agency, be intimidating. For this reason, I didn't love that when I was briefing Director John Walters during the George W. Bush Administration that I had to look directly into this large-framed poster of Winston Churchill's stern face staring back at me. It's not that I don't admire Churchill's amazing leadership of Britain during World War II, quite the contrary. However, the combination of Churchill's face, plus the message on the poster, added to my stress. The message, about the war, was simple: "Deserve to Win." The phrase has really stuck in my mind.

It's easy for policy experts to say their issue or cause deserves a lot more money and attention. Everyone in Washington is always pushing for more: more resources, more staff, more high-level attention from the White House. That's just the nature of life inside the beltway—everyone always wants more. Generally, agencies must think incrementally. Resources are always limited, and it is extremely difficult not only to get increased funding approved by the Office of Management and Budget and included in the president's annual budget request, but also to secure full congressional appropriations for everything proposed, especially new initiatives. Even if successful, that's just one year, support must be fought for and sustained every year. Programs have to garner broad and sustained political support, or they become targets for elimination, a potential bill-payer for someone else's priority. Even if programs produce good outcomes, if supporters have not built a large and deep enough coalition of supporters, in the Executive Branch, Congress and among state and local officials and NGOs, successful programs with solid evaluations for effectiveness can become targets for downsizing or elimination.

Later, in a subsequent administration when I was the acting ONDCP Director occupying the same office as Director Walters, I decorated the office differently, but I didn't forget Churchill's phrase. To gain financial and political support for the drug issue, to fairly earn the attention and focus of the President, press, and the public, one needs a wise policy, concrete plans designed to produce measurable results, and a broad coalition of support. You need to make your case that you *deserve to win* in the fierce annual battle for resources in Washington. Supporters of a larger effort to help those impacted by drugs, as I am, need to make a very strong argument that this increased investment will pay off for the country.

Hard Lesson: We have vastly underfunded the drug crisis response and must invest wisely now, or will pay much more later

Congress and the executive branch have taken several important steps forward to expand federal drug programs as the scope of the opioid epidemic became clearer. Nonetheless, the type of problem we have now is far different from what the United States faced in previous epidemics. The explosion of opioid use triggered by Purdue Pharma massively expanded the number of

Americans who were misusing opioids and has caused a "once in a century" tidal wave of an epidemic. Today the drug-consuming population faces a drug supply often containing lethal amounts of fentanyl combined with a wide range of other substances. The risk of an overdose is no longer a relatively rare event for a person who uses drugs daily, but rather a regular occurrence. The time horizon to save such individuals from death is limited. The programs required to assist those with an opioid use disorder, including the many that are co-using methamphetamine, cocaine, alcohol, or other substances, require significant up-front investments. Considering the risks, investments in prevention and early intervention programs are critical, as are initiatives to sustain and strengthen treatment, recovery, and justice system programs. We can't do everything, but we must do much more. Programs must be well-designed, validated by evaluation, skillfully implemented, produce a measurable return on investment, and be continuously improved so that supporters can rally around the program and drive funding requests through the federal government's annual budget process.

Bolstering the Management and Assessment of Drug Policies

Famed business author Jim Collins, wrote a short book that highlights some of the specific challenges faced by public-interest oriented organizations, called *Good to Great and the Social Sectors*.[1] Such organizations, whether governmental or not, cannot rely on profit to measure success. Rather, they must develop alternative mechanisms to assess their impact and calibrate their operational priorities.

It's a mistake to think that just pouring money into a program is going to be effective in addressing complex social problems like drugs. Further, without a disciplined approach, it is extremely difficult to justify appropriations and sustain support from either federal or state governments. I have made an argument about the need to invest more funds to combat the drug problem, but there are no blank checks or free lunches. Drug programs, like other taxpayer funding initiatives, can't exist just to make us feel like we are doing something, they must produce measurable results. To get these results government officials and program directors at every level must drive change in an environment where they do not have long-term control over their budget (managed by Congress and state legislatures), nor the freedom to hire and fire their staff (controlled both by funding limits and strict governmental hiring processes). Jim Collins said it well:

> A great organization is one that delivers superior performance and makes a distinctive impact over a long period of time. For a business, financial returns are a perfectly legitimate measure of performance. For a social sector organization, however, performance must be assessed relative to mission, not financial returns.... What matters is not finding a perfect indicator but settling upon a consistent and intelligent method of assessing your output results, and then tracking your trajectory with rigor.[2]

This diffuse power structure, in Collins nomenclature, creates implementation obstacles that must be overcome. Further, the overlapping health and justice issues, the rapidly evolving drug supply, the constantly emerging research, as well as the international challenges that many at the federal level must grapple with, create a great deal of complexity. In addition, the short-term grant structure that funds many drug programs generates uncertainty in employees' lives and distracts from program implementation. Anybody who knows that at the end of the fiscal year they can be out of a job must spend a lot of time applying for new grants and can't focus exclusively on their day-to-day work. Nonetheless, Collins' guidance on the need for government-funded programs to carefully assess results, track progress, and calibrate success is critical for the long-term sustainability of drug programs. Government funded programs can and must improve in this area.

Combating Costly Delays in Utilizing Evidence-Based Policies

The long delays in implementing evidence-based policies are a problem in many fields, with drug policy certainly being no exception. In terms of clinical practice in healthcare it is often said that it takes an average of seventeen years for research evidence to be implemented.[3] There is wide variation in implementing evidence-driven changes in drug policy among states due to the diffusion of decision-making at the federal, state, and local levels. This is an under-appreciated aspect of debates over drug policy. Of course, it's easier for journalists, think tanks, and elected officials to focus on what happens in Washington. But states have a large role in deciding which health and justice programs will be funded and implemented.

State drug officials, like federal ones, must find ways to garner and sustain support for evidence-based policies and programs while operating in their own different political and policy environments, which can vary greatly from the one in which federal agencies operate. Easy access to medications for opioid use disorders, syringe service programs, sober and supportive housing, Good Samaritan laws, and contingency management approaches for drug treatment, for example, may be obvious priorities at ONDCP, SAMHSA, and CDC, but regardless of the robust evaluation evidence, they can be a tough sell in many states and localities.

With the federal government's support and resources, and through the new action-forcing mechanisms I am proposing below, there needs to be an intensified focus on deploying evidence-based programs (EBPs). This is a long overdue reform. As well described by Jeneen Interlandi in *The New York Times*:

> The United States has invested billions of dollars in addiction research in the past 50 years. That work, though hardly perfect, has yielded scores of insights about which treatments do and don't work for which use disorders. It has led to hundreds of randomized trials parsing the relative benefits of cognitive behavioral therapy, motivational interviewing, and contingency management. And it has helped produce a small roster of medications, especially to treat alcohol addiction and opioid addictions. . . . All of these treatments are clinically useful. Medication and therapy can't cure addiction any more than insulin injections can cure diabetes, but when used correctly—ideally, in concert—they can nudge people into remission and help keep them there longer. And yet, almost none of these treatments are in widespread use.[4]

Leaders must find a path forward toward robust implementation of research-validated policies more quickly while overcoming or working around obstacles that are impeding better results. This effort would be aided not just by more resources but also by more precise information on returns on investment, long-term outcome data, and compelling, user-friendly information to help those who want to implement evidence-based policies confirm program effectiveness and persuade skeptics. We will turn to political and implementation challenges later in the chapter, but let's first take a hard look at the resources issue.

Dollars and Sense—Thinking About How Much to Spend

It would be fair to ask me, as the person who led the drafting of more national drug control strategies than anyone else in ONDCP's 38-year history, why there are not more bold new initiatives incorporated into this key bi-annual White House document. The answer is that the government's internal review process usually scales down the scope of ambition. However, in the case of the 2017-2018 *Commission on Combating Drug Addiction and the Opioid Crisis*, led by then New Jersey Governor Chris Christie (the other members were Patrick Kennedy, Bertha Madras, Pam Bondi, Roy Cooper, and Charlie Baker), for which I served as Executive Director, there were no such constraints. The bipartisan Commission worked with the career staff at ONDCP to produce strong recommendations that did not have to withstand the grueling interagency clearance process and reached Congress and the public with a good effect on future legislation.

Nonetheless, every year there is a new federal drug budget proposal as part of the President's budget into which agencies must work hard to get their priorities included. The nearly $50 billion federal drug budget includes everything, prevention, treatment, recovery, and drug enforcement, as well as border interdiction and international programs. From "leaf to street" as we used to say when we were thinking about coca and cocaine and not synthetics such as fentanyl and methamphetamine. Certainly, it's a lot of money, much of which goes to states to run programs and deliver services. But the drug problem is a vast, complicated, difficult challenge that impacts many millions of Americans. Failing to equip state and local governments to take on the problem at the earliest possible points of intervention leads to enormous downstream costs.

Think of the benefits to school districts identifying those struggling with adverse childhood experiences and getting them help when they are 5 years old, instead of waiting until they are in their late teens. By then, that once small boy or girl could have a criminal record, a pattern of illicit drug use, and a poor academic record—all of which could have been prevented with an early intervention. Those long-term costs for society and to the individual are enormous. It is much cheaper, smarter, and kinder to intervene earlier.

To provide some perspective on the drug budget, here is what the United States government spends on other large governmental problems. For Fiscal Year 2025, the President proposed $884 billion for defense spending, $1.54 trillion for Social Security, $936 billion for Medicare, $587 billion for Medicaid, $73 billion for the entire Department of Housing and Urban Development, $64 billion for the State Department, and $129 billion for the Department of Veterans Affairs.[5] The total federal budget request was $7.3 trillion.

A bit more than half of the proposed 2025 drug budget is for demand reduction, which includes $2.9 billion for prevention and $21.8 billion for treatment. Supply side programs are divided between domestic law enforcement ($12.2 billion), interdiction ($6.5 billion), and international programs ($1 billion). It's both a big chunk of money and not enough.

It's challenging to get a sense of what is the "right" amount to spend on the drug problem. One way to gain a perspective on this question is through analysis and economic modeling, which estimate the cost of the problem to American society. In the case of the opioid epidemic, the costs are substantial. Utilizing an approach[6] developed by the Centers for Disease Control and Prevention (CDC), the Joint Economic Committee of Congress estimated the opioid epidemic cost the United States nearly $1.5 trillion in 2020 alone.[7] This cost is *thirty times* what the federal government spends each year on all its drug programs.

The CDC methodology was based on combining incidences of fatal opioid overdoses from the National Vital Statistics System and the rate of opioid use disorder from the National Survey of Drug Use and Health. Then costs were added up for health care, criminal justice, lost productivity, reduced quality of life, and loss of life. HHS has pre-existing guidelines on how to value, in terms of financial cost, loss of life and disease. In part these estimates end up being so high because many of the people who experience fatal overdoses have many years left to work, earn income, and pay taxes.

These are imperfect estimates; they reflect one way to look at a complex problem. Some would argue that this type of approach can overestimate costs. However, there is also a case to be made that these costs are underestimated, because the data used to estimate drug consumption from the (NSDUH) appears to undercount those with an opioid use disorder due to the difficulty of getting an accurate estimate of illicit drug use by chronic drug consumers.

NSDUH is a valuable study of broad population trends, and one that is worth preserving, but it's a survey that historically has missed many consumers who are justice-involved, homeless, or otherwise unreachable by researchers. It is just these types of people that tend to have the highest rates of illicit drugs such as fentanyl. NSDUH has been updating their methodology and now estimates in their survey published in 2025 that 4.8 million Americans have an opioid use disorder while a total of 7.8 million misuse opioids.[8] The country very much needs a regular study that captures this hard to reach population. In the meantime, policymakers at the federal state level lack an accurate assessment of the drug that is killing the most Americans and imposing the greatest costs on society. One recent study suggests that illicit fentanyl use is twenty-five times larger than NSDUH's 2022 estimate – 7.5 percent of the population rather than 0.3 percent.[9]

So even if the $1.5 trillion a year estimate of the cost of the opioid epidemic is imperfect, it does indicate that the cascading consequences of the opioid epidemic throughout society are very deep, and the response would benefit from increased investments. However, one cannot assume that any expenditure on anti-drug programs will produce major savings. Analytical work on producing as precise data as possible on the return on investment (ROI) for the range of interventions would help guide policymakers to make more informed decisions going forward.

For example, if you imagine a treatment program serving 100 people that spends $10,000 a year for wrap around services, housing support, medications, job training, etc., that's a $1 million cost to run the program. If fifty of those 100 patients reach sustained recovery, start working and paying taxes, that generates a lot of savings that grow year by year, benefiting the government's bottom line at every level and almost surely far more than the $1 million cost of the program. Savings are generated by avoiding costs, such as emergency responses for overdoses, disease transmission, and criminal justice costs for arrest, prosecution, and incarceration, etc. But because of the way government budgeting works, those savings do not go to finance the treatment program—that highly effective program that is saving the government a lot of money still receives its financial support via a complex decision-making process through which legislators and administrators determine how to address their budget choices each year.

So, this type of reality, played out in terms of many thousands of programs in the fifty states and 3,000 counties across the country, leaves us in a confusing situation. We are collectively investing large amounts of money across a spectrum of initiatives, yet a fair assessment of the current scope of the problem and the highly visible unmet needs, as well as the continuing high overdose rates, tells us what we are doing is insufficient. As highlighted throughout this book, even as important areas of investment are producing good results and already saving taxpayers significant amounts of money, they are not reaching nearly enough of the population in need to substantially drive down the overall substance use disorder rate.

Although this conclusion could be described more precisely with better ROI analysis, my view, based on the continued historically elevated consequences of illicit drug use, is that effective programs are simply not getting scaled nationally, due to the realities of federal budgeting constraints. The country needs to find a way out of this conundrum.

Overcoming the Curse of Knowledge

In the introduction, I referenced the curse of knowledge to highlight how easy it is when one sees an inspiring model program to believe, incorrectly, that it's a straightforward process to get that program to every community it could help. It makes sense that experts in drug policy visit model programs and work to spread the word about how impactful they can be. However, to paraphrase *The Shallows* author Nicholas Carr, these drug policy experts—who have already learned a lot about addiction programs and thought deeply about the subject—experience very specific and individualized "intellectual vibrations within their own mind"[10] based on *what they have already learned* through many years of work and study. Drug policy experts can experience an amazing epiphany when they see an innovative approach and instantly become convinced that it must be utilized everywhere. Another person, say a city manager, a police executive, or a state official without a similar deep background in drug policy, likely would not experience the same reaction if visiting the program or when reading about it. Unfortunately, just getting the word out about a great idea, or showing it to someone once, isn't sufficient to generate the enthusiasm, resources, and organizational capacity to get model programs replicated in another part of the country. As business strategist Guy Kawaski said, "Ideas are easy. Implementation is hard."[11]

It usually takes a fair bit of policy and program infrastructure to enable widespread implementation of new ideas. When the country was fighting crack cocaine and wanted to lock up crack dealers and chronic consumers, it took many steps. Congress and state legislatures enacted tough sentencing laws, funded support for state and local law enforcement, built prisons, and expanded court capacity to process millions of arrestees into prison. Local justice systems reformulated how they operated to achieve the objective of a national tough on drugs campaign. Similarly, when the country belatedly turned to addressing the HIV/AIDs crisis, it massively turned on the spigot of financial support to fund research and support and treat patients and initiated an array of new programs and refined them over time, including through the Ryan White Comprehensive AIDS Resources Emergency (CARE) Act, enacted in August 1990.

When you meet with people running an effective program that's saving lives, their excitement is contagious. But during those visits we are only seeing the tip of the iceberg of all the funding streams, organizations and individuals involved in getting that program funded and implemented. There is always much more to the story. It's much harder than it looks. Yes, a visitor can be impressed and grasp that the program is working. But spreading a model program nationwide still requires careful planning, new resources, coalition building, persistent political support, and skilled implementation.

Implementation Science and the Real Policy Cycle

There is a growing research base around policy and program implementation that helps to explain why, despite successful efforts to develop EBPs in behavioral health fields, there remains, as referenced above, a troubling "science-practice" gap "in which community-based services spanning many fields are unlikely to routinely incorporate EBPs."[12] Fortunately, the relatively new field of implementation science has been chipping away at overcoming this challenge.

Implementation science can be defined as "the scientific study of methods to promote the systematic uptake of research findings and other evidence-based practices into routine practice, and hence, to improve the quality and effectiveness of health services and care."[13] It offers specific solutions to closing gaps between academic research and real-world practice. Although the field is still evolving, it has determined[14] that effective implementation:

- Requires an *assessment* of needs prior to starting implementation,
- Depends on the *readiness* of participating individuals and organizations,
- Necessitates the *adaptation* of an intervention based on local circumstances,
- Counts on *capacity building* among all stakeholders involved—internal as well as external,
- Entails developing an *infrastructure* to support implementation through planning, team building, and the alignment of component parts,
- Demands *continuous monitoring* of and support to implementers—ideally through embedded feedback mechanisms.

It has become routine, and often required as a condition of grant funds, that program administrators collect data on program effectiveness. But implementation science emphasizes that it is also necessary to collect data specifically on implementation effectiveness, not just program outcomes. Without knowing if an EBP is appropriately implemented, one cannot know with confidence why a program was effective or why it failed, nor how to improve subsequent replications. Obstacles to implementation "can include social, cultural, political, organizational, financial, and individual factors. Implementation science provides a means of understanding these barriers and can help to identify strategies that best be employed to overcome them."[15]

Local context and circumstances are critical to understanding how to effectively implement evidence-based practices. So, unfortunately, one can't just duplicate a model program, even one with a very strong evidence base, and drop it, cookie-cutter fashion, into every community where it is needed. That doesn't mean programs can't be scaled and spread nationally, only that it takes more work, focus, and effort to get it done.

A traditional policy cycle, as taught in public policy schools, incorporates "agenda-setting, analysis, formulation, implementation, and monitoring."[16] However, looking squarely at drug policy challenges today, I would define the *real-world drug policy process* that should guide us as follows:

1. Generate high-quality **knowledge** to validate model programs effectiveness and demonstrate a substantial ROI for a particular drug policy.
2. Establish a strong **legislative** basis to support programs at federal and state level.
3. Acquire sustained **resources** sufficient to spread model programs nationwide over time.
4. Build a policy, political, and grass-roots **coalition** to maintain support for the program.
5. Ensure effective national and local **implementation** and continuous improvement of the program through oversight both inside and outside of government.

Unfortunately, this type of process is rarely followed. Drug policy programs do not receive the financial and political support they need to thrive and grow nationally on an adequate scale. However, if we examine the critical drug policy gaps targeted efforts can be made to close them.

Closing the Drug Policy Gaps

Certainly, I am not suggesting that the United States must increase its drug budget to over a trillion dollars a year to match an estimate of the costs. No country budgets that way. There are always many problems and costs for the government to grapple with—all of which compete for limited funds. Also, there is an absorption/capacity problem in increasing spending at too high a rate. Programs need to be built, and that takes time and requires expert staffing which exists in a limited supply. But I am suggesting that it is urgent to begin seriously addressing the most critical needs in a comprehensive, methodical way. It is also important, both in terms of effectiveness, that the government acquires more precise ROI data so that the funding can be fairly justified as a legitimate expense to the public, and to ensure that programs can be continuously scrutinized and improved. Government should not be in the business of spending taxpayer money so it looks good or feels good, it must produce results.

Intelligence professionals often talk about the gaps between what we know about a certain national security challenge and what we want to or need to know. In this type of "gap analysis" experts would highlight what is lacking and then offer recommendations on how to close these gaps to enable senior officials to make good decisions. Let me summarize the major drug policy gaps, which are aligned with the *real-world drug policy process* defined above that should guide us.

1. **Knowledge Gaps**—Across the spectrum of drug policy issues, there has been a great deal learned via model programs, high-quality research, and the collective experience of grappling with the opioid epidemic over the past twenty-five years. But gaps remain. Core drug research is well funded through NIDA, but new research is needed in certain areas, especially on how to best persuade people to take the first steps toward engaging in some level of treatment and on more effectively addressing polydrug use. We also need to understand how to best reduce relapse rates during or after treatment, as well as to avoid the significant discontinuation rate of buprenorphine and methadone use within the first "weeks or months"[17] of treatment and to generally increase retention in all types of treatment. Further study on how to best utilize new addiction medication delivery mechanisms, such as weekly and monthly injections of

buprenorphine and six-month surgically inserted time-released concentrated forms of buprenorphine or naltrexone would be useful. Much of the research on marijuana, based on low-potency, products is outdated. We need to know more about those who have developed dependence on high potency forms of the drug, including edibles. On the other hand, as the NIDA Director wrote in 2022, some key areas are well researched already. Dr. Nora Volkow explained there is already sufficient research to justify widespread adoption of naloxone distribution, medications for opioid use disorders, contingency management to treat stimulant use disorders, syringe service programs, and prevention initiatives.[18] ROI information and implementation data remain spotty and require much more focus across the board.

2. **Legislative Gaps** – Most of the recommendations of this book will require legislative action. Federal and state legislation is needed not just to establish new governmental organizations, programs, and funding streams, but also to reform outdated approaches. National legislation is necessary to establish federal agency homes for key initiatives, with internal staffing and long-term, at least three-year, renewable, grant-making capacity. Many states may need new or updated legislation. For example, states should strengthen Good Samaritan laws to ensure people who call police to help those suffering an overdose don't face legal consequences, to authorize syringe service programs, and to legalize drug checking services so people seeking to avoid deadly substances such as fentanyl can get the information they need. Too often these laws, when they do exist, are "written in complex and confusing language that officers and people who use drugs do not fully understand."[19] States must find ways to address legislative gaps more systematically and to better adhere to research-based best practices.
3. **Resource Gaps**—Most difficult of all is the growing chasm between the resources federal, state, and local agencies require to address the type of drug problem we have today and what is available. Understanding this gap and thinking through a reasonable, practical, and sustainable way to address it is critical. In a country with many health and social needs competing for limited public dollars, this is a particularly challenging topic. However, if the United States wants to reduce addiction and overdose and save resources over the long term,

we must invest in major new initiatives and much more seriously take on the worst drug crisis in American history. As highlighted at the start of the book, an additional $10 billion a year opioid crisis fee for the pharmaceutical industry would generate funds to close this gap.

4. **Coalition Gaps**—The United States is a massive country—urban, rural, and suburban—with great variability in the politics and priorities among us. On big issues like drug policy, it is possible to build strong and deep coalitions, but it takes work. As we have seen from the defunding of previous national drug prevention and important data collection initiatives, drug programs can become vulnerable to elimination. Critical to protect effective initiatives is the creation of a successful coalition, including bipartisan support and backing from national associations. Major priorities in addressing today's drug threats need an external *Center of Excellence* outside the government to tend to the political coalition that brought the program into existence and to continue to refine programs through research, technical assistance, and training. Government offices can manage grant programs and policy making, but added stability is gained by an outside government partner who can hire permanent staff, work closely with the field, build relationships of their own with Congress and the media, and avoid a loss of momentum when there are political or personnel changes in the executive branch.
5. **Implementation Gaps**—All of us who work in this field, especially long-term policy wonks (like your author) who get excited about model programs, need to begin to seriously care about studying, tracking, and improving program implementation. Yes, a lot of technical assistance and training, best practices guidance, and case studies already exist. That's a good start. But it hasn't been enough. Intensive efforts to study implementation and continuously adapt and improve government funded programs are required. The drug problem is too difficult and is evolving too rapidly to have confidence that federally funded programs are working as well as they could. If federally funded programs cannot set up systems to improve on implementation, progress will be too slow to build momentum, and federal funding won't be sustainable. Decision makers need the data to show that investments will pay off for the American people in terms of concrete, cost-effective results.

Establishing Return-on-Investment Teams in Federal and State Anti-Drug Offices

It is a widespread political and practical reality that there is always more energy behind funds for direct service rather than for government staffing. Every Congressional district is enthusiastic about getting more treatment centers or drug enforcement task forces funded, but few are lobbying for more analytical capacity within government agencies. This is a shock to nobody in Washington, it's a fact of life. Nonetheless, the scale of the threat, the large amount of money already spent on drug-related programs, and the need for more, requires it.

A 2024 brief from *Pew Charitable Trusts* highlights that even when states collect useful information to support data-driven decision-making, many states do not act on this knowledge. Among their recommendations to remedy this failure is for states to allocate funding "specifically for staffing."[20] Agreed, but we shouldn't wait around for dozens of state legislatures to execute this logical suggestion. I believe this is one of the areas where a modest commitment of new federal funds to states can make a big difference in supporting states to utilize existing funding streams to put existing knowledge to work where it can help the most.

Every state needs its own small, expert level, *return on investment team* specifically to work on the drug problems that are harming its citizens. No disrespect is meant to the hard-working civil servants at the state level already tasked with administering federal grants, state funds, and opioid abatement proceeds. They get the money out the door, write grant proposals, put together fact sheets, presentations, briefing papers, and talking points needed by their state leaders. However, inter-disciplinary teams skilled in economics, program goal setting and tracking, public administration and implementation science are required to quantify the impact of programs, identify areas that need improvement, and to propose targeted research projects to fill knowledge and data gaps.

This type of work will not only strengthen existing programs but would also provide solid data to share with Congress, the Government

Accountability Office, the media, and the public. Let's be honest, it's not right for any government agency to keep asking for more money from taxpayers if they can't demonstrate their programs are producing results. Although I have argued that Congress should not be too hasty in shutting down programs that have identified flaws, rather it should seek to reform them, but ultimately it is up to those who run programs to fix them, or they will face the reality that their funds will be cut, and their program eliminated.

It is unusual to propose the use of federal anti-drug funds to finance state anti-drug analytical staffing. Often such staffing is one of those categories that are strictly prohibited by federal grant rules. Understandably, Congress doesn't want states to divert funds intended for programs to be misused. For this reason, a dedicated federal program with clear guidelines is needed specifically to enable states to fund with federal dollars small ROI teams that will work for their lead state drug policy decision-makers. The federal government would *not* control these staff, they would be local officials paid with federal grant dollars to analyze state drug programs, assess ROI of current programs, identify gaps, and give data-based advice to their state agencies. A few basic data collection and sharing protocols should be developed so states can credibly compare data and learn from each other, but otherwise states could use their team as they see fit.

A federal ROI drug program office should be established at ONDCP to conduct analysis on a national level and to facilitate regular exchanges between national and state ROI teams, and among states, either by region or issue. Frankly, the cost is quite modest compared with the current almost $50 billion a year drug budget. At about a million dollars per state, plus the same for Washington D.C. and Puerto Rico, and a few million to run the program at ONDCP, the total cost would be about $100 million a year. States, with a million dollars, could hire five full-time staff and have a few hundred thousand dollars left over for targeted research grants to assess their own programs through rapid research. This effort should identify key gaps, highlight the need for new legislation, and build support for programs that produce the best results. Programs not found to produce a solid ROI could be reformed, reduced, or eliminated.

State decision-makers with responsibility for leading efforts on how to spend their federal anti-drug dollars have a difficult job. They need analytical experts skilled at assessing how to use the funds with maximum impact, and able to advise when policy shifts are in the state's interest. The leader of this team should become one of their top advisors on state drug spending. As a classic business book highlights: "Leaders do not succeed alone. A leader's potential is determined by those closest to them."[21] This was described as "The Law of the Inner Circle." Those worried about improving the impact of investments in addressing the opioid crisis need to keep this in mind and ensure that state drug policy leaders have within their inner circle top quality, expert advisors on how then can maximize real-world results.

Further, the combination of federal and state analysis of specific programs, the sharing of data, and the increased reporting on such matters will cumulatively increase the availability of actionable knowledge about drug program effectiveness. Certain issues, such as the cost and benefits of treatment programs, how long people stay in treatment, which programs produce the best results at the lowest cost, will be valuable for all to know. Further, this data and analysis will enable much more refined projections of what the costs would be for services to reach all that need it, and the total net ROI. For example, if every state prisoner with an opioid use disorder received treatment in prison, and re-entry assistance upon release, knowing how much it would cost—and how much the state would save from reduced recidivism—could be quite useful. These estimates would empower federal and state officials to make more informed decisions in investing taxpayer funds.

It's true that this type of program research and analysis could be done at the federal level through existing agencies. However, getting the analysis closer to decision makers in state capitals would be better. The state experts could brief officials and testify before the legislature and utilize their local knowledge and relationships within the state to make their case more effectively on how to best utilize state-controlled funds. They can also talk directly to state and locally based NGOs, activists, parents' groups, foundations, professional groups and others seeking more impactful state drug policies. Such experts can infuse into all those who work on drug policy in a state knowledge of the latest research, evidence, and cost-effectiveness—knowledge that is urgently needed for such a complex, sensitive and important topic.

The Need for Drug Policy Centers of Excellence Outside Government

I highlighted above the importance of major government initiatives having a strong outside government partner. I want to expand on the idea because it is a critical one. Those of us passionate about drug policy must recognize that competition for dollars is always tough and attention for any issue or program is limited. There are many issues and crises that pull government officials away from long-standing problem such as drugs. This limited attention span, combined with the never-ending fight over the size of one's slice of the budget pie, makes for a dangerous game. One year's exciting and important new program can easily face cuts to fund new priorities. Another way to say this is that the battle to sustain a program is *never* permanently won, it must be re-fought every year. Only the strong survive.

Although many in the executive branch and Congress firmly support anti-drug funding, that support can never be taken for granted. It comes down to the people working on the program, the harried appropriations staffers, the overwhelmed civil servants, and the exhausted agency heads. Also, these individuals get new jobs or retire, and administrations turn over. "At the federal government level, the vast majority of agencies have political appointees in leadership positions, and the tenure of such leaders typically lasts between twenty and thirty months . . . you cannot assume positive changes will survive leadership transitions."[22]

I can almost laugh about it now, but when I was running ONDCP in President Trump's first term, we had a lot of turnover in political positions. When ONDCP's Chief of Staff suddenly resigned, the twenty-four-year-old politically appointed Deputy Chief of Staff of the agency, Taylor Weyeneth, was assigned some of the Chief of Staff's duties by me. I didn't really have a choice, since he was the only political appointee on hand. Although he never made any significant decisions on behalf of ONDCP and was not involved in policy making, *The Washington Post* made Taylor the poster boy for inexperienced appointees.[23] He was a nice young man and did a solid job as a White House liaison, which is what he was hired for. It was probably a mistake for me to have communicated the staff changes internally at the agency in writing. I was not thrilled to see my memo on the front page of the newspaper. Live and learn.

New political appointees will always have a learning curve, and organizations and associations without a range of supporters for their priority federal programs shouldn't count on continued support if they lost their only friend in government. The champion who helped create a program in a cabinet department or on Capitol Hill could suddenly leave their job, representing a mortal threat to an initiative that has not built a robust coalition. However, there is a way to mitigate this risk, and that is to establish a strong base of support for the initiative *outside* government. Sometimes these outside groups, which I will refer to as "Centers of Excellence" are established organically by NGOs and funded by private donations, and other times they receive small government grants.

There are many very important NGOs in the drug policy space. If you see a large NGO working in drug policy, say a national association or group that has annual conferences, puts on webinars, develops a robust website, maintains an active social media profile, publishes reports and studies, and holds meetings with government officials at federal and state level, that is a Center of Excellence. Established NGOs, such as the Community Anti-Drug Coalitions of America (CADCA), the national drug treatment court association (All Rise), the Association of Recovery in Higher Education (ARHE), Faces & Voices of Recovery and the National Council for Mental Wellbeing already serve as Centers of Excellence in their respective areas. Some of these groups receive federal funding to provide training and technical assistance in their policy space. New initiatives need new groups, or better funded existing groups, to serve as champions for their issue areas. The federal government would be smart to carve out a small portion of program appropriations to fund such Centers of Excellence directly.

These Centers of Excellence provide needed services and expertise and help those on the ground to start up a local program in a city or town. A Center of Excellence, such as Faces and Voices of Recovery, especially if supported by a dedicated federal funding stream, can provide invaluable information to newly established Recovery Community Organizations. Those new local organizations will need to go through the typical growing pains of any new startup. They must set up an office, website, and a fiduciary to pay their bills and do their banking, hire staff, and develop basic internal policies. These are the kinds of things that an NGO Center of Excellence can support, accelerating the startup process and helping to get the program up and running.

But there's more. This Center of Excellence also serves as the voice of the program to Congress and the executive branch. They are the squeaky wheel demanding attention. Yes, they are, among other things, a lobbying group. There is no shame in that; big oil, big pharma, big tech, all have their team of lobbyists. Why shouldn't a program set up to serve people in recovery have a Washington representative that can speak for their group and their cause? There are rules about how lobbying is done, so I am not suggesting that Congress and the executive branch literally provide funds so organizations can hire people to lobby them for more funding, rather I am suggesting that government provide core funding for a dedicated NGO to be built with close ties to supporters of the program, including those in the field executing the programs on a local level.

With modest startup funds from the government, the NGO will be able to raise funds from non-governmental sources if they need lobbyists. Political lobbying is not the main purpose of the organization. Rather, they will keep the initiative in the public eye through their other activities. They will host events, produce reports, and keep interested components of the government informed about what they are doing. But when a threat to the program's funding base emerges, and it will—because that's the world we live in—they will know how to organize and respond effectively to counter the threat.

Let me emphasize that these Centers of Excellence should not be just boosters of their work. It is important that embedded into their DNA by the legislative guidance they receive from Congress should be a commitment to continuous improvement of the program they support. A strong NGO, strengthened and stabilized by some core federal funding, must not be shy about assessing performance and providing direction to the field about following best practices and critiquing local programs that are *not* utilizing evidence-based approaches. In fact, a key reason to federally fund these programs is to make them *strong enough to do hard things*. Every large national initiative, as they grow to have hundreds of local programs in the field, will see a range of excellence, with some doing great and others falling short. To protect the entire enterprise, the Center of Excellence must help strengthen weak programs, using their leverage as the national NGO for the initiative to push hard for improvements and utilize its expertise to offer needed technical assistance and training.

Our Madisonian constitutional system of government is complex and difficult. Those of us in government learn to be skilled in working the system, getting our way, and winning the bureaucratic game. But winning is not the only point; it's also important to get things right. When I read Barton Gellman's book about former Vice President Dick Cheney, *Angler*, it deeply reinforced this idea for me. Cheney, Gellman explains, skillfully built support for the things he wanted to get done not just at the senior level, but deep in the bureaucracy. If there was an options paper coming up to the President, Vice President Cheney wanted his staff to talk to people writing up all the different options, to shape them to point toward the outcome Cheney sought. At first, I thought wow, this is a great tip, I'm going to steal it and put it to use. Then I read how this was done with the options paper regarding the management of the aftermath of the Iraq war, which limited the planning role by the State Department. As it turned out, this short-circuiting of the policy process had some bad results. It's a concept to keep in mind. I am not arguing that it is just important to win, but also to get things right, again, to deserve to win. The Centers of Excellence must have this objective built into their mission.

These dedicated Centers of Excellence must serve as "self-correcting" mechanisms, with the mission, will, moral authority and capacity to identify and address weaknesses in the programs they support and believe in. Rather than serving just as program promoters, the Centers of Excellence have an incentive to protect the entire enterprise by intervening quickly to help when a local program is struggling. In his 2024 book—*Nexus*—Yuval Noah Harari, described how early scientific institutions were established specifically with an incentive structure to ensure objective truth and data drive research findings and explicitly commit to reviewing and updating any errors. He wrote: "What makes scientific institutions self-correcting mechanisms particularly strong is that scientific institutions are not just willing to admit institutional errors and ignorance, they are actively seeking to expose them."[24] Centers of Excellence in drug policy need to be funded to perform this same mission so that the country can ensure that large federal investments in combating the drug crisis produce consistent results and struggling local programs are fixed before the whole initiative is damaged or defunded.

It's true that the scale and scope of these Centers of Excellence are quite small compared to large federal departments, but their focus, sustainability, established relationships, and personal commitment of their staff can make a huge difference. The fifteen Centers of Excellence proposed throughout the book will ensure that a few experienced and committed experts in key drug policy areas are always around to offer advice to government officials at every level. The cultural anthropologist Margaret Mead said, "Never doubt that a small group of thoughtful, committed citizens can change the world; indeed, it's the only thing that ever has."[25]

Building Drug Policy Coalitions to Improve and Support Drug Programs Nationwide

As previously highlighted, it's a big country, with fifty states, 3,000 counties, and 20,000 cities and towns that all play an important role in drug policy decision-making. There are also 3,500 local health agencies and 17,000 law enforcement agencies interacting every day with people who use and/or sell drugs. The drug crisis is massive, and the response hugely underfunded, but that is not the only problem. There has been a fragmentation of the response. Major policy and program areas require focused, systematic, coordinated efforts. There is a way to combat this fragmentation, and that is to build a strong *coalition* of federal, state, and local officials, along with non-governmental organizations, researchers, writers, private companies, and practioners that work in each key issue area.

As General McCaffrey used to tell us at ONDCP, this is America; nobody is in charge, and that's the way we like it. What he meant was that there are intentionally built into our constitutional democracy overlapping and conflicting spheres of influence, creating inefficiencies in addressing large national problems. We can't totally fix that problem, but it can and must be thoughtfully mitigated through weaving together a coalition in key drug policy issue areas.

Dedicated Centers of Excellence can help to build up such coalitions through linking together government agencies, NGOs, professional associations, foundations, researchers, technical assistance providers, and private companies working on specific initiatives. I believe it's important for the government to seed NGOs with a few million a year to help ensure that these organizations can continue to operate long-term. Such funding offers stability in operations and staffing to organizations and reduces the pressure to rely exclusively on donations, corporate sponsorships, or membership fees, which can vary year by year. In a nearly $50 billion drug budget, $140 million a year for funding NGO Centers of Excellence is a critical, essential investment. These centers are necessary to ensure key drug policy interventions are keeping up with the evolving drug problem, are producing implementable and measurable results, and informing key stakeholders about their work.

Let me illustrate the issue with the example of drug treatment courts. There are about 4,000 drug treatment courts in the country, with about 30,000 people working in them every day. There are executive branch and Congressional staff that support some modest-sized grants to help fund drug courts, a national association of drug court professionals (All Rise) and the courts themselves spread around the country. All Rise serves as the Center of Excellence, hosting an annual training conference, producing reports and documents, including an academic journal (*Advancing Justice*), and offering guidance to individual courts, both directly and via resources on their regularly updated website.

The association is closely connected to its membership, and as a trusted source of expertise, can directly inform individual treatment courts when they are falling short. Further, All Rise follows not just what is happening in and around drug courts, but also national trends, and is able to anticipate the need for new programs, policies, and guidance and to assess and respond to criticism as necessary, through direct action. An effective Center of Excellence surfaces problems and presses its members to solve them, rather than allowing them to fester and harm the entire effort.

Anti-drug programs and policies need such a Center of Excellence because of the fragmentation built into our country's governance. The federal government can and should contribute to addressing fragmentation in how it manages and supports national grant programs, but a federal agency based in D.C. can't solve this problem on its own. Here is a brief list of fragmentation factors: short-term grants, failure to effectively disseminate research findings, inadequate funding, insufficient staffing at every level and siloed efforts in different jurisdictions, even if they are right next to each other.

There are also coherence factors that can mitigate fragmentation. These include longer-term grants, issue-focused user-friendly summaries of the latest research findings, robust program funding that provides a living wage for the workforce, mentoring of new staff by experienced administrators and as highlighted above, support for Centers of Excellence. We must do a much better job in recognizing and addressing fragmentation factors and build in coherence factors to ensure that coordination and collaboration obstacles are addressed. If the country can "defrag" coordination within the core drug priorities described throughout this book by building robust coalitions around key policy priorities, it will significantly speed up the adoption of best practices and produce better results across the board.

Reinforcing Leadership of Drug Agencies

This chapter has focused on the importance of generating better data and ensuring more rigorous implementation and assessment of programs. But it is also important to support federal appointees to get up to speed on these complex, multifaceted, and sometimes controversial drug issues.

There are many talented people leading drug policy at the federal level. But even those with strong backgrounds in education and experience would benefit from more focused efforts to accelerate their learning curves. Political appointees in the drug policy field often have a good background for their jobs. But as mentioned above, the overlapping health and justice issues, the rapidly evolving drug supply, the constantly emerging research, and evidence on the effectiveness of different policies, as well as the range of global issues that many at the federal level have to regularly address are a lot to deal with.

In our system, political appointees get their jobs through a combination of their professional background and their political connections. Many federal appointees are quite logically recruited from state agencies, the winning presidential campaign, or Congressional offices. All need and deserve time to settle into their new jobs. It is natural that such appointees have a learning curve to get up to speed, supported in most places by experienced civil servants that can help show them the ropes. Most appointees may need to learn, or at least get a refresher on the latest research-based evidence on effective drug policy practices. But the opioid crisis—with its staggering fatalities, rapidly evolving drug supply, and urgent need to save lives—requires a much faster learning curve.

There is no magic solution to these challenges, since as a democracy, we will always have a rotation of senior federal officials in key policy jobs. However, there are some important steps that can and should be taken to shrink learning curves, identify and train potential future appointees, and better support them in more effectively implementing drug policy. Below is a recommendation calling for the establishment of a dedicated "boot camp" to ensure the leaders charged with addressing the drug crisis know what they have to do when they step into their office on day one. The country needs drug policy leaders up to speed on what works. "Unfortunately, policymakers sometimes ignore[26] the very studies their organizations have funded and are just not sufficiently aware of the research-based evidence available to them. There is a lot to keep track of, and new research reports and data are arriving daily. Federal and state officials need more help to better serve the people they work for.

The political leadership and the civil servants who work at ONDCP in the White House have a special responsibility to maintain expert level knowledge across the spectrum of drug issues. Central to achieving this objective is ensuring that every new administration can rely on career experts who have built deep knowledge of all areas of drug policy and developed relationships with staff working in other agencies, state government, and NGOs that work on drug issues. As of 2026, most of the large group of staff hired and trained by General McCaffrey in the 1990s, including your author, have completed their government service. They need to be replaced by a new generation of experts to join the skilled cadre still there, to guide the agency through the evolving opioid crisis. I believe the office needs to return to 100 total staff—an increase of about one-third—as per the recommendations in this book, the office takes on new responsibilities to meet the challenges posed by today's drug crisis. I also believe that if the ONDCP Director is going to truly serve effectively, as intended by the statute creating the office, as the top advisor to the President on drug policy, he or she should be included in the Cabinet. ONDCP is the coordinator of the far-flung, complex, and almost $50 billion annual anti-drug effort. To lead the Drug Czar needs the talent, resources, and status equal to the other top officers of the government.

Recommendations

26. **Establish a *Drug Policy Return on Investment Team* for each state and at the White House Drug Czar's Office**

    The opioid/polydrug crisis is costly and complex; policymakers need precise information about the most efficient way to make progress. ONDCP should be authorized and funded by Congress to establish the new team, led by a new Assistant Director for ROI and staffed by economists and experts from other disciplines to conduct studies, and produce reports to advise federal, state, and local policymakers on the drug programs that produce the best outcomes. Further, where there are knowledge gaps in terms of cost-effectiveness of a particular intervention, this team should have some dedicated research funds to pay for needed studies, and/or to partner with other federal agencies to generate the necessary data. Similarly, it should fund states to establish their own ROI teams to assess state priorities, programs, and gaps that need to be addressed. Working together, federal and state ROI teams can produce a far more precise picture of where anti-drug funds need to be invested and better estimate how much it will cost to produce desired outcomes. *Congress should create and fund at $5 million a year a new Drug Policy Return on Investment Team at ONDCP and appropriate $95 million for the agency to provide to states, plus Washington D.C. and Puerto Rico, annual grants to establish their own ROI teams.*

27. **Build a *Real-Time Drug Data System* to Track Rapidly Changing Drug Use Trends Nationwide**

    The federal support for modern, private sector quality data collection is woefully inadequate to the highly consequential drug problem, forcing government officials to make funding and programmatic decisions often on two-year-old data. Further, the heaviest consuming population, such as those that are justice-involved or homeless, are massively undercounted in current data systems, giving the country a distorted, overly optimistic view of problematic drug use. In addition, long-term data of how individuals fare after completing treatment is virtually non-existent, as are accurate estimates of the quantities of drugs consumed. We must do better. Techniques such as wastewater studies of drug use are relatively inexpensive to build out, since water treatment plants already sample and test the water across the country. Such an approach can track near real-time not just consumption of illicit drugs but also rates of naloxone utilization, which are difficult to capture since there are now far fewer 911 calls for an ambulance after a nonfatal overdose (which is how the government tracks nonfatal overdoses). It is long since time to move beyond pilot projects and to permanently fund a nationwide drug wastewater analysis system along with other initiatives to fill significant knowledge gaps. Focused analysis of arrestees in jails around the country, as accomplished by the Arrestee Drug Abuse Monitoring program (ended in 2014), should be revived. Collectively, this type of information enables local authorities to respond more rapidly to new drug threats and allocate health resources where they are most needed. As described by several of the country's most experienced drug researchers in their 2025 article: "What is most shocking is that more than a decade after opioid-related deaths began their terrible rise, the federal government did not see fit to launch a single new primary data collection effort to monitor the nature and extent of opioid supply or use."[27] This must change. *ONDCP should be directed via Executive Order to lead an interagency group to assess current needs, develop a five-year plan for a modernized drug data system, and report the results to Congress. At least $100 million in additional annual Congressional appropriations is required for this overdue initiative to ensure policymakers at the federal and state levels can target their efforts based on an accurate and current assessment of the drug threat.*

28. **Accelerate advances in drug policy program implementation science**

The fifteen Centers of Excellence proposed in this book will have important responsibilities to build coalitions, share information, and support continuous improvement and program implementation. However, it is also prudent that a small office be established at ONDCP to support the centers' work related to the latest findings of implementation science. The ONDCP office will facilitate exchanges between these centers, promote common approaches to data collection, and bring experts together virtually or in person to meet and share ideas around drug program implementation. In addition, the ONDCP office can advise federal research agencies on implementation knowledge gaps that need to be addressed and keep national drug program agencies informed of the latest findings from implementation science. *Congress should appropriate $25 million annually for ONDCP to run a National Coordination Center on Drug Policy Implementation Science that will work directly with all drug policy Centers of Excellence and host exchanges, webinars, and conferences to support program implementation.*

29. **Fund an intensive *Drug Policy Boot Camp* for new government appointees**

During the political transition, ONDCP should contract with a university to develop a weeklong intensive overview of drug policy for new appointees. Instructors and experts will provide presentations, panel discussions, answer questions, and identify mentors for continued dialogue with the new appointees as they prepare and take on their new responsibilities. It's true that agency career staff also provide a wealth of information to their incoming teams, but the perspective of outside experts and former officials will be complementary to what the agency can provide. Further, the boot camp will be an opportunity for new officials to get to know each other before they formally start their jobs and get caught up in the grueling daily schedule of meetings, Congressional briefings and hearings, travel, conferences, budgeting, and the other requirements of a senior policy official. A similar, but state-specific program should also be developed and offered to new state drug policy officials. *Congress should appropriate $10 million a year to ONDCP to provide a three-year renewable grant to a university to develop and host the Drug Policy Boot Camp and cover the costs of ongoing mentoring and training to drug policy officials year-round. Funds could also be utilized to provide training to state and local officials, to host public educational events, produce publications, and host a web site based on the boot camp curriculum.*

Chapter Summary

11

The Fentanyl Generation

Protecting Youth from Today's Dangerous Drug Threats

Chapter Introduction: Straight Talk for Dangerous Times

I don't believe in scare tactics. The research on drug prevention clearly shows that it is not effective with adolescents. Telling them something is going to destroy their lives or kill them conflicts with their sense of autonomy. Further, substance use, not just alcohol and marijuana, but also taking prescription pills, is common enough among their peers to undermine such fear-messaging. Meaning that if some authority tells them—or they interpret what they hear—as "take drugs and it will wreck your life and maybe kill you" they quickly learn that many young people do use drugs and avoid such tragic consequences. A fair understanding of prevention science is to avoid scaremongering as ineffective. Nonetheless, the danger is all too real. It's for this very reason that I am so worried about today's high school students and young adults, whether they are in college or not. The risk profile young people are exposed to today is, in fact, severe and life-threatening. We must work very hard to find ways to deliver that message effectively to teenagers, and not assume that what messages are compelling for adults are effective with adolescents.

With my long career commitment to drug policy, in this area I am, admittedly, an unusual parent. I'm scared for my kids. I tell them how dangerous the drug supply has become now that it is poisoned with fentanyl. I warn them never to accept a prescription drug from anyone, no matter how well they know them, and to only use a medically prescribed and pharmacy-filled prescription. Still, I worry. Any person, including any young person, can have a difficult day—a bad night's sleep, a breakup with a significant other, a bout of anxiety, or a high-stakes test that requires an all-nighter. We shouldn't live in a world where one mistake can send someone to their grave, but we very much do. Our young people have it rough; they shouldn't take any chances with drugs. But of course, taking chances has long been a core part of what being young is all about.

So, I worry, not just for my kids, but for kids across the country. I think of the families, the moms, and dads I have met who lost children—whether as teenagers or as adults. When I meet with them, I see the grief in their faces, and I feel it in my bones. It haunts me, because I know our country did not do everything it could have done to protect their children. Just the fact that those parents can get out of bed each day to go on with their lives amazes me. That they can repeatedly share their family's heartbreaking story with government officials in the hopes of helping others blows me away. One mom, Carol Beyer, whom I have become friends with through my work, has lost two sons to fatal overdoses. Yet she goes on, as an activist and an organizer, to try to help others.

Can we hope that the drug situation will get better, and the incredible level of risk will decline? No, I don't think so. The synthetic drug revolution is here and it's not going away. The chain of events, started by Purdue Pharma's reckless and greedy marketing of prescription opioids and addicting so many Americans to opioids, opened Pandora's box and directly led to this moment. It's a straight line. The drug supply's transition from OxyContin, to broader heroin use, and then to fentanyl, today often mixed with stimulants and in fraudulent prescription drugs of all kinds, is impossible to reverse. Focused enforcement can help reduce the risk, but not eliminate it. I hope I'm wrong, but the current threat is so great that we must act like we will be living with this type of problem indefinitely.

Informing adolescents of the risks they face through school prevention programs and media messaging is essential, but it's just the start of what is needed. Let's make sure every teenager gets the facts, but prevention science points toward early childhood as the most critical time.

Experiences during elementary and middle school can set kids on a problematic trajectory in terms of risky behavior, including but not limited to substance misuse. We must do both, protect today's adolescents, but also move upstream to better insulate younger kids from the environment in which they will grow up.

When I served as Acting Drug Czar, I worked closely with Cabinet colleagues to develop a detailed multibillion-dollar drug demand reduction initiative. It was an ambitious proposal, appropriate for the daunting consequences of the opioid crisis. Unfortunately, after a series of high-level meetings and extensive planning, it was derailed over cost concerns. The failure to get this approved was quite a disappointment for me and those inside government, and several top prevention experts from outside government, who advised me on the effort, who helped to put it together. If it had been enacted, I am confident that it would have made a real difference. Nonetheless, I will always be grateful to then DHS Secretary John Kelly's support in getting us as far as we did. The unmet need is still there.

Hard Lesson: Youth face a terrifying risk of overdose—new prevention and early intervention programs are needed to protect them

Increased drug overdose rates among young people are deeply troubling. The opioid epidemic, spreading and evolving for two decades, although long impacting young people, has now penetrated our schools. The threat posed by the wide variety of fraudulent prescription pills containing fentanyl marketed to young people via the internet poses a mortal risk to this generation of young people. All the generations to follow will likely face the same, or perhaps even a more serious threat. Adolescents seeking to cope with an array of behavioral health, family, and societal challenges need so much more help than they are receiving. Although urgent threats face us across the range of drug issues, the one to our young people is acute, especially knowing that there is a great deal that can be done to help that is not yet happening.

Understanding the World in Which Today's Adolescents Are Growing Up

When you get a chance to spend time in high school, either as a parent, teacher, volunteer, or a government official, it's obvious that there is a lot going on. Classes, sports, labs, theater, test-taking, college advising, and of course, the fun, friendship, and cliques which develop among young people. But it's also true that in this swirl of youthful activity and energy, some kids are struggling. Recognizing who needs help is not always easy. First off, kids who are using drugs or alcohol don't walk around thinking they have a "drug problem." It would be simpler to identify and help them if they did. Rather, many of these kids have a "life problem," and they are utilizing drugs or alcohol to self-medicate as a coping mechanism to deal with stress, anxiety, or depression. As discussed further below, at times, such life problems could be rooted in serious childhood trauma, neglect, or abuse.

There are young people, of course, who consume drugs or alcohol who do not develop serious addiction problems. Since they are underage, all this use is illegal and inappropriate. But I think it's important to acknowledge that not all substance misuse is a sign of a substance use disorder. However, it is nonetheless risky behavior and troubling enough for adults to do all they can to discourage consumption. Youthful experimentation, not inevitably, but often enough, leads to bigger trouble down the road. Identifying underage substance use or other behavioral health issues should be a priority in schools. It is not always easy to find those who need help and guide them back on track before serious consequences mount. But the investment in time and resources to intervene early is well worth it. Delay can be costly, in more ways than one.

A few years back, there was a television show on Netflix called *13 Reasons Why* about the suicide of a high schooler. It demonstrated a teenage girl's mounting problems—which included some substance use–and the failure of the girl's friends, the school, or her parents to effectively help her. The show was controversial, and experts advised that families should watch the show with their children, so that's what we did. After our family watched it, including the very sad end of the show and the lead character's suicide, I talked to my teenage daughter. Knowing her and her warm and wonderful friends well, I asked her about whether it was realistic that this girl's friends didn't do more to help her. What she told me was: "Dad, what you have to remember is that it's really hard to tell the difference between normal teenage angst and something that is super-serious." It's a good point, and I have kept it in mind over the years.

The kid who ends up committing suicide, or who is going to overdose and die, doesn't have a sign on their back that says, "help me now before it's too late." Rather, they are going through their busy high school lives with school, family responsibilities, work, parties, friends, and romantic relationships, and dealing with the normal teenager's emotional ups and downs. We should not assume that it's a simple matter to identify those who need assistance and or to get them to come forward to ask for help. Yet, that doesn't mean there isn't a lot more that can be done.

When I was serving as ONDCP's Acting Director I visited a very impressive high school in Johnstown, Pennsylvania, where I had a chance to talk to the staff and students about substance use problems and what the school was doing to protect their kids. I was encouraged by what they were doing. That day I went through a naloxone training with some of the students, staff, and community members at the school. Despite their wide range of programming, the senior school staff were worried about their students. They explained that often kids were on track academically but were struggling at home. Many were part of families that had been impacted by the economic problems in an area that had not adjusted to the decline of the coal industry.

Further, many of their students had a parent or guardian who had developed a serious substance misuse problem or had become involved with the justice system. The school tried to support these kids by keeping their school building open as long as possible for clubs, sports, and social activities, providing food for those not getting enough at home, and bringing in counseling for those who needed it. Too often, they told me, even young people who had shown great academic promise ended up dropping out to care for a family member or to work to support them. Some of their students were among the estimated 321,566 children nationwide who lost their mom or dad from a fatal drug overdose between 2011-2021.[1] A recent study found that nationwide, almost one in four children, a total of 19 million, were living in a household with a parent with a substance use disorder.[2]

When I left Johnstown after that visit, I had one thought in my mind: we must do more. Schools need more behavioral health counselors, social workers, nurses, and evidence-based prevention programs that better equip young people with the skills they need to cope with challenges they face, including, but not limited to, drugs and alcohol. Why aren't we doing more? It's an important question.

Drug prevention is funded primarily through the federal government. These programs are the longstanding (recently renamed) Substance Use Prevention, Treatment, and Recovery Services and the newer State Opioid Response block grant program. To its credit, Congress has been expanding these grants over the past five years. Nonetheless, total drug prevention spending, inclusive of these grants and other federal programs, is just under $3 billion a year, or 6.5 percent of the total drug budget. This is not nearly enough to address the current need in the fentanyl era.

Further, due to the massive opioid emergency every state faces, a portion of prevention funding has been diverted to fund the purchase and distribution of naloxone. This is understandable, but it has diluted resources available to pay for the essential evidence-based youth drug prevention and early intervention initiatives. Now that Congress is explicitly funding naloxone distribution, federal grants designed for youth prevention efforts should be utilized as intended.

This gap between what needs to be invested in drug prevention and what is provided is more serious because the Obama Administration and Congress eliminated[3] the $294 million annual spending for the Safe and Drug Free Schools Program, which went directly to state educational agencies. Its elimination as the opioid crisis was rapidly growing was very unfortunate. About one-third of this funding was reallocated to other prevention programs. This program was designed to prevent both drug use and youth violence. It wasn't a perfect program—there were evaluations of it that pointed out that some schools were funding non-evidence-based programs. But the existence of such a robust funding stream, direct to schools for drug prevention, would be so useful today. It would have been better if, instead of eliminating the program, it had been reformed, sustained, and available to focus on today's threats. A new program must now be established to support schools directly in hiring the staff and funding the programs urgently needed to keep our kids safe.

Youth drug overdose rates rose sharply since 2019, but more recently stabilized. About twenty adolescents suffer a fatal overdose each week.

This does not reflect an increase in overall drug use rates by young people, but rather the presence of fentanyl in widely used counterfeit prescription pills, including opioids and benzodiazepines such as Xanax and Valium.[4]

Ensuring that Drug Prevention Programs Work to Drive Down Drug Use

As troubling as the risk is, there is tremendous potential to help many more children. It's amazing how much prevention science has advanced compared to earlier eras of scaremongering and propaganda. As described in a comprehensive report by the *Partnership to End Addiction*:

> It is becoming increasingly clear that the seeds of addiction risk and resilience are planted very early in life, necessitating a shift in the traditional approach to substance use prevention. We now know that experiences in infancy and early-to-middle childhood, coupled with biological and larger social vulnerabilities, set the stage for how children will fare as they age . . . even small interventions can successfully shift the course of risk for a child. By intervening earlier and more broadly, we can prevent substance use and its negative consequences.[5]

A multi-layered approach, one that provides age-appropriate programming throughout a young person's education, is needed to maximize protection. This includes supporting new parents and their young children and then building on those efforts in middle school to build resilience for risks that will increase as youth advance through their school systems

Prevention programs are generally divided into three categories. Universal or primary prevention is implemented widely—for every student in a school. Selective, or secondary prevention, focuses on those groups that are considered at higher risk of developing a substance use disorder, such as those who have demonstrated behavioral or academic difficulties, or have a family history of addiction. Indicated, or tertiary prevention, is more tightly focused on those who are already struggling to address major risk factors and who have initiated substance misuse. At each of these levels, "the goal is to maximize factors that protect against engaging in substance use and developing addiction."[6]

Adolescence "represents the height of vulnerability for experimentation with and initiation of substance use and for the consequences of such use, including the risk of developing addiction."[7] This doesn't mean that it's the ideal time to initiate drug prevention. To understand the critical need to invest much earlier in prevention, far before initial substance use, it's important to shine a light on the risks we are exposing adolescents to by failing to invest in building up protective factors much earlier in their young lives.

By the time they finish high school, nearly half of students have used marijuana, and nearly one-fifth have used other drugs. Dr. Robert Dupont has quite appropriately pointed out that doesn't mean that the trend line for overall substance misuse has been consistently rising; in fact, it's quite the opposite. Past month *non-use* has risen to two-thirds of twelfth graders.[8] This is an encouraging trend when comparing use levels in the 1980s. Still, that leaves a lot of young people at risk. Although a variety of behavioral health problems are widespread and it is not always easy to identify who is at greatest risk, there are some factors Dr. Dupont emphasizes that can offer useful guidance to counselors, teachers, and families:

> The most high-risk picture for the development of addiction is not difficult to define. When a person with a high genetic vulnerability (such as having parents or siblings who are addicted to alcohol and other drugs), a co-occurring mental health disorder and/or impulsive character traits is exposed to a highly addictive drug taken by a high-risk route of administration (smoking or injecting) in a setting that promotes drug intoxication … the gun of addiction is loaded.[9]

As has been recently discussed in the media and explored in academic research, a growing number of young people are struggling with their mental health, making them vulnerable to substance misuse. Many adolescents "have experienced worsened emotional health, increased stress, and a lack of peer connection . . ." that have led to "self-harm and eating disorders"[10] and suicide attempts.

Certain groups, including sexual minorities from the LGBTQ+ community (of all ages) face a two to three times higher rate of substance use than heterosexuals.[11] American Indian and Alaska Natives are also at significant risk—experiencing the highest drug-related deaths between 2013—2017, compared with all other racial groups.[12] American Indian adolescents between the age of twelve and seventeen experienced almost double the nonmedical use of prescription drugs compared to the national average (6.1 percent compared to 3.3 percent).[13] Specific age-appropriate interventions designed to support these higher-risk groups would be logical for school systems to consider. Drug prevention and intervention programs for pre-adolescent children should, however, be available to everyone since they are designed to broadly improve behavioral health and address both mental health challenges and substance misuse risk.

The Failure to Reach Most Young People with Effective Drug Prevention Programs

There are a lot of wonderful, concerned community members who urgently want to protect kids from substance use and the terrifying risk of overdose. There are also many organizations, whether non-profits or private companies, who are marketing specific proprietary prevention programs to school districts. However, those determining where to dedicate limited drug prevention resources have to be careful about which programs they select and ensure that any programs they fund have a strong record of success.

This is not to say that there are not some excellent programs that have received solid evaluations. Effective programs don't just inform kids about the risks of drug use, but also work to foster problem-solving, impulse control, strategies for coping with challenges, effective communication, and building healthy peer relationships and engagement in school. Prevention interventions can have a positive impact on drug use and other parameters such as better emotional and mental health.[14] As adults, children with poor self-control can have an elevated risk for substance use disorders. They are also more likely to have poorer health, possess fewer financial resources, and be convicted of a criminal offense.[15]

Those making the decision on which drug prevention or behavioral health supporting program to fund would be wise to consult the available research and utilize independent reviews of the literature. One initiative, *Blueprints for Healthy Youth Development* developed by the University of

Colorado Boulder, has established high "standards for identifying evidence-based programs and has acted in a way similar to the FDA—evaluating evidence, data and research to determine which programs meet their high standard of proven efficacy."[16] Their analysis takes into account the *quality* of evaluation studies, intervention *impact*, intervention *specificity*—meaning that the program worked to impact the targeted behavior, and the degree to which programs have all the materials ready for *dissemination*. The latest information on a wide range of programs is regularly updated on a website (blueprintsprograms.org). A search on this site for substance use lists ninety-seven programs, with fifteen identified as model programs and an additional 82 rated as promising. With this wealth of information so easily available, no school administrator should be tempted to spend their drug prevention dollars on untested programs.

In April of 2025 the National Academies of Sciences, Engineering and Medicine published a comprehensive *Blueprint for a National Prevention Infrastructure for Mental, Emotional, and Behavioral Health*.[17] They wisely call on the government to close research and data gaps, train and support the workforce, develop an economic model that can capture the downstream ROI, reduce reliance on incarceration, establish at HHS a Center for Mental Health Promotion, and to increase federal funding on prevention.

The country needs to establish sufficient funding streams to make sure every student in the United States gets to benefit from drug prevention. However, it's vital that such programs, due to either resource shortages or lack of knowledge about early child development, are not reserved just for adolescents. Building an effective web of protection for kids requires a significant investment in protecting them earlier in their lives, much earlier.

Going Upstream to Help Children Earlier

Yes, we must respond to drug use at whatever age it occurs, but it is essential to not invest all our prevention dollars on "downstream" activities that "react to problems once they've occurred. Upstream efforts aim to prevent those problems from happening."[18] As Dan Heath explains in his book on this topic, downstream work can be more tangible—it reflects a reaction to a problem right in front of us. Upstream successes are less visible, "you'll never know who you helped.... Your victories are written in data, starring invisible heroes who save invisible victims."[19] Nonetheless, the payoff is dramatic.

Back in 1997, the original study on adverse childhood experiences (ACEs) was published and shared important findings on how early encounters with trauma, chronic stress, neglect, or abuse can have significant implications as children grow up. This research found that the more ACEs identified, the greater the risk to the child. The study, which was not focused specifically on substance misuse but on a wide range of health consequences, found that prevalence and risk of alcoholism and injection drug use rose substantially for those with four or more ACEs."[20] These early childhood wounds leave a mark, causing many kids to be especially vulnerable to unhealthy coping strategies when they face the typical challenges of adolescence. Multiple studies have identified a significant association between ACEs and substance use. By reducing children's exposure to ACEs and intervening early when they do occur, we can lower the risks of addiction, overdose, and a range of behavioral and mental-health problems.

It's important to highlight that many young people are resilient and can overcome all kinds of childhood difficulties to lead full lives. Certainly, we do not want to stigmatize anyone who was exposed to painful early experiences, but the reality is that many such children, if identified early, can receive a range of impactful support and counseling. Their families could also receive help. Although many adverse experiences are linked to what happens in the family home, larger societal problems, including endemic poverty and unstable housing, are critical factors that cannot be ignored. In addition to the specific behavioral health-related recommendations in this chapter, there is no question that broader measures to help impoverished families would be of great assistance in mitigating trauma.

As important as the ACEs analysis is, one of the original authors of the ACEs study has cautioned about the risks of overreliance on an ACE score. The "questions from the ACE study cannot fully assess the frequency, intensity, or chronicity of exposure to an ACE ... the ACE score is not suitable for screening individuals and assigning risk for use in decision making about need for services or treatment."[21] Further, it is important to balance the focus on factors which undermine healthy development, such as trauma, with an understanding of the wide range of positive experiences that can prevent or mitigate difficult early childhood experiences.

The CDC provides a list of family and other protective factors,[22] that can reduce risk and strengthen kids ability to avoid or overcome ACEs, which include the following:

- Families who create safe, stable, and nurturing relationships mean that children have a consistent family life where they are safe, taken care of, and supported,
- Children who have positive friendships and peer networks,
- Children who do well in school,
- Children who have caring adults outside the family who serve as mentors or role models,
- Families where caregivers have steady employment,
- Families where caregivers engage in parental monitoring, supervision, and consistent enforcement of rules,
- Families where parents and caregivers work through conflicts peacefully,
- Families that engage in fun, positive activities together.

There are a variety of evidence-based policies and programs that help to foster these protective factors and build childhood resilience. These efforts include such logical initiatives as: funding more school psychologists and counselors; building child resilience in preschool and continuing it each year; requiring and reimbursing pediatric screening for ACEs in children; and increasing focus on very early identification and treatment of mental health and other behavioral health problems. Unfortunately, the United States, underinvests in these programs and too often waits until behavior problems emerge among teenagers, missing out on critical opportunities to have an impact much earlier.

This is the type of problem that requires a long-term focus since it produces results many years after programs are funded and instituted. The country must consider the grave threats children will face as they grow into adolescence and build the capacity to invest in them today. In addition to the great benefits to children and families, intervening early with family support and counseling is far cheaper than paying for a prison cell, emergency overdose responses, and potentially multiple rounds of evidence-based addiction treatment. As stated in the Partnership's report: "This leaves us in the repeated and tragic position of having to respond in an urgent and costly fashion to addiction . . ."[23]

Remarkably, recent research has shown that early childhood interventions showed significant differences in the offspring of individuals (now parents) who had received the prevention intervention in childhood. The Seattle Social Development Project, a study of the Raising Healthy Children program, was delivered in elementary grades 1 through 6. Participants were followed up longitudinally. The children of individuals who received the initial prevention intervention were observed to have improved early-childhood developmental functioning, lower teacher-rated behavioral problems, higher teacher-rated academic skills and performance, and lower child-reported risk behaviors.[24] Prevention interventions that foster self-control and successful coping strategies can bring persistent benefits, including less drug use, better health, and higher incomes.[25]

In the drug and violence prevention fields, there is an understandable focus on "high-risk" young people. The reality is, however, that every child benefits from programs to build resilience, many are at risk, and the costs of such early interventions are minimal compared to the costs that manifest in adolescence and beyond. At high school age and older we are, of course, worried about keeping people safe, but investment in early childhood health programs is a very wise investment. The costs are modest, the benefits clear. These initiatives are not strictly speaking "anti-drug programs," but they represent the set of activities that will do the most to reduce drug use initiation, addiction, and overdose. It's not the only thing that has to be done, but it's a good place to start. As kids grow, there is more that can and should be done.

Further, it's important to keep in mind the need to ensure children develop this resilience before they gain control of their own smartphone. Jonathan Haidt in his 2024 book, *The Anxious Generation*, makes the case that frequent use of smartphones and social media by young adolescents is causing harm. He reports that by 2022, 46 percent of adolescents were online almost constantly and notes that Gen Z is the first generation to have "gone through puberty hunched over smartphones and tablets, having fewer face-to-face conversations and shoulder-to-shoulder adventures with their friends." These experiences are occurring at a critical time, "when the brain is more vulnerable to the effects of sustained stressors, which can tilt the adolescent into mental disorders such as generalized anxiety disorder, depression, eating disorders, and substance abuse." This, he explains, makes adolescence both a time of risk "but also a window of opportunity for advancing adolescents' health and well-being."[26] It's a formative opportunity that families, communities, and the country don't want to miss.

Why Getting Kids Excited By Sports, Hobbies, Artistic Pursuits and Other Fun Stuff Stops Drug Use from Starting

When I first read about Iceland's drug prevention program in 2017, it blew me away. The article was called "How Iceland Got Teens to Say No to Drugs."[27] It describes how this small, northern European island country of 375,000 people performed a drug policy miracle. Through sports and recreational programs, developed to fit young people's interests in the localities where they lived, Iceland managed to drive down alcohol use among fifteen–sixteen-year-olds from its peak level of 42 percent in 1998 to a far lower level in a few years, and kept it at 5 percent through 2016. This kind of public policy success is extremely rare and exciting. My first thought was how in the world did they do this, and my second thought was, could we ever do this in the United States? Let me take the second question first, and then describe the rather straightforward elements of their program.

My excitement at learning about something so effective to help young people is something that endures. But any hope that Congress could be convinced to fund recreational programs in local communities was quickly dashed when I thought about how things work in the United States. Recreational programs for youth are seen today as a matter for state and local governments, schools, and communities to fund and organize themselves. However, as I investigated the subject more deeply, it turns out this wasn't always the case.

During the depression and under President Franklin Roosevelt's New Deal, there was a widespread national effort to construct public swimming pools. More than 1,000 were built. Until the successes of the civil rights movements mounted, these pools were segregated and designated almost exclusively for the white majority. When a 1954 Supreme Court decision and the subsequent Civil Rights Act of 1964 made segregation illegal, many whites were not willing to share public pools with African Americans. Instead, they chose to build their own private or community pools in the rapidly growing suburbs, as well as recreation centers that charged admission and were not easily accessible by public transportation. Public funding for recreational facilities that could be used by all dried up. The existing pools deteriorated from lack of maintenance, and in some cases were filled in with concrete so nobody could use them. It's an ugly chapter in American history.

There has been much written about white flight to the suburbs, the continuing deficit of quality facilities of all kinds—schools, housing, hospitals, and recreational facilities—in minority communities. As described in Heather McGhee's inciteful book:

> entire communities lost out on once public amenities considered essential to making democracy real. Today we don't even notice the absence of grand resort community pools where grass grows over former sites. There are no plaques to tell the story of how racism drained the pools. But the spirit that drained these public resources lives on. The impulse to exclude now manifests in a subtler fashion, more often reflected in a pool of resources rather than a literal one.[28]

This is a painful legacy, but it doesn't mean the ability to publicly fund recreational resources has to be permanently impaired, especially when it is taking such a toll on the behavioral health of children. Although this type of initiative on any significant scale seems daunting, big problems need big solutions. As the data continues to come in about youth overdoses, as well as the worrying increase in suicides and a broader mental health crisis, I believe the country can summon the will to invest in our kids' futures. Not just for them, but for all of us and the world they will inherit. This is something that can be justified by the severe and costly behavioral health crisis and through a hard-headed assessment of the potential substantial return on investment. Let's look at how Iceland did it.

Lessons from Iceland's Groundbreaking National Drug Prevention Initiative

It started not in Iceland, but closer to home, with a simple idea from an American psychology professor, Harvey Milkman. In his doctoral dissertation, Milkman concluded that people who used drugs were choosing whether they used a sedative like heroin or a stimulant like amphetamines depending on how they responded to stress. Heroin users sought to numb themselves from stress, while amphetamine users were looking for ways to actively confront it. Based on his dissertation, Milkman was recruited by NIDA to serve on a team looking at why people start and continue to consume drugs. In doing this work, he realized that just as taking drugs impacted the brain in particular ways, based on the substances selected, so did various activities. Then the idea hit him. "Why not orchestrate a social movement around natural highs: around people getting high on their own brain chemistry—because it seems obvious to me that people want to change"[29] how they feel, but without the negative effects of drugs.

In 1992, Milkman and colleagues won a grant to establish Project Self Discovery, which provided teenagers in Denver, Colorado natural high alternatives to drugs and low-level crime. Kids over age fourteen were referred to the program who didn't seem to need drug treatment, but who had behavioral problems with minor substance misuse or petty crime. Milkman explains: "We didn't say to them, you're coming in for treatment. We said we'll teach you anything you want to learn, music, dance, hip hop, art, martial arts." What they were interested in would align with their preferences in dealing with stress and anxiety. Life skills training was also provided to help them improve how they thought about themselves and how they connected with other people.

Milkman was invited to Iceland to share his work. Later, he was asked to serve as a consultant to the first residential drug treatment center for adolescents in Tindar, Iceland. National government officials decided to take the emerging initiative nationwide. Working with Icelandic collaborators, they developed what would become the Icelandic Prevention Model (IPM).

Iceland surveyed every 14-, 15-, and 16-year-old in the country, asking questions about substance use, family relationships, and social and recreational activities. A few important protective factors emerged from the survey that were associated with low levels of substance use. These included participating in structured activities, such as sports at least three times a week; total time spent with parents; feeling cared about at school; and not being out late at night. Utilizing the survey results, a new program was introduced. National funding was increased for organized sports, music, art, dance, and other structured activities. A user-friendly voucher system was established for families so every young person could participate, regardless of income. Evaluations in Iceland, and replications in other countries, have shown excellent results and validated the concept that: "Peer, family, and structured leisure domains are protective against substance use."[30] But also, it's fair to say that piloting the model in different environments would require careful assessment to ensure an effective adaptation. An overview of how to establish a firm evidence-based going forward to support a transfer of the IPM was recently published."[31]

This type of intervention holds enormous promise for the United States to reduce the risks of dangerous, potentially lethal, drug use by adolescents. It also has the additional benefit of helping remedy the huge deficit of organized youth recreational activity in long-neglected minority communities. Below, I will recommend a national pilot modeled on the IPM, focused on school districts that face both a high rate of drug misuse and a deficit of recreational activities. I hope one day that every community in the country has the resources to support sports and recreational activities for young people, but for now, let's get started in helping those most in need and build out nationally if the program delivers for the U.S.A. as it has for Iceland.

How to Unleash America's Creative Talent for A New Anti-Drug Media Campaign

Anti-drug media campaigns have long been a staple of anti-drug efforts, both nationally and locally. Nobody wants to return to the days of the ugly, and decidedly non-evidence-based propaganda of Harry Anslinger, nor the well-intended, but now outdated Nancy Reagan "just say no" program. But with today's advances in prevention science and the incredible penetration of social media in the lives of adolescents, it's important to build a well-funded program run by an organization with a strong commitment to science and equipped to regularly update content, assess results, and continuously improve its media messages.

Like many other interventions, media campaigns vary in effectiveness. They must be produced with care and tested through private sector developed advertising effectiveness tools. These tools are improving in today's digital economy. If every phone app today can tell what kind of TV shows I watch and when I am getting ready to buy a new car or appliance, surely, they can be put to work to validate anti-drug media ads. My attitude toward anti-drug media campaigns is simple: I am for whatever works with kids. The state of the science suggests that scare-mongering ads that drugs are going to kill you, even when true, tend not to be effective. Regardless, those of us long past our adolescence must support the latest effectiveness research and count on the experts at designing these ads to keep up with rapidly changing trends.

Like other parents, I have long been impressed with the ability of kids to produce high-quality and entertaining short videos on their phones, often with music, graphics, and cool sound effects. It would be great to put that talent to work to benefit a national anti-drug social media campaign. So, in addition to a professionally run program, the government should provide a modest amount of funding for states to run competitions for the most innovative student-made ads, as judged by experts in prevention science. Every school in the state could nominate its best student-produced ad and send it to a statewide competition, with the top entries advancing to a national competition and an annual awards ceremony in Washington. Student created anti-drug videos would generate enthusiasm in schools and have the added benefit of educating those communities about the current drug threat and bringing people together to both watch the youth created ads and talk about the challenge.

The ability of young people to influence each other is an important mechanism to tap into. One study highlighted that training students to utilize their own social media accounts to communicate drug education messages was found to be impactful. The "Living the Example" program's peer-to-peer approach enable a relatively small number of youth ambassadors to "reach a large audience with authentic, targeted prevention messages, given the widespread use of social networking platforms."[32] This evaluation found that the initiative reduced substance use intentions among high school students.

Drug prevention messaging campaigns have a long history in the United States. Some have been effective, and others have had minimal impact or may have even increased drug use. These campaigns must be carefully tested, managed, and updated as necessary. Establishing a permanent federal government office with sufficient funding to administer the program and continually study results is essential. A Center of Excellence outside government can help keep the effort focused and educate Congress and the public about these programs, while also providing technical assistance to state and local anti-drug media campaigns.

As I have argued not just throughout this chapter, but throughout the whole book, these investments in addressing the drug crisis will not just save lives but will reduce government expenditures over time. The mounting costs of today's drug crisis should put us on notice—we can either find a way to cover the costs of these investments now—or most certainly will pay a higher price later. Below are the recommendations on what is required to protect today's and tomorrow's, generation from the risks in this difficult world they will inherit.

Recommendations

30. **<u>Ensure that every school provides high-quality drug prevention programs to all students</u>**

    There is an urgent need to move our approach to behavioral health upstream to discourage early drug use, identify those children with untreated trauma, and to intervene earlier with kids and families that need help. The likely cost savings and transformational impact on the lives of students by helping them when they are young are immense. The failure to provide all young people with quality drug prevention education is a reckless strategy considering the lethality of the drug supply. This program is best managed at HHS. *A budget of $400 million is proposed for HHS to provide funds directly to school districts* *around the country, based on need. Ten million should be dedicated to funding an NGO Center of Excellence to provide technical assistance and training to schools on drug prevention at every age.*

31. **Provide recreational, athletic, and social activities for kids in counties with high addiction rates**

In many areas of the country the lack of sufficient community resources for youth sports, clubs, and other in-person recreational activities undermines the development of children and puts them at risk for a range of problems, including substance misuse. A *Behavioral Health Community Activities Program* should be established to begin to remedy this very consequential deficit. Communities with the greatest need should form a geographically coherent local coalition to seek and receive five-year, renewable grants to fund a major expansion of youth activities. Those selected to receive grants would hire a program executive director who will work under the supervision of an advisory board including health officials, recreational agencies, and city, town, and county officials. Grant funds can be used to build new facilities or rehabilitate existing ones, to offer parents vouchers for various programs, to survey youth on activities they are interested in and to fund local agencies, NGOs, or private companies to run youth activities programs. *A budget of $350 million is proposed for this program, to be administered by the CDC. Up to $10 million should be dedicated to establishing an NGO Center of Excellence to provide technical assistance and training to grantees.*

32. **Establish a New 'National Youth Anti-Drug Media Campaign' with cutting-edge, private sector approaches, including artificial intelligence**

Positive, impactful, focus-group tested messages designed to combat drug use need to regularly reach young people through traditional and social media. Although some of the existing programs are laudable, their scale is insufficient compared to the need and the threat. The campaign should have a national brand that becomes as widely known to kids as Nike, Spotify, Apple, McDonald's and Coca-Cola. The program should provide regularly updated content informed by feedback from target audiences, survey research, and focus groups. The program should encourage youth to interact with the content through their own social media accounts. Targeting of messages and assessment of results should be informed by emerging artificial intelligence tools. This will allow the use of much more real-time data on current risks to young people and a focus on geographic areas of highest need. *A budget of $200 million is proposed for the CDC to administer the program, with the support of an advisory group from other agencies and outside organizations with expertise in this area. A portion of the funds should be used to run statewide and national contests for youth to create their own ads, with the winning entries integrated into the national campaign. Five million should be dedicated to establishing an NGO Center of Excellence to support the initiative.*

Chapter Summary

Conclusion

The Final Hard Lesson: There is no easy button—the opioid crisis can only be solved by bringing innovative health and justice interventions to the millions of Americans who need them

When I first heard House Narcotics Committee Chairman Charlie Rangel and other advocates for treatment call for "treatment on demand" back in the 1980s, the phrase rubbed me the wrong way. Back then, I thought of treatment slots as a scarce and expensive resource that ought to be distributed only to the most deserving. Meaning those who were not committing crimes, who had pledged to stop their drug use, and who had come forward to humbly request assistance. Illegal drug consumers should not be able to "demand it." Over the years, however, as I learned more about addiction, spent time with those impacted by drugs, and visited with those working in treatment, recovery, prison re-entry, drug courts, and street outreach to drug consumers, I have changed my mind.

Today's drug supply is so lethal and unpredictable that the country must make a wide range of treatment and low-threshold health and social services available on a drop-in basis, or on demand. Treatment should be available whenever, wherever, and however people who need it want it. What I call Engagement and Support Centers, specifically set up to help those with substance use problems, need to offer, without pre-conditions, the full range of treatment, recovery, health, and social services to everyone who wants help to reduce their drug use and overdose risk. The benefits to those struggling with addiction, and to the wider society from this type of full service center, are clear.

It's important also that the justice system provide a range of entry points into treatment. The country's 4,000 drug courts provide long-term supervised treatment to those who have been arrested for crimes driven by their addiction, but almost always well beyond drug possession offenses. Police facilitated deflection to treatment gives officers an important alternative to arrest and an opportunity to foster life-transforming changes for those in need. I have recommended that other community leaders—coaches, school nurses, faith leaders—also have access to paid treatment slots to provide to those they know who could benefit from them. Drug treatment in jails or prisons needs to be a priority for the large percentage of inmates with an untreated drug problem. These programs need to be greatly expanded, while they are continually assessed to further improve them. Innovation is happening at jails and prisons to provide methadone and buprenorphine and other treatment services, but more is needed, including the use of long-acting injectable medications which only require weekly or monthly administration, and counseling services to advance progress in recovery before release.

The way prison reentry is often managed for many with a substance use disorder who have served their sentence should trouble the conscience of every American, especially those charged with running these facilities. Anyone who completes a prison sentence must have, in those critical first weeks when they return to the community and are at acute risk of a fatal overdose, reliable access to housing, health care, recovery support, social services and fair opportunities for paid work. Reentry from jail should not be, as it has become for far too many, a death sentence. The same supports are needed for all those who complete a treatment program, regardless of whether they are involved in the justice system or not. Transitions such as these are risky for those with a history of substance use, and they need to be supported by professional case managers to ensure they go smoothly and safely.

The drug enforcement and interdiction workforce continues to work hard to disrupt the drug supply, relying on new technology at border entry points, investigations of dangerous drug trafficking organizations, and deploying a range of diplomatic, programmatic, and financial tools.

Reforms are needed, such as the development of a new international drug treaty that focuses on synthetics to rapidly ban the constantly evolving drugs and chemicals utilized by drug traffickers. Bilateral programs and the presence of American agents and experts based abroad are needed to support critical countries, especially Mexico. Greater utilization of targeted financial sanctions, as well as expanded rewards programs to generate hard-to-get insider information, are needed throughout the illicit drug supply chain. However, international efforts alone cannot solve this crisis. The costs and consequences at home will continue to rise without an expanded domestic effort.

The opioid crisis, now including the misuse of a variety of drugs in combination with opioids, such as methamphetamine and cocaine, is also shockingly costly. It removes people from the workforce our economy needs, damages communities, and often requires expensive emergency medical and criminal justice system interventions. Why have we not solved this yet? The many reasons why we have not fully taken on the opioid crisis have been explored throughout this book, but much of it is tied back to the stigma that is projected onto those struggling with addiction. The country has not adequately funded the needed response, nor modernized its approach to take on today's urgent challenges.

Perhaps too many have looked the other way, not wanting to deal with this complicated problem. It's important to see the drug crisis for what it is, something that impacts us all. People struggling with addiction come from all types of backgrounds, they are present in every sector of society, in our neighborhoods and workplaces, in our schools and places of worship. Those with a substance use disorder may have taken a wrong turn, could be grappling with some childhood trauma, and may have made some mistakes. Those of us who have avoided a significant substance use problem should count our blessings, but should not look away from the immense suffering.

This problem is daunting, but not impossible to address. The recommendations throughout the book offer a map to guide us out of the opioid crisis. I have emphasized the need for a larger federal effort, but there is no need for state and local officials, advocacy groups, private foundations, and individual citizens to wait. Most of the solutions supported in the book's thirty-two recommendations can be advanced on the local level now, using existing federal grants, state dollars, opioid abatement funds, or private donations. What we shouldn't do is think there is nothing we can do, when that is so clearly not the case.

Almost every year, whoever serves as the country's Drug Czar provides a keynote address to the Rx and Illicit Drug Summit, which was founded by Congressman Hal Rogers in 2012. At the annual conference, there is not just a wide range of officials and practitioners attending, but also parents who have lost a child to a fatal overdose. In April of 2017, in Atlanta, I met with about two dozen moms and dads gathered around a long table in a hotel boardroom. They took turns to tell me about their kids, how they first became involved with drugs, what they did to try to help them, and why it wasn't enough to save their son or daughter. Many tears flowed over the hour or so we spent together. What I took from these conversations was how much additional help should be available to support those in need, as well as an intensified sense of urgency for the country to save many more American families from this nightmare. While still in government, I did my best – I wish I could have done more. Now that I am out, I remember that time with the families, and I want to help carry their powerful message forward.

We absolutely can prevent the deaths of thousands more lives over the next decade, reduce the number of grieving families, and address addiction problems far earlier, when they are easier to resolve. This is not easy, but certainly is possible.

The research-based knowledge to effectively combat the opioid crisis already exists, but the country has yet to summon the will, resources, or compassion to do so. We have been fighting the drug war for a long time. We may wish we were done with drugs, but drugs are not done with us. It is time to directly take on the hard lessons from the past and restructure the War on Drugs across the board. Most importantly, as individuals and as a society, if we want to save the lives of people who are struggling with addiction, if we want them to seek and accept help, we have to offer them not shame, not stigma, not "tough love" but the real love they need and deserve.

The 12 HARD LESSONS FOR TODAY'S DRUG WAR (full list)

1. We must confront the two original sins of the Drug War—racism and stigma—to effectively combat today's crisis.
2. Drug policies and programs, built for the crack cocaine epidemic, must be overhauled for the opioid crisis.
3. Big Pharma's reckless marketing of opioids has severely and permanently worsened America's drug problem.
4. Restrictions on opioid painkillers were recklessly applied and led to many unnecessary drug overdose deaths.
5. Most chronic drug users will only voluntarily enter treatment via "harm-reduction-informed" approaches that support a gradual pursuit of recovery.
6. Treatment and justice system initiatives are not sufficient to solve the crisis; we also need a nationwide recovery support system.
7. Mass incarceration damages communities—to combat drugs, police must rebuild frayed relationships and adopt a much more targeted approach.
8. Police, courts, and jails can only reduce chronic drug use and overdoses through coordinated initiatives with health agencies.
9. Supply control is wickedly difficult—a disciplined focus is needed on the most dangerous drug threats.
10. We have vastly underfunded the drug crisis response and must invest wisely now, or we will pay much more later.
11. Youth face a terrifying risk of overdose—new prevention and early intervention programs are needed to protect them.
12. There is no easy button—the opioid crisis can only be solved by bringing innovative health and justice interventions to the millions of Americans who need them.

List of Recommendations and Proposed Budget to Fund Them

Recommendations	Funding
1. Establish an *Opioid Crisis Memorial Museum and Education Center* in Washington D.C.*	$100 million
2. Create a bipartisan *Congressional Committee on Drug Policy Reform* to modernize outdated laws.	-
3. Impose *a lifetime ban* on pharmaceutical employment for the few dozen top FDA officials responsible for drug approval.	$5m
4. Generate $10 billion via an *opioid crisis fee* on the pharmaceutical industry.	(+$10 billion)
5. Reform and rename prescription drug monitoring programs (PDMPs).*	100 million
6. Designate officials to produce *drug policy risk assessments* for major initiatives.	-
7. Study state drug policy changes before national implementation.	$100 million
8. Fund 1,000 *Engagement and Support Centers* for those with a substance use disorder.*	**$1.8 billion**
9. Hire 100,000 *recovery coaches and peer counselors.**	**$1 billion**
10. Conduct surveys of drug users and first responders to identify the most effective strategies for increasing voluntary entry into addiction treatment.	$50 million
11. Increase access to medications for addiction—including long-acting injectables—while investing in artificial intelligence and studying psychedelics.*	$100m
12. Build a recovery-friendly America in communities, colleges, and workplaces.*	$500 million
13. Increase the availability of recovery and supportive housing.*	**$2 billion**
14. Combat illicit drug sales without mass incarceration by carefully studying drug markets and targeting the most dangerous dealers for arrest.*	$500 million
15. Establish a *DEA Covert Drug Markets Division* to disrupt internet/social media drug sales.	$200 million

(*Continued*)

(Continued)

Recommendations	Funding
16. Sentence drug offenders based on their role in a trafficking organization, not the weight of the drugs.	-
17. Authorize limited expungement of felony drug convictions.*	$10 million
18. Restrict reckless marijuana marketing, educate youth about health risks of high-potency THC products and federally decriminalize marijuana possession.	$100 million
19. Bring police, health agencies, and NGOs together to support *deflection to treatment* as an alternative to arrest of chronic drug consumers.*	**$1 billion**
20. Create 500 *treatment first drug courts* to reduce overdoses of addicted drug offenders.*	$250 million
21. Establish 50 *Treatment Coordination Task Forces* through ONDCP in areas of greatest need.	$250 million
22. Reinforce DHS's ability to conduct complex drug cartel investigations.	$200 million
23. Target trafficker vulnerabilities through international financial sanctions.*	$50 million
24. Fund a ten-year bilateral anti-drug partnership with Mexico.	$500 million
25. Negotiate a new international drug treaty to more rapidly ban new synthetic drugs and chemicals used by traffickers.	-
26. Establish at ONDCP and for each state *Drug Policy Return on Investment Teams*.	$100 million
27. Build a real-time national drug data system, led by ONDCP, to track rapidly changing drug use trends.	$100 million
28. Establish a *National Center on Drug Policy Implementation Science* at ONDCP.	$25 million
29. Fund an intensive *Drug Policy Boot Camp* for new government appointees.	$10 million
30. Ensure that every student participates in a high-quality, evidence-based drug-prevention program.*	$400 million
31. Launch a national initiative to expand youth recreational opportunities in counties with the highest addiction rates.*	$350 million
32. Establish a *National Youth Anti-Drug Media Campaign* using cutting-edge, private-sector strategies.*	$200 million
TOTAL	**$10 billion**

* Recommendation includes establishment of an outside of government Center of Excellence

Notes

Introduction

1 "Drugs of Abuse—2022," DEA, December 2, 2022, https://www.dea.gov/documents/2022/2022-12/2022-12-02/drugs-abuse-2022.
2 Substance Abuse and Mental Health Services Administration, "Highlights for the 2024 National Survey on Drug Use and Health," Report, 2025.
3 For a definition of an opioid use disorder (OUD) see: https://www.psychiatry.org/patients-families/addiction/opioid-use-disorder/opioid-use-disorder. The Diagnostic and Statistical Manual of Mental Disorders, (DSM-5) describes OUD as a pattern of opioid use leading to problems or distress, where at least two of the following occurring within a twelve-month period: 1. Taking larger amounts or taking drugs over a longer period than intended. 2. Persistent desire or unsuccessful efforts to cut down or control opioid use. 3. Spending a great deal of time obtaining or using the opioid or recovering from its effects. 4. Craving, or a strong desire or urge to use opioids. 5. Problems fulfilling obligations at work, school or home. 6. Continued opioid use despite having recurring social or interpersonal problems. 7. Giving up or reducing activities because of opioid use. 8. Using opioids in physically hazardous situations such as driving while under the influence of opiates. 9. Continued opioid use despite ongoing physical or psychological problem likely to have been caused or worsened by opioids. 10. Tolerance (i.e., need for increased amounts or diminished effect with continued use of the same amount). 11. Experiencing withdrawal (opioid withdrawal syndrome) or taking opioids (or a closely related substance) to relieve or avoid withdrawal symptom. Other drug use disorders, or alcohol use disorders, are defined similarly with 11 factors. Those with two to three factors have a mild SUD, four to five moderate, six or more severe.

4 Chris Barber, "Public Enemy Number One: A Pragmatic Approach to America's Drug Problem," Richard Nixon Foundation, December 19, 2019, https://www.nixonfoundation.org/2016/06/26404/.
5 Heather McGhee, *The Sum of Us: What Racism Costs Everyone and How We Can Prosper Together* (Profile Books, 2021).
6 Merianne R. Spencer et al., "Drug Overdose Deaths in the United States, 2002–2022," *NCHS Data Brief*, February 2024, https://www.cdc.gov/nchs/data/databriefs/db491.pdf.
7 Shatterproof, Ipsos Public Affairs, and Indiana University, "Shatterproof Addiction Stigma Index Report," 2024, https://www.shatterproof.org/sites/default/files/2024-09/Final%20SASI%202024.pdf.
8 American Society of Addiction Medicine, "Definition of Addiction," *American Society of Addiction Medicine* (American Society of Addiction Medicine, 2019), https://www.asam.org/docs/default-source/quality-science/asam's-2019-definition-of-addiction-(1).pdf?sfvrsn=b8b64fc2_2.
9 Owen Flanagan, *What it is Like to be an Addict.* (Oxford University Press, 2025).
10 Gabor Maté and Daniel Maté, *The Myth of Normal: Trauma, Illness & Healing in a Toxic Culture* (Random House, 2022).
11 Ibid.
12 Douglas B. Marlowe, "Behavioral Responsivity: Toward Evidence-Based Practice Standards for Substance-Related Crime." *Ohio St. J. Crim. L.* 19 (2021): 351.
13 Fernando Montero, Philippe Bourgois, and Joseph Friedman, "Potency-Enhancing Synthetics in the Drug Overdose Epidemic: Xylazine ('Tranq'), Fentanyl, Methamphetamine, and the Displacement of Heroin in Philadelphia and Tijuana," *Journal of Illicit Economies and Development* 4, no. 2 (January 1, 2022): 204–22, https://doi.org/10.31389/jied.122.
14 Yutong Li et al., "Co-involvement of Stimulants With Opioids in North America: A 'silent Epidemic,'" *PLOS Mental Health.* 2, no. 7 (July 16, 2025): e0000319, https://doi.org/10.1371/journal.pmen.0000319.
15 Bridget M. Kuehn, "Fentanyl Drives Startling Increases in Adolescent Overdose Deaths," *JAMA* 329, no. 4 (January 24, 2023): 280, https://doi.org/10.1001/jama.2022.23563.
16 Chip Heath and Dan Heath, *Made to Stick: Why Some Ideas Survive and Others Die* (Random House, 2007).

17 Ibid.

18 Lena H. Sun and Scott Higham, "Trump Proposes Steep Cuts to White House 'Drug Czar' Office Amid Opioid Crisis," *The Washington Post*, May 24, 2023,https://www.washingtonpost.com/national/health-science/trump-proposes-steep-cuts-to-white-house-drug-czar-office-amid-opioid-crisis/2017/05/05/b666cd48-31bc-11e7-8674-437ddb6e813e_story.html.

19 Sam Mermin, Rebekah Falkner, and Katie Greene, "Understanding Opioid Settlement Spending Plans across States: Key Components and Approaches," NASHP, February 28, 2023, https://nashp.org/understanding-opioid-settlement-spending-plans-across-states-key-components-and-approaches/.

20 From $4.2 billion to $12.1 billion, see https://tracreports.org/tracdea/findings/national/drugbudn.html. By way of comparison, overall drug spending in the five years after the emergence of fentanyl, from 2014 to 2018, increased by 54 percent. See https://www.statista.com/statistics/618857/total-federal-drug-control-spending-in-us/.

21 Office of Disease Prevention and Health Promotion, "Incarceration —Healthy People 2030," September 6, 2022, https://health.gov/healthypeople/priority-areas/social-determinants-health/literature-summaries/incarceration.

22 Steven L Proctor and Philip L. Herschman. "The continuing care model of substance use treatment: What works, and when is 'enough,' 'enough?'" *Psychiatry journal* 2014, no. 1 (2014): 692423.

23 Carlo C. DiClemente, *Addiction and Change, Second Edition: How Addictions Develop and Addicted People Recover* (Guilford Press, 2017).

24 Richard G. Frank, "Medicaid Cuts Kick Down on People Caught in the Opioid Epidemic," Scientific American, March 18, 2025, https://www.scientificamerican.com/article/medicaid-cuts-kick-down-on-people-caught-in-the-opioid-epidemic/.

25 Natalie Kitroeff and Paulina Villegas, "Mexican Cartels Lure Chemistry Students to Make Fentanyl," *The New York Times*, December 1, 2024, https://www.nytimes.com/2024/12/01/world/americas/mexico-fentanyl-chemistry-students.html.

26 Raphael E. Cuomo. *Crave: The Hidden Biology of Addiction and.* (Independently published, June 10, 2025).

27 Jeffrey Foote et al., *Beyond Addiction: How Science and Kindness Help People Change* (Simon and Schuster, 2014).

Chapter 1

1 "The Power of the Poppy: Exploring Opium through 'The Wizard of Oz,'" National Museum of American History, n.d., https://americanhistory.si.edu/blog/opium-through-wizard-oz.
2 Hasan Pathan and John P. Williams, "Basic Opioid Pharmacology: An Update," *British Journal of Pain* 6, no. 1 (February 1, 2012): 11–16, https://doi.org/10.1177/2049463712438493.
3 DEA, "Drug Fact Sheet," April 2020, https://www.dea.gov/sites/default/files/2020-06/Narcotics-2020.pdf, accessed June 10, 2023.
4 "Mrs. Winslow's Soothing Syrup," DEA Museum, n.d., https://museum.dea.gov/museum-collection/collection-spotlight/artifact/soothing-syrup, accessed May 28, 2023.
5 Dan Lewis, "What Happened to the Cocaine In Coca-Cola?," *Business Insider*, February 27, 2012, https://www.businessinsider.com/what-happened-to-the-cocaine-in-coca-cola-2012-2.
6 Samuel Hopkins Adams, *The Great American Fraud* (1907). See The Great American Fraud (archive.org).
7 David Farber, *The War on Drugs: A History* (New York University Press, 2021), 24 ("The Advent of the War on Drugs").
8 "Drug Conventions," United Nations: Office on Drugs and Crime, n.d., Drug Conventions (unodc.org), accessed June 10, 2023. (See chapter 9 on why the current crisis requires a fourth Convention).
9 United Nations: Office on Drugs and Crime, "This Day in History: The Shanghai Opium Commission, 1909," n.d., https://www.unodc.org/unodc/en/frontpage/this-day-in-history-the-shanghai-opium-commission-1909.html, accessed June 10, 2023.
10 David F. Musto, *The American Disease: Origins of Narcotic Control* (Oxford University Press, 1999).
11 Ibid.
12 David T. Courtwright, "Preventing and Treating Narcotic Addiction—A Century of Federal Drug Control," *The New England Journal of Medicine* 373, no. 22 (November 26, 2015): 2095–7, https://doi.org/10.1056/nejmp1508818.
13 Ibid.
14 In the 21st century, most countries have adopted more balanced drug policies and have brought discussions of drug demand reduction issues into the United Nations in a variety of forums.

15 Nancy Campbell, J. P. Olsen, and Luke Walden, *The Narcotic Farm: The Rise and Fall of America's First Prison for Drug Addicts* (2008), https://openlibrary.org/books/OL29525090M/Narcotic_Farm.
16 "The Twelve Steps," Alcoholics Anonymous, n.d., https://www.aa.org/the-twelve-steps.
17 "Records of the Drug Enforcement Administration [DEA]," October 12, 2016, https://www.archives.gov/research/guide-fed-records/groups/170.html, accessed June 11, 2023. The early history of the federal office responsible for narcotics under the Harrison Act reflects a series of bureaucratic changes.
18 Alexandra Chasin, *Assassin of Youth: A Kaleidoscopic History of Harry J. Anslinger's War on Drugs* (University of Chicago Press, 2016).
19 Matthew R. Pembleton, *Containing Addiction: The Federal Bureau of Narcotics and the Origins of America's Global Drug War* (Emerald Group Publishing Limited, 2017).
20 Ibid., 6.
21 US Census Bureau, "1930 Census: Volume 2. Population, General Report, Statistics by Subjects," Census.gov, October 8, 2021, https://www.census.gov/library/publications/1933/dec/1930a-vol-02-population.html, accessed November 26, 2023.
22 Pembleton, *Containing Addiction*, 45.
23 Hash Marihuana & Hemp Museum, "Assassin of Youth," February 6, 2023, https://hashmuseum.com/en/collection/reefer-madness/assassin-of-youth/.
24 An audio recording of the song can be found here: https://www.youtube.com/watch?v=Web007rzSOI.
25 See https://chasingthescream.com/.
26 See https://www.imdb.com/title/tt8521718/.
27 Johann Hari, "The Hunting of Billie Holiday," *POLITICO Magazine*, January 17, 2015, https://www.politico.com/magazine/story/2015/01/drug-war-the-hunting-of-billie-holiday-114298/, accessed June 11, 2023.
28 Farber, *The War on Drugs*, 25.
29 Ibid.
30 Pembleton, *Containing Addiction*, 59.
31 Beverly Gage, *G-Man: J. Edgar Hoover and the Making of the American Century* (Simon and Schuster, 2023).
32 Laura Mansnerus, "Timothy Leary, Pied Piper of Psychedelic 60's, Dies at 75," *The New York Times*, June 1, 1996, https://www.nytimes.com

/1996/06/01/us/timothy-leary-pied-piper-of-psychedelic-60-s-dies-at -75.html.

33 Julia Naftulin, "Kacey Musgraves Says She Was on LSD Listening to Bach When She Came Up with the Idea for her New Album 'Star-Crossed,'" *Business Insider*, September 9, 2021, https://www .businessinsider.com/kacey-musgraves-listening-to-bach-on-lsd -inspired-star-crossed-2021-9.

34 Psychedelic.Support, "10 Celebrity Experiences with Psychedelics," June 8, 2023, https://psychedelic.support/resources/celebrity-experiences-with-psychedelics/.

35 Rich Tenorio, "How the Sackler Family Built a Pharma Dynasty and Fueled an American Calamity," *The Times of Israel*, July 5, 2021, https:// www.timesofisrael.com/how-the-sackler-family-built-a-pharma -dynasty-and-fueled-an-american-calamity/, accessed November 26, 2023.

36 Gary Woods, "Mother's Little Helper," *The British Journal of Psychiatry* 208, no. 6 (June 1, 2016): 555, https://doi.org/10.1192/bjp.bp.115 .177295.

37 Mical Raz, "Treating Addiction or Reducing Crime? Methadone Maintenance and Drug Policy under the Nixon Administration," *Journal of Policy History* 29, no. 1 (December 15, 2016): 58–86, https://doi.org /10.1017/s089803061600035x.

38 Robert L. DuPont and Richard N. Katon, "Development of a Heroin-Addiction Treatment Program. Effect on Urban Crime," *PubMed* 216, no. 8 (May 24, 1971): 1320–4, https://pubmed.ncbi.nlm.nih.gov /5108449, accessed June 18, 2023.

39 Raz, "Treating Addiction or Reducing Crime?"

40 "Remarks About an Intensified Program for Drug Abuse Prevention and Control," The American Presidency Project, n.d., https://www .presidency.ucsb.edu/documents/remarks-about-intensified-program -for-drug-abuse-prevention-and-control.

41 Ibid.

42 Ibid.

43 Ibid.

44 Michael Massing, "Nixon Had It Right," *Washington Post*, November 8, 1998, https://www.washingtonpost.com/archive/opinions/1998/11/08/ nixon-had-it-right/357a87d4-2c96-428f-8698-fae0f749be13/, accessed June 18, 2023.

45 Dan Baum, *Smoke and Mirrors: The War on Drugs and the Politics of Failure* (Boston: Little, Brown, 1996).

46 "Document—Richard Nixon, 'What Has Happened to America?' Reader's Digest (October 1967)—American Horizons 3E Dashboard Resources—Learning Link," accessed June 18, 2023.

47 Dan Baum, "Legalize It All," *Harper's Magazine*, March 31, 2016, https://harpers.org/archive/2016/04/legalize-it-all/.

48 I had dinner with Jaffe and a long discussion about Nixon era drug policy on April 9, 2017.

49 Email from author from Robert Dupont, received June 12, 2023.

50 Kathleen Crapanzano et al., "The Association between Perceived Stigma and Substance Use Disorder Treatment Outcomes: A Review," *Substance Abuse and Rehabilitation* 10 (December 1, 2018): 1–12, https://doi.org/10.2147/sar.s183252.

51 Emma E. McGinty and Colleen L. Barry, "Stigma Reduction to Combat the Addiction Crisis—Developing an Evidence Base," *The New England Journal of Medicine* 382, no. 14 (April 2, 2020): 1291–2, https://doi.org/10.1056/nejmp2000227.

52 Ibid.

53 Kara Thieleman, Joanne Cacciatore, and Allen Frances, "Rates of Prolonged Grief Disorder: Considering Relationship to the Person Who Died and Cause of Death," *Journal of Affective Disorders* 339 (October 1, 2023): 832–7, https://doi.org/10.1016/j.jad.2023.07.094.

Chapter 2

1 "Inaugural Address," March 14, 2003, https://georgewbush-whitehouse.archives.gov/news/inaugural-address.html.

2 David Farber, *Crack: Rock Cocaine, Street Capitalism, and the Decade of Greed* (Cambridge University Press, 2022), 17.

3 Dylan Love, "Meet The Science and Tech Geniuses Who Got High and Solved Amazing Problems," *Business Insider*, August 22, 2013, https://www.businessinsider.com/scientists-and-geniuses-who-used-drugs-2013-8#thomas-edison-cocaine-6.

4 Farber, *Crack*, 48.

5 Domestic Council (US) Drug Abuse Task Force, *White Paper on Drug Abuse: A Report to the President*, US Government Printing Office, 1975, accessed June 19, 2023 at Google books.

6 Michael Hedges, "'Benign' Drug of the '70s Is a Scourge in the '90s," *Deseret News*, June 29, 2019, https://www.deseret.com/1999/8/24

/19462324/benign-drug-of-the-70s-is-a-scourge-in-the-90s, accessed July 7, 2023.

7 Thomas Conner, "Ex Writes About Life with Fleetwood Mac, the Guitarist's Physical Abuse and All That Cocaine," September 30, 2007, https://www.thomasconner.info/clips/ex-writes-about-life-with-fleetwood-mac-the-guitarists-physical-abuse-and-all-that-cocaine.

8 Michael Demarest, "Cocaine: Middle Class High," *TIME*, July 6, 1981, https://content.time.com/time/magazine/article/0,9171,922619,00.html, accessed June 18, 2023.

9 Ibid.

10 See "Burnin' Up" - Richard Pryor - YouTube.

11 Farber, *Crack*, 57.

12 Ibid., 62.

13 Roland G. Fryer et al., "Measuring Crack Cocaine and Its Impact," *Economic Inquiry* 51, no. 3 (January 2, 2013): 1651–81, https://doi.org/10.1111/j.1465-7295.2012.00506.x.

14 "Remarks in New Orleans, Louisiana, at the Annual Meeting of the International Association of Chiefs of Police," The American Presidency Project, n.d., https://www.presidency.ucsb.edu/documents/remarks-new-orleans-louisiana-the-annual-meeting-the-international-association-chiefs.

15 Michael Isikoff, "Drugs Top Problem in U.S., Poll Finds," *The Washington Post*, August 15, 1989.

16 Peter H. Reuter and Patricia A. Ebener, "Cocaine: The First Decade," *RAND Issue Paper* 6000 (1999).

17 John W. Kingdon and Eric Stano, *Agendas, Alternatives, and Public Policies*, vol. 45 (Boston: Little, Brown, 1984).

18 Peter Kerr, "Anatomy of the Drug Issue: How, After Years, It Erupted," *The New York Times*, November 17, 1986, https://www.nytimes.com/1986/11/17/us/anatomy-of-the-drug-issue-how-after-years-it-erupted.html, accessed June 19, 2023.

19 Dan Baum, *Smoke and Mirrors: The War on Drugs and the Politics of Failure* (Little, Brown, 1996).

20 Elise Viebeck, "How an Early Biden Crime Bill Created the Sentencing Disparity for Crack and Cocaine Trafficking," *Washington Post*, July 29, 2019, https://www.washingtonpost.com/politics/how-an-early-biden-crime-bill-created-the-sentencing-disparity-for-crack-and-cocaine-trafficking/2019/07/28/5cbb4c98-9dcf-11e9-85d6-5211733f92c7_story.html.

21 Farber, *The War on Drugs: A History*, 54.

22 Office of Justice Programs, Drug Control: Highlights of P.L. 99-570, Anti-Drug Abuse Act of 1986, n.d., https://www.ojp.gov/media/document/56996, accessed July 18, 2023. This summary is drawn from the CRS summary of the law.

23 Jonathan Easley, "The Day the Drug War Really Started," *Salon*, June 19, 2011, https://www.salon.com/2011/06/19/len_bias_cocaine_tragedy_still_affecting_us_drug_law, accessed July 9, 2023.

24 The Sentencing Project, "50 Years and a Wake Up—The Sentencing Project," October 12, 2023, https://www.sentencingproject.org/advocacy/50-years-and-a-wake-up-ending-the-mass-incarceration-crisis-in-america/, accessed July 9, 2023.

25 Farber, *The War on Drugs: A History*, chapter by Peter C. Pihos, "The Local War on Drugs."

26 David T. Courtwright, *Dark Paradise* (Harvard University Press, 2009).

27 Elayne E. Greenberg, "Unshackling Plea Bargaining from Racial Bias," *Social Science Research Network*, January 1, 2020, https//doi.org/10.2139ssrn.3634786.

28 Philip J. Levchak, "Stop-and-Frisk in New York City: Estimating Racial Disparities in Post-Stop Outcomes," *Journal of Criminal Justice* 73 (March 1, 2021): 101784, https://doi.org/10.1016/j.jcrimjus.2021.101784.

29 New York Civil Liberties Union, "Stop-and-Frisk Data," July 26, 2023, https://www.nyclu.org/en/stop-and-frisk-data.

30 New York City Police Department, "Crime Stats—Historical," n.d., https://www.nyc.gov/site/nypd/stats/crime-statistics/historical.page.

31 Michael Massing, *The Fix* (University of California Press, 2000).

32 Jeff Leen, "Gary Webb Was No Journalism Hero, Despite What 'Kill the Messenger' Says," *Washington Post*, April 16, 2023, https://www.washingtonpost.com/opinions/gary-webb-was-no-journalism-hero-despite-what-kill-the-messenger-says/2014/10/17/026b7560-53c9-11e4-809b-8cc0a295c773_story.html.

33 Susan Okie, "The Epidemic that Wasn't," *The New York Times*, January 26, 2009, https://www.nytimes.com/2009/01/27/health/27coca.html.

34 John J. DiIulio Jr., "The Coming of the Super-Predators," The Weekly Standard, January 20, 1996, https://www.washingtonexaminer.com/weekly-standard/the-coming-of-the-super-predators.

35 Elizabeth Becker, "As Ex-Theorist on Young 'Superpredators,' Bush Aide Has Regrets," *The New York Times*, February 9, 2001, https://www.nytimes.com/2001/02/09/us/as-ex-theorist-on-young-superpredators-bush-aide-has-regrets.html.

36 Farber, *Crack*, 229.

37 Collateral Consequences Inventory | National Inventory of Collateral Consequences of Criminal Conviction (nationalreentryresourcecent er.org). This database shows both federal and state-specific collateral consequences.

Chapter 3

1 Patrick Radden Keefe, *Empire of Pain: The Secret History of the Sackler Dynasty* (New York: Anchor Books, 2022).
2 Jane Porter and Hershel Jick, "Addiction Rare in Patients Treated with Narcotics," *The New England Journal of Medicine* 302, no. 2 (January 10, 1980): 123, https://doi.org/10.1056/nejm198001103020221, accessed October 22, 2022.
3 Russell K. Portenoy and Kathleen M. Foley, "Chronic Use of Opioid Analgesics in Non-malignant Pain: Report of 38 Cases," *Pain* 25, Issue 2 (1986): 171–86, ISSN 0304-3959, https://doi.org/10.1016/0304-3959(86)90091-6, https://www.sciencedirect.com/science/article/pii/0304395986900916, accessed October 22, 2022.
4 PharmaNewsIntelligence, "Understanding US Food and Drug Administration (FDA) Approval Processes," April 20, 2022, https://pharmanewsintel.com/features/understanding-us-food-and-drug-administration-fda-approval-processes.
5 Keefe, *Empire of Pain*, 225.
6 https://twitter.com/benjamin_rubin/status/1462971152939335684.
7 Harriet Ryan, Lisa Girion, and Scott Glover, "'You Want a Description of Hell?' OxyContin's 12-Hour Problem," Los Angeles Times, May 5, 2016, https://www.latimes.com/projects/oxycontin-part1/, accessed March 11, 2023.
8 Suzanne K. Vosburg et al., "Assessment of a Formulation Designed to Be Crush-Resistant in Prescription Opioid Abusers," *Drug and Alcohol Dependence* 126, no. 1–2 (November 1, 2012): 206–15, https://doi.org/10.1016/j.drugalcdep.2012.05.013.
9 James P. Orlowski and Leon Wateska, "The Effect of Pharmaceutical Firm Enticements on Physician Prescribing Patterns. There's No Such Thing as a Free Lunch," *Chest* 102, no. 1 (1992): 270–3.
10 Jonathan Marks, "Lessons from Corporate Influence in the Opioid Epidemic: Toward a Norm of Separation," *Journal of Bioethical Inquiry* 17, no. 2 (June 2020): 173–89. https://doi.org/10.1007/s11673-020

-09982-x. Epub 2020 Jul 13. PMID: 32661741; PMCID: PMC7357445. https://www.ncbi.nlm.nih.gov/pmc/articles/PMC7357445/, accessed October 23, 2022.

11 See links to three episodes and the database of materials posted at https://www.judgeforyourselves.com/info/.

12 Art Van Zee, "The Promotion and Marketing of OxyContin: Commercial Triumph, Public Health Tragedy," *American Journal of Public Health* 99, no. 2 (2009): 221–7.

13 Keefe, *Empire of Pain*, 237–8.

14 Mike Mariani, "How the American Opiate Epidemic Was Started by One Pharmaceutical Company," *The Week*, March 4, 2015, https://theweek.com/articles/541526/how-american-opiate-epidemic-started-by-one-pharmaceutical-company.

15 Keefe, *Empire of Pain*.

16 Malcolm Gladwell, *Revenge of the Tipping Point: Overstories, Superspreaders, and the Rise of Social Engineering* (Hachette UK, 2024).

17 Chris Hamby, "Giant Companies Took Secret Payments to Allow Free Flow of Opioids." *The New York* Times, December 17, https://www.nytimes.com/2024/12/17/business/pharmacy-benefit-managers-opioids.html.

18 Jonathan Marks, "Lessons from Corporate Influence in the Opioid Epidemic: Toward a Norm of Separation," *Journal of Bioethical Inquiry* 17 (2020): 173–89.

19 Douglas Farrago, "Maybe the Opioid Crisis Wasn't Our Fault? Duh," *Authentic Medicine*, October 6, 2021, https://authenticmedicine.com/2021/10/maybe-the-opioid-crisis-wasnt-our-fault-duh/, accessed October 23, 2022.

20 Kristina Fiore, "Opioid Crisis: Scrap Pain as 5th Vital Sign?" *MedPage Today*, April 19, 2016, https://www.medpagetoday.com/publichealthpolicy/publichealth/57336, accessed October 23, 2022.

21 "White House Office of National Drug Control Policy (ONDCP) Announces Record Reduction in Poppy Cultivation and Potential Heroin Production in Mexico," The White House, July 31, 2020, https://trumpwhitehouse.archives.gov/briefings-statements/ondcp-announces-record-reduction-poppy-cultivation-potential-heroin-production-mexico/.

22 Gardiner Harris, *No More Tears: The Dark Secrets of Johnson & Johnson.* (Random House, 2025).

23 O. Hayden Griffin and Bryan Lee Miller, "OxyContin and a Regulation Deficiency of the Pharmaceutical Industry: Rethinking State-Corporate Crime," *Critical Criminology* 19, no. 3 (September 17, 2010): 213–26, https://doi.org/10.1007/s10612-010-9113-9.

24 Substance Abuse and Mental Health Services Administration, *Key Substance Use and Mental Health Indicators in the United States: Results from the 2024 National Survey on Drug Use and Health*, https://www.samhsa.gov/data/data-we-collect/nsduh-national-survey-drug-use-and-health/national-releases.

25 Ibid.

26 "How Big Is the U.S. Pharmaceutical Industry?," December 6, 2022, https://www.zippia.com/answers/how-big-is-the-us-pharmaceutical-industry/.

Chapter 4

1 Irving Lester Janis, *Groupthink: Psychological Studies of Policy Decisions and Fiascoes* (Cengage Learning, 1983).

2 Jane E. Brody, "The Hidden Drug Epidemic among Older People," *The New York Times*, December 17, 2019, https://www.nytimes.com/2019/12/16/well/live/the-hidden-drug-epidemic-among-older-people.html.

3 Marilyn Bulloch, "The Evolution of the PDMP," *Pharmacy Times*, March 5, 2021, https://www.pharmacytimes.com/view/the-evolution-of-the-pdmp.

4 Julia Dickson-Gómez et al., "Effects of Implementation and Enforcement Differences in Prescription Drug Monitoring Programs in 3 States: Connecticut, Kentucky, and Wisconsin," *Substance Abuse: Research and Treatment* 15 (January 1, 2021): 117822182199234, https://doi.org/10.1177/1178221821992349.

5 Andrew Joseph, "'A Blizzard of Prescriptions': Documents Reveal New Details about Purdue's Marketing of OxyContin," *STAT*, July 25, 2023, https://www.statnews.com/2019/01/15/massachusetts-purdue-lawsuit-new-details/, accessed October 21, 2022.

6 Katherine Ellen Foley, "Big Pharma Is Taking Advantage of Patent Law to Keep OxyContin from Ever Dying," *Quartz*, July 20, 2022, https://qz.com/1125690/big-pharma-is-taking-advantage-of-patent-law-to-keep-oxycontin-from-ever-dying, accessed November 6, 2022.

7 William N. Evans, Ethan M. J. Lieber, and Patrick Power, "How the Reformulation of OxyContin Ignited the Heroin Epidemic," *The Review of Economics and Statistics* 101, no. 1 (March 1, 2019): 1–15, https://doi.org/10.1162/rest_a_00755, accessed November 6, 2022.

8 David Powell, Abby Alpert, and Rosalie Liccardo Pacula, "A Transitioning Epidemic: How the Opioid Crisis Is Driving the Rise in Hepatitis C," *Health Affairs* 38, no. 2 (February 1, 2019): 287–94, https://doi.org/10.1377/hlthaff.2018.05232, accessed October 23, 2022.

9 Anuj Shah et al., "Characteristics of Initial Prescription Episodes and Likelihood of Long-Term Opioid Use—United States, 2006–2015," *MMWR Morbidity and Mortality Weekly Report* 66, no. 10 (2017): 265–9, https://doi.org/10.15585/mmwr.mm6610a1.

10 Charles Lebaron, *Greed to Do Good: The Untold Story of CDC's Disastrous War on Opioids: A CDC Physician's Personal Account* (Amplify Publishing, 2024).

11 Terry Spencer, "Florida 'Pill Mills' Were 'Gas on Fire' of Opioid Crisis," *AP News*, July 20, 2019, https://apnews.com/article/west-virginia-fires-health-wv-state-wire-us-news-0ced46b203864d8fa6b8fda6bd97b60e, accessed October 15, 2022.

12 Michael J. Mooney, "Are There Really More Pain Clinics in Broward than McDonald's?" *New Times Broward-Palm Beach*, March 2, 2010, https://www.browardpalmbeach.com/news/are-there-really-more-pain-clinics-in-broward-than-mcdonalds-6451705.

13 Later, there were some efforts to organize better health care in the aftermath of a pill mill shutdown. The Center for Disease Control and Prevention's Opioid Rapid Response Program piloted in 2018 and then expanded. For more information see https://www.cdc.gov/overdose-prevention/orrp/index.html.

14 Julia Dickson-Gómez et al., "The Effects of Opioid Policy Changes on Transitions from Prescription Opioids to Heroin, Fentanyl and Injection Drug Use: A Qualitative Analysis," *Substance Abuse Treatment, Prevention, and Policy* 17, no. 1 (July 21, 2022), https://doi.org/10.1186/s13011-022-00480-4, accessed October 17, 2022.

15 Simone Balestra et al., "Behavioral Responses to Supply-Side Drug Policy during the Opioid Epidemic," NBER Working Paper No. 29596, December 1, 2021, https://doi.org/10.3386/w29596, accessed October 15, 2022.

16 "Prescription Opioid Use Is a Risk Factor for Heroin Use," National Institute on Drug Abuse, February 25, 2022, https://nida.nih.gov/publications/research-reports/prescription-opioids-heroin/prescription-opioid-use-risk-factor-heroin-use, accessed November 11, 2022.

17 Bipartisan Policy Center, *Tracking Federal Funding to Combat the Opioid Crisis*, 2019, https://bipartisanpolicy.org/download/?file=/wp-content/uploads/2019/03/Tracking-Federal-Funding-to-Combat-the-Opioid-Crisis.pdf.
18 Bradley A. Blakeman, "States are the Laboratory of Democracy," *The Hill*, May 7, 2020, https://thehill.com/opinion/judiciary/496524-states-are-the-laboratories-of-democracy/, accessed October 21, 2022.

Chapter 5

1 Anand Giridharadas, *The Persuaders: At the Front Lines of the Fight for Hearts, Minds, and Democracy* (Vintage, 2022).
2 Substance Abuse and Mental Health Services Administration (SAMHSA), "Advisory: Low Barrier Models of Care for Substance Use Disorders," November 2023, https://store.samhsa.gov/sites/default/files/advisory-low-barrier-models-of-care-pep23-02-00-005.pdf.
3 Colleen L. Barry et al., "Estimating Demand for Primary Care-based Treatment for Substance and Alcohol Use Disorders," *Addiction* 111, no. 8 (May 15, 2016): 1376–84, https://doi.org/10.1111/add.13364.
4 Pia M. Mauro et al., "Use of Medication for Opioid Use Disorder among US Adolescents and Adults with Need for Opioid Treatment, 2019," *JAMA Network Open* 5, no. 3 (March 23, 2022): e223821, https://doi.org/10.1001/jamanetworkopen.2022.3821.
5 Andrew Tatarsky, *Harm Reduction Psychotherapy: A New Treatment for Drug and Alcohol Problems* (Jason Aronson, 2007), 185.
6 Gabor Mate and Daniel Mate, *The Myth of Normal: Trauma, Illness & Healing in a Toxic Culture* (Random House, 2022).
7 Centers for Disease Control and Prevention, *Preventing Adverse Childhood Experiences: Leveraging the Best Available Evidence* (Atlanta: National Center for Injury Prevention and Control, Centers for Disease Control and Prevention, 2019), https://www.cdc.gov/violenceprevention/pdf/preventingACES.pdf.
8 Sally Satel, "'What Is It Like to Be an Addict?' Review: The Danger of a Safe Feeling," *The Wall Street Journal*, April 29, 2025, https://www.aei.org/op-eds/what-is-it-like-to-be-an-addict-review-the-danger-of-a-safe-feeling/.

9 This section relies on the generous input and advice from Steve Hanson, the former Associate Commissioner of the New York State Office of Alcoholism and Substance Abuse Services.

10 Lucinda A. Grande, Dave Cundiff, Mark K. Greenwald, MaryAnne Murray, Tricia E. Wright, and Stephen A. Martin. "Evidence on Buprenorphine Dose Limits: A Review," *Journal of Addiction Medicine* 17, no. 5 (2023): 509-16.

11 Shoshana Walter, "It Was a Promising Addiction Treatment. Many Patients Never Got It.," *The New York Times*, August 7, 2025, https://www.nytimes.com/2025/08/07/magazine/suboxone-buprenorphine-opioid-addiction-drugs.html.

12 Shoshana Walter, *Rehab: An American Scandal* (Simon and Schuster, 2025).

13 Alicia Ault, "Praise for Final Methadone, Buprenorphine Rule," *Medscape*, February 8, 2024, https://www.medscape.com/viewarticle/praise-final-methadone-buprenorphine-rule-2024a10002un?icd=login_success_email_match_fpf.

14 Lindsey R. Hammerslag et al., "Telemedicine Buprenorphine Initiation and Retention in Opioid Use Disorder Treatment for Medicaid Enrollees," *JAMA Network Open* 6, no. 10 (October 18, 2023): e2336914, https://doi.org/10.1001/jamanetworkopen.2023.36914.

15 R. Kathryn McHugh, Bridget A. Hearon, and Michael W. Otto, "Cognitive Behavioral Therapy for Substance Use Disorders," *Psychiatric Clinics of North America* 33, no. 3 (September 1, 2010): 511–25, https://doi.org/10.1016/j.psc.2010.04.012.

16 Soumya Karlamangla, "California Tries Paying Drug Users to Stay," *The New York Times*, August 29, 2023, https://www.nytimes.com/2023/08/29/us/california-drug-program-gift-cards.html, accessed November 29, 2023.

17 Addiction Policy Forum, "National Organizations Urge the White House to Lift the Contingency Management Funding Cap," December 19, 2024, https://www.addictionpolicy.org/post/national-organizations-urge-the-white-house-to-lift-the-contingency-management-funding-cap.

18 Stephanie Souza, "SAMHSA Updates Guidelines for Contingency Management: Maximum Incentives Increased to $750," American Academy of Addiction Psychiatry, January 10, 2025, https://www.aaap.org/samhsa-updates-guidelines-for-contingency-management-maximum-incentives-increased-to-750/.

19 The acronym stands for Self-Management and Recovery Training, see Patt Denning and Jeannie Little, *Over the Influence, Second Edition: The Harm Reduction Guide to Controlling Your Drug and Alcohol Use* (Guilford Publications, 2017).
20 Janet Zwick, Hannah Appleseth, and Stephan Arndt, "Stigma: How it Affects the Substance Use Disorder Patient," *Substance Abuse Treatment, Prevention, and Policy* 15 (2020): 1–4.
21 Leonieke C. van Boekel et al., "Stigma among Health Professionals towards Patients with Substance Use Disorders and Its Consequences for Healthcare Delivery: Systematic Review," *Drug and Alcohol Dependence* 131, no. 1–2 (July 1, 2013): 23–35, https://doi.org/10.1016/j.drugalcdep.2013.02.018.
22 Valerie A. Earnshaw, "Stigma and Substance Use Disorders: A Clinical, Research, and Advocacy Agenda," *American Psychologist* 75, no. 9 (December 1, 2020): 1300–11, https://doi.org/10.1037/amp0000744.
23 Jennifer Murphy and Brenda L. Russell, "Stigma Reduction through Addiction and Naloxone Education," *Journal of Criminal Justice Education* 34, no. 2 (May 9, 2022): 185–98, https://doi.org/10.1080/10511253.2022.2068632.
24 Tatarsky, *Harm Reduction Psychotherapy*.
25 Ibid., 342.
26 Jerome Adams, "Making the Case for Syringe Services Programs," *Public Health Reports* 135, no. 1_suppl (July 1, 2020): 10S–12S, https://doi.org/10.1177/0033354920936233.
27 Marcelo Fernandez-Vina et al., "State Laws Governing Syringe Services Programs and Participant Syringe Possession, 2014—2019," *Public Health Reports* 135, no. 1_suppl (July 1, 2020): 128S–137S, https://doi.org/10.1177/0033354920921817.
28 Taeko Frost et al., "'We'll Be Able to Take Care of Ourselves'—A Qualitative Study of Client Attitudes toward Implementing Buprenorphine Treatment at Syringe Services Programs," *Substance Abuse* 42, no. 4 (October 1, 2021): 983–9, https://doi.org/10.1080/08897077.2021.1901173.
29 Andrea Jakubowski et al., "Implementation of Buprenorphine Services in NYC Syringe Services Programs: A Qualitative Process Evaluation," *Harm Reduction Journal* 19, no. 1 (July 10, 2022), https://doi.org/10.1186/s12954-022-00654-0.
30 Shashi N. Kapadia et al., "A Harm Reduction Approach to Treating Opioid Use Disorder in an Independent Primary Care Practice: A Qualitative Study," *Journal of General Internal Medicine* 36, no. 7

(January 19, 2021): 1898–905, https://doi.org/10.1007/s11606-020-06409-6.

31 Sheila P. Vakharia, *The Harm Reduction Gap: Helping Individuals Left Behind by Conventional Drug Prevention and Abstinence-only Addiction Treatment* (Taylor & Francis, 2024).

32 Richard G. Frank, "Medicaid Cuts Kick Down on People Caught in the Opioid Epidemic," *Scientific American*, March 18, 2025, https://www.scientificamerican.com/article/medicaid-cuts-kick-down-on-people-caught-in-the-opioid-epidemic/.

33 Community Catalyst, "Peers Speak Out: Priority Outcomes for Substance Use Treatment and Services," February 27, 2023, https://communitycatalyst.org/resource/peers-speak-out/.

34 "Core Competencies for Peer Workers," SAMHSA, October 3, 2023, https://www.samhsa.gov/brss-tacs/recovery-support-tools/peers/core-competencies-peer-workers.

35 Damon Centola, *Change: How to Make Big Things Happen* (Little, Brown Spark, 2021).

36 Nils Gesser, Archana Bodas LaPollo, Alexander J. Peters, Doris Weiland, Steven Belenko, and Lauren Perron, "To Be Part of the Fully Functional Team, There Need to Be Clear Roles," *Journal for Advancing Justice* IV (2022): 23–52.

37 Melanie Whitter and Jose Silva, "The Substance Use Workforce Crisis: Drivers, Challenges, and Promising Strategies," NASADAD, April 2025, https://nasadad.org/wp-content/uploads/2025/04/The-Substance-Use-Workforce-Crisis-Drivers-Challenges-and-Promising-Strategies_POST-2.pdf.

38 Jessica Taylor et al., "Substance Use Disorder Bridge Clinics: Models, Evidence, and Future Directions," *Addiction Science & Clinical Practice* 18, no. 1 (April 14, 2023), https://doi.org/10.1186/s13722-023-00365-2.

39 Patrick J. Kennedy and Stephen Fried, *Profiles in Mental Health Courage* (Penguin, 2024).

40 Brent Gibson et al., *A Baseline Report on the Operation of the First Recognized Overdose Prevention Centers in the United States* (OnPoint NYC, 2023), https://onpointnyc.org/wp-content/uploads/2023/12/ONPOINTNYC_OPCREPORT_small-web1.pdf, accessed December 16, 2023.

41 Matthew Choi, "Crenshaw's Psychedelic PTSD Treatment Bill Passes," *The Texas Tribune*, February 6, 2024, https://www.texastribune.org/2023/12/14/ndaa-congress-psychedelics-ptsd-dan-crenshaw/.

42 Fúlvio Rieli Mendes et al., "Classic and Non-classic Psychedelics for Substance Use Disorder: A Review of Their Historic, Past and Current Research," *Addiction Neuroscience* 3 (September 1, 2022): 100025, https://doi.org/10.1016/j.addicn.2022.100025.

43 Juliana Marino Maia et al., "Therapeutic Potential of Psychedelics: History, Advancements, and Unexplored Frontiers," *Progress in Neuro-Psychopharmacology and Biological Psychiatry* 131 (April 1, 2024): 110951, https://doi.org/10.1016/j.pnpbp.2024.110951.

44 Bessel A. van der Kolk et al., "Effects of MDMA-Assisted Therapy for PTSD on Self-Experience," *PLOS ONE* 19, no. 1 (January 10, 2024): e0295926, https://doi.org/10.1371/journal.pone.0295926.

45 Ibid.

46 Erin O'Brien, "FDA Accepts, Grants Priority Review of NDA for MDMA-Assisted Therapy for PTSD," *Psychiatric Times*, February 13, 2024, https://www.psychiatrictimes.com/view/fda-accepts-grants-priority-review-of-nda-for-mdma-assisted-therapy-for-ptsd.

47 Andrew Jacobs, "F.D.A. Declines to Approve MDMA Therapy, Seeking More Study," *The New York Times*, August 9, 2024, https://www.nytimes.com/2024/08/09/health/fda-mdma-ptsd-delay.html.

48 Will Stone, "As the FDA Evaluates Ecstasy Treatment for PTSD, Questions Mount About the Evidence," *NPR*, May 13, 2024, https://www.npr.org/sections/health-shots/2024/05/13/1250580932/ecstasy-mdma-ptsd-fda-approval.

49 Center for Drug Evaluation and Research, "FDA Alerts Health Care Professionals of Potential Risks Associated with Compounded Ketamine Nasal Spray," U.S. Food and Drug Administration, February 16, 2022, https://www.fda.gov/drugs/human-drug-compounding/fda-alerts-health-care-professionals-potential-risks-associated-compounded-ketamine-nasal-spray.

50 "Compounding FAQs," https://www.pharmacist.com/Practice/Patient-Care-Services/Compounding/, accessed March 24, 2024.

51 Center for Drug Evaluation and Research, "FDA Warns Patients and Health Care Providers About Potential Risks Associated with Compounded Ketamine Products, Including Oral Formulations, for the Treatment of Psychiatric Disorders," U.S. Food and Drug Administration, October 10, 2023, https://www.fda.gov/drugs/human-drug-compounding/fda-warns-patients-and-health-care-providers-about-potential-risks-associated-compounded-ketamine.

52 Josh Campbell, "Autopsy Shows Matthew Perry Died of 'Acute Effects of Ketamine,'" CNN.Com, December 16, 2023, https://www.cnn.com/2023/12/15/entertainment/matthew-perry-autopsy-report/index.html.
53 "Psilocybin (Magic Mushrooms)," National Institute on Drug Abuse, March 4, 2024, https://nida.nih.gov/research-topics/psilocybin-magic-mushrooms#what-is-psilocybin.
54 Robin J. Murphy, Suresh Muthukumaraswamy, and Harriet De Wit, "Microdosing Psychedelics: Current Evidence From Controlled Studies," *Biological Psychiatry: Cognitive Neuroscience and Neuroimaging*, January 1, 2024, https://doi.org/10.1016/j.bpsc.2024.01.002.
55 Shayla Love, "When Does a High Become a Trip?" *The Atlantic*, October 20, 2024, https://www.theatlantic.com/health/archive/2024/10/psychedelic-trip-high-hallucination-medicine/680314/.
56 Andrew Jacobs, "Texas OK's $50 Million for Ibogaine Research," *The New York Times*, June 14, 2025, https://www.nytimes.com/2025/06/14/health/texas-psychedelics-ibogaine-veterans.html.
57 Ernesto Londono, *TRIPPY: The Perils and Promise of Medicinal Psychedelics* (Celadon Books, 2024).
58 Benjamin Li et al., "Special Report: The Art of Treating Complex Substance Use Disorders," *Psychiatric News* 59, no. 8 (July 22, 2024), https://doi.org/10.1176/appi.pn.2024.08.8.33.
59 "Prospective Study of Masimo NSS-2 BRIDGE; as a Non-Pharmacological Treatment for Acute Opioid Withdrawal Symptoms," *Pain Management Nursing* 24, no. Issue 2 (April 2023): 238–9, https://doi.org/10.1016/j.pmn.2023.02.022.
60 "Smart Intervention: A Next-Gen IoT Device for Combatting Drug Addiction," IEEE Xplore Conference Publication, June 5, 2024.
61 Diana Emilia Martínez-Fernández et al., "The Effect of Eye Movement Desensitization and Reprocessing (EMDR) Therapy on Reducing Craving in Populations with Substance Use Disorder: A Meta-analysis," Research Square (Research Square), May 9, 2024, https://doi.org/10.21203/rs.3.rs-4391211/v1.
62 "Ray Kurzweil on How AI Will Transform the Physical World," *The Economist*, June 17, 2024, https://www.economist.com/by-invitation/2024/06/17/ray-kurzweil-on-how-ai-will-transform-the-physical-world.
63 Dario Amodei, "Dario Amodei—Machines of Loving Grace," October 1, 2024, https://darioamodei.com/machines-of-loving-grace.
64 Dong Chen et al., "Artificial Intelligence Approaches for Anti-Addiction Drug Discovery," *Digital Discovery*,January 1, 2025, https://doi.org/10.1039/d5dd00032g.

65 Ajayi Rhoda, "AI-Powered Innovations for Managing Complex Mental Health Conditions and Addiction Treatments," *International Research Journal of Modern Engineering and Technology Science* 7, no. 1 (2025): 87.

Chapter 6

1 Sarah King, "An Escalated Defense: Sheriff Karl Leonard Unveils SMART Program to Treat Inmates' Opioid Addiction," *Chesterfield Observer*, May 25, 2022, https://www.chesterfieldobserver.com/articles/an-escalated-defense-sheriff-karl-leonard-unveils-smart-program-to-treat-inmates-opioid-addiction/.

2 "Helping Addicts Recover Progressively (HARP)," Brandeis Opioid Resource Connector, https://opioid-resource-connector.org/index.php/program-model/helping-addicts-recover-progressively-harp#collapse-contentfield. Their analysis found 28.4 percent of HARP graduates were arrested, compared to 45.4 percent of non-graduates.

3 "Criminal Justice DrugFacts," National Institute on Drug Abuse, 2020, https://nida.nih.gov/publications/drugfacts/criminal-justice.

4 Shabbar I. Ranapurwala et al., "Opioid Overdose Mortality among Former North Carolina Inmates: 2000–2015," *American Journal of Public Health* 108, no. 9 (September 1, 2018): 1207–13, https://doi.org/10.2105/ajph.2018.304514.

5 David Eddie et al., "Reasons to Be Cheerful: Personal, Civic, and Economic Achievements after Resolving an Alcohol or Drug Problem in the United States Population," *Psychology of Addictive Behaviors* 35, no. 4 (June 1, 2021): 402–14, https://doi.org/10.1037/adb0000689.

6 "Medicaid's Role in Addressing Social Determinants of Health," RWJF, (February 1, 2019), https://www.rwjf.org/en/insights/our-research/2019/02/medicaid-s-role-in-addressing-social-determinants-of-health.html.

7 David Best and Emily A. Hennessy, "The Science of Recovery Capital: Where Do We Go From Here?," *Addiction* (Abingdon. Print) 117, no. 4 (December 1, 2021): 1139–45, https://doi.org/10.1111/add.15732.

8 Hinckley A. Jones-Sanpei, Debbie L. Humphries, and Richard J. Nance. "Financial Capability Building in the Treatment of Substance-Related and Addictive Disorders: A Co-Creation and Engagement Approach to Intervention Development." *Journal for Advancing Justice*: V 5, 2024.

9 Ernest Becker, *The Denial of Death* (Simon and Schuster, 2007).

10 Shelby Arnold et al. "Recovery-Oriented Cognitive Therapy: A Testable Framework to Promote Successful Long-Term Recovery From Substance Use Challenges for Justice-Involved Individuals." *Journal for Advancing Justice*: V 5, 2024.
11 Matthew Desmond, *Evicted: Poverty and Profit in the American City* (Penguin UK, 2016).
12 Jerusalem Demsas, "Community Input Is Bad, Actually," *The Atlantic*, April 22, 2022 https://www.theatlantic.com/ideas/archive/2022/04/community-input-bad-actually/629609.
13 Ezra Klein & Derek Thompson, D., *Abundance. (*Simon and Schuster, 2025).
14 "Examining Concerns of Patient Brokering and Addiction Treatment Fraud," Hearing Before the Subcommittee on Oversight and Investigations of the Committee on Energy and Commerce, House of Representatives, December 12, 2017, Serial No. 115–87. Written testimony of Dave Aronberg, 45, https://www.govinfo.gov/content/pkg/CHRG-115hhrg28931/pdf/CHRG-115hhrg28931.pdf.
15 Dave Aronberg, and David R. Campbell, *Fighting the Florida shuffle: The Inside Story of Corruption in the Drug Treatment Industry and How One Community Found the Solution* (Simon and Schuster, 2025).
16 Deborah Padgett, Benjamin Henwood, and Sam Tsemberis, *Housing First* (Oxford University Press, 2016), viii–ix. Kindle Edition.
17 Ibid.
18 Patricia O'Campo et al., "Health and Social Outcomes in the Housing First Model: Testing the Theory of Change," *EClinicalMedicine* 47 (May 1, 2022): 101387, https://doi.org/10.1016/j.eclinm.2022.101387.
19 Monique Gill, Kyle Jones, Ritu Ghosal, James M. Scanlan, and Emily J. Cox, "Housing and Reentry: A Mixed-Method Evaluation of a Low-Cost Community-Based Intervention for Increasing Access to Housing Post Incarceration," *Journal for Advancing Justice* IV (2022): 23–52.
20 See https://recoveryisgoodbusiness.com/why-hire-people-in-recovery/.
21 Tanya de Sousa and Meghan Henry, *The 2024 Annual Homelessness Assessment Report (AHAR) to Congress*, 2024. https://www.huduser.gov/portal/sites/default/files/pdf/2024-AHAR-Part-1.pdf.
22 Substance Abuse and Mental Health Services Administration, "Highlights for the 2024 National Survey on Drug Use and Health," Report, 2025.
23 See https://www.belden.com/hubfs/resources/other/belden_pathways-case-study-final.pdf?hsLang=en.

24 Fors Marsh, "2022 Workplace Substance Use Disorder Recovery Survey," October 12, 2023, https://www.forsmarsh.com/2023/03/23/2022-workplace-recovery-survey/.
25 Rachael M. Billock, Andrea L. Steege, and Arialdi M. Miniño, "Drug Overdose Mortality by Usual Occupation and Industry: 46 States and New York City, United States, 2020," August 22, 2023, https://doi.org/10.15620/cdc:128631.
26 Fors Marsh, *Workplace Recovery Survey 2025*, in *The Voice of Human Resources*, vol. 2 (2025), https://www.forsmarsh.com/wp-content/uploads/2025/04/Recovery-Friendly-Workplaces-Survey-2025.pdf.
27 CBHSQ Data, "2023 NSDUH Detailed Tables," July 2024, https://www.samhsa.gov/data/report/2023-nsduh-detailed-tables.
28 See https://recoveryschools.org/.
29 John Kelly et al., "New Kid on the Block: An Investigation of the Physical, Operational, Personnel, and Service Characteristics of Recovery Community Centers in the United States," *Journal of Substance Abuse Treatment* 111 (April 1, 2020): 1–10, https://doi.org/10.1016/j.jsat.2019.12.009.
30 Cenikor Foundation, "2024 Annual Report," Cenikor, September 25, 2024, https://www.cenikor.org/annual-report/.

Chapter 7

1 Marc Mauer and Tracy Huling, "Young Black Americans and the Criminal Justice System: Five Years Later," *Sentencing Project*, 1995.
2 The Sentencing Project, "50 Years and a Wake Up," October 12, 2023, https://www.sentencingproject.org/advocacy/50-years-and-a-wake-up-ending-the-mass-incarceration-crisis-in-america/.
3 The Andrew Goodman Foundation, "Historical Archives," Andrew Goodman Foundation, December 6, 2022, https://andrewgoodman.org/historical-archives/.
4 Michelle Alexander, *The New Jim Crow* (The New Press, 2012).
5 Mark Kleiman, *When Brute Force Fails: How to Have Less Crime and Less Punishment* (Princeton University Press, 2009).
6 Ryan Hampton, *Fentanyl Nation: Toxic Politics and America's Failed War on Drugs* (St. Martin's, 2024).

7 Council on Criminal Justice, *Task Force on Long Sentences: Final Report, Rec 7 —"How Long Is Long Enough*?" March 21, 2023, https://counciloncj.foleon.com/tfls/long-sentences-final-report/recommendation-7/.

8 Marta Nelson, Samuel Feineh, and Maris Mapolski, *A New Paradigm for Sentencing in the United States* (New York: Vera Institute of Justice, 2023).

9 John Pfaff, *Locked in: The True Causes of Mass Incarceration-and How to Achieve Real Reform* (Hachette UK, 2017).

10 NIDA, "Criminal Justice Drug Facts," National Institutes of Health, U.S. Department of Health and Human Services, accessed June 14, 2025, https://nida.nih.gov/publications/drugfacts/criminal-justice.

11 Reuben Jonathan Miller, *Halfway Home: Race, Punishment, and the Afterlife of Mass Incarceration* (New York: Little, Brown and Company, 2021).

12 Elayne E. Greenberg, "Unshackling Plea Bargaining from Racial Bias," *Journal of Criminal Law and Criminology* 111 (2021): 93.

13 Philip J. Levchak, "Stop-and-Frisk in New York City: Estimating Racial Disparities in Post-stop Outcomes," *Journal of Criminal Justice* 73 (2021): 101784.

14 New York Civil Liberties Union, "Stop-and-Frisk Data," July 26, 2023, https://www.nyclu.org/en/stop-and-frisk-data.

15 "Crime Stats - Historical," New York City Police Department, n.d., https://www.nyc.gov/site/nypd/stats/crime-statistics/historical.page.

16 Bailey Maryfield, "Implicit Racial Bias," *Justice Research and Statistics Association*, December 2018, https://jrsa-factsheet-implicit-racial-bias-libre.pdf, accessed December 2, 2023.

17 Kim Taylor-Thompson and Anthony C. Thompson, *Progressive Prosecution: Race and Reform in Criminal Justice* (New York University Press, 2022). From chapter by William C. Snowden, "Rethinking How Prosecutors Deal with Race and Implicit Bias." Ibid., 160–1.

18 Tali Sharot and Cass R. Sunstein, *Look Again: The Power of Noticing What Was Always There* (Simon and Schuster, 2024).

19 Congressional Research Service, "Offender Reentry: Correctional Statistics, Reintegration into the Community, and Recidivism," March 31, 2016, https://crsreports.congress.gov/product/pdf/RL/RL34287/25, accessed November 30, 2023.

20 Victoria Law, *Prisons Make Us Safer: And 20 Other Myths about Mass Incarceration* (Haymarket Books, 2021).

21 "Overdose Deaths and Jail Incarceration—National Trends and Racial Disparities," Vera Institute of Justice, January 26, 2021, https://www.vera.org/publications/overdose-deaths-and-jail-incarceration/national-trends-and-racial-disparities.

22 Shabbar I. Ranapurwala et al., "Opioid Overdose Mortality among Former North Carolina Inmates: 2000–2015," *American Journal of Public Health* 108, no. 9 (September 1, 2018): 1207–13, https://doi.org/10.2105/ajph.2018.304514.

23 Kleiman, *When Brute Force Fails*, 179.

24 Office of U.S. Senator Tammy Baldwin, "Senators Baldwin, Braun Introduce Bipartisan Reentry Act to Help Reduce Drug Overdoses," March 30, 2023, https://www.baldwin.senate.gov/news/press-releases/senators-baldwin-braun-introduce-bipartisan-reentry-act-to-help-reduce-drug-overdoses.

25 Centers for Medicare & Medicaid Services, "About Section 1115 Demonstrations," https://www.medicaid.gov/medicaid/section-1115-demonstrations/about-section-1115-demonstrations/index.html.

26 Evelyne P. Baumrucker, "Medicaid and Incarcerated Individuals," Congressional Research Service, August 24, 2023, https://crsreports.congress.gov/product/pdf/IF/IF11830, accessed April 6, 2024.

27 United States Commission on Marihuana and Drug Abuse, *Marihuana: A Signal of Misunderstanding: First Report*, Appendix, 1972. https://books.google.com/books?id=PjbGxgEACAAJ.

28 Mike Bebernes, "Why Hasn't Legal Weed Killed the Marijuana Black Market," *Yahoo News*, December 16, 2022, https://news.yahoo.com/why-hasnt-legal-weed-killed-the-marijuana-black-market-224158722.html?, accessed August 6, 2023.

29 Connor Griffin, "Thousands of Illegal Marijuana Grow Sites, Some Linked to Mexican Drug Cartels, Litter Precious Public Lands Across Northern California," *Louisville Courier Journal*, June 1, 2023, https://www.courier-journal.com/in-depth/news/investigations/2023/06/01/illegal-marijuana-grows-linked-to-mexican-cartels-fueling-a-wildlife-purge-in-the-west/69948360007/, accessed August 6, 2023.

30 National Institute on Drug Abuse, "Cannabis Potency Data," June 6, 2023, https://nida.nih.gov/research/research-data-measures-resources/cannabis-potency-data, accessed August 6, 2023.

31 "2024 National Survey on Drug Use and Health (NSDUH) Releases," CBHSQ Data, July 2025, https://www.samhsa.gov/data/data-we-collect/nsduh-national-survey-drug-use-and-health/national-releases/2024.

32 Grant T. Baldwin et al., "Current Cannabis Use in the United States: Implications for Public Health Research," *American Journal of Public Health* 114, no. S8 (October 23, 2024): S624–27, https://doi.org/10.2105/ajph.2024.307823.

33 Centers for Disease Control and Prevention, "Addiction: Health Effects of Marijuana," October 19, 2019, https://www.cdc.gov/marijuana/health-effects/addiction.html, accessed August 6, 2023.

34 Ken C. Winters and Holly B. Waldron. "Cannabis, Psychosis, and the Teen Brain." In *Mind the Children: How to Think About the Youth Mental Health Collapse*, edited by Naomi Schaefer Riley and Sally Satel, American Enterprise Institute, 2025.

35 National Institute on Drug Abuse, "Is There a Link Between Marijuana Use and Psychiatric Disorders?" May 8, 2023, https://nida.nih.gov/publications/research-reports/marijuana/there-link-between-marijuana-use-psychiatric-disorders, accessed August 6, 2023.

36 Patricia Pinto-Garcia, "Cannabinoid Hyperemesis Syndrome and 'Scromiting': What You Should Know," *GoodRx Health*, March 8, 2023, https://www.goodrx.com/health-topic/cannabis/cannabinoid-hyperemesis-syndrome-scromiting, accessed August 6, 2023.

37 Megan Twohey et al., "As America's Marijuana Use Grows, So Do the Harms," *The New York Times*, October 4, 2024, https://www.nytimes.com/2024/10/04/us/cannabis-marijuana-risks-addiction.html?searchResultPosition=1.

38 Stephanie Armour, "For Marijuana Users, Even Legalization Doesn't Guarantee Safety," *Wall Street Journal*, February 20, 2024, accessed April 13, 2024.https://www.wsj.com/health/healthcare/for-marijuana-users-even-legalization-doesnt-guarantee-safety-ef1660a5?msockid=10a290e949ad6d2c0e4883d148506c20.

39 Luke Halpern, Assistant Editor, "Potential Drug for Mitigation of Cannabis Withdrawal Symptoms Receives FDA Fast Track Designation," *Pharmacy Times*, February 14, 2025,https://www.pharmacytimes.com/view/potential-drug-for-mitigation-of-cannabis-withdrawal-symptoms-receives-fda-fast-track-designation.

40 Muhammad Afzal and Panos Panagiotopoulos, "Data in Policing: An Integrative Review," *International Journal of Public Administration*, May 30, 2024, 1–20, https://doi.org/10.1080/01900692.2024.2360586.

41 Anthony A. Braga and David M. Kennedy, *A Framework for Addressing Violence and Serious Crime: Focused Deterrence, Legitimacy, and Prevention* (Cambridge University Press, 2021).

42 Steven D. Levitt and Stephen J. Dubner, *Freakonomics Rev Ed: A Rogue Economist Explores the Hidden Side of Everything*

(WmMorrow, 2006). See Chapter 3: "Why Do Drug Dealers Still Live with Their Moms?"

43 David Boyum and Peter Reuter, *An Analytic Assessment of U.S. Drug Policy* (AEI Press, 2005).

44 "Program Profile: High Point Drug Market Intervention," *CrimeSolutions*, National Institute of Justice, 2014. https://crimesolutions.ojp.gov/ratedprograms/361#pd.

45 National Network for Safe Communities, "The High Point Drug Market Intervention Strategy (2009)," November 27, 2018, https://nnscommunities.org/guides/the-high-point-drug-market-intervention-strategy-2009/.

46 Nicholas Corsaro, Rodney K. Brunson, and Edmund F. McGarrell, "Evaluating a Policing Strategy Intended to Disrupt an Illicit Street-Level Drug Market," *Evaluation Review* 34, no. 6 (December 1, 2010): 513–48, https://doi.org/10.1177/0193841x10389136.

47 Anthony A Braga and David M. Kennedy, *A Framework for Addressing Violence and Serious Crime: Focused Deterrence, Legitimacy, and Prevention* (Cambridge University Press, 2021).

48 Charles Fain Lehman, "Drug Policing in the 21st Century," Manhattan Institute, May 23, 2024, https://manhattan.institute/article/drug-policing-in-the-21st-century.

49 David Kennedy and J. Ben-Menachem, "Using DMI to Combat Covert Opioid Markets," *Police Chief*, March 2018.

50 Drug Enforcement Administration, "National Drug Threat Assessment 2024," May 24, 2024, https://www.dea.gov/documents/2024/2024-05/2024-05-24/national-drug-threat-assessment-2024.

51 Maria Cramer and Amir Hamja, "What Happened When a Brooklyn Neighborhood Policed Itself for Five Days," *International New York Times*, 2023, https://www.nytimes.com/2023/06/04/nyregion/brooklyn-brownsville-no-police.html?searchResultPosition=1, accessed June 4, 2023.

52 E.J. Dionne Jr, "The Good News About Murder," *The Washington Post*, July 31, 2025, https://www.washingtonpost.com/opinions/2025/07/31/crime-murder-trump-biden-pandemic/?itid=sr_0_27ddeaf1-3f46-402d-8f00-1a8162be26ea.

53 Alex Vitale, *The End of Policing* (Verso Books, 2021).

54 Centers for Disease Control and Prevention, "Provisional Drug Overdose Data," n.d., https://www.cdc.gov/nchs/nvss/vsrr/drug-overdose-data.htm, accessed September 13, 2025.

55 Oregon Health Authority, "Too Early to Tell: The Challenging Implementation of Measure 110 Has Increased Risks, but the

Effectiveness of the Program Has yet to Be Determined," Report 2023-03, January 2023, https://sos.oregon.gov/audits/Documents/2023-03.pdf.

56 Tony Schick and Conrad Wilson, "Oregon Leaders Hampered Drug Decriminalization Effort," *ProPublica*, February 16, 2024, https://www.propublica.org/article/oregon-leaders-hampered-drug-decriminalization-effort.

57 Keith Humphreys and Rob Bovett, "Why Oregon's Drug Decriminalization Failed," *The Atlantic*, March 17, 2024, https://www.theatlantic.com/ideas/archive/2024/03/oregon-drug-decriminalization-failed/677678/.

Chapter 8

1 See https://paariusa.org/about-us/.

2 Jac Charlier, "Want to Reduce Drugs in Your Community? You Might Want to Deflect Instead of Arrest," *Police Chief Magazine*, September 2015, 30–1. Charlier is Executive Director of TASC's Center for Health and Justice.

3 Joe McGallagly and Neil McKeganey, "Does Robust Drug Enforcement Lead to an Increase in Drug Users Coming Forward for Treatment?" *Drugs: Education, Prevention and Policy* 20, no. 1 (2013): 1–4.

4 Sally Satel, "Dark Genies, Dark Horizons: The Riddle of Addiction," *Liberties: A Journal of Culture and Politics*, April 14, 2021, https://libertiesjournal.com/articles/dark-genies-dark-horizons-the-riddle-of-addiction/.

5 Hanna Pickard, "Responsibility Without Blame for Addiction," *Neuroethics* 10, no. 1 (January 7, 2017): 169–80, https://doi.org/10.1007/s12152-016-9295-2.

6 Jon Ross and Bruce Taylor, "Designed to Do Good: Key Findings on the Development and Operation of First Responder Deflection Programs," *Journal of Public Health Management and Practice* 28, no. Supplement 6 (November 1, 2022): S295–301, https://doi.org/10.1097/phh.0000000000001578.

7 Jac Charlier, "Deflection: A Powerful Crime-Fighting Tool that Improved Community Relations," *Police Chief*, 2017.

8 Jessica Reichert, Brandon Del Pozo, and Bruce Taylor, "Police Stigma toward People with Opioid Use Disorder: A Study of Illinois Officers," *Substance Use & Misuse* 58, no. 12 (2023): 1493–504.

9 Jessica Reichert et al., "Guiding Officers to Deflect Citizens to Treatment: An Examination of Police Department Policies in Illinois," *Health & Justice* 11, no. 1 (February 8, 2023), https://doi.org/10.1186/s40352-023-00207-y.

10 Bureau of Justice Assistance, "Report of the National Survey to Assess First Responder Deflection Programs in Response to the Opioid Crisis," May 2021, https://bja.ojp.gov/library/publications/report-national-survey-assess-first-responder-deflection-programs-response.

11 TASC—Center for Health and Justice, "Law Enforcement Deflection Frameworks: A Decision Making Tool for Police Leaders," January 2017, https://ptaccollaborative.org/wp-content/uploads/2019/11/TASC_Deflection-Framework___Tool_Jan-2017.pdf, accessed November 30, 2023.

12 Police, Treatment, and Community Collaborative (PTACC), "The Six Pathways of Deflection and Pre-Arrest Diversion," 2023, https://ptaccollaborative.org/wp-content/uploads/2023/01/PTACC-6-Pathways-of-Deflection-Onepager.pdf.

13 H. Gene Hern et al., "Prehospital Buprenorphine Treatment for Opioid Use Disorder by Paramedics: First Year Results of the EMS Buprenorphine Use Pilot," *Prehospital Emergency Care* 27, no. 3 (May 13, 2022): 334–42, https://doi.org/10.1080/10903127.2022.2061661.

14 National Institute of Justice, "The Drug Court Movement," July 1995, https://www.ojp.gov/pdffiles/drgctmov.pdf, accessed November 30, 2023.

15 Shelli B. Rossman et al., *The Multi-Site Adult Drug Court Evaluation: Executive Summary* (Urban Institute Justice Policy Center, 2011),https://www.ojp.gov/pdffiles1/nij/grants/237108.pdf, accessed December 19, 2023.

16 Drug Policy Alliance, "Moving Away from Drug Courts: Toward a Health-Centered Approach to Drug Use," New York, 2014.

17 Joanne Csete, "United States Drug Courts and Opioid Agonist Therapy: Missing the Target of Overdose Reduction," *Forensic Science International: Mind and Law* 1 (November 1, 2020): 100024, https://doi.org/10.1016/j.fsiml.2020.100024.

18 Maia Szalavitz, "Claims That Drug Decriminalization in Oregon Isn't Working Are Short-Sighted," *The New York Times*, August 29, 2023, https://www.nytimes.com/2023/08/29/opinion/arrest-drug-treatment-addiction.html.

19 All Rise, "Adult Treatment Court Best Practice Standards," May 27, 2025, https://allrise.org/publications/standards/.

20 Shannon M. Carey, Jacqueline van Wormer, and Adrian Johnson, "Responding to a State of Emergency: The Creation of a New Triage to Treatment Court Model to Address the Opioid Crisis," *Journal for Advancing Justice* IV (2022): 5–22.
21 Michael D. Clark and Teresa Chandler, "There May Not Be a Tomorrow: Immediacy, Motivational Interviewing, and Opioid Intervention Courts," *Federal Probation* 86 (2022): 18.
22 Bradley Ray et al., "Spatiotemporal Analysis Exploring the Effect of Law Enforcement Drug Market Disruptions on Overdose, Indianapolis, Indiana, 2020–2021," *American Journal of Public Health* 113, no. 7 (July 1, 2023): 750–8, https://doi.org/10.2105/ajph.2023.307291, accessed June 8, 2023.
23 McGallagly and McKeganey, "Does Robust Drug Enforcement Lead to an Increase in Drug Users Coming Forward for Treatment?"
24 Centers for Disease Control and Prevention, "Mitigate Drug Overdose Risks Among Patients Experiencing Disrupted Access to Prescribers," December 1, 2022, https://www.cdc.gov/opioids/opioid-rapid-response-program.html, accessed November 30, 2023.

Chapter 9

1 Nick Oza, "THE WALL: Drug Smuggling Long," October 3, 2017, https://www.azcentral.com/picture-gallery/news/politics/border-issues/2017/08/14/the-wall-drug-smuggling-long/104592040/.
2 Arturo Martinez, "Tunnels at US-Mexico Border Show Smugglers' Deep Commitment," *Voice of America*, May 24, 2017, https://www.voanews.com/a/tunnels-at-us-mexico-border-show-smugglers-deep-commitment/3869064.html.
3 United States Trade Representative, "Mexico," n.d., https://ustr.gov/countries-regions/americas/mexico.
4 Thomas Graham, "Mexican Cartels Are Fifth-Largest Employers in the Country, Study Finds," *The Guardian*, September 21, 2023, https://www.theguardian.com/world/2023/sep/21/mexico-cartels-fifth-largest-employer-study.
5 Jonathan P. Caulkins and Bishu Giri, "Fentanyl at the Gates: Comparing Large Seizures at the U.S.–Mexican and U.S.–Canadian Borders," *Manhattan Institute*, July 1, 2025, https://manhattan.institute/article/

fentanyl-at-the-gates-comparing-large-seizures-at-the-u-s-mexican-and-u-s-canadian-borders.

6 United Nations Office on Drugs and Crime, "World Drug Report 2025," June 26, 2025, https://www.unodc.org/unodc/en/data-and-analysis/world-drug-report-2025.html.

7 United States citizens comprised 86 percent of fentanyl trafficking convictions in 2021, as noted in https://thirdway.imgix.net/pdfs/the-truth-about-fentanyl-trafficking.pdf.

8 https://www.cbp.gov/newsroom/stats/typical-day-fy2022.

9 Kylie Murdock, "The Truth About Fentanyl Trafficking," *Third Way*, April 12, 2023, https://thirdway.imgix.net/pdfs/the-truth-about-fentanyl-trafficking.pdf, accessed November 30, 2023.

10 Rick Davis, *Billion Dollar Highway: Arizona Interstate 19* (independently published, 2018).

11 City Paper Staff, "Cocaine Production Hits Record High, Colombia's Coca Crop at 253,000 Hectares," *The City Paper Bogotá*, June 26, 2025, https://thecitypaperbogota.com/news/cocaine-production-hits-record-high-colombias-coca-crop-at-253000-hectares/.

12 A significant portion of recent cocaine overdoses also involves Fentanyl.

13 Adam Isacson, "U.S.-Mexico Border Methamphetamine Seizures," *WOLA Border Oversight*, November 20, 2023, https://borderoversight.org/2023/10/04/border-methamphetamine-seizures/.

14 https://www.dea.gov/resource-center/meth-lab-maps-archives.html.

15 DEA, "2017 National Drug Threat Assessment," October 2017, 69, https://www.dea.gov/sites/default/files/2018-07/DIR-040-17_2017-NDTA.pdf, accessed November 30, 2023.

16 Kristine Phillips, "U.S. Border Officers Told a Mexican Teen to Drink Liquid Meth. His Family Received $1 Million for His Death," *Washington Post*, October 26, 2021, https://www.washingtonpost.com/news/post-nation/wp/2017/03/21/u-s-border-agents-made-a-mexican-teen-drink-liquid-meth-his-family-won-1-million-for-his-death/?utm_term=.ea74405e9381.

17 Esmé E. Deprez, "Deadly Chinese Fentanyl Is Creating a New Era of Drug Kingpins," *Bloomberg.com*, May 22, 2018, https://www.bloomberg.com/news/features/2018-05-22/deadly-chinese-fentanyl-is-creating-a-new-era-of-drug-kingpins.

18 U.S. Department of Homeland Security, "Department of Homeland Security Unveils Artificial Intelligence Roadmap, Announces Pilot Projects to Maximize Benefits of Technology, Advance Homeland Security Mission," March 18, 2024, https://www.dhs.gov/

news/2024/03/18/department-homeland-security-unveils-artificial-intelligence-roadmap-announces.

19 Vanda Felbab-Brown, "China and Synthetic Drugs Control: Fentanyl, Methamphetamines," *Brookings*, November 7, 2022, https://www.brookings.edu/articles/china-and-synthetic-drugs-control-fentanyl-methamphetamines-and-precursors/.

20 Tim Thompson, "How Much Does Colombian Coffee Cost? Shipped Directly to You?" *Buy Organic Coffee*, May 9, 2018, https://buyorganiccoffee.org/1672/how-much-does-colombian-coffee-cost/.

21 Scott Stewart, "From Colombia to New York City: The Narconomics of Cocaine," *Business Insider/STRATFOR*, June 27, 2016, http://www.businessinsider.com/from-colombia-to-new-york-city-the-economics-of-cocaine-2015-7.

22 Leo Beletsky and Corey S. Davis, "Today's Fentanyl Crisis: Prohibition's Iron Law, Revisited," *International Journal of Drug Policy* 46 (August 1, 2017): 156–9, https://doi.org/10.1016/j.drugpo.2017.05.050.

23 Felbab-Brown, "China and Synthetic Drugs Control."

24 Jack Riley, *Drug Warrior: Inside the Hunt for El Chapo and the Rise of America's Opioid Crisis* (Hachette UK, 2019).

25 DEA. "2025 National Drug Threat Assessment," May 2025. https://www.dea.gov/sites/default/files/2025-07/2025NationalDrugThreatAssessment.pdf.

Chapter 10

1 James Collins, *Good to Great and the Social Sectors: Why Business Thinking is Not the Answer* (Harper Collins, 2005).

2 Ibid.

3 Zoë Slote Morris, Steven Wooding, and Jonathan Grant, "The Answer Is 17 Years, What Is the Question: Understanding Time Lags in Translational Research," *Journal of the Royal Society of Medicine* 104, no. 12 (December 1, 2011): 510–20, https://doi.org/10.1258/jrsm.2011.110180.

4 Jeneen Interlandi, "48 Million Americans Live with Addiction. Here's How to Get Them Help That Works," *The New York Times*, December 13, 2023, https://www.nytimes.com/2023/12/13/opinion/addiction-policy-treatment-opioid.html, accessed December 18, 2023.

5 Office of Management and Budget, *Budget of the U.S. Government: Fiscal Year 2025* (U.S. Government Publishing Office, 2024), https://www.whitehouse.gov/wp-content/uploads/2024/03/budget_fy2025.pdf.
6 Curtis S. Florence, Feijun Luo, and Ketra Rice, "The Economic Burden of Opioid Use Disorder and Fatal Opioid Overdose in the United States, 2017," *Drug and Alcohol Dependence* 218 (January 1, 2021): 108350, https://doi.org/10.1016/j.drugalcdep.2020.108350.
7 Joint Economic Committee Democrats, "The Economic Toll of the Opioid Crisis Reached Nearly $1.5 Trillion in 2020," September 28, 2022, https://www.jec.senate.gov/public/index.cfm/democrats/issue-briefs?ID=CE55E977-B473-414F-8B88-53EB55EB7C7C, accessed July 7, 2023.
8 David Powell and Mireille Jacobson, (2025). Estimates of illicit opioid use in the US. *JAMA Health Forum*, *6*(5), e250809. https://doi.org/10.1001/jamahealthforum.2025.0809.
9 Substance Abuse and Mental Health Services Administration, "Highlights for the 2024 National Survey on Drug Use and Health," Report, 2025.
10 Nicholas Carr, *The Shallows: What the Internet Is Doing to Our Brains* (W. W. Norton & Company, 2020).
11 Guy Kawasaki, *The Art of the Start 2.0: The Time-Tested, Battle-Hardened Guide for Anyone Starting Anything* (Penguin, 2015).
12 Bianca Albers, Aron Shlonsky, and Robyn Mildon, *Implementation Science 3.0* (Springer, 2020), 538.
13 Ibid., 35.
14 Ibid., 28.
15 Ibid., 328.
16 Khaled Draghmeh, Mark S. Gold, and Brian Fuehrlein, "A Review of Relapse in Opioid Use Disorder," *Current Addiction Reports* 12, no. 1 (June 11, 2025), https://doi.org/10.1007/s40429-025-00672-5.
17 Noella Edelmann and Valerie Albrecht, "The Policy Cycle: A Framework for Knowledge Management of Practitioners' Expertise and Role in Participatory Processes," *Frontiers in Political Science* 5 (2023): 4, 1223013. https://doi.org/10.3389/fpos.2023.1223013.
18 Nora Volkow, "Five Areas Where 'More Research' Isn't Needed to Curb the Overdose Crisis," National Institute on Drug Abuse, August 31, 2022, https://nida.nih.gov/about-nida/noras-blog/2022/08/five-areas-where-more-research-isnt-needed-to-curb-overdose-crisis.
19 Nicholas Richardson et al., "National Survey Findings on Law Enforcement Agency Drug Response Practices, Overdose Victim

Outcomes, and Good Samaritan Laws," *Drug and Alcohol Dependence* 248 (July 1, 2023): 109916, https://doi.org/10.1016/j.drugalcdep.2023.109916.

20 The Pew Charitable Trusts, "How States Use Opioid Use Disorder Treatment Measures to Inform Decision-Making," May 28, 2024, https://www.pewtrusts.org/en/research-and-analysis/issue-briefs/2024/05/how-states-use-opioid-use-disorder-treatment-measures-to-inform-decision-making.

21 John C. Maxwell, *The 21 Irrefutable Laws of Leadership: Follow Them and People Will Follow You* (HarperCollins Leadership, 2022).

22 Richard A. Spires, *Government Can Deliver: A Practitioner's Guide to Improving Agency Effectiveness and Efficiency* (BookLocker.com, Inc., 2023).

23 Robert O'Harrow Jr, "Meet the 24-year-old Trump Campaign Worker Appointed to Help Lead the Government's Drug Policy Office," *The Washington Post*, January 15, 2018.

24 Yuval Noah Harari, *Nexus: A Brief History of Information Networks from the Stone Age to AI* (Random House, 2024).

25 Patrick R. Leddin, Shawn D. Moon, and Patrick Leddin, *Building a Winning Culture in Government: A Blueprint for Delivering Success in the Public Sector* (Mango Media Inc., 2018).

26 Barbara Andraka-Christou. "Federal Policymakers Should Read the Drug Policy Research They Funded." *The ASAM Weekly*, July 2025, https://www.asam.org/publications-resources/the-asam-weekly/detail/2025/07/09/the-asam-weekly-for-july-8th--2025.

27 Jonathan P. Caulkins, Greg Midgette, and Peter Reuter, "Improving Opioid Use Estimates Through Multiple Data Sources," *JAMA Health Forum* 6, no. 5 (May 9, 2025): e250806, https://doi.org/10.1001/jamahealthforum.2025.0806.

Chapter 11

1 Christopher M. Jones et al., "Estimated Number of Children Who Lost a Parent to Drug Overdose in the US From 2011 to 2021," *JAMA Psychiatry*, 2024, https://doi.org/10.1001/jamapsychiatry.2024.0810.

2 Sean Esteban McCabe, et al, "US Children Living with a Parent With Substance Use Disorder." JAMA Pediatrics, Published online May 12, 2025. doi:10.1001/jamapediatrics.2025.0828.

3 Jon Greenberg, "PolitiFact—Did Obama Cut $300 Million for School Safety? Not Really," Politifact, March 9, 2018, https://www.politifact.com/factchecks/2018/mar/09/ted-cruz/did-obama-cut-300-million-school-safety-not-really/.

4 Joseph Friedman and Scott E. Hadland, "The Overdose Crisis Among U.S. Adolescents," *The New England Journal of Medicine* (Print), January 6, 2024, https://doi.org/10.1056/nejmp2312084.

5 Linda Richter, "Rethinking Substance Use Prevention: An Earlier and Broader Approach," Partnership to End Addiction, September 19, 2023, https://drugfree.org/reports/rethinking-substance-use-prevention-an-earlier-and-broader-approach/.

6 Ibid., 15.

7 Ibid., 5.

8 Richard A. Miech, "National Survey Results on Drug Use, 1975–2004," December 2024, https://monitoringthefuture.org/wp-content/uploads/2024/12/mtf2025.pdf.

9 Robert Dupont, *Chemical Slavery: Understanding Addiction and Stopping the Drug Epidemic* (Createspace Independent Publishing Platform, 2018).

10 Nirmita Panchal, Robin Rudowitz, and Cynthia Cox, "Recent Trends in Mental Health and Substance Use Concerns among Adolescents," *KFF*, June 28, 2022, https://www.kff.org/mental-health/issue-brief/recent-trends-in-mental-health-and-substance-use-concerns-among-adolescents/.

11 Substance Abuse and Mental Health Services Administration, "Lesbian, Gay, and Bisexual Behavioral Health: Results from the 2021 and 2022 National Surveys on Drug Use and Health (SAMHSA Publication No. PEP23-07-01-001)," Center for Behavioral Health Statistics and Quality, Substance Abuse and Mental Health Services Administration, 2023, https://www.samhsa.gov/data/report/LGB-Behavioral-Health-Report-2021-2022.

12 Claradina Soto et al., "Substance and Behavioral Addictions among American Indian and Alaska Native Populations," *International Journal of Environmental Research and Public Health* 19, no. 5 (March 3, 2022): 2974, https://doi.org/10.3390/ijerph19052974.

13 American Psychological Association, "Substance Abuse/Addiction in Native American Youth," n.d., https://www.apa.org/pi/oema/resources/ethnicity-health/native-american/substance-use.

14 J. David Hawkins, Rick Kosterman, Richard F. Catalano et al., "Promoting Positive Adult Functioning through Social Development

Intervention in Childhood: Long-Term Effects from the Seattle Social Development Project—Correction," *Archives of Pediatrics & Adolescent Medicine* 159, no. 5 (May 1, 2005): 469, https://doi.org/10.1001/archpedi.159.5.469.

15 Terrie E. Moffitt et al., "A Gradient of Childhood Self-Control Predicts Health, Wealth, and Public Safety," *Proceedings of the National Academy of Sciences of the United States of America* 108, no. 7 (January 24, 2011): 2693–8, https://doi.org/10.1073/pnas.1010076108.

16 Sharon Mihalic and Delbert S. Elliott, "Evidence-Based Programs Registry: Blueprints for Healthy Youth Development," *Evaluation and Program Planning* 48 (February 1, 2015): 124–31, https://doi.org/10.1016/j.evalprogplan.2014.08.004.

17 *Blueprint for a National Prevention Infrastructure for Mental, Emotional, and Behavioral Disorders. National Academies Press eBooks*, 2025. https://doi.org/10.17226/28577.

18 Dan Heath, *Upstream: The Quest to Solve Problems Before They Happen* (Avid Reader Press / Simon & Schuster, 2020).

19 Ibid.

20 Vincent J. Felitti et al., "REPRINT OF: Relationship of Childhood Abuse and Household Dysfunction to Many of the Leading Causes of Death in Adults: The Adverse Childhood Experiences (ACE) Study," *American Journal of Preventive Medicine* 56, no. 6 (June 1, 2019): 774–86, https://doi.org/10.1016/j.amepre.2019.04.001.

21 Robert F. Anda, Laura Porter, and David W. Brown, "Inside the Adverse Childhood Experience Score: Strengths, Limitations, and Misapplications," *American Journal of Preventive Medicine* 59, no. 2 (August 1, 2020): 293–5, https://doi.org/10.1016/j.amepre.2020.01.009.

22 Centers for Disease Control and Prevention, "Risk and Protective Factors," June 29, 2023, https://www.cdc.gov/violenceprevention/aces/riskprotectivefactors.html.

23 Linda Richter PhD, "Rethinking Substance Use Prevention: An Earlier and Broader Approach," Partnership to End Addiction, September 19, 2023, https://drugfree.org/reports/rethinking-substance-use-prevention-an-earlier-and-broader-approach/.

24 Karl G. Hill et al., "Outcomes of Childhood Preventive Intervention across 2 Generations," *JAMA Pediatrics* 174, no. 8 (August 1, 2020): 764, https://doi.org/10.1001/jamapediatrics.2020.1310.

25 Moffitt et al., "A Gradient of Childhood Self-Control Predicts Health, Wealth, and Public Safety."

26 Jonathan Haidt, *The Anxious Generation: How the Great Rewiring of Childhood Is Causing an Epidemic of Mental Illness* (Random House, 2024).

27 Emma Young, "How Iceland Got Teens to Say No to Drugs," *The Atlantic*, January 19, 2017, https://www.theatlantic.com/health/archive/2017/01/teens-drugs-iceland/513668/.

28 Heather McGhee, *The Sum of Us: What Racism Costs Everyone and How We Can Prosper Together* (Profile Books, 2021).

29 Ibid.

30 Tara Woodward et al., "Risk & Protective Factors for Youth Substance Use across Family, Peers, School, & Leisure Domains," *Children and Youth Services Review* 151 (August 1, 2023): 107027, https://doi.org/10.1016/j.childyouth.2023.107027.

31 Ina M. Koning et al., "Implementation of the Icelandic Prevention Model: A Critical Discussion of Its Worldwide Transferability," *Drugs: Education, Prevention and Policy* 28, no. 4 (December 23, 2020): 367–78, https://doi.org/10.1080/09687637.2020.1863916.

32 W. Douglas Evans et al., "Peer-to-Peer Social Media as an Effective Prevention Strategy: Quasi-Experimental Evaluation," *JMIR Mhealth and Uhealth* 8, no. 5 (May 6, 2020): e16207, https://doi.org/10.2196/16207.

Bibliography

"About Section 1115 Demonstrations | Medicaid," (February 1, 2019). https://www.medicaid.gov/medicaid/section-1115-demonstrations/about-section-1115-demonstrations/index.html.

Adams, Jerome. "Making the Case for Syringe Services Programs." *Public Health Reports* 135, no. 1_suppl (July 1, 2020): 10S--12S. https://doi.org/10.1177/0033354920936233.

Adams, Samuel Hopkins. *The Great American Fraud*. Collier's Weekly,1905.

Addiction Policy Forum. "National Organizations Urge the White House to Lift the Contingency Management Funding Cap." December 19, 2024. https://www.addictionpolicy.org/post/national-organizations-urge-the-white-house-to-lift-the-contingency-management-funding-cap.

Afzal, Muhammad, and Panos Panagiotopoulos. "Data in Policing: An Integrative Review." *International Journal of Public Administration*, (May 30, 2024), 1–20. https://doi.org/10.1080/01900692.2024.2360586.

Ajayi, Rhoda. "AI-powered innovations for managing complex mental health conditions and addiction treatments." *Int Res J Modern Eng Technol Sci* 7, no. 1 (2025): *Int Res J Modern Eng Technol Sci* 7, no. 1 (2025): 87.

All Rise. "Adult Treatment Court Best Practice Standards," December 20, 2023. https://allrise.org/publications/standards/.

Albers, Bianca, Aron Shlonsky, and Robyn Mildon. *Implementation Science 3.0*. Springer, 2020.

Alexander, Michelle. *The New Jim Crow*. The New Press, 2012.

American Psychological Association. "Substance Abuse/Addiction in Native American Youth," 2014. https://www.apa.org/pi/oema/resources/ethnicity-health/native-american/substance-use.

American Society of Addiction Medicine. "Definition of Addiction." *American Society of Addiction Medicine*, 2019. https://www.asam.org/docs/default-source/quality-science/asam's-2019-definition-of-addiction-(1).pdf?sfvrsn=b8b64fc2_2.

Amodei, Dario. "Dario Amodei—Machines of Loving Grace," October 1, 2024. https://darioamodei.com/machines-of-loving-grace.

Anda, Robert F., Laura Porter, and David W. Brown. "Inside the Adverse Childhood Experience Score: Strengths, Limitations, and

Misapplications." *American Journal of Preventive Medicine* 59, no. 2 (August 1, 2020): 293–5. https://doi.org/10.1016/j.amepre.2020.01.009.

Andraka-Christou, Barbara. "Federal Policymakers Should Read the Drug Policy Research They Funded." *The ASAM Weekly.* July 8th, 2025. https://www.asam.org/publications-resources/the-asam-weekly/detail/2025/07/09/the-asam-weekly-for-july-8th--2025.

Aronberg, Dave, and David R. Campbell. *Fighting the Florida Shuffle: The Inside Story of Corruption in the Drug Treatment Industry and How One Community Found the Solution*. Simon & Schuster, 2025.

Armour, Stephanie. "For Marijuana Users, Even Legalization Doesn't Guarantee Safety." *Wall Street Journal,* February 20, 2024. Accessed April 13, 2024. https://www.wsj.com/articles/for-marijuana-users-even-legalization-doesnt-guarantee-safety-ef1660a5.

Arnold, Shelby; Pinto, Lindsey; Grant, Paul; Lustig, Nicola et al. "Recovery-Oriented Cognitive Therapy: A Testable Framework to Promote Successful Long-Term Recovery From Substance Use Challenges for Justice-Involved Individuals." *Journal for Advancing Justice*: V 5, 2024.

Ault, Alicia. "Praise for Final Methadone, Buprenorphine Rule." *Medscape*, February 8, 2024. https://www.medscape.com/viewarticle/praise-final-methadone-buprenorphine-rule-2024a10002un?icd=login_success_email_match_fpf.

Baldwin, Grant T., Alana Vivolo-Kantor, Brooke Hoots, Douglas R. Roehler, and Jean Y. Ko. "Current Cannabis Use in the United States: Implications for Public Health Research." *American Journal of Public Health* 114, no. S8 (October 23, 2024): S624–27. https://doi.org/10.2105/ajph.2024.307823.

Baldwin, Tammy. "Senators Baldwin, Braun Introduce Bipartisan Reentry Act to Help Reduce Drug Overdoses." Press release, Office of U.S. Senator Tammy Baldwin, March 30, 2023. https://www.baldwin.senate.gov/news/press-releases/baldwin-braun-reentry-act.

Balestra, Simone, Helge Liebert, Nicole Maestas, and Tisamarie B. Sherry. "Behavioral Responses to Supply-Side Drug Policy during the Opioid Epidemic," December 1, 2021. https://doi.org/10.3386/w29596.

Barber, Chris. "Public Enemy Number One: A Pragmatic Approach to America's Drug Problem." *Richard Nixon Foundation*, December 19, 2019. https://www.nixonfoundation.org/2016/06/26404/.

Barry, Colleen L., Andrew J. Epstein, David A. Fiellin, Liana Fraenkel, and Susan H. Busch. "Estimating Demand for Primary Care-based Treatment for Substance and Alcohol Use Disorders." *Addiction* 111, no. 8 (May 15, 2016): 1376–84. https://doi.org/10.1111/add.13364.

Balawajder, Elizabeth Flanagan, Lori Ducharme, Bruce G. Taylor, Phoebe A. Lamuda, Marynia Kolak, Peter D. Friedmann, Harold A. Pollack, and John A. Schneider. "Barriers to Universal Availability of Medications for Opioid Use Disorder in US Jails." *JAMA network open* 8, no. 4 (2025): e255340-e255340.

Baum, Dan. "Legalize It All." *Harper's Magazine*, March 31, 2016. https://harpers.org/archive/2016/04/legalize-it-all/.

Baum, Dan. *Smoke and Mirrors: The War on Drugs and the Politics of Failure.* Little, Brown, 1996.

Baumrucker, Evelyne P. "Medicaid and Incarcerated Individuals." Congressional Research Service, August 24, 2023. https://crsreports.congress.gov/product/pdf/IF/IF11830. Accessed April 6, 2024.

Blueprint for a National Prevention Infrastructure for Mental, Emotional, and Behavioral Disorders. National Academies Press eBooks, 2025. https://doi.org/10.17226/28577.

Bebernes, Mike. "Why Hasn't Legal Weed Killed the Marijuana Black Market." *Yahoo News*, December 16, 2022.

Becker, Elizabeth. "As Ex-theorist on Young 'Superpredators,' Bush Aide has Regrets." *New York Times*, February 9, 2001.

Becker, Ernest. *The Denial of Death.* Page 247. Simon and Schuster, 2007.

Beletsky, Leo, and Corey S. Davis. "Today's Fentanyl Crisis: Prohibition's Iron Law, Revisited." *International Journal of Drug Policy* 46 (August 1, 2017): 156–9. https://doi.org/10.1016/j.drugpo.2017.05.050.

Best, David, and Emily A. Hennessy. "The Science of Recovery Capital: Where Do We Go From Here?" *Addiction (Abingdon. Print)* 117, no. 4 (December 1, 2021): 1139–45. https://doi.org/10.1111/add.15732.

Billock, Rachael M., Andrea L. Steege, and Arialdi M. Miniño. "Drug Overdose Mortality by Usual Occupation and Industry: 46 States and New York City, United States, 2020," August 22, 2023. https://doi.org/10.15620/cdc:128631.

Bipartisan Policy Center. *Tracking Federal Funding to Combat the Opioid Crisis.* Website, 2019. bipartisanpolicy.org/download/?file=/wp-content/uploads/2019/03/Tracking-Federal-Funding-to-Combat-the-Opioid-Crisis.pdf.

Blakeman, Bradley A. "States are the Laboratory of Democracy." *The Hill*, May 7, 2020.

Boyum, David, and Peter Reuter. *An Analytic Assessment of U.S. Drug Policy.* AEI Press, 2005.

Braga, Anthony A., and David M. Kennedy. *A Framework for Addressing Violence and Serious Crime: Focused Deterrence, Legitimacy, and Prevention*. Cambridge University Press, 2021.

Brody, Jane E. "The Hidden Drug Epidemic among Older People." *The New York Times*, December 17, 2019. https://www.nytimes.com/2019/12/16/well/live/the-hidden-drug-epidemic-among-older-people.html.

Brooks, Jennifer, and Star Tribune. "Incarcerated Counselors Draw on Their Own Experiences to Help Others Through Recovery." *Star Tribune*, January 18, 2024. https://www.startribune.com/lino-lakes-minnesota-prison-peer-support-counselors/600336676/.

Bulloch, Marilyn. PharmD, FCCM, BCPS. "The Evolution of the PDMP." *Pharmacy Times*, March 5, 2021. https://www.pharmacytimes.com/view/the-evolution-of-the-pdmp.

Bureau of Justice Assistance. "Report of the National Survey to Assess First Responder Deflection Programs in Response to the Opioid Crisis," May 2021. https://bja.ojp.gov/library/publications/report-national-survey-assess-first-responder-deflection-programs-response.

Bureau of Justice Statistics. "Public Opinion about Drugs," n.d. https://bjs.ojp.gov/drugs-and-crime-facts/public-opinion-about-drugs.

Campbell, Josh. "Autopsy Shows Matthew Perry Died of 'Acute Effects of Ketamine.'" *CNN.Com*, December 16, 2023. https://www.cnn.com/2023/12/15/entertainment/matthew-perry-autopsy-report/index.html.

Campbell, Nancy, J. P. Olsen, and Luke Walden. *The Narcotic Farm: The Rise and Fall of America's First Prison for Drug Addicts*, 2008. https://openlibrary.org/books/OL29525090M/Narcotic_Farm.

Carey, Shannon M., Jacqueline van Wormer, and Adrian Johnson. "Responding to a State of Emergency: The Creation of a New Triage to Treatment Court Model to Address the Opioid Crisis." *Journal for Advancing Justice* IV (2022): 5–22.

Carr, Nicholas. *The Shallows: What the Internet Is Doing to Our Brains*. W. W. Norton & Company, 2020.

Caulkins, Jonathan P., and Bishu Giri. "Fentanyl at the Gates: Comparing Large Seizures at the U.S.–Mexican and U.S.–Canadian Borders." *Manhattan Institute*, July 1, 2025.https://manhattan.institute/article/fentanyl-at-the-gates-comparing-large-seizures-at-the-u-s-mexican-and-u-s-canadian-borders.

Caulkins, Jonathan P., Greg Midgette, and Peter Reuter. "Improving Opioid Use Estimates Through Multiple Data Sources." *JAMA Health Forum* 6, no. 5 (May 9, 2025): e250806. https://doi.org/10.1001/jamahealthforum.2025.0806.

CBHSQ Data. "2023 NSDUH Detailed Tables," June 7, 2024. https://www.samhsa.gov/data/report/2023-nsduh-detailed-tables.

CDC. "Addiction | Health Effects | Marijuana," October 19, 2019. https://www.cdc.gov/marijuana/health-effects/addiction.html.

CDC. "Mitigate Drug Overdose Risks Among Patients Experiencing Disrupted Access to Prescribers," December 1, 2022. Accessed November 30, 2023. https://www.cdc.gov/opioids/opioid-rapid-response-program.html.

CDC. "Risk and Protective Factors | Violence Prevention|Injury Center," June 29, 2023. https://www.cdc.gov/violenceprevention/aces/riskprotectivefactors.html.

Cenikor Foundation. *2024 Annual Report*, September 25, 2024. https://www.cenikor.org/annual-report/.

Centers for Disease Control and Prevention. *Preventing Adverse Childhood Experiences: Leveraging the Best Available Evidence*. Atlanta: National Center for Injury Prevention and Control, CDC and Prevention, 2019. https://www.cdc.gov/violenceprevention/pdf/preventingACES.pdf

Centola, Damon. *Change: How to Make Big Things Happen*, Little, Brown Spark, 2021.

Charlier, Jac. "Deflection: A Powerful Crime-Fighting Tool that Improved Community Relations." *Police Chief*, 2017.

Charlier, Jac. "Want to Reduce Drugs in Your Community? You Might Want to Deflect Instead of Arrest." *Police Chief Magazine*, September 2015, 30–1.

Chasin, Alexandra. *Assassin of Youth: A Kaleidoscopic History of Harry J. Anslinger's War on Drugs*. University of Chicago Press, 2016.

Choi, Matthew. "Crenshaw's Psychedelic PTSD Treatment Bill Passes." *The Texas Tribune*, February 6, 2024. https://www.texastribune.org/2023/12/14/ndaa-congress-psychedelics-ptsd-dan-crenshaw/.

Chen, Dong, Jian Jiang, Nicole Hayes, Zhe Su, and Guo-Wei Wei. "Artificial Intelligence Approaches for Anti-Addiction Drug Discovery." *Digital Discovery*, January 1, 2025. https://doi.org/10.1039/d5dd00032g.

Clark, Michael D., and Teresa Chandler. "There May Not Be a Tomorrow: Immediacy, Motivational Interviewing, and Opioid Intervention Courts." *Federal Probation* 86 (2022): 18.

Collins, James. *Good to Great and the Social Sectors: Why Business Thinking is Not the Answer*. Harper Collins, 2005.

Community Catalyst. *Peers Speak Out: Priority Outcomes for Substance Use Treatment and Services*, February 27, 2023. https://communitycatalyst.org/resource/peers-speak-out/.

"Compounding FAQs." Pharmacist.com, American Pharmacists Association. https://www.pharmacist.com/Practice/Patient-Care-Services/Compounding/.

Congressional Research Service. *Offender Reentry: Correctional Statistics, Reintegration into the Community, and Recidivism*. https://crsreports.congress.gov/product/pdf/RL/RL34287/25.

Conner, Thomas. "Ex Writes About Life with Fleetwood Mac, the Guitarist's Physical Abuse and All That Cocaine." *Chicago Sun-Times*, September 30, 2007. https://www.thomasconner.info/clips/ex-writes-about-life-with-fleetwood-mac-the-guitarists-physical-abuse-and-all-that-cocaine.

Corsaro, Nicholas, Rodney K. Brunson, and Edmund F. McGarrell. "Evaluating a Policing Strategy Intended to Disrupt an Illicit Street-Level Drug Market." *Evaluation Review* 34, no. 6 (December 1, 2010): 513–48. https://doi.org/10.1177/0193841x10389136.

Courtwright, David T. *Dark Paradise*. Harvard University Press, 2009.

Courtright, David T. "Preventing and Treating Narcotic Addiction—A Century of Federal Drug Control." *The New England Journal of Medicine* 373, no. 22 (November 26, 2015): 2095–7. https://doi.org/10.1056/nejmp1508818.

Cramer, Maria, and Amir Hamja. "What Happened When a Brooklyn Neighborhood Policed Itself for Five Days." *International New York Times*, 2023.

Crapanzano, Kathleen, Rebecca Hammarlund, Bilal Ahmad, Natalie Hunsinger, and Rumneet Kullar. "The Association between Perceived Stigma and Substance Use Disorder Treatment Outcomes: A Review." *Substance Abuse and Rehabilitation* 10 (December 1, 2018): 1–12. https://doi.org/10.2147/sar.s183252.

CrimeSolutions, National Institute of Justice. "Program Profile: High Point Drug Market Intervention." 2014. https://crimesolutions.ojp.gov/ratedprograms/361.

New York City Police Department. "Historical Crime Data." n.d. https://www.nyc.gov/site/nypd/stats/crime-statistics/historical.page.

Criminal Justice Drug Facts, National Institute on Drug Abuse; National Institutes of Health; U.S. Department of Health and Human Services.

Csete, Joanne. "United States Drug Courts and Opioid Agonist Therapy: Missing the Target of Overdose Reduction." *Forensic Science International: Mind and Law* 1 (November 1, 2020): 100024. https://doi.org/10.1016/j.fsiml.2020.100024.

Cuomo, Raphael E. Crave: *The Hidden Biology of Addiction and Cancer*. Independently Published, June 10, 2025.

Davis, Rick. *Billion Dollar Highway: Arizona Interstate 19*. Independently Published, 2018.

DEA. "2017 National Drug Threat Assessment," October 2017. https://www.dea.gov/sites/default/files/2018-07/DIR-040-17_2017-NDTA.pdf, accessed November 30, 2023.

DEA. "2025 National Drug Threat Assessment," May 2025. https://www.dea.gov/sites/default/files/2025-07/2025NationalDrugThreatAssessment.pdf, accessed June 14, 2025.

DEA. "Drugs of Abuse—2022," December 2, 2022. https://www.dea.gov/documents/2022/2022-12/2022-12-02/drugs-abuse-2022.

Demarest, Michael. "Cocaine: Middle Class High." *TIME*, July 6, 1981. https://content.time.com/time/magazine/article/0,9171,922619,00.html.

Demsas, Jerusalem. "Community Input Is Bad, Actually." *The Atlantic*, April 22, 2022. https://www.theatlantic.com/ideas/archive/2022/04/community-input-bad-housing-policy/629637/.

Denning, Patt and Jeannie Little, *Over the Influence, Second Edition: The Harm Reduction Guide to Controlling Your Drug and Alcohol Use*. Guilford Publications, 2017.

Deprez, Esmé E. "Deadly Chinese Fentanyl Is Creating a New Era of Drug Kingpins." *Bloomberg.com*, May 22, 2018. https://www.bloomberg.com/news/features/2018-05-22/deadly-chinese-fentanyl-is-creating-a-new-era-of-drug-kingpins.

Desmond, Matthew. *Evicted: Poverty and Profit in the American City*. Penguin, 2016.

De Sousa, Tanya, and Meghan Henry. *The 2024 Annual Homelessness Assessment Report (AHAR) to Congress*, 2024. https://www.huduser.gov/portal/sites/default/files/pdf/2024-AHAR-Part-1.pdf.

Dickson-Gómez, Julia, Erika Christenson, Margaret R. Weeks, Carol L. Galletly, Jennifer Wogen, Antoinette Spector, Madelyn McDonald, and Jessica Ohlrich. "Effects of Implementation and Enforcement Differences in Prescription Drug Monitoring Programs in 3 States: Connecticut, Kentucky, and Wisconsin." *Substance Abuse: Research and Treatment* 15 (January 1, 2021): 117822182199234. https://doi.org/10.1177/1178221821992349.

Dickson-Gómez, Julia, Sarah Krechel, Antoinette Spector, Margaret R. Weeks, Jessica Ohlrich, Danielle Green, and Jianghong Li. "The Effects of Opioid Policy Changes on Transitions from Prescription Opioids to Heroin, Fentanyl and Injection Drug Use: A Qualitative Analysis." *Substance Abuse Treatment, Prevention, and Policy* 17, no. 1 (July 21, 2022). https://doi.org/10.1186/s13011-022-00480-4.

DiClemente, Carlo C. *Addiction and Change, Second Edition: How Addictions Develop and Addicted People Recover*. Guilford Press, 2017.

DiIulio, John J., Jr. "The Coming of the Super-Predators." *The Weekly Standard*, November 27, 1995. https://www.washingtonexaminer.com/magazine/1558817/the-coming-of-the-super-predators.

Dionne, E.J., Jr. "The Good News About Murder." *The Washington Post*, July 31, 2025. https://www.washingtonpost.com/opinions/2025/07/31/crime-murder-trump-biden-pandemic/?itid=sr_0_27ddeaf1-3f46-402d-8f00-1a8162be26ea.

Domestic Council (US) Drug Abuse Task Force. *White Paper on Drug Abuse: A Report to the President*. US Government Printing Office, 1975.

Draghmeh, Khaled, Mark S. Gold, and Brian Fuehrlein. "A Review of Relapse in Opioid Use Disorder." *Current Addiction Reports* 12, no. 1 (June 11, 2025). https://doi.org/10.1007/s40429-025-00672-5.

"Drug Fact Sheet." DEA, April 2020.

Drug Policy Alliance. "Moving Away from Drug Courts: Toward a Health-Centered Approach to Drug Use." New York, 2014.

DuPont, Robert L. *Chemical Slavery: Understanding Addiction and Stopping the Drug Epidemic*. Createspace Independent Publishing Platform, 2018.

DuPont, Robert L., and Richard N. Katon. "Development of a Heroin-Addiction Treatment Program. Effect on Urban Crime." *PubMed* 216, no. 8 (May 24, 1971): 1320–4. https://pubmed.ncbi.nlm.nih.gov/5108449.

Earnshaw, Valerie A. "Stigma and Substance Use Disorders: A Clinical, Research, and Advocacy Agenda." *American Psychologist* 75, no. 9 (December 1, 2020): 1300–11. https://doi.org/10.1037/amp0000744.

Easley, Jonathan. "The Day the Drug War Really Started." *Salon*, June 19, 2011. https://www.salon.com/2011/06/19/len_bias_cocaine_tragedy_still_affecting_us_drug_law/.

The Economist. "Ray Kurzweil on How AI will Transform the Physical World." *The Economist*, June 17, 2024. https://www.economist.com/by-invitation/2024/06/17/ray-kurzweil-on-how-ai-will-transform-the-physical-world.

Eddie, David, William L. White, Corrie L. Vilsaint, Brandon G. Bergman, and John F. Kelly. "Reasons to Be Cheerful: Personal, Civic, and Economic Achievements after Resolving an Alcohol or Drug Problem in the United States Population." *Psychology of Addictive Behaviors* 35, no. 4 (June 1, 2021): 402–14. https://doi.org/10.1037/adb0000689.

Edelmann, Noella, and Valerie Albrecht. "The Policy Cycle: A Framework for Knowledge Management of Practitioners' Expertise and Role in Participatory Processes." *Frontiers in Political Science* 5 (2023): 1223013. https://doi.org/10.3389/fpos.2023.1223013.

Evans, W. Douglas, Elizabeth Andrade, Michaela Pratt, Alexandra Mottern, Sergio Jorge Chávez, Anthony Calzetta-Raymond, and Jiayan Gu. "Peer-to-Peer Social Media as an Effective Prevention Strategy: Quasi-Experimental Evaluation." *JMIR Mhealth and Uhealth* 8, no. 5 (May 6, 2020): e16207. https://doi.org/10.2196/16207.

Evans, William N., Ethan M. J. Lieber, and Patrick Power. "How the Reformulation of OxyContin Ignited the Heroin Epidemic." *The Review of Economics and Statistics* 101, no. 1 (March 1, 2019): 1–15. https://doi.org/10.1162/rest_a_00755.

Farber, David. *Crack: Rock Cocaine, Street Capitalism, and the Decade of Greed*. Cambridge University Press, 2022.

Farber, David. *The War on Drugs: A History*. New York University Press, 2021.

Farrago, Douglas. "Maybe the Opioid Crisis Wasn't Our Fault? Duh." *Authentic Medicine*, October 6, 2021. https://authenticmedicine.com/2021/10/maybe-the-opioid-crisis-wasnt-our-fault-duh/.

Felbab-Brown, Vanda. "China and Synthetic Drugs Control: Fentanyl, Methamphetamines." *Brookings*, November 7, 2022.

Felitti, Vincent J., Robert F. Anda, Dale Nordenberg, David F. Williamson, Alison M. Spitz, Valerie J. Edwards, Mary P. Koss, and James S. Marks. "Reprint of Relationship of Childhood Abuse and Household Dysfunction to Many of the Leading Causes of Death in Adults: The Adverse Childhood Experiences (ACE) Study." *American Journal of Preventive Medicine* 56, no. 6 (June 1, 2019): 774–786. https://doi.org/10.1016/j.amepre.2019.04.001.

Fernandez-Vina, Marcelo, Nadya Prood, Adam Herpolsheimer, Joshua Waimberg, and Scott Burris. "State Laws Governing Syringe Services Programs and Participant Syringe Possession, 2014-2019." *Public Health Reports* 135, no. 1_suppl (July 1, 2020): 128S–137S. https://doi.org/10.1177/0033354920921817.

Fiore, Kristina. "Opioid Crisis: Scrap Pain as 5th Vital Sign?" *MedPage Today*, April 19, 2016. https://www.medpagetoday.com/publichealthpolicy/publichealth/57336#:~:text=In%202001%2C%20the%20Joint%20Commission,was%20that%20pain%20was%20undertreated.

Flanagan, Owen. *What Is It Like to Be an Addict?* Oxford University Press, 2025.

Florence, Curtis S., Feijun Luo, and Ketra Rice. "The Economic Burden of Opioid Use Disorder and Fatal Opioid Overdose in the United States, 2017." *Drug and Alcohol Dependence* 218 (January 1, 2021): 108350. https://doi.org/10.1016/j.drugalcdep.2020.108350.

Foley, Katherine Ellen. “Big Pharma Is Taking Advantage of Patent Law to Keep OxyContin from Ever Dying.” *Quartz*, July 20, 2022. https://qz.com/1125690/big-pharma-is-taking-advantage-of-patent-law-to-keep-oxycontin-from-ever-dying.

Foote, Jeffrey, Carrie Wilkens, Nicole Kosanke, and Stephanie Higgs. *Beyond Addiction: How Science and Kindness Help People Change*. Simon and Schuster, 2014.

Fors Marsh. *2022 Workplace Substance Use Disorder Recovery Survey*, October 12, 2023. https://www.forsmarsh.com/2023/03/23/2022-workplace-recovery-survey/.

Fors Marsh. *Workplace Recovery Survey 2025*, March 18, 2025. In *The Voice of Human Resources* (Vol. 2). https://www.forsmarsh.com/wp-content/uploads/2025/04/Recovery-Friendly_Workplaces_Survey_2025.pdf.

Frank, R. G. *Medicaid Cuts Kick Down on People Caught in the Opioid Epidemic*. Scientific American, March 18, 2025. https://www.scientificamerican.com/article/medicaid-cuts-kick-down-on-people-caught-in-the-opioid-epidemic/.

Friedman, Joseph, and Scott E. Hadland. “The Overdose Crisis Among U.S. Adolescents.” *New England Journal of Medicine* 390 (January 6, 2024). https://doi.org/10.1056/nejmp2312084.

Frost, Taeko, Sarah Deutsch, Shoshana D. Brown, Ellen Lemien, Chinazo O. Cunningham, and Aaron D. Fox. “‘We’ll Be Able to Take Care of Ourselves’—A Qualitative Study of Client Attitudes toward Implementing Buprenorphine Treatment at Syringe Services Programs.” *Substance Abuse* 42, no. 4 (October 1, 2021): 983–9. https://doi.org/10.1080/08897077.2021.1901173.

Fryer, Roland G., Paul Heaton, Steven D. Levitt, and Kevin M. Murphy. “Measuring Crack Cocaine and Its Impact.” *Economic Inquiry* 51, no. 3 (January 2, 2013): 1651–81. https://doi.org/10.1111/j.1465-7295.2012.00506.x.

Gage, Beverly. *G-Man: J. Edgar Hoover and the Making of the American Century*. Simon and Schuster, 2023.

Gesser, Nils, Archana Bodas LaPollo, Alexander J. Peters, Doris Weiland, Steven Belenko, and Lauren Perron. “To Be Part of the Fully Functional Team, There Need to Be Clear Roles.” *Journal for Advancing Justice* IV (2022): 23–52.

Gibson, Brent et al. *A Baseline Report on the Operation of the First Recognized Overdose Prevention Centers in the United States*. OnPoint NYC, 2023. https://onpointnyc.org/wp-content/uploads/2023/12/ONPOINTNYC_OPCREPORT_small-web1.pdf.

Gill, Monique, Kyle Jones, Ritu Ghosal, James M. Scanlan, and Emily J. Cox. "Housing and Reentry: A Mixed-Method Evaluation of a Low-Cost Community-Based Intervention for Increasing Access to Housing Post Incarceration." *Journal for Advancing Justice* IV. (2022): 53–64.

Giridharadas, Anand. *The Persuaders: At the Front Lines of the Fight for Hearts, Minds, and Democracy*. Vintage, 2022.

Gladwell, Malcolm. *Revenge of the Tipping Point: Overstories, Superspreaders and the Rise of Social Engineering*. Hachette UK, 2024.

Graham, Thomas. "Mexican Cartels Are Fifth-largest Employers in the Country, Study Finds." *The Guardian*, September 22, 2023. https://www.theguardian.com/world/2023/sep/21/mexico-cartels-fifth-largest-employer-study.

Grande, L. A., Cundiff, D., Greenwald, M. K., Murray, M., Wright, T. E., & Martin, S. A. "Evidence on Buprenorphine Dose Limits: A Review." *Journal of Addiction Medicine* 17, no. 5 (2023): 509 -516. https://doi.org/10.1097/ADM.0000000000001189.

Greenberg, Elayne E. "Unshackling Plea Bargaining from Racial Bias." *Social Science Research Network*, January 1, 2020. https://doi.org/10.2139/ssrn.3634786.

Greenberg, Jon. "Did Obama Cut $300 Million for School Safety? Not Really." Politifact, March 9, 2018. https://www.politifact.com/factchecks/2018/mar/09/ted-cruz/did-obama-cut-300-million-school-safety-not-really/.

Griffin, Connor. "Thousands of Illegal Marijuana Grow Sites, Some Linked to Mexican Drug Cartels, Litter Precious Public Lands Across Northern California." *Louisville Courier Journal*, June 1, 2023.

Griffin, O. Hayden, and Bryan Lee Miller. "OxyContin and a Regulation Deficiency of the Pharmaceutical Industry: Rethinking State-Corporate Crime." *Critical Criminology* 19, no. 3 (September 17, 2010): 213–26. https://doi.org/10.1007/s10612-010-9113-9.

Haidt, Jonathan. *The Anxious Generation: How the Great Rewiring of Childhood Is Causing an Epidemic of Mental Illness*. Random House, 2024.

Halpern, Luke. "Potential Drug for Mitigation of Cannabis Withdrawal Symptoms Receives FDA Fast Track Designation." *Pharmacy Times*, February 14, 2025.

Hampton, Ryan. *Fentanyl Nation: Toxic Politics and America's Failed War on Drugs*, St. Martin's, 2024.

Harris, G. *No More Tears: The Dark Secrets of Johnson & Johnson*. Random House, 2025.

Hamby, C. "Giant Companies Took Secret Payments to Allow Free Flow of Opioids." *The New York Times*, December 17, 2024. https://www.nytimes.com/2024/12/17/business/pharmacy-benefit-managers-opioids.html.

Hammerslag, Lindsey R., Aimee Mack, Redonna K. Chandler, Laura Fanucchi, Daniel J. Feaster, Marc R. Larochelle, Michelle R. Lofwall et al. "Telemedicine Buprenorphine Initiation and Retention in Opioid Use Disorder Treatment for Medicaid Enrollees." *JAMA Network Open* 6, no. 10 (October 18, 2023): e2336914. https://doi.org/10.1001/jamanetworkopen.2023.36914.

Harari, Yuval Noah. *Nexus: A Brief History of Information Networks from the Stone Age to AI*. Random House, 2024.

Hari, Johann. "The Hunting of Billie Holiday." *POLITICO Magazine*, January 17, 2015. https://www.politico.com/magazine/story/2015/01/drug-war-the-hunting-of-billie-holiday-114298/.

Hash Marihuana & Hemp Museum. "Assassin of Youth—Hash Marihuana & Hemp Museum," February 6, 2023. https://hashmuseum.com/en/collection/reefer-madness/assassin-of-youth/.

Hawkins, J. David, Rick Kosterman, Richard F. Catalano et al. "Promoting Positive Adult Functioning through Social Development Intervention in Childhood: Long-Term Effects from the Seattle Social Development Project—Correction." *Archives of Pediatrics & Adolescent Medicine* 159, no. 5 (May 1, 2005): 469. https://doi.org/10.1001/archpedi.159.5.469.

Heath, Chip, and Dan Heath. *Made to Stick: Why Some Ideas Survive and Others Die*. Random House, 2007.

Heath, Dan. *Upstream: The Quest to Solve Problems Before They Happen*. Avid Reader Press / Simon & Schuster, 2020.

Hedges, Michael. "'Benign' Drug of the '70s Is a Scourge in the '90s." *Deseret News*, June 29, 2019. https://www.deseret.com/1999/8/24/19462324/benign-drug-of-the-70s-is-a-scourge-in-the-90s.

"Helping Addicts Recover Progressively (HARP)." Brandeis Opioid Resource Connector, n.d. https://opioid-resource-connector.org/index.php/program-model/helping-addicts-recover-progressively-harp.

Hern, H. Gene, Vanessa Soares Lara, David Goldstein, Mariah M. Kalmin, S. Kidane, Steven Shoptaw, Ori Tzvieli, and Andrew A. Herring. "Prehospital Buprenorphine Treatment for Opioid Use Disorder by Paramedics: First Year Results of the EMS Buprenorphine Use Pilot." *Prehospital Emergency Care* 27, no. 3 (May 13, 2022): 334–42. https://doi.org/10.1080/10903127.2022.2061661.

Hill, Karl G., Joanne Bailey, Christine M. Steeger, J. David Hawkins, Richard F. Catalano, Rick Kosterman, Mark Epstein, and Robert D. Abbott. "Outcomes of Childhood Preventive Intervention Across 2 Generations." *JAMA Pediatrics* 174, no. 8 (August 1, 2020). https://doi.org/10.1001/jamapediatrics.2020.1310.

Humphreys, Keith, and Rob Bovett. "Why Oregon's Drug Decriminalization Failed." *The Atlantic*, March 17, 2024. https://www.theatlantic.com/ideas/archive/2024/03/oregon-drug-decriminalization-failed/677678/.

IEEE Conference Publication | IEEE Xplore. "Smart Intervention: A Next-Gen IoT Device for Combatting Drug Addiction," June 5, 2024.

"Inaugural Address," March 14, 2003. https://georgewbush-whitehouse.archives.gov/news/inaugural-address.html.

"Incarceration—Healthy People 2030." Health.gov, n.d. https://health.gov/healthypeople/priority-areas/social-determinants-health/literature-summaries/incarceration.

Interlandi, J., and D. Winter. "Opinion | 48 Million Americans Live with Addiction. Here's How to Get Them Help that Works." *The New York Times*, December 15, 2023. https://www.nytimes.com/2023/12/13/opinion/addiction-policy-treatment-opioid.html.

Isacson, Adam. "U.S.-Mexico Border Methamphetamine Seizures." *WOLA Border Oversight*, November 20, 2023. https://borderoversight.org/2023/10/04/border-methamphetamine-seizures/.

Jacobs, Andrew. "F.D.A. Declines to Approve MDMA Therapy, Seeking More Study." *The New York Times*, August 9, 2024. https://www.nytimes.com/2024/08/09/health/fda-mdma-ptsd-delay.html.

Jacobs, Andrew. "Texas OK's $50 Million for Ibogaine Research." *The New York Times*, June 14, 2025. https://www.nytimes.com/2025/06/14/health/texas-psychedelics-ibogaine-veterans.html.

Jakubowski, Andrea, Caroline Rath, Alex Harocopos, Monique Wright, Alice Welch, Jessica Kattan, Czarina N. Behrends, Teresa López-Castro, and Aaron D. Fox. "Implementation of Buprenorphine Services in NYC Syringe Services Programs: A Qualitative Process Evaluation." *Harm Reduction Journal* 19, no. 1 (July 10, 2022). https://doi.org/10.1186/s12954-022-00654-0.

Janis, Irving Lester. *Groupthink: Psychological Studies of Policy Decisions and Fiascoes*. Houghton Mifflin, 1982.

Joint Economic Committee Democrats. "The Economic Toll of the Opioid Crisis Reached Nearly $1.5 Trillion in 2020," September 28, 2022. https://www.jec.senate.gov/public/index.cfm/democrats/issue-briefs?ID

=CE55E977-B473-414F-8B88-53EB55EB7C7C. Accessed December 1, 2023.

Jones, Christopher M., Kun Zhang, Beth Han, Gery P. Guy, Jan Losby, Emily B. Einstein, Miriam Delphin-Rittmon et al. "Estimated Number of Children Who Lost a Parent to Drug Overdose in the US From 2011 to 2021." *JAMA Psychiatry*, 2024. https://doi.org/10.1001/jamapsychiatry.2024.0810.

Jones-Sanpei, Hinckley A., Debbie L. Humphries, and Richard J. Nance. "Financial Capability Building in the Treatment of Substance-Related and Addictive Disorders: A Co-Creation and Engagement Approach to Intervention Development." *Journal for Advancing Justice*: 3.

Joseph, Andrew. "'A Blizzard of Prescriptions': Documents Reveal New Details about Purdue's Marketing of OxyContin." *STAT*, July 25, 2023. https://www.statnews.com/2019/01/15/massachusetts-purdue-lawsuit-new-details/.

Kapadia, Shashi N., Judith L. Griffin, Justine Waldman, Nicolas R. Ziebarth, Bruce R. Schackman, and Czarina N. Behrends. "A Harm Reduction Approach to Treating Opioid Use Disorder in an Independent Primary Care Practice: A Qualitative Study." *Journal of General Internal Medicine* 36, no. 7 (January 19, 2021): 1898–905. https://doi.org/10.1007/s11606-020-06409-6.

Karlamangla, Soumya. "California Tries Paying Drug Users to Stay." *The New York Times*, August 29, 2023. https://www.nytimes.com/2023/08/29/us/california-drug-program-gift-cards.html.

Kawasaki, Guy. *The Art of the Start 2.0: The Time-Tested, Battle-Hardened Guide for Anyone Starting Anything*. Penguin, 2015.

Keefe, Patrick Radden. *Empire of Pain: The Secret History of the Sackler Dynasty*. Anchor Books, 2022.

Kelly, John, Nilofar Fallah-Sohy, Corrie L. Vilsaint, Lauren A. Hoffman, Leonard A. Jason, Robert L. Stout, Julie V. Cristello, and Bettina B. Hoeppner. "New Kid on the Block: An Investigation of the Physical, Operational, Personnel, and Service Characteristics of Recovery Community Centers in the United States." *Journal of Substance Abuse Treatment* 111 (April 1, 2020): 1–10. https://doi.org/10.1016/j.jsat.2019.12.009.

Kennedy, David, and J. Ben-Menachem. "Using DMI to Combat Covert Opioid Markets." *Police Chief*, March 2018.

Kennedy, Patrick J., and Stephen Fried. *Profiles in Mental Health Courage*. Penguin, 2024.

Kerr, Peter. "Anatomy of the Drug Issue: How, After Years, it Erupted." *The New York Times*, November 17, 1986. https://www.nytimes.com/1986/11/17/us/anatomy-of-the-drug-issue-how-after-years-it-erupted.html.

King, Sarah. "An Escalated Defense: Sheriff Karl Leonard Unveils SMART Program to Treat Inmates' Opioid Addiction." *Chesterfield Observer*, May 25, 2022. https://www.chesterfieldobserver.com/articles/an-escalated-defense-sheriff-karl-leonard-unveils-smart-program-to-treat-inmates-opioid-addiction/.

Kingdon, John W., and Eric Stano. *Agendas, Alternatives, and Public Policies*. Vol. 45. Boston: Little, Brown, 1984.

Kitroeff, N., and P. Villegas. "Mexican Cartels Lure Chemistry Students to Make Fentanyl." *The New York Times*, December 1, 2024. https://www.nytimes.com/2024/12/01/world/americas/mexico-fentanyl-chemistry-students.html.

Kleiman, Mark. *When Brute Force Fails: How to Have Less Crime and Less Punishment*. Princeton University Press, 2009.

Klein, Ezra & Thompson, Derek. *Abundance*. Simon and Schuster, 2025.

Koning, Ina M., Charlotte De Kock, P. Van Der Kreeft, Andrew Percy, Zila M. Sanchez, and Gregor Burkhart. "Implementation of the Icelandic Prevention Model: A Critical Discussion of Its Worldwide Transferability." *Drugs: Education, Prevention and Policy* 28, no. 4 (December 23, 2020): 367–78. https://doi.org/10.1080/09687637.2020.1863916.

Kuehn, Bridget M. "Fentanyl Drives Startling Increases in Adolescent Overdose Deaths." *JAMA* 329, no. 4 (January 24, 2023): 280. https://doi.org/10.1001/jama.2022.23563.

Law, Victoria. *"Prisons Make Us Safer": And 20 Other Myths about Mass Incarceration*. Beacon Press, 2021.

Lebaron, Charles. *Greed to Do Good: The Untold Story of CDC's Disastrous War on Opioids: A CDC Physician's Personal Account*. Amplify Publishing, 2024.

Lehman, Charles Fain. "Drug Policing in the 21st Century." *Manhattan Institute*, May 23, 2024. https://manhattan.institute/article/drug-policing-in-the-21st-century.

Leddin, Patrick R., Shawn D. Moon, and Patrick Leddin. *Building a Winning Culture in Government: A Blueprint for Delivering Success in the Public Sector*. Mango Media Inc., 2018.

Leen, Jeff. "Gary Webb Was No Journalism Hero, Despite What 'Kill the Messenger' Says." *Washington Post*, April 16, 2023. https://www

.washingtonpost.com/opinions/gary-webb-was-no-journalism-hero-despite-what-kill-the-messenger-says/2014/10/17/026b7560-53c9-11e4-809b-8cc0a295c773_story.html.

Levchak, Philip J. "Stop-and-Frisk in New York City: Estimating Racial Disparities in Post-Stop Outcomes." *Journal of Criminal Justice* 73 (March 1, 2021): 101784. https://doi.org/10.1016/j.jcrimjus.2021.101784.

Levitt, Steven D., and Stephen J. Dubner, *Freakonomics Rev Ed: A Rogue Economist Explores the Hidden Side of Everything*. WmMorrow, 2006.

Lewis, Dan. "What Happened to The Cocaine in Coca-Cola?" *Business Insider*, February 27, 2012. https://www.businessinsider.com/what-happened-to-the-cocaine-in-coca-cola-2012-2.

Li, Benjamin, Thanh Thuy Truong, Daryl Shorter, and Nidal Moukaddam. "Special Report: The Art of Treating Complex Substance Use Disorders." *Psychiatric News* 59, no. 08 (July 22, 2024). https://doi.org/10.1176/appi.pn.2024.08.8.33.

Li, Yutong, Derek V. Pierce, Shelly Vik, Kathryn Dong, Scott Patten, Yanbo Zhang, Jake Hayward, Andrew J. Greenshaw, and Bo Cao. "Co-involvement of Stimulants With Opioids in North America: A 'Silent Epidemic.'" *PLOS Mental Health*. 2, no. 7 (July 16, 2025): e0000319. https://doi.org/10.1371/journal.pmen.0000319.

Londono, Ernesto. *TRIPPY: The Perils and Promise of Medicinal Psychedelics*. Celadon Books, 2024.

Love, Dylan. "Meet The Science and Tech Geniuses Who Got High and Solved Amazing Problems." *Business Insider*, August 22, 2013. https://www.businessinsider.com/scientists-and-geniuses-who-used-drugs-2013-8#thomas-edison-cocaine-6.

Love, Shayla. "When Does a High Become a Trip?" *The Atlantic*, October 20, 2024. https://www.theatlantic.com/health/archive/2024/10/psychedelic-trip-high-hallucination-medicine/680314/.

Maia, Juliana Marino, Bruna Stefane Alves De Oliveira, Luiz G. S. Branco, and Renato Nery Soriano. "Therapeutic Potential of Psychedelics: History, Advancements, and Unexplored Frontiers." *Progress in Neuro-Psychopharmacology and Biological Psychiatry* 131 (April 1, 2024): 110951. https://doi.org/10.1016/j.pnpbp.2024.110951.

Mansnerus, Laura. "Timothy Leary, Pied Piper of Psychedelic 60's, Dies at 75." *The New York Times*, June 1, 1996. https://www.nytimes.com/1996/06/01/us/timothy-leary-pied-piper-of-psychedelic-60-s-dies-at-75.html.

Mariani, Mike. "How the American Opiate Epidemic was Started by One Pharmaceutical Company." *The Week*, 2015.

Marks, Jonathan H. "Lessons from Corporate Influence in the Opioid Epidemic: Toward a Norm of Separation." *Journal of Bioethical Inquiry* 17 (2020): 173–89.

Marlowe, Douglas B. "Behavioral Responsivity: Toward Evidence-Based Practice Standards for Substance-Related Crime." *Ohio St. J. Crim. L.* 19 (2021): 351.

Martinez, Arturo. "Tunnels at US-Mexico Border Show Smugglers' Deep Commitment." *Voice of America*, May 24, 2017. https://www.voanews.com/a/tunnels-at-us-mexico-border-show-smugglers-deep-commitment/3869064.html.

Martínez-Fernández, Diana Emilia, Andrea P. Garzón-Partida, Irene G. Aguilar-García, Joaquín García-Estrada, Sonia Luquin, and David Fernández-Quezada. "The Effect of Eye Movement Desensitization and Reprocessing (EMDR) Therapy on Reducing Craving in Populations With Substance Use Disorder: A Meta-analysis." *Research Square (Research Square)*, May 9, 2024. https://doi.org/10.21203/rs.3.rs-4391211/v1.

McCabe, S. E., McCabe, V. V., & Schepis, T. S. (2025). "US children living with a parent with substance use disorder." *JAMA Pediatrics*. https://doi.org/10.1001/jamapediatrics.2025.0828

Maryfield, Bailey. "Implicit Racial Bias." *Justice Research and Statistics Association*, December 2018. https://jrsa-factsheet-implicit-racial-bias-libre.pdf.

Massing, Michael. "Nixon Had It Right." *Washington Post*, November 8, 1998. https://www.washingtonpost.com/archive/opinions/1998/11/08/nixon-had-it-right/357a87d4-2c96-428f-8698-fae0f749be13/.

Massing, Michael. *The Fix*. University of California Press, 2000.

Maté, Gabor, and Daniel Maté. *The Myth of Normal: Trauma, Illness & Healing in a Toxic Culture*. Random House, 2022.

Mauer, Marc, and Tracy Huling. "Young Black Americans and the Criminal Justice System: Five Years Later." *Sentencing Project*, 1995, 251–66.

Mauro, Pia M., Sarah Gutkind, Erin M. Annunziato, and Hillary Samples. "Use of Medication for Opioid Use Disorder among US Adolescents and Adults with Need for Opioid Treatment, 2019." *JAMA Network Open* 5, no. 3 (March 23, 2022): e223821. https://doi.org/10.1001/jamanetworkopen.2022.3821.

Maxwell, John C. *The 21 Irrefutable Laws of Leadership: Follow Them and People Will Follow You*. HarperCollins Leadership, 2022.

McGallagly, Joe, and Neil McKeganey. "Does Robust Drug Enforcement Lead to an Increase in Drug Users Coming Forward for Treatment?" *Drugs: Education, Prevention and Policy* 20, no. 1 (2013): 1–4.

McGhee, Heather. *The Sum of Us: What Racism Costs Everyone and How We Can Prosper Together*. Profile Books, 2021.

McGinty, Emma E., and Colleen L. Barry. "Stigma Reduction to Combat the Addiction Crisis—Developing an Evidence Base." *The New England Journal of Medicine* 382, no. 14 (April 2, 2020): 1291–2. https://doi.org/10.1056/nejmp2000227.

McHugh, R. Kathryn, Bridget A. Hearon, and Michael W. Otto. "Cognitive Behavioral Therapy for Substance Use Disorders." *Psychiatric Clinics of North America* 33, no. 3 (September 1, 2010): 511–25. https://doi.org/10.1016/j.psc.2010.04.012.

Mendes, Fúlvio Rieli, Cristiane Dos Santos Costa, Victor Distefano Wiltenburg, Gabriela Morales-Lima, João Ariel Bonar Fernandes, and Renato Filev. "Classic and Non-classic Psychedelics for Substance Use Disorder: A Review of Their Historic, Past and Current Research." *Addiction Neuroscience* 3 (September 1, 2022): 100025. https://doi.org/10.1016/j.addicn.2022.100025.

Mermin, Sam, Rebekah Falkner, and Katie Greene. "Understanding Opioid Settlement Spending Plans across States: Key Components and Approaches." *NASHP*, February 28, 2023. https://nashp.org/understanding-opioid-settlement-spending-plans-across-states-key-components-and-approaches/.

Miech, Richard A. "National Survey Results on Drug Use, 1975-2004," December 2024. https://monitoringthefuture.org/wp-content/uploads/2024/12/mtf2025.pdf.

Mihalic, Sharon, and Delbert S. Elliott. "Evidence-Based Programs Registry: Blueprints for Healthy Youth Development." *Evaluation and Program Planning* 48 (February 1, 2015): 124–31. https://doi.org/10.1016/j.evalprogplan.2014.08.004.

Miller, Reuben Jonathan. *Halfway Home: Race, Punishment, and the Afterlife of Mass Incarceration*. Little, Brown and Company, 2021.

Moffitt, Terrie E., Louise Arseneault, Daniel W. Belsky, Nigel Dickson, Robert J. Hancox, HonaLee Harrington, Renate Houts et al. "A Gradient of Childhood Self-Control Predicts Health, Wealth, and Public Safety." *Proceedings of the National Academy of Sciences of the United States of America* 108, no. 7 (January 24, 2011): 2693–8. https://doi.org/10.1073/pnas.1010076108.

Montero, Fernando, Philippe Bourgois, and Joseph Friedman. "Potency-Enhancing Synthetics in the Drug Overdose Epidemic: Xylazine ('Tranq'), Fentanyl, Methamphetamine, and the Displacement of Heroin in Philadelphia and Tijuana." *Journal of Illicit Economies and Development* 4, no. 2 (January 1, 2022): 204–22. https://doi.org/10.31389/jied.122.

Mooney, Michael J. "Are There Really More Pain Clinics in Broward than McDonald's?" *New Times Broward-Palm Beach*, March 2, 2010. https://www.browardpalmbeach.com/news/are-there-really-more-pain-clinics-in-broward-than-mcdonalds-6451705.

Morris, Zoë Slote, Steven Wooding, and Jonathan Grant. "The Answer Is 17 Years, What Is the Question: Understanding Time Lags in Translational Research." *Journal of the Royal Society of Medicine* 104, no. 12 (December 1, 2011): 510–20. https://doi.org/10.1258/jrsm.2011.110180.

"Mrs. Winslow's Soothing Syrup | DEA Museum," n.d. https://museum.dea.gov/museum-collection/collection-spotlight/artifact/soothing-syrup.

Murdock, Kylie. "The Truth About Fentanyl Trafficking." *Third Way*, April 12, 2023.

Murphy, Jennifer, and Brenda L. Russell. "Stigma Reduction through Addiction and Naloxone Education." *Journal of Criminal Justice Education* 34, no. 2 (May 9, 2022): 185–98. https://doi.org/10.1080/10511253.2022.2068632.

Murphy, Robin J., Suresh Muthukumaraswamy, and Harriet De Wit. "Microdosing Psychedelics: Current Evidence from Controlled Studies." *Biological Psychiatry: Cognitive Neuroscience and Neuroimaging*, January 1, 2024. https://doi.org/10.1016/j.bpsc.2024.01.002.

Musto, David F. *The American Disease: Origins of Narcotic Control*. Oxford University Press, 1999.

Naftulin, Julia. "Kacey Musgraves Says She Was on LSD Listening to Bach When She Came Up with the Idea for Her New Album 'Star-crossed.'" *Business Insider*, September 9, 2021. https://www.businessinsider.com/kacey-musgraves-listening-to-bach-on-lsd-inspired-star-crossed-2021-9.

"National Drug Threat Assessment 2024." DEA, May 24, 2024. https://www.dea.gov/documents/2024/2024-05/2024-05-24/national-drug-threat-assessment-2024.

National Institute on Drug Abuse. "Cannabis Potency Data," June 6, 2023. https://nida.nih.gov/research/research-data-measures-resources/cannabis-potency-data.

National Institute on Drug Abuse. "Drug Facts: Criminal Justice," 2020. Criminal Justice DrugFacts | National Institute on Drug Abuse (NIDA).

National Institute on Drug Abuse. "Is There a Link between Marijuana Use and Psychiatric Disorders?" May 8, 2023. https://nida.nih.gov/publications/research-reports/marijuana/there-link-between-marijuana-use-psychiatric-disorders.

National Institute on Drug Abuse. "Prescription Opioid Use Is a Risk Factor for Heroin Use | National Institute on Drug Abuse," February 25, 2022. https://nida.nih.gov/publications/research-reports/prescription-opioids-heroin/prescription-opioid-use-risk-factor-heroin-use.

National Institute on Drug Abuse. "Psilocybin (Magic Mushrooms)," March 4, 2024. https://nida.nih.gov/research-topics/psilocybin-magic-mushrooms#what-is-psilocybin.

National Institute of Justice. "The Drug Court Movement." ojp.gov, July 1995. https://www.ojp.gov/pdffiles/drgctmov.pdf.

"National Inventory of Collateral Consequences of Criminal Conviction," n.d. https://niccc.nationalreentryresourcecenter.org/.

National Museum of American History. "The Power of the Poppy: Exploring Opium through 'The Wizard of Oz,'" n.d. https://americanhistory.si.edu/blog/opium-through-wizard-oz.

National Network for Safe Communities (NNSC). "The High Point Drug Market Intervention Strategy (2009)," November 27, 2018. https://nnscommunities.org/guides/the-high-point-drug-market-intervention-strategy-2009/.

Nelson, Marta, Samuel Feineh, and Maris Mapolski. *A New Paradigm for Sentencing in the United States*. New York: Vera Institute of Justice, 2023.

New York Civil Liberties Union. "Stop-and-Frisk Data," July 26, 2023. https://www.nyclu.org/en/stop-and-frisk-data.

Nixon, Richard "'What Has Happened to America?' Reader's Digest (October 1967) - American Horizons 3e Dashboard Resources - Oxford Learning Link," n.d. https://learninglink.oup.com/access/content/schaller-3e-dashboard-resources/document-richard-nixon-what-has-happened-to-america-readers-digest-october-1967.

O'Brien, Erin. "FDA Accepts, Grants Priority Review of NDA for MDMA-Assisted Therapy for PTSD." *Psychiatric Times*, February 13, 2024. https://www.psychiatrictimes.com/view/fda-accepts-grants-priority-review-of-nda-for-mdma-assisted-therapy-for-ptsd.

O'Campo, Patricia, Vicky Stergiopoulos, Owen K. Davis, James Lachaud, Rosane Nisenbaum, James R. Dunn, Naveed Ahmed, and Sam Tsemberis. "Health and Social Outcomes in the Housing First Model: Testing the Theory of Change." *EClinicalMedicine* 47 (May 1, 2022): 101387. https://doi.org/10.1016/j.eclinm.2022.101387.

Office of Justice Programs. "Drug Control: Highlights of P.L. 99-570, Anti-Drug Abuse Act of 1986." n.d. https://www.ojp.gov/media/document/56996.

Office of Management and Budget. *Budget of the U.S. Government: Fiscal Year 2025*. United States Government, 2024.

O'Harrow, Robert, Jr. "Meet the 24-year-old Trump Campaign Worker Appointed to Help Lead the Government's Drug Policy Office." *The Washington Post*, January 15, 2018.

Okie, Susan. "The Epidemic that Wasn't." *The New York Times*, January 26, 2009.

Oregon Health Authority. "Too Early to Tell: The Challenging Implementation of Measure 110 Has Increased Risks, but the Effectiveness of the Program Has yet to Be Determined." Report 2023-03, January 2023. https://sos.oregon.gov/audits/Documents/2023-03.pdf.

Orlowski, James P., and Leon Wateska. "The Effects of Pharmaceutical Firm Enticements on Physician Prescribing Patterns: There's no Such Thing as a Free Lunch." *Chest* 102, no. 1 (1992): 270–3.

Oza, Nick. "THE WALL: Drug Smuggling Long," October 3, 2017. https://www.azcentral.com/picture-gallery/news/politics/border-issues/2017/08/14/the-wall-drug-smuggling-long/104592040/.

Padgett, Deborah, Benjamin F. Henwood, and Sam J. Tsemberis. *Housing First: Ending Homelessness, Transforming Systems, and Changing Lives*. Oxford University Press, 2016.

Panchal, Nirmita et al. "Recent Trends in Mental Health and Substance Use Concerns among Adolescents." *KFF*, June 28, 2022. https://www.kff.org/mental-health/issue-brief/recent-trends-in-mental-health-and-substance-use-concerns-among-adolescents/.

Pathan, Hasan, and John P. Williams. "Basic Opioid Pharmacology: An Update." *British Journal of Pain* 6, no. 1 (February 1, 2012): 11–16. https://doi.org/10.1177/2049463712438493.

Pembleton, Matthew R. *Containing Addiction: The Federal Bureau of Narcotics and the Origins of America's Global Drug War*. Emerald Group Publishing Limited, 2017.

Pew Charitable Trusts. "How States Use Opioid Use Disorder Treatment Measures to Inform Decision-Making." The Pew Charitable Trusts, May 28, 2024. https://www.pewtrusts.org/en/research-and-analysis/issue-briefs/2024/05/how-states-use-opioid-use-disorder-treatment-measures-to-inform-decision-making.

Pickard, Hanna. "Responsibility Without Blame for Addiction." *Neuroethics* 10, no. 1 (January 7, 2017): 169–80. https://doi.org/10.1007/s12152-016-9295-2.

Pfaff, John. *Locked in: The True Causes of Mass Incarceration-and How to Achieve Real Reform*. Hachette UK, 2017.

PharmaNewsIntelligence. "Understanding US Food and Drug Administration (FDA) Approval Processes," April 20, 2022. https://

pharmanewsintel.com/features/understanding-us-food-and-drug-administration-fda-approval-processes.

Phillips, Kristine. "U.S. Border Officers Told a Mexican Teen to Drink Liquid Meth. His Family Received $1 Million for His Death." *Washington Post*, October 26, 2021.

Pinto-Garcia, Patricia. "Cannabinoid Hyperemesis Syndrome and 'Scromiting': What You Should Know." *GoodRx Health*, March 8, 2023.

Portenoy, Russell K., and Kathleen M. Foley. "Chronic Use of Opioid Analgesics in Non-Malignant Pain: Report of 38 Cases." *Pain* 25, no. 2 (May 1, 1986): 171–86. https://doi.org/10.1016/0304-3959(86)90091-6.

Porter, Jane, and Hershel Jick. "Addiction Rare in Patients Treated with Narcotics." *The New England Journal of Medicine* 302, no. 2 (January 10, 1980): 123. https://doi.org/10.1056/nejm198001103020221.

Powell, David, Abby Alpert, and Rosalie Liccardo Pacula "A Transitioning Epidemic: How the Opioid Crisis Is Driving the Rise in Hepatitis C." *Health Affairs* 38, no. 2 (February 1, 2019): 287–94. https://doi.org/10.1377/hlthaff.2018.05232.

Powell, D., & Jacobson, M. (2025). "Estimates of illicit opioid use in the US." *JAMA Health Forum*, 6(5), e250809. https://doi.org/10.1001/jamahealthforum.2025.0809.

Proctor, Steven L., and Philip L. Herschman. "The continuing care model of substance use treatment: What works, and when is 'enough,' 'enough?'" *Psychiatry journal* 2014, no. 1 (2014): 69242.

"Prospective Study of Masimo NSS-2 BRIDGE; as a Non-Pharmacological Treatment for Acute Opioid Withdrawal Symptoms." *Pain Management Nursing* 24, no. Issue 2 (April 2023): 238–9. https://doi.org/10.1016/j.pmn.2023.02.022.

Police, Treatment, and Community Collaborative (PTACC). "The Six Pathways of Deflection and Pre-Arrest Diversion," 2023. https://ptaccollaborative.org/wp-content/uploads/2023/01/PTACC-6-Pathways-of-Deflection-Onepager.pdf.

Ranapurwala, Shabbar I., Meghan Shanahan, Apostolos A. Alexandridis, Scott Proescholdbell, Rebecca B. Naumann, Daniel Edwards, and Stephen W. Marshall. "Opioid Overdose Mortality among Former North Carolina Inmates: 2000–2015." *American Journal of Public Health* 108, no. 9 (September 1, 2018): 1207–13. https://doi.org/10.2105/ajph.2018.304514.

Ray, Bradley, Steven J. Korzeniewski, George Mohler, Jennifer Carroll, Brandon Del Pozo, Grant Victor, Philip Huynh, and Bethany J. Hedden. "Spatiotemporal Analysis Exploring the Effect of Law Enforcement Drug Market Disruptions on Overdose, Indianapolis, Indiana, 2020–2021."

American Journal of Public Health 113, no. 7 (July 1, 2023): 750–8. https://doi.org/10.2105/ajph.2023.307291.

Raz, Mical. “Treating Addiction or Reducing Crime? Methadone Maintenance and Drug Policy under the Nixon Administration.” *Journal of Policy History* 29, no. 1 (December 15, 2016): 58–86. https://doi.org/10.1017/s089803061600035x.

“Records of the Drug Enforcement Administration [DEA],” October 12, 2016. https://www.archives.gov/research/guide-fed-records/groups/170.html.

Reichert, Jessica, Sharyn Adams, Jirka Taylor, and Brandon Del Pozo. “Guiding Officers to Deflect Citizens to Treatment: An Examination of Police Department Policies in Illinois.” *Health & Justice* 11, no. 1 (February 8, 2023). https://doi.org/10.1186/s40352-023-00207-y.

Reichert, Jessica, Brandon Del Pozo, and Bruce Taylor. “Police Stigma toward People with Opioid Use Disorder: A Study of Illinois Officers.” *Substance Use & Misuse* 58, no. 12 (2023): 1493–504.

Reuter, Peter H., and Patricia A. Ebener. “Cocaine: The First Decade.” *RAND Issue Paper* 6000 (1999).

Reuters. “Colombia Potential Cocaine Output Rose 24% in 2022—UN.” *Reuters*, September 11, 2023.

“Richard Nixon Remarks About an Intensified Program for Drug Abuse Prevention and Control. | The American Presidency Project,” n.d. https://www.presidency.ucsb.edu/documents/remarks-about-intensified-program-for-drug-abuse-prevention-and-control.

Richardson, Nicholas, Bradley Ray, Hope Smiley McDonald, Corey S. Davis, and Alex H. Kral. “National Survey Findings on Law Enforcement Agency Drug Response Practices, Overdose Victim Outcomes, and Good Samaritan Laws.” *Drug and Alcohol Dependence* 248 (July 1, 2023): 109916. https://doi.org/10.1016/j.drugalcdep.2023.109916.

Richter, Linda. “Rethinking Substance Use Prevention: An Earlier and Broader Approach.” Partnership to End Addiction, September 19, 2023. https://drugfree.org/reports/rethinking-substance-use-prevention-an-earlier-and-broader-approach/.

Riley, Jack. *Drug Warrior: Inside the Hunt for El Chapo and the Rise of America’s Opioid Crisis*. Hachette UK, 2019.

“Ronald Reagan Remarks in New Orleans, Louisiana, at the Annual Meeting of the International Association of Chiefs of Police” *The American Presidency Project*, n.d. https://www.presidency.ucsb.edu/documents/remarks-new-orleans-louisiana-the-annual-meeting-the-international-association-chiefs.

Ross, Jon, and Bruce Taylor. "Designed to Do Good: Key Findings on the Development and Operation of First Responder Deflection Programs." *Journal of Public Health Management and Practice* 28, no. Supplement 6 (November 1, 2022): S295–301. https://doi.org/10.1097/phh.0000000000001578.

Rossman, S. B., J. K. Roman, J. M. Zweig, M. Rempel, and C. H. Lindquist. *The Multi-site Adult Drug Court Evaluation: Executive Summary*. Washington, DC: Urban Institute Justice Policy Center, 2011.

RWJF. "Medicaid's Role in Addressing Social Determinants of Health," (February 1, 2019) https://www.rwjf.org/en/insights/our-research/2019/02/medicaid-s-role-in-addressing-social-determinants-of-health.html.

Ryan, Harriet, Lisa Girion, and Scott Glover. "'You Want a Description of Hell?' OxyContin's 12-Hour Problem #InvestigatingOxy." *L.A. Times*, May 5, 2016.

Schick, Tony, and Conrad Wilson. "Oregon Leaders Hampered Drug Decriminalization Effort." *ProPublica*, February 16, 2024. https://www.propublica.org/article/oregon-leaders-hampered-drug-decriminalization-effort.

Shah, A., C. J. Hayes, and B. C. Martin. "Characteristics of Initial Prescription Episodes and Likelihood of Long-Term Opioid Use—United States, 2006–2015." *MMWR Morbidity and Mortality Weekly Report* 66, no. 10 (2017): 265–9. https://doi.org/10.15585/mmwr.mm6610a1.

Sharot, Tali, and Cass R. Sunstein. *Look Again: The Power of Noticing What Was Always There*. Simon and Schuster, 2024.

Shatterproof, Ipsos Public Affairs, and Indiana University. "Shatterproof Addiction Stigma Index Report," 2024. https://www.shatterproof.org/sites/default/files/2024-09/Final%20SASI%202024.pdf.

Souza, Stephanie. "SAMHSA Updates Guidelines for Contingency Management: Maximum Incentives Increased to $750." American Academy of Addiction Psychiatry, January 10, 2025.https://www.aaap.org/samhsa-updates-guidelines-for-contingency-management-maximum-incentives-increased-to-750/.

Soto, Claradina, Amy E. West, Guadalupe Ramos, and Jennifer B. Unger. "Substance and Behavioral Addictions among American Indian and Alaska Native Populations." *International Journal of Environmental Research and Public Health* 19, no. 5 (March 3, 2022): 2974. https://doi.org/10.3390/ijerph19052974.

Spencer, Merianne R., Matthew F. Garnett, Arialdi M. Miniño, U.S. Department of Health and Human Services, Centers for Disease Control and Prevention, and National Center for Health Statistics. "Drug

Overdose Deaths in the United States, 2002–2022." *NCHS Data Brief*, February 2024. https://www.cdc.gov/nchs/data/databriefs/db491.pdf.

Spencer, Terry. "Florida 'Pill Mills' Were 'Gas on the Fire' of Opioid Crisis." *AP News*, July 20, 2019. https://apnews.com/article/west-virginia-fires-health-wv-state-wire-us-news-0ced46b203864d8fa6b8fda6bd97b60e

Spires, Richard A. *Government Can Deliver: A Practitioner's Guide to Improving Agency Effectiveness and Efficiency*. BookLocker.com, Inc., 2023.

Staff, City Paper. "Cocaine Production Hits Record High, Colombia's Coca Crop at 253,000 Hectares." *The City Paper Bogotá*, June 26, 2025. https://thecitypaperbogota.com/news/cocaine-production-hits-record-high-colombias-coca-crop-at-253000-hectares/.

Stewart, Scott. "From Colombia to New York City: The Narconomics of Cocaine." *Business Insider/STRATFOR*, June 27, 2016. http://www.businessinsider.com/from-colombia-to-new-york-city-the-economics-of-cocaine-2015-7.

Stone, Will. "As The FDA Evaluates Ecstasy Treatment for PTSD, Questions Mount About the Evidence." *NPR*, May 13, 2024. https://www.npr.org/sections/health-shots/2024/05/13/1250580932/ecstasy-mdma-ptsd-fda-approval.

Substance Abuse and Mental Health Services Administration (SAMHSA). "Advisory: Low Barrier Models of Care for Substance Use Disorders," November 2023. https://store.samhsa.gov/sites/default/files/advisory-low-barrier-models-of-care-pep23-02-00-005.pdf.

Sun, Lena H., and Scott Higham. "Trump Proposes Steep Cuts to White House 'Drug Czar' Office Amid Opioid Crisis." *The Washington Post*, May 24, 2023.https://www.washingtonpost.com/national/health-science/trump-proposes-steep-cuts-to-white-house-drug-czar-office-amid-opioid-crisis/2017/05/05/b666cd48-31bc-11e7-8674-437ddb6e813e_story.html.

Substance Abuse and Mental Health Services Administration (SAMHSA). "Core Competencies for Peer Workers," October 3, 2023. https://www.samhsa.gov/brss-tacs/recovery-support-tools/peers/core-competencies-peer-workers.

Substance Abuse and Mental Health Services Administration. "Key Substance Use and Mental Health Indicators in the United States: Results From the 2024 National Survey on Drug Use and Health." *Substance Abuse and Mental Health Services Administration*, 2025. https://www.samhsa.gov/data/sites/default/files/reports/rpt56287/2024-nsduh-annual-national-report.pdf.

Substance Abuse and Mental Health Services Administration. "Lesbian, Gay, and Bisexual Behavioral Health: Results from the 2021 and 2022 National

Surveys on Drug Use and Health (SAMHSA Publication No. PEP23-07-01-001)." *Center for Behavioral Health Statistics and Quality, Substance Abuse and Mental Health Services Administration*, 2023. https://www.samhsa.gov/data/report/LGB-Behavioral-Health-Report-2021-2022.

Substance Abuse and Mental Health Services Administration (SAMHSA). "SAMHSA Announces National Survey on Drug Use and Health (NSDUH) Results Detailing Mental Illness and Substance Use Levels in 2021," January 4, 2023. https://www.samhsa.gov/newsroom/press-announcements/20230104/samhsa-announces-nsduh-results-detailing-mental-illness-substance-use-levels-2021.

Satel, Sally. 'What Is It like to Be an Addict?' Review: The Danger of a Safe Feeling." *The Wall Street Journal*, April 29, 2025. https://www.aei.org/op-eds/what-is-it-like-to-be-an-addict-review-the-danger-of-a-safe-feeling/.

Satel, Sally. 'Liberties, A Journal of Culture and Politics. "Dark Genies, Dark Horizons: The Riddle of Addiction." *Liberties*, April 14, 2021. https://libertiesjournal.com/articles/dark-genies-dark-horizons-the-riddle-of-addiction/.

Szalavitz, Maia. "Opinion | Claims That Drug Decriminalization in Oregon Isn't Working Are Short-Sighted." *The New York Times*, August 29, 2023. https://www.nytimes.com/2023/08/29/opinion/arrest-drug-treatment-addiction.html.

TASC - Center for Health and Justice. "Law Enforcement Deflection Frameworks: A Decision Making Tool for Police Leaders," January 2017. https://ptaccollaborative.org/.

Tatarsky, Andrew. *Harm Reduction Psychotherapy: A New Treatment for Drug and Alcohol Problems*. Jason Aronson, 2007.

Taylor, Jessica, Sarah E. Wakeman, Alexander Y. Walley, and Laura Kehoe. "Substance Use Disorder Bridge Clinics: Models, Evidence, and Future Directions." *Addiction Science & Clinical Practice* 18, no. 1 (April 14, 2023). https://doi.org/10.1186/s13722-023-00365-2.

Taylor-Thompson, Kim, and Anthony C. Thompson. *Progressive Prosecution: Race and Reform in Criminal Justice*. New York University Press, 2022.

Tenorio, Rich. "How the Sackler Family Built a Pharma Dynasty and Fueled an American Calamity." *The Times of Israel*, July 5, 2021. https://www.timesofisrael.com/how-the-sackler-family-built-a-pharma-dynasty-and-fueled-an-american-calamity/. Accessed November 26, 2023.

The Andrew Goodman Foundation. "Historical Archives." Andrew Goodman Foundation, December 6, 2022. https://andrewgoodman.org/historical-archives/.

The Sentencing Project. "50 Years and a Wake Up," October 12, 2023. https://www.sentencingproject.org/advocacy/50-years-and-a-wake-up-ending-the-mass-incarceration-crisis-in-america/.

"The Twelve Steps | Alcoholics Anonymous," n.d. https://www.aa.org/the-twelve-steps.

The White House. "White House Office of National Drug Control Policy (ONDCP) Announces Record Reduction in Poppy Cultivation and Potential Heroin Production in Mexico," July 31, 2020. https://trumpwhitehouse.archives.gov/briefings-statements/ondcp-announces-record-reduction-poppy-cultivation-potential-heroin-production-mexico/.

Thieleman, Kara, Joanne Cacciatore, and Allen Frances. "Rates of Prolonged Grief Disorder: Considering Relationship to the Person Who Died and Cause of Death." *Journal of Affective Disorders* 339 (October 1, 2023): 832–7. https://doi.org/10.1016/j.jad.2023.07.094.

Thompson, Tim. "How Much Does Colombian Coffee Cost? | Shipped Directly to You?," *Buy Organic Coffee*, May 9, 2018. https://buyorganiccoffee.org/1672/how-much-does-colombian-coffee-cost/.

Twohey, Megan et al. "As America's Marijuana Use Grows, So Do the Harms." *The New York Times*, October 4, 2024. https://www.nytimes.com/2024/10/04/us/cannabis-marijuana-risks-addiction.html?searchResultPosition=1.

United Nations: Office on Drugs and Crime. "Drug Conventions," n.d. Drug Conventions (unodc.org).

United Nations: Office on Drugs and Crime. "This Day in History: The Shanghai Opium Commission, 1909," n.d. https://www.unodc.org/unodc/en/frontpage/this-day-in-history-the-shanghai-opium-commission-1909.html.

United States Commission on Marihuana and Drug Abuse. *Marihuana: A Signal of Misunderstanding: First Report*. Signet, The New Americam Library Incorporated, 1972. https://books.google.com/books?id=PjbGxgEACAAJ.

United States Trade Representative. "Mexico," n.d. https://ustr.gov/countries-regions/americas/mexico.

U.S. Census Bureau. "1930 Census: Volume 2. Population, General Report, Statistics by Subjects." Census.gov, October 8, 2021. https://www.census.gov/library/publications/1933/dec/1930a-vol-02-population.html.

U.S. Department of Homeland Security. "Department of Homeland Security Unveils Artificial Intelligence Roadmap, Announces Pilot Projects to Maximize Benefits of Technology, Advance Homeland Security Mission | Homeland Security," March 18, 2024. https://www.dhs.gov/news/2024

/03/18/department-homeland-security-unveils-artificial-intelligence-roadmap-announces.
US Food and Drug Administration. "FDA Alerts Health Care Professionals of Potential Risks Associated With Compounded Ketamine Nasal Spray." 2022.
United Nations: Office on Drugs and Crime. "World Drug Report 2025," June 26, 2025. https://www.unodc.org/unodc/en/data-and-analysis/world-drug-report-2025.html.
Vakharia, Sheila P. *The Harm Reduction Gap: Helping Individuals Left Behind by Conventional Drug Prevention and Abstinence-only Addiction Treatment*. Taylor & Francis, 2024.
Van Boekel, Leonieke C., Evelien P. M. Brouwers, Jaap Van Weeghel, and H. F. L. Garretsen. "Stigma among Health Professionals towards Patients with Substance Use Disorders and Its Consequences for Healthcare Delivery: Systematic Review." *Drug and Alcohol Dependence* 131, no. 1–2 (July 1, 2013): 23–35. https://doi.org/10.1016/j.drugalcdep.2013.02.018.
Van Der Kolk, Bessel A., Julie B. Wang, Rachel Yehuda, Leah Bedrosian, Allison R. Coker, Charlotte Harrison, Michael C. Mithoefer, Berra Yazar-Klosinski, Amy Emerson, and Rick Doblin. "Effects of MDMA-assisted Therapy for PTSD on Self-experience." *PLOS ONE* 19, no. 1 (January 10, 2024): e0295926. https://doi.org/10.1371/journal.pone.0295926.
Van Zee, Art. "The Promotion and Marketing of OxyContin: Commercial Triumph, Public Health Tragedy." *American Journal of Public Health* 99, no. 2 (2009): 221–7.
Vera Institute of Justice. "Overdose Deaths and Jail Incarceration—National Trends and Racial Disparities," January 26, 2021. https://www.vera.org/publications/overdose-deaths-and-jail-incarceration/national-trends-and-racial-disparities.
Viebeck, Elise. "How an Early Biden Crime Bill Created the Sentencing Disparity for Crack and Cocaine Trafficking." *Washington Post*, July 29, 2019. https://www.washingtonpost.com/politics/how-an-early-biden-crime-bill-created-the-sentencing-disparity-for-crack-and-cocaine-trafficking/2019/07/28/5cbb4c98-9dcf-11e9-85d6-5211733f92c7_story.html.
Vitale, Alex. *The End of Policing*. Verso Books, 2021.
Volkow, Nora. "Five Areas Where 'More Research' Isn't Needed to Curb the Overdose Crisis." *National Institute on Drug Abuse*, August 31, 2022. https://nida.nih.gov/about-nida/noras-blog/2022/08/five-areas-where-more-research-isnt-needed-to-curb-overdose-crisis.
Vosburg, Suzanne K., Jermaine D. Jones, Jeanne M. Manubay, Judy Ashworth, Irma H. Benedek, and Sandra D. Comer. "Assessment of a

Formulation Designed to Be Crush-Resistant in Prescription Opioid Abusers." *Drug and Alcohol Dependence* 126, no. 1–2 (November 1, 2012): 206–15. https://doi.org/10.1016/j.drugalcdep.2012.05.013.

Walter, Shoshana. "It Was a Promising Addiction Treatment. Many Patients Never Got It." *The New York Times*, August 7, 2025. https://www.nytimes.com/2025/08/07/magazine/suboxone-buprenorphine-opioid-addiction-drugs.html.

Walter, Shoshana. *Rehab: An American Scandal* (Simon and Schuster, 2025).

Whitter, Melanie and Jose Silva, "The Substance Use Workforce Crisis: Drivers, Challenges, and Promising Strategies," *NASADAD*, April 2025, https://nasadad.org/wp-content/uploads/2025/04/The-Substance-Use-Workforce-Crisis-Drivers-Challenges-and-Promising-Strategies_POST-2.pdf.

Winters, Ken C. and Waldron, Holly B. "Cannabis, Psychosis, and the Teen Brain." In *Mind the Children: How to Think About the Youth Mental Health Collapse*, edited by Naomi Schaefer Riley and Sally Satel, American Enterprise Institute, 2025.

Woods, Gary. "Mother's Little Helper." *The British Journal of Psychiatry* 208, no. 6 (June 1, 2016): 555. https://doi.org/10.1192/bjp.bp.115.177295.

Woodward, Tara et al., "Risk & Protective Factors for Youth Substance Use across Family, Peers, School, & Leisure Domains." *Children and Youth Services Review* 151 (August 1, 2023): 107027. https://doi.org/10.1016/j.childyouth.2023.107027.

Young, Emma. "How Iceland Got Teens to Say No to Drugs." *The Atlantic*, January 19, 2017. https://www.theatlantic.com/health/archive/2017/01/teens-drugs-iceland/513668/.

Zippia. "How Big Is the U.S. Pharmaceutical Industry?" December 6, 2022. https://www.zippia.com/answers/how-big-is-the-us-pharmaceutical-industry/.

Zwick, Janet, Hannah Appleseth, and Stephan Arndt. "Stigma: How it Affects the Substance Use Disorder Patient." *Substance Abuse Treatment, Prevention, and Policy* 15 (2020): 1–4.

Index

About the Author

Drawing on his extensive experience at the forefront of national drug policy, including a year as Acting Director of the White House Office of National Drug Control Policy (ONDCP), **Richard J. Baum** offers unparalleled insight into the complexities of America's opioid crisis. While leading ONDCP in the position referred to as the Drug Czar and serving as the President's principal advisor on drug policy, Baum was also the Executive Director of the President's Opioid Commission. In this role, he directly oversaw the development of the Commission's reports and recommendations, gaining a deep understanding of the multifaceted challenges and failures in addressing this epidemic.

During his twenty-eight years at ONDCP he also spearheaded the development of six iterations of ONDCP's flagship document, the National Drug Control Strategy. This document outlines priorities for nineteen federal agencies regarding prevention, treatment, recovery, enforcement and interdiction. He also led the creation of key strategies addressing transnational organized crime, Southwest border drug trafficking, and synthetic drugs, demonstrating a comprehensive grasp of the evolving drug landscape. These experiences have provided him with the critical perspectives that inform his book, *Inside America's Opioid Crisis: 12 Hard Lessons for Today's Drug War.*

Baum's expertise has been sought after by policymakers and professionals alike. He has testified before Congress and served as a keynote speaker at national and international conferences focused on drugs, crime, and health. Prior to his distinguished career at ONDCP, Baum worked as a Congressional Staff Member during the crack cocaine epidemic and as a researcher on crime and drug policy. He holds advanced degrees from Georgetown University and the University of Colorado and currently serves as an Adjunct Professor of Public Policy at Georgetown

University's McCourt School, where he designed and teaches a graduate course on drug policy. His deep engagement with policy, research, and education underscores his commitment to finding effective solutions to the nation's drug challenges. His extensive network and deep understanding make him a vital voice in analyzing the challenges of today's drug war.

www.ingramcontent.com/pod-product-compliance
Ingram Content Group UK Ltd.
Pitfield, Milton Keynes, MK11 3LW, UK
UKHW021905150926
475560UK00003B/196

9 781538 186404